Managing Fraud Risk

A Practical Guide for Directors and Managers

Managing Fraud Risk

A Practical Guide for Directors and Managers

Steve Giles

WILEY

A John Wiley & Sons, Ltd, Publication

This edition first published 2012
Copyright © 2012 Stephen Giles

Registered office
John Wiley & Sons Ltd, The Atrium, Southern Gate, Chichester, West Sussex, PO19 8SQ, United Kingdom

For details of our global editorial offices, for customer services and for information about how to apply for permission to reuse the copyright material in this book please see our website at www.wiley.com

Library of Congress Cataloging- in- Publication Data

Giles, Stephen, 1957- author.
  Managing fraud risk : a practical guide for directors and managers / Stephen Giles.
      pages cm
  Includes bibliographical references and index.
  ISBN 978-0-470-97945-7 (hardback)
1. Fraud–Prevention. 2. Commercial crime–Prevention. 3. Risk management. I. Title.
  HV6691.G53 2012
  658.4'73–dc23
                                                                    2012018034

ISBN 978-0-470-97945-7 (hbk) ISBN 978-1-118-38729-0 (ebk)
ISBN 978-1-119-96043-0 (ebk) ISBN 978-1-119-96042-3 (ebk)

A catalogue record for this book is available from the British Library

Typeset in 10/12pt Palatino Roman by Thomson Digital, New Delhi, India.
Printed and bound by CPI Group (UK) Ltd., Croydon, CRO4YY

To my parents, Hilda and Norman Giles
and to my wife Val, the love of my life

Contents

Acknowledgements

I want to thank everybody who has contributed in any way to the publication of this book. An impossible task of course, because this necessarily includes so many people. For example, everyone who has attended one of my lectures, workshops or training courses is absolutely included because they have all made a contribution– every time I deliver a talk on fraud I learn something myself from the comments, observations and stories coming from the members of the audience. I only hope that those of you who have listened to my talks have enjoyed them as much as I have enjoyed giving them.

Also included in the thanks are the numerous professionals that I have worked with on fraud assignments over the years. This begins with the old Polly Peck investigation team – too many to name everyone here but the core team comprised: John Aizelwood, Lucy Bracken, Adam Downing, John Forbes, Alice Hayes, Gill Head, Will Inglis, Piyesh Patel, David Pollock and Phil Weston. Particular thanks go to a small number of experts from various specialisms and disciplines from whom I learned so much in my early years of working on fraud cases: Christopher Morris and Fergus Falk; Mark Tantam and Martin Muirhead; David Oliver QC; Paul Gordon-Saker and Simon Castley; and Ian Johnson. More recently I have done much training, lecturing and conference work and I want to thank Dr John Mitchell and Keith Checkley for encouraging me to do so and for providing the initial introductions.

I have spent much of the last 20 years combating fraud and financial crime in one form or another. As a result, my views and attitudes have been shaped primarily by my experiences but they have also been influenced by a wide variety of material from many sources during that time: the general business press; online news services; professional magazines; surveys and reports on crime statistics and trends. In addition, there are many, many books written on fraud and on financial crime generally, a fair number of which I have read. It is my opinion that the most important single source about internal fraud and the risks posed to business organisations of all types is provided by the Association of Certified Fraud Examiners. My ideas have been informed by the many articles published by the Association over the last 20 years, in particular those written by the Association's founder and fraud expert Dr Joseph T Wells.

Turning specifically now to the book, there are eight business associates and colleagues of mine who agreed to be interviewed for the purposes of the book and so have given their valuable time and observations, for which I am so grateful. None of them would claim to be a fraud expert but their interviews give a fascinating insight into the practical problems of dealing with fraud that all organisations have to manage in the modern world. Because of the sensitive subject matter, I have agreed to keep the identity of the interviewees under wraps. In alphabetical order, by given names only, they are: Adrian; Bernard; Charles; Frazer; Jerry; Martin; Sharon; and Teresa. I also value the comments of Jeffrey Robinson, the financial crime author and journalist during our long-range discussion about the book, courtesy of Skype.

Special thanks go to my friend Julie Collins. The interviews were recorded and Julie kindly agreed to type them all up for me, a task which no doubt took many hours to complete. I am very grateful to her for all her time and patience.

There are a number of people who have helped me to shape the book. The whole process started with the original idea from Jenny McCall who commissioned me to write a book on fraud for John Wiley and Sons. The team at Wiley then took on the process of first reviewing and commenting on my manuscript and then secondly turning the manuscript into the published book. My thanks go to them all, in particular to Gemma Valler and Tess Allen for their continued support and advice throughout.

I also received ideas on the cover design from my very talented niece, Katie Giles. I was greatly reassured also to have her brother, and Manchester United supporter, Adam confirm that my various references to football made sense to him—Adam knows more about football than anyone that I have ever met. It was great fun talking to them both about the book and I want to thank Katie and Adam very much for all their help.

My thanks go also to (unpaid, at least by me!) business coach Charles Kingsmill for his continuous encouragement over the writing period, splendid drawing of the diagrams and constructive criticism and advice over many hours spent together, not all of them entirely sober.

Finally and most importantly I want to say a very big "thank you" to my wife Val who has been the source of so much steadfast support for me whilst writing this book and in everything else that I have tried to do since we were married. I remember reading somewhere that the ultimate success in life is that one's spouse likes and respects you more as each year goes by. I happen to agree and by that measure, more than any other, I hope to be every bit as successful as Val is.

In the end I take full responsibility for my writing. This book, including all the views, opinions, stories and mistakes, is mine alone.

Introduction

Making me an offer that I can't refuse

"I have a proposition for you, Steve." It is October 1990 and I am sitting in an office close to Fleet Street in the heart of London. My boss, one of the senior partners of the accounting firm Touche Ross (now known as Deloitte) has asked to see me. He is in the process of outlining the events surrounding the headline corporate scandal that has featured so prominently in the media in recent weeks. He tells me that there has been a significant development in the High Court today that is likely to have important implications for the firm and, if I am interested, for me too. I am listening.

My boss is a small, dapper man with forthright views and little small talk. He assumes that I am aware of the headlines concerning the rumours and events surrounding the high-flying and hitherto very successful international company Polly Peck International Plc ("Polly Peck"), which has seen the company's share price, quoted on the London Stock Exchange, collapse in recent days. I simply nod. He then brings me up to date with the latest news: the directors have been removed and we are to investigate what had been going on. I look surprised so he explains further. He has just learned that the High Court has agreed to an application from the company's directors and creditors to place Polly Peck in "administration", a legal arrangement whereby the company's affairs will be reorganised and an orderly disposal of its assets made for the benefit of all the creditors. This process will be overseen by an outside administrator rather than by the board of directors. The High Court has appointed three highly experienced insolvency accountants to take charge of the company: Michael Jordan and Richard Stone of Coopers & Lybrand Deloitte (now PricewaterhouseCoopers) and Christopher Morris of Touche Ross. Unusually, the responsibilities of the administrators are to be split, so that Messrs Jordan and Stone are going to run the continuing operations of the business day-to-day whilst Mr Morris is charged with handling any claims made against Mr Asil Nadir personally. Mr Nadir is the Chairman and Chief Executive of Polly Peck.[1]

He doesn't have to tell me about the background to all this. The Polly Peck rise and fall saga has dominated the news in recent weeks. From small beginnings it had become the best-performing share of the 1980s on any world stock market. Now, in the last month it has suddenly run out of cash and its bankers are unwilling to extend it any more credit. How could this have happened? The circumstances of the collapse look suspicious and of course the press is full of gossip and rumours. One of the rumours is that the crisis is the result of large-scale corporate fraud.

My boss is getting to the point of the meeting now. He says that the Polly Peck investigation is likely to be a long project involving a large number of staff (managers, qualified accountants and junior staff, some just out of university). It will be a difficult job to manage. It will also be a very high-profile case – fraud investigations into publicly listed companies always attract a lot of attention from the media. So the firm is looking for someone to organise and run the investigation team as the case develops. He and his fellow partners think that I am the right person for the job – am I interested in taking it on? He tells me that I will be dealing with leading lawyers and fraud specialists and will report directly to some of the senior partners in the firm. Of course, if I decide to accept, a fraud investigation on this scale will certainly take up 100% of my time. All my existing workload (my group manager role, my portfolio of audit clients, my student recruitment work etc.) will have to be re-allocated. This needs to be done very quickly – who do I think is the best person to take over the various roles?

As he continues to talk it is rapidly becoming clear to me that the decision has already been made. This is not an exploratory discussion. I am expected to say "yes", to accept the job and get on with managing it. This is how things happen in a big firm and I don't really have an option. Actually, this is not a problem for me and I am happy enough with most of what I have heard. There is only one thing that is bothering me. At the end of the meeting I say to my boss: "Christopher, thank you for the opportunity, all of this sounds fine and I am really looking forward to it. There is just one thing . . . I don't know much about corporate fraud at all."

Opening remarks

That was my introduction to the world of fraud and it points to one of the main reasons for writing this book. Most of the directors and managers that I work with today seem to have no more understanding of fraud and its key characteristics (what it is, who commits it and why, what are the most effective controls to prevent and detect it and how to investigate it to obtain the best results) than I did back in 1990. Fraud remains a blind-spot so far as most businesses are concerned. This is both frustrating and almost unbelievable given the extent of the risk that fraud poses to the profits and reputations of every organisation and also the proven methodologies that exist today for reducing this risk.

It might seem surprising that when I started work on the Polly Peck case I had only the vaguest ideas about corporate fraud even though at that time I had been a qualified chartered accountant for over seven years. Please remember, however, that the times were very different then and that financial crime, although it has of course always existed, was not looked at with the same analytical rigour that it is today. Since 1990 there have been many corporate fraud scandals that have hit the headlines and shaken investor confidence around the world: Polly Peck, Barings Bank, Enron, WorldCom, Allied Irish Banks, Parmalat, Société Générale, Hollinger, Refco, Galleon, Satyam and Madoff to name but a few. These headline cases did much to initiate and influence changes in financial crime legislation, regulation, standards and convention around the world, examples being: a Code of Corporate Governance in the UK; the Sarbanes-Oxley Act ("SOX") in the US; increasingly stringent anti-money laundering and counter-terrorist financing regulations for financial institutions worldwide; and tougher international auditing standards. Why is it that all of this "noise" has not led to greater awareness of fraud risk in business today, in particular amongst the directors and managers working in the public and private sectors?

Jeffrey Robinson, the financial crime expert and best-selling international author, has no doubts regarding the answer to this question. I met Jeffrey in 2010 when I chaired a conference in Gibraltar organised by the Gibraltar Association of Compliance Officers ("GACO") under the heading "Risk on the Rock". Jeffrey was the keynote speaker. When I told him later that I was writing this book and asked him whether he thought there was any greater awareness of fraud in the business community today than 20 years ago his answer was straightforward: absolutely not. When I asked why he thought directors and senior managers were not better prepared these days, Jeffrey replied "Because they are stupid and in denial." Although I would not phrase it in quite this way, I happen to agree with him.

I have worked on many fraud cases since 1990 and this has enabled me to develop expertise in this area. But my experiences have also shown me that most business people, whether they are owners, directors, managers or employees, have no more idea about fraud than I had back in 1990. Essentially, this will remain true unless, and until, such time as they are hit by a fraud themselves and have to deal with the consequences directly. The reality is that most of us only become aware of the dangers of fraud once either we personally or the organisations that we work for have fallen victim to a fraudster. We are then required to react to events, often quickly and under conditions of extreme pressure. Consequently, fraud is almost always approached reactively, in crisis mode which is why it remains one of the most poorly managed areas of business risk today.

This is both disappointing and unnecessary as so much work has been carried out into corporate fraud since the early 1990s. This book provides business with a summary of this work, backed up with practical tips and examples throughout – it is in effect a practical guide, a route-map showing the best ways for directors and managers to navigate around the various threats to their organisations by taking a strategic, proportionate and risk-based approach.

About this book

The book is organised around 10 Chapters. Each one covers an important aspect of fraud and ends by setting out five key learning points for directors and managers. The book is peppered with examples from headline cases and my own experience, together with practical tips and advice.

This is a unique book, both because of its practical approach and because of its business focus. It analyses corporate fraud, not from a theoretical, legal or investigative point of view but from a business perspective. The book concentrates on internal, occupational fraud and places it firmly in its proper business context, that of risk management. This is a business book that summarises for directors and managers the modern anti-fraud approach. It provides them with a menu of options from which to choose those methodologies, controls and techniques that are most suited to the individual circumstances of their organisations so that they can manage fraud risk effectively.

The book's other key feature is its practical approach. This extends well beyond my own thoughts and experiences. It combines all that I have learned in over 20 years of fighting fraud as investigator, consultant and lecturer with the perceptions, experiences and observations of many hundreds of business people to produce a menu of anti-fraud options for directors and managers to choose from.

How is this possible? Well, to start with, examples from my own experiences are given throughout the book, in particular the short narratives of incidents from every stage of my career that are set out at the start of each Chapter. Also in Chapter 9 there is a detailed case study of a major fraud that I investigated a number of years ago. All of these examples are made suitably anonymous. I have then built this by incorporating the views of other business people into the book in two ways: first, by including extracts from interviews conducted specifically for this book with a number of directors and managers who I have come to know over the years, drawn from various jurisdictions and from different business sectors; and secondly through the medium of the answers that I have received to the Fraud Awareness Quiz, something that I have used to stimulate discussion and debate amongst delegates in training sessions on financial crime risk management around the world. Each Chapter in the book contains one question from the Quiz, together with the answers. The way that delegates answer the questions provides a useful insight into just how aware (or otherwise) of fraud risk the directors and managers who run business organisations today are in practice.

So, there are three layers of practical experience in this book: my own; those of my delegates on courses; and those of my interviewees. I give a brief overview of each layer below, beginning with my own experience.

1. Personal experiences

Background

I am a chartered accountant by profession, qualifying in 1983 and later specialising in forensic accounting and risk management work during the 1990s. Before I did so, I was working as a senior audit manager for the accountancy firm Touche Ross (now operating under the global brand name of "Deloitte") in London. My experience up to that point was very traditional for a professional accountant: I had done a lot of auditing (I was managing an extensive portfolio of audit clients when the Polly Peck team was set up) and had also worked on a number of projects involving financial due diligence and investigations work. Like most of my colleagues at the time I had relatively little experience or knowledge of corporate fraud.

All this changed for me with the Polly Peck case. Since 1990 when this investigation started, I have been involved in the fight against financial crime in various roles as investigator, consultant and lecturer, working in many jurisdictions around the world. I regard myself as being very fortunate in the cases and projects that I have worked on and the people that I have met along the way. Fraud is generally a fascinating area of work.

The Polly Peck case

As indicated above, my experience of handling fraud-related assignments began with the Polly Peck case in 1990. I was the operations manager of the team pulled together by Touche Ross to investigate this headline scandal centring on the circumstances surrounding the collapse of Polly Peck, a huge international conglomerate, leaving debts of some £1.3 billion owing to creditors.

I worked on the Polly Peck investigation for over two years. Throughout this time Touche Ross tried to recover money owed to the creditors of Polly Peck principally by bringing legal actions against a number of parties who, we alleged, had either been negligent or had failed properly to discharge a duty of care owed to the company. This was part of the civil litigation process in the UK. At the same time the Serious Fraud Office ("SFO") was investigating Mr Nadir and ultimately brought charges against him under the criminal litigation process. Although our civil litigation was based upon the presumption that the creditors of Polly Peck had lost money because of the malpractice of Mr Nadir, it was the SFO that brought criminal charges of false accounting and theft against him in a separate legal action. Mr Nadir denied the charges. Almost unbelievably (and in circumstances described below) the criminal case against Mr Nadir has now been re-opened and his trial commenced in London on 23 January 2012.[2] It is not therefore appropriate to include any detailed analysis of the case in this book. However, an overview is provided below, together with brief examples, used to illustrate various points made elsewhere in the book.

Polly Peck had enjoyed considerable commercial success during the 1980s under the charismatic leadership of its driving force, Chairman and Chief Executive, the Turkish-Cypriot entrepreneur Asil Nadir. The group had its corporate headquarters in Berkeley Square in the fashionable West End of London but it was a global trading conglomerate embracing textiles, electronics and the packaging and sale of citrus fruits, especially those grown in Turkey and in the self-proclaimed Turkish Republic of Northern Cyprus ("TRNC"). Mr Nadir had successfully floated the company on the London Stock Exchange in 1986 and when Polly Peck subsequently acquired a significant part of the Del Monte operations, the share price soared and long-term growth seemed assured. However, the success of Polly Peck was always closely linked to the personality and reputation of its Chairman, Mr Nadir. Astonishingly, when stories began to circulate in the summer of 1990 that the UK authorities were investigating the personal affairs of Mr Nadir and that, in turn, he was seeking to take the company back into private ownership, investor confidence in Polly Peck dipped sharply. When news broke that the authorities had raided Mr Nadir's private offices the share price collapsed. Hence, the directors were compelled to go to the High Court to request that the company be placed in administration.

I learned many lessons about corporate fraud and how to investigate it from the Polly Peck case. The Touche Ross team was headed up by Christopher Morris and Fergus Falk, both highly experienced in insolvency and financial investigation work respectively. The firm also recruited a barrister from the SFO and a specialist fraud investigator. Both became integral parts of the investigation team and helped to give it relevant experience and expertise. I learned much about the legal process in the UK, not least from working closely with David Oliver, QC and other pre-eminent lawyers when putting together civil litigation cases with the objective of recovering money for creditors. Also important were the key aspects of investigation techniques, evidence gathering and security threats and procedures that I learned from working with specialists in these areas on the case. However, I learned three over-arching lessons about corporate fraud from the Polly Peck case that I have never forgotten. These lessons will re-surface at various times throughout the book and they can be summarised as follows:

- First, the need to retain a high degree of professional scepticism at all times during a fraud investigation. All information obtained, even that from intuitively reliable sources (such as directors and senior managers or the audited report and accounts) should be tested and corroborated by independent supporting evidence before it is used for forensic purposes;

- Secondly, to understand the critical importance of culture and control consciousness when assessing the fraud risk in an organisation. Fundamental to this is that the key generic anti-fraud controls of segregation of duties, delegated authority levels and access controls to data actually work in practice at all levels of a business including the very top around the boardroom table; and

- Thirdly, to realise that all litigation is contingent and that the verdict of the courts can never be predicted with certainty. It is always a very difficult and time-consuming process to bring a fraud case to a successful conclusion before a court of law. Sometimes it is an impossible one.

Our work on the Polly Peck investigation was brought to a premature close in 1993 soon after Mr Nadir absconded from the UK in contravention of his bail conditions just before he was due to stand trial, charged by the SFO with fraud and theft amounting to £34 million. He flew in a private aircraft to his native Northern Cyprus in May of that year. The breakaway de facto Turkish Republic of Northern Cyprus ("TRNC") had been established following the Turkish invasion of Cyprus in 1974. In 1993 it was not recognised by any country in the world other than by Turkey, a situation that remains unchanged today. Certainly the UK has never had an extradition treaty with the TRNC. Consequently, Mr Nadir was able to remain there, apparently living in some luxury in his villa in the town of Lapta close to Kyrenia. He lived in exile in the TRNC for 17 years before returning to the UK on 26 August 2010 in an attempt to prove his innocence and clear his name. Mr Nadir's criminal trail finally began on 23 January 2012.

Forensic work

Following the winding down of the Polly Peck case, I and most of my colleagues on the investigation team became part of the newly-formed Forensic Department at Touche Ross. As a result, we were able to put the skills and experience we gained at Polly Peck to good effect on other fraud-related assignments. I myself worked on a broad range of forensic projects over the next five years, gaining excellent experience of different aspects of financial crime in the UK, in Continental Europe and in the US. The work was varied. Some of the assignments were high profile (including reporting to governments) and all were challenging. I will give examples from this experience at various points in the book but the work included: managing fraud investigations;

producing quantum of loss statements for litigation and arbitration purposes; proactive fraud advisory services for clients; corporate threat assessment and analysis projects; and managing investigations on behalf of some of the firm's financial services clients in the areas of anti-money laundering and asset tracing.

Before moving on, I just want to say a brief word at this stage about the term forensic accounting, which will re-appear later in the book. The word "forensic" in this context means doing work to a standard that would be required to satisfy a court of law or of arbitration. We in the forensic team at Touche Ross in the 1990s liked to think that it was our old boss, Fergus Falk, who invented the term because he thought it was a "sexier" alternative to the fairly bland "Litigation Support Services" which was the name of the old department. Every other major accountancy firm at the time provided litigation support services. Certainly, Fergus was very successful thereafter in differentiating Touche Ross from the competition and in attracting a lot of business to the firm and its new forensic team. Of course, the growing reputation of the firm for expertise in fraud-related work helped. This was gained not only from the Polly Peck case but also from another high profile fraud case carried out by Touche Ross at that time – the investigation into the collapse of Bank of Credit and Commerce International in 1991 (this became a huge investigation that was to end up spanning over a decade).

Life after Touche Ross

I left Touche Ross in 1997 to set up a forensic accounting business. Working with partners, colleagues and associates I continued to work primarily on financial crime assignments and risk-related projects for the next ten years or so in an investigative and consultancy capacity. We advised some of the biggest companies in the UK and worked on a wide range of projects in the UK, the US and in Continental Europe. Again, I will use specific examples from this period at various stages in the book. Increasingly on these projects I found myself working with multi-disciplinary teams comprising at different times: lawyers, internal auditors, ex-police and/or ex-customs investigators, information technology and security specialists. The objective was often to help senior managers and the board to obtain the best possible solution to unusual business problems. Forensic investigation skills were almost always required at the outset of these projects. However, senior managers were increasingly looking for recommendations on how to prevent and deter similar problems from happening in the future and also for advice on new controls and techniques for detecting fraud quickly and efficiently.

In response, I started to develop a number of fraud awareness-raising training sessions for some of my clients in the early years of this century and I have built on this ever since. Today, I lecture in the UK and around the world on a variety of subjects. In addition to fraud and financial crime, I address the broader business issues of corporate governance, risk management, audit and compliance and business ethics. I have enjoyed working with many organisations to put on events and training courses, in particular over the last five years or so. I started in the UK by joining the lecturing panel at Quorum Training and began working abroad by becoming a member of the teaching faculty at Euromoney Training and DC Gardiner. Since then, I have developed and expanded my training network and have worked with other professional organisations including: the London Stock Exchange; the Association of Certified Chartered Accountants; Risk Audit; the Institute of Chartered Secretaries and Administrators; Faculty-One; and Lessons Learned Ltd. When working abroad I have been delighted to work with a number of dedicated local trade associations including the Gibraltar Association of Compliance Officers ("GACO") and the Malta Institute of Accountants.

It has been a real pleasure for me to have worked in so many jurisdictions around the world doing this kind of work involving research, training courses, conference work and lectures. This experience leads directly to one of the other key feature of the book – input from the delegates attending these events.

2. Courses, delegates and the Fraud Awareness Quiz

Training experience

From 2006 onwards the balance of my work has gradually changed from primarily being an investigator and consultant who did a little awareness training to being primarily a lecturer, facilitator and trainer who still does some consultancy work. The training covers the broad business areas of corporate governance, risk management and business ethics. However, my background as a forensic accountant gives me great experience and expertise in financial crime generally and in fraud risk management in particular. My first courses were developed in this area and I still do more lecturing on aspects of financial crime risk than on any other topic.

Different jurisdictions

It has been my privilege and great pleasure to lecture and run courses in many different jurisdictions around the world. A good proportion of this is UK-based of course. I have much experience of training delegates in London and elsewhere in the UK in terms of both public and in-house courses as well as speaking at many conferences. This extends to the Crown Dependencies of the Channel Islands (the bailiwicks of Jersey and Guernsey) and the Isle of Man. I have had the pleasure of travelling often to the British overseas territory of Gibraltar and working in a variety of roles there: appearing at conferences, providing both public and in-house training courses and also consulting advice largely to Gibraltar's successful and growing financial services sector.

I also have extensive experience of working with people and organisations from outside of the broad UK jurisdiction. To take the European context first, business people from the continental mainland, notably from Russia, the Ukraine, France and Switzerland, attend my courses in the UK as delegates from time to time. I have lectured and run training courses in a variety of other European countries also: Germany, Spain, Greece, Luxembourg, Iceland and Malta. Finally in terms of my European experience, I have run internal training courses for Greek, Swedish and Danish banks and for a large pharmaceutical company based in Switzerland. I have also gained some experience of working in jurisdictions further east, which can be very different to those in Europe, by lecturing and running workshops in Mauritius, Singapore and Mongolia. Finally, I have spent some considerable time lecturing and working in jurisdictions across the Atlantic Ocean to the west of the UK: running courses in the United States based in New York and Miami; participating in a whole variety of events (speaking at conferences, running public courses and giving in-house training for financial institutions and corporations in the energy sector) in the Caribbean island of Trinidad and Tobago and also in the Bahamas; and I have run in-house training for a large Brazilian multinational energy corporation based in Rio de Janeiro.

Fraud Awareness Quiz

I firmly believe that the insights that I have gained from the many hundreds of delegates that I have worked with over the years help to give this book a truly international dimension. One of the ways this is conveyed in the book is through the medium of the Fraud Awareness Quiz.

I always try to encourage as much discussion and debate with the delegates as possible, whether on courses or at conferences. One of the most effective ways of doing this is to make use of quizzes on the subject concerned, either at the beginning of the course or later in the day at a suitable point. When working with delegates on the subject of fraud I like to begin the course by asking them to complete the Fraud Awareness Quiz. I have developed this Quiz over a number of years, altering the questions slightly over time but generally aiming to ensure that each one addresses an important aspect of fraud. The answers to the Quiz given by delegates and the subsequent discussion around the room then serve as a bridge to the formal presentation of the subject, with slides and notes, for the remainder of the day.

The Fraud Awareness Quiz has proved to be highly popular with delegates. There are 10 questions in the Quiz. The answers to these questions given by the delegates vary of course but I have noticed discernible trends over the years and these trends enable me to draw some conclusions about how the issue of fraud is dealt with in practice by organisations around the world. The Quiz is set out in full at the end of this introduction. Each of the 10 Chapters in the book contains one of the Quiz questions, with the answers and comments from delegates being summarised as part of the analysis of the subject under discussion in each particular Chapter.

3. Interviews and interviewees

The third layer of fraud knowledge and awareness is provided by a series of extracts from interviews that I have conducted for this book with a number of business associates and contacts with whom I have worked at various times over the last 20 years. These individuals are experienced business people from a variety of industries, each with different experiences and areas of expertise. They are not fraud specialists. The interviewees comprise, in no particular order: two senior managers from different UK retail banks; an ex-international Compliance Officer and current senior manager of a financial services firm; an entrepreneur and ex-senior executive of a large US corporation; a former head of internal audit and current audit committee member; a senior manager in the UK public sector; a deputy CEO of an international financial services company; and the owner and Managing Director of a medium-sized manufacturing company based in the UK.

Each has his or her own perspective on fraud. I am very grateful for their time in giving the interviews, extracts from which appear at various stages of the book. Each person provides knowledgeable and practical business insights from their own experiences, sometimes giving very trenchant and even controversial views based on examples from their organisations. Fraud is an intrinsically sensitive subject and this can sometimes act as an inhibitor to discussion. So, in order to facilitate the interview process I have stipulated from the outset ground rules designed to preserve the anonymity of each of the interviewees. This applies particularly in Chapter 9 of the book where the investigation of fraud is discussed and where a number of fraud cases, some taken from the interviews, are set out. Accordingly, I refer to each interviewee by their given name only in the book. Their organisations are not mentioned by name at all. Similarly, the extracts relating to specific fraud events and investigations are anonymous.

In alphabetical order the interviewees are: Adrian; Bernard; Charles; Frazer; Jerry; Martin; Sharon and Teresa. To each one of you I say a big "thank you".

Concepts and focus

This is a business book about occupational fraud. Specifically, it is a practical guide, an instruction manual showing the various methods and techniques available to directors and managers to prevent, deter, detect and investigate fraud within an organisation. It provides strategic guidance and also more tactical assistance in terms of the most effective anti-fraud controls, the ones that have been shown to work best in practice to reduce the risks. There is no one methodology that is guaranteed to be "fraud-proof". Every business situation is unique, so that for every organisation there will be a specific approach that is better suited and more efficient than all the others.

So, this is a practical book, designed to raise awareness of internal fraud and to provide a variety of different options on how to manage it, always with the emphasis on taking a proportionate, risk-based approach. It is not a traditional book about fraud. It does not go into the threats posed by outsiders, whether they are computer hackers or members of organised crime gangs, in any great detail. Nor does it concentrate on the legal and regulatory side as it applies to fraud or have as its prime focus how to investigate fraud. Whilst these areas all receive some attention in the book, I am coming at this problem primarily from a practical business angle, not from an investigatory angle. The book's main concentration is on how organisations can best prevent, deter and detect fraud – the creation of an effective controls framework to manage fraud risk.

As mentioned, I believe that there is a big need for this type of practical fraud risk management in business today. When looking back over my own involvement in fighting financial crime over the last 20 years, I often think that despite all the headline scandals, all the books written about corporate fraud, all the behavioural research carried out on motives for fraud and all the anti-fraud training courses run and attended, the way that most organisations approach fraud risk today remains essentially the same as it always was – reactive, haphazard and ineffective. During the 1990s it was often said that fraud was one of the great "unmanaged risks" in business. It concerns me that this might still be true today. If it is, then this is a dangerous situation indeed because fraud risks have increased markedly since Polly Peck went into administration in terms both of the likelihood of a fraud event happening and the extent of the probable impact if it did so on the victim company. The likelihood of fraud always increases when the economy downturns whilst the potential scale of losses from fraud today is huge and the damage to an organisation's reputation can be irreparable. Directors and managers can no longer afford to allow fraud to remain a blind-spot in their business.

Fraud: the gorilla in the room?

When I talk to clients or to delegates on my courses, the great majority have no difficulty in agreeing with the proposition, when prompted, that fraud risk has increased since the financial crisis of 2007–09. However, if I begin the discussion by asking what extra controls or procedures have been introduced in their organisation in the last three years to counter increased fraud threats, I tend to get a very different reply – it is almost always a hesitant and muted response. It is pretty clear to me that most business entities have not increased their anti-fraud measures to match the increased fraud risk at all. Instead, many organisations will have, in effect, reduced them. This is because middle managers feature heavily in most recent corporate redundancy programmes designed to reduce staff numbers and so save costs – exactly the people who provide crucial segregation of duty controls. Smart controls, which could be used to bridge this widening gap, are often ignored, not because of cost but through a combination of a lack of awareness and a failure of willpower and commitment by directors and managers to take tough action. This management failure could carry its own risk for those individuals at the top in business because, should their own organisations fall victim to fraud, they could well be accused of negligence.

There can be no real excuses today for directors and managers not being well aware of fraud risk. The various fraud threats, both to all of us as individuals in our personal lives and to organisations in a business context are all around us and are clearly visible. Although this book deals with occupational fraud in organisations I thought it would provide some interesting perspective at the outset to look briefly at fraud in the broader context.

Once I had been approached to write this book by John Wiley and Sons and had been given the go-ahead in August 2010, I decided to keep a record of the instances of financial crime, fraud-related articles and other pieces as publicised in the media over the next seven months. In fact, there were so many that I have had to summarise drastically. I set out below some of the evidence for the visibility of fraud during the period August 2010–February 2011 inclusive, divided into three components: fraud as reported by the international media; fraud highlighted by the national media in the UK; and the specific case of Bernie Madoff, the biggest fraudster of our times, which is where we begin.

1. The Bernie Madoff effect

Today we live in the post-Madoff era. The sheer size and longevity of Mr Madoff's $65 billion Ponzi scheme have had a huge impact on areas of the financial services industry in particular and have captured the imagination of the public. Mr Madoff was arrested in December 2008 and was sentenced to 150 years in prison in June 2009. Stories about him and his fraud continued to feature heavily in the business press in 2010 and 2011 and also about the suicide of Mark Madoff, one of his two sons; about the raft of legal suits brought by Irving Picard, the court-appointed liquidator against major financial institutions such as JP Morgan, HSBC, UBS and others for alleged breach of fiduciary duty; and about the action taken by the US authorities to charge others with complicity in Mr Madoff's fraud. Despite Mr Madoff insisting that he had carried out the fraud by himself, a total of five others (four former employees and the auditor) had pleaded guilty to criminal charges by December 2011, with a further five ex-employees facing charges which they deny.

When reading these stories about the activities of Mr Madoff I am constantly reminded of the fictional character Augustus Melmotte, the "gigantic swindler" of Anthony Trollope's nineteenth century novel *The Way We Live Our Lives Now.*[3] Like Mr Madoff in New York, the fictional Melmotte is portrayed as a colossal figure in London society of the 1870s, an individual with a reputation for financial wizardry based on high investment returns, who was able to use this to build an aura of exclusivity around his affairs. The clear impression given in the novel is that everyone, including members of the English aristocracy, considered it to be a privilege to be accepted as Melmotte's client and therefore to be able to invest money with the great man. It was the same with Mr Madoff in the United States (and, reflecting the global nature of business today, around the world too). Although an outsider and coming to London from France with a somewhat chequered history, Melmotte is portrayed by Trollope as turning into a high-profile socialite, entertaining the Emperor of China at his home and even being elected Member of Parliament for the seat of Westminster! It was similar with Madoff, who rose from modest beginnings to enjoy high profile status in New York society.

There are some important differences of course (Melmotte is a character from fiction after all): Melmotte remained essentially an outsider (he arrived in London from Paris and his French connections were frowned on by many characters in the novel, perhaps even more so than was his "shady" business history) whilst Mr Madoff was an integral part of Jewish society in New York and Florida; some of Melmotte's victims are portrayed in the book as recovering quickly and not suffering great financial hardship, whilst over 16,000 claims have been lodged by people with Mr Picard, the majority of whom have lost very significant amounts of money as victims of the Madoff fraud; and for Melmotte, when he is finally convinced that his forgeries will be exposed imminently, there is only one way out – he chooses to kill himself, ending his life with a dose of prussic acid rather than be revealed to the world as the great swindler that he is. Bernie Madoff, of course, is not a character from nineteenth century fiction and he is very much alive today. When the financial crisis finally made his Ponzi scheme untenable, rather than take his own life he confessed his fraud to his sons, who handed him over to the authorities. He subsequently admitted his crimes in court and is now serving a sentence of 150 years in jail.

2. Corporate fraud highlighted by the international media

There were many references to aspects of corporate fraud discussed in the media around the world during the period August 2010–February 2011. I have summarised six of these below to illustrate both the international dimension and also the high profile nature of recent events in the fraud arena:

- The US authorities launched a major anti-fraud initiative called Operation Broken Trust. This resulted in over 340 cases of fraud being investigated, involving total funds of $8.5 billion. Eighty-seven fraudsters were jailed as a result.

- In France, Jerome Kerviel, the former trader on the Delta One derivatives desk at Société Générale Bank was found guilty of forgery, breach of trust and unauthorised computer use by a court in Paris. His unauthorised, unhedged trading activities resulted in losses to the bank of Euro 4.9 billion when they were unwound in January 2008. Monsieur Kerviel admitted his guilt to the unauthorised computer use charge but claimed he was always acting in the bank's interest, that his supervisors knew what he was doing throughout, and that they encouraged him to break the rules in order to make money for the bank. The court rejected Monsieur Kerviel's claims that the prevailing culture of greed at the bank contributed to the losses and put all the blame on him. He was sentenced to five years in jail (two of which were suspended) and ordered to repay all of the Euro 4.9 billion losses. Monsieur Kerviel is to appeal against the sentence.

- In Italy, the trials of the directors and senior managers of Parmalat, the Italian dairy group which collapsed in 2003 after its results were found to be riddled with fraud to the value of Euro 14 billion, were concluded. Calisto Tanzi, the former CEO of Parmalat, was found guilty of fraudulent bankruptcy and criminal conspiracy and was given an 18-year jail sentence. Fausto Tonna, the former Finance Director was jailed for 14 years. Thirteen other executives were found guilty, whilst two were acquitted.

- In India, 2011 has seen the unfolding of a major corruption scandal involving the telecoms industry and the Indian government which has undermined investor confidence and threatens to cripple legislative activity. It is believed by many to be the biggest fraud scam in India's history. Dubbed "2G Gate" in India, it involves the award of lucrative second generation mobile phone licenses in 2008 by Mr Andimuthu Raja, the former Indian telecoms minister (who is now under arrest) to various companies, not via a competitive bidding process but on a "first come first served" basis in return, it is alleged, for bribes. The result, predictably, was that favoured companies won the licences at prices far below market rates in 2008. A government auditor has concluded that the Indian Exchequer was deprived of $40 billion in potential lost revenues as a result. Mr Raja has been charged with conspiracy, forgery and fraud.

- The UK's Bribery Act 2010 has been described as the most draconian piece of company law to be passed in Britain in the last 100 years. It came into effect on 1 July 2011. Taking its lead from the Foreign Corrupt Practices Act ("FCPA") in the US and the United Nations Convention against Corruption ("UNCAC"), it is intolerant of all forms of bribery and goes further than previous measures, in particular in its robust stance against corporate corruption. The FCPA and similar measures concentrate on the bribery of foreign public officials. The Bribery Act, however, introduces a new corporate offence of failing to prevent bribery, the only defence to this being that a company had "adequate procedures" in place to prevent and deter bribes being paid on its behalf. Like the FCPA, the Bribery Act has extra-territorial jurisdiction so that it is attracting interest and attention from companies outside of the UK also. We will return to the Bribery Act, along with the FCPA, in Chapter 5 but suffice to conclude at this stage that it has already been the subject of much publicity in the UK and around the world.

- In Russia, Michael Khodorkovsky, the ex-CEO of Yukos went on trial for a second time. At his first trial, he had been found guilty of fraud and tax evasion. This time, despite his protestations that the trial and judicial process was politically motivated, he was convicted of massive oil theft and money laundering and was given an extra six years in jail. Many consider this to have been a victory for the Russian leader Vladimir Putin, and an indicator that Russian justice is anything but strong and impartial. However, as Mr Putin himself said: "A thief must sit in jail."

3. General fraud highlighted by the national media in the UK

The press in the UK has taken the view for many years that fraud is a "hot topic" and cases involving financial crime are always sure to receive a high level of coverage in the country's media generally. I can confirm this personally from the results of a small piece of research that I carried out when at Touche Ross. In 1996, I looked at the popularity of fraud as a storyline in terms of its coverage in the "quality press" newspapers in the UK at that time. The coverage was staggeringly high. In fact, I could only find one subject with significantly more hits than "fraud" in my review and that was "Tony Blair". The topicality of this subject should be no surprise because 1996 was the year before Mr Blair first became Prime Minister in an electoral landslide and there was of course huge interest in him and his "New Labour project" at that time. The interest shown by journalists in fraud was clearly also very significant in that year and has remained so some 15 years later. Set out below are, again, six examples drawn from the UK media in 2010–2011 selected to show different aspects of the "fraud story" that is both widely varied and has high visibility to ordinary members of the public:

- To start, there is perhaps the most sensational case of expenses fraud of all time. At the time of writing, four former Members of Parliament and two Members of the House of Lords (Messrs Chayter, Illsley, Devine and Morley, together with the peers Lord Taylor and Lord Hanningfield) have been found guilty by the Criminal Court in 2011 of false accounting in relation to their expense claims. All have received prison sentences. This was the culmination of a major political scandal in the UK caused by the disclosure of widespread manipulation by Members of Parliament of the various allowances and expenses that were available to them. The scandal provoked outrage throughout the country, though only a small number of cases involved criminality. The individual circumstances of each of the six convictions are all different but the case of Mr Morley will serve as a good example. Mr Morley is, as a former government minister, the most high profile parliamentarian to be jailed. He was sentenced to 16 months' imprisonment in May 2011 for claiming more than £30,000 in false mortgage payments. He admitted two charges of false accounting and was told by the judge that he was guilty of "blatant dishonesty". He abused the expenses system not only by over-claiming the mortgage interest on his second home for a number of years but also by continuing to submit claims for 18 months after his mortgage had been repaid! Criminal investigations into the activities of a small number of other former MPs are ongoing at the time of writing and could result in additional trials.

- There has been much publicity given to the tougher stance taken by UK authorities to clamp down on market abuse and fraud in financial services. As an example, the following insider trading prosecution was widely reported. In February 2011 Christian Littlewood, who worked for Shore Capital and was a former Dresdner Kleinwort banker, was jailed for 40 months for insider dealing, the longest prison sentence handed down for the crime in the UK after a long investigation by the Financial Services Authority ("FSA"). Littlewood conspired with his wife Angie and a third accomplice, Helmy Omar Sa'aid, who had emigrated from Singapore in 2002, to make illegal profits using a simple but effective way of disguising trades. For nearly eight years inside information was passed from Littlewood to Sa'aid to invest illegally – the FSA investigated 51 deals amounting to £5.5 million of suspicious trading. Initially, the FSA could find no connection between Littlewood and Sa'aid. However, the investigators did uncover large cash transfers between an individual named Siew-Yoon Lew and both Littlewood and Sa'aid. It was only when they checked Angie Littlewood's marriage certificate that they solved the puzzle – Ms Lew and Mrs Littlewood were in fact the same person![4]

- At the other end of the scale, benefit fraud schemes always attract the attention of the UK press, even when the amounts involved are not large. This report in the Times newspaper in August 2010 is typical: "A 61-year-old man who fraudulently claimed nearly £20,000 in disability benefits was secretly filmed taking part in a jazz dancing competition by investigators from the Department of Work and Pensions."

- Insurance scams also make good newspaper copy. In August 2010 the *Daily Mail* newspaper reported that two brothers, Rezwan and Rehan Javed, were found guilty of masterminding a "crash for cash" fraud that cost the insurance industry up to £12 million. They paid drivers up to £500 a time to stage vehicle collisions thereby opening the way to greatly inflated insurance claims. The scam worked as follows: first, the crash occurred when the driver, paid by the Javeds, would brake suddenly causing the innocent motorist behind to drive into the back of the car; next the driver would coerce the innocent motorist into admitting liability; then the owner of the car, also working with the Javeds, would use their firm (North West Claims Centre) to pursue costs against the innocent motorist, giving the crash details to the insurer and declaring non-liability; costs are then submitted (salvage, storage, repairs, care hire and injury) at around £17,000 a time; finally, as liability is not in question, the claim would be settled. The scheme was only uncovered after one driver repeatedly used the same roundabout on a busy road to stage collisions. Workers in an office block overlooking the roundabout recognised him as the "victim" of a number of rear-end shunts and informed the authorities.

- Football is the national sport in the UK. It should be no surprise therefore to learn that the media gave blanket coverage to the allegations of institutional corruption within FIFA, the governing body for football worldwide, circulating at this time. Following the failure of England's bid to host the football World Cup in 2018, claims that FIFA executives were involved in giving or receiving bribes surrounding the bidding process for the 2018 World Cup (and also the bidding process for the 2022 World Cup) became widespread, notably in the UK when Lord Triesman, the former Football Association Chairman, gave details of alleged "improper and unethical" behaviour among FIFA executives in an appearance before the House of Commons Culture, Media and Sport Committee. Subsequently, two executive members, Jack Warner and Mohamed bin Hammam, were accused of attempting to buy votes for Mr bin Hammam's successful bid to stage the 2022 World Cup finals in Qatar by offering 25 leaders of Caribbean football associations $40,000 each in cash. Following an investigation by FIFA's Ethics Committee, Mr Warner resigned from all his positions in international football and Mr bin Hammam was banned from all football-related activity for life, which he is currently appealing against.

- Finally, an example taken not from the national press but from the local community – my own golf club in fact! Mass-marketing fraud – approaches and promotions from people and organisations that we do not know promising fabulous offers – is something that almost all of us will have experienced at some stage. Many of us (not all by any means) understand that if something appears to be too good to be true it generally is just that. Organised criminals remain determined and creative in thinking up new schemes and increasingly are looking to "help" victims rather than simply play upon their greed. The copy email below is a good example of this. It was sent by the Secretary of my club to all club members warning them of one of the latest scams doing the rounds in the run-up to Christmas 2010 – note the routine nature of the service to be provided and the international dimension of the fraudsters:

> Can you circulate this around especially as Christmas is fast approaching – it has been confirmed by the Royal Mail. The Trading Standards Office are making people aware of the following scam:
>
> A card is posted through your door from a company called PDS (Parcel Delivery Service) suggesting that they were unable to deliver a parcel and that you need to contact them on 0906 6611911 (a Premium rate number).
>
> DO NOT call this number, as this is a mail scam originating from Belize.
>
> If you call the number and you start to hear a recorded message you will already have been billed £315 for the phone call.
>
> If you do receive a card with these details, then please contact Royal Mail Fraud on 020 7239 6655.

Closing remarks

I believe that this book provides an essential guide for all directors and managers at this time. Fraud poses a significant and growing risk to all types of organisations today – public sector, private sector and across jurisdictions – in terms of its potential impact on both their finances and their reputation. It must not remain a business blind-spot, especially at the present time when the tough economic climate has meant that fraud risks have increased significantly.

This book addresses this issue directly. It makes extensive use of real-life examples throughout to show how organisations can best deal with fraud. It advocates taking a proportionate, risk-based approach and provides practical advice that will enable fraud threats to be managed as efficiently and effectively as possible.

The Fraud Awareness Quiz is set out on the following pages. It also features throughout the book. Each Chapter contains one of the questions from the Quiz and the answers are also included in the narrative of each Chapter. Why not take the Quiz yourself? You might be surprised at some of the questions – and also at some of your answers!

Enjoy the book.

FRAUD AWARENESS QUIZ

1. Who is responsible for preventing and detecting fraud in your organisation?

2. What is fraud and what percentage of annual turnover are losses from fraud estimated to cost a typical organisation each year? Give three practices or types of behaviour that you consider to be examples of fraud.

3. What percentage of employees do you consider to be totally honest?

4. What percentage (by value) of internal fraud is committed by women?

5. What are the first two words or phrases that come into your mind when you hear the term "corporate governance"?

6. When assessing controls there are two fundamental questions that you should always ask. What are they?

7. What anti-fraud controls and techniques does your organisation currently use to prevent fraud from occurring?

8. Fraud occurs in all business sectors and is detected through a variety of means. What do you think is the most common way that fraud is discovered?

9. Who is responsible for investigating fraud in your organisation?

10. Imagine that you are the Head of Internal Audit and are faced with the following situation: by chance you learn that one of your sales executives provided false and inflated academic qualifications on his CV and application form when he applied to join the company two years ago. Since he joined he has made an excellent impression and last year he hit all his bonus targets making him one of the company's most highly rated managers. What do you do?

1 Responsibility

Fraud Awareness Quiz – Question 1
Who is responsible for preventing and detecting fraud in your organisation?

_____

What a mess – how could all this have been allowed to happen?

I am sitting in the boardroom of our new offices in Covent Garden, London. It is March 1991. I am about to present the monthly update report on the progress of the Polly Peck case to Christopher Morris, Fergus Falk and the various other partners and lawyers who together comprise the senior members of the Touche Ross investigation team. It is almost six months since Christopher was first appointed as joint administrator of Polly Peck, charged specifically with investigating the circumstances of the collapse of the company and the activities of its then Chairman and Chief Executive, Asil Nadir. Much has happened since then.

The investigation team has been working hard and the partners are not yet aware of all of the results. I know that what I have to say in this meeting will have a big impact. There are three parts to my report.

I begin by giving an update on the new offices, reminding everyone about the background. We moved in earlier in the month on the advice of our security consultants. These men work for a specialist firm and come highly recommended by the police. They are mainly from an army background in military security and defence intelligence and, having left the army, they are now the acknowledged experts in the UK in all aspects of corporate security and counter-surveillance. Their first piece of advice is to tell us that we need our own premises, separate from Touche Ross's existing buildings. Their reasoning is simple: the locations of the firm's main offices in various buildings around London are all well-known; they present an obvious target for the other side were they to want to discover what we were up to; and the team needed its own secure, self-contained and secret premises from which to run the investigation most effectively. Obviously, as we are now working in the new offices, we took their advice. Somebody in the meeting asks how we came to choose this particular suite of offices. I say that the security advisers located it for us by means of a fairly basic but effective vetting process. They obtained a list of premises with available office space to rent in central London and then proceeded to visit each office. Their technique was very simple. They arrived unannounced at each office in turn, always dressed smartly in business suits and carrying clip-boards. They proceeded to walk through the buildings until challenged. They were looking for the building where the challenge process was both quick and robust. The Covent Garden offices passed these tests (the other buildings visited did not) and they advised us to take them. I then mention the second, more prosaic advantage of being here, which is that these premises have a lot of storage space and we are certainly going to need it, given all the evidence that we are rapidly accumulating on the case. The offices are now the base for the entire investigation team. Everyone agrees with me that they are ideal for our purposes. I say one more thing about the new premises: everyone can speak openly and freely in today's meeting because the security consultants came in earlier this morning and carried out a "sweep" of the boardroom to make sure that it is free of any surveillance bugs or listening devices. There are a number of nervous smiles around the room at this news.

I now turn to the more serious matter of what looks like some major control weaknesses at Polly Peck. The team has made progress with one of the key areas of the investigation – asset tracing. We have already come across an array of money transfers out of the London head office bank account. As a court-appointed administrator, Mr Morris has the power to compel each of Polly Peck's various bankers to supply details and paperwork of all transactions going across the account. All the requests for this information have now been sent out and the replies from the banks are starting to come in. Our analysis and review work is at an early stage but there is one feature that is starting to cause us some concern. We can identify a series of large cash payments going out of the account, all for round-sum amounts (e.g. £100,000 or £150,000 or £250,000 etc.). These payments have been posted in Polly Peck's books to the inter-company account with Unipac, the group's main trading subsidiary in the TRNC. However, from the initial review of the information received from the banks, it seems that much of the money does not arrive there! The money appears to be transferred initially to accounts in the Channel Islands, from where it is splintered and diverted to a variety of other destinations, all in accordance with instructions from Polly Peck. We will be able to confirm these destinations when we receive all the documentation from the banks in due course. I mention also that the purpose of these transfers is entirely unclear at present. Why does Unipac, a very profitable company (at least, according to the accounts) apparently need so much cash from London? There is silence in the room now. I come to the most disturbing part. It seems that all of these transfers were approved by Mr Nadir himself and were paid away on his sole signature. Mr Nadir was able to do this because, we believe, he enjoyed sole cheque signing powers, to an unlimited amount, on the Polly Peck bank accounts. If this is indeed the case, then there were no effective controls over his use of corporate funds whatsoever, despite Polly Peck being a listed company.

I can see that this news has certainly got everyone's attention. There is more to come.

My third point is to inform everyone about the contents of a report just in from our undercover investigators in the TRNC. I need to say something about these undercover investigators. Originally, we had assumed that members of the investigation team would soon be travelling to the TRNC to review the Polly Peck group assets there. Questions of the ownership of assets in the TRNC and their recoverability were proving to be far from straightforward. For example, we could see from the accounting documentation that tens of millions of pounds of Polly Peck money were apparently located in the TRNC, held on deposit with two local banks. The joint administrators wrote to these two banks, instructing them to remit this money to London, only to receive replies expressing regret that they were unable to comply with the instructions because the funds were "blocked". This sounded highly suspicious and clearly we needed to resolve the position. However, our security consultants strongly advised against any members of the investigation team travelling to the TRNC. In their view, when the stakes were as high as this, nothing could be ruled out. The UK has no extradition treaty with the TRNC and it was even possible that if any of the team went out there the individuals might not be allowed to leave. Given the regard with which Mr Nadir was held in the TRNC and by the government there also, our security experts felt that it was not beyond credulity that any Touche Ross representatives working in the TRNC might be detained at the end of their visit to be used as bargaining chips in subsequent negotiations. So, rather than travel ourselves we decided to hire two investigators to take a look at the situation on the ground in the TRNC, in a covert capacity. Accordingly, the investigators had travelled secretly to the TRNC three weeks ago and we received their first report only the day before.

So, I take the meeting through the key points in the investigators' report. I know that they will be as shocked at its contents as all of us who read it yesterday were. I say that the investigators have visited the two banks in the TRNC that claim to be holding Polly Peck's money. Photographs of the banks are attached to the report and I hand these out around the table. The banks look small, shabby and run down even, not places that give confidence that they should be holding millions of of Polly Peck's funds. I now come to the most alarming part of the report. The investigators looked at the ownership structure of the banks. It seems that each of them is owned by Mr Nadir personally! Everyone in the room is now looking around at each other.

These are all senior accountants and lawyers, with years of experience of looking into corporate collapses and scandals. So, a number of them no doubt suspected that something like this had been going on. However, the reality still comes as a big shock to most people in the room. This looks like an obvious and significant conflict of interest which further undermines the controls over cash at Polly Peck. Fergus Falk says something quietly, almost to himself, but it captures exactly what we are all feeling: "Well, well, well, what a mess – how could all this have been allowed to happen?"

Introduction

Fraud is a significant risk to the profits and reputation of all businesses today. The starting point for any organisation in fighting fraud effectively is a clear understanding of where responsibility for managing this risk lies. Fergus Falk's comment, back in 1991, was absolutely the key question – exactly who was responsible for the problems that we were uncovering at Polly Peck? This Chapter provides directors and managers with an overview, a framework within which effective governance, risk management and internal controls can be developed. Structural weaknesses existed in the controls framework at Polly Peck, weaknesses that Mr Nadir was able to exploit.

This Chapter starts with a look at how the delegates on my courses and workshops over the years have answered the responsibility question in the Quiz. The answers enable us to draw a number of conclusions on areas where businesses can improve their approach. Next, we look at the powerful Responsibility Framework and consider the governance, risk and controls theory that underpins it. There is then a section introducing the topic of the responsibility of auditors (both internal and external) in preventing and detecting fraud. This is an important area because audit responsibility is often misunderstood and also, in practice, many organisations place too much reliance on traditional audit techniques to fight fraud. Finally, the Chapter closes with an overview of the modern approach to managing fraud: it is a strategic, risk-based approach that is rooted in governance mechanisms, with resources devoted to "upstream activities" of prevention and deterrence, backed up by modern detective techniques and access to specialist investigation resources.

This Chapter emphasises from the outset the importance of factors such as corporate culture, tone at the top and awareness of risk in the successful management of fraud threats.

As an example of best practice in strategic fraud risk management, consider the following comments in an extract from my interview with Frazer. Frazer is a senior manager in a large government department in the UK's public sector. I began the interview by asking him what level of priority was given to fraud in his organisation. This is his reply:

> Fraud risk management has been reported by the Chair of the Audit and Risk Committee as one of the top three priorities for our board, so it's given very high priority. It's primarily driven by guidance on how we manage public finances and we are required to have in place a process for understanding and managing cases of fraud so it's managing public money. Our Accounting Officer is accountable to make sure we have that and it is treated extremely seriously by our most senior officers.

There is a very powerful message here. Directors and managers need to understand that, although anti-fraud controls are crucial (and these are discussed at length throughout the book) the culture, tone and risk profile of their business will provide the entire context in which these controls are set.

Another important point (and one of my key messages) is that if fraud is to be managed successfully, it must not be looked at in isolation but rather it should be put in its proper context of business risk. All organisations need a proper understanding and assessment of fraud risk within their own business profiles in order to be able to design effective and proportionate controls to manage the various threats that fraud poses both to their profits and to their reputation. This is the essence of taking a risk-based approach.

Before we go on to discuss the risk-based approach, we begin with the Quiz and the answers to Question 1.

Answers to the Quiz

Fraud Awareness Quiz – Question 1
Who is responsible for preventing and detecting fraud in your organisation?

The first question of the Quiz addresses the issue of responsibility directly. The answers given by delegates on my courses and the points arising in the subsequent discussions provide me with a good indicator of how effective fraud prevention, deterrence and detection is likely to be within the individual organisations represented in the room on a particular day. When taken together over the years, these answers provide a useful insight into a number of general attitudes to fraud that are common in business organisations today that can lead to vulnerabilities in day-to-day practice.

The answers given to the question will vary of course depending on the mix of experience and backgrounds of delegates on any one day. Nevertheless, there are similarities and patterns from which conclusions may be drawn. Set out below are the most often repeated comments and discussion points that I have heard, in order of frequency:

- **"Everyone".** Most delegates write down one word as their answer to this question – everyone. This is now by far the most popular response I get in any discussions around responsibility, not only when discussing fraud specifically but also in a wider risk management context too. It was not always so: 12 years ago when I started lecturing on fraud most people would nominate specific individuals or departments such as "Internal Audit" or "Security" or "Compliance" or even the Money Laundering Reporting Officer as having responsibility. Today there is much greater awareness of the power and effectiveness of getting everybody in an organisation involved in the fight against fraud. However, the one-word answer of "everyone" can seem to be a little routine, a little superficial sometimes. It needs to be tested further (see below). In addition, a more forensic approach to the question of where responsibility lies in business is required.

- **"Internal Audit".** Many delegates believe that internal auditors have specific responsibility for preventing and detecting fraud. Interestingly, external audit is almost never put forward as an answer. "Internal audit" is of course most often given as an answer by those delegates who are themselves internal auditors. In the subsequent discussions it is sometimes unclear on what experience their answer is based, because most of these delegates admit that they do not themselves carry out specific anti-fraud auditing. Many have been involved in investigating frauds that have occurred but this is not the same thing – it is reactive work, responding to a specific situation revealed by a tip-off or otherwise. It is not proactive fraud prevention and detection work. We will look at aspects of fraud investigations in Chapter 9 of the book but it is important at this stage to emphasise that if internal auditors are going to be involved as fraud investigators they need two things to be effective in that role. First, they need some tailored investigation training – on the rules of evidence, on how to handle themselves when conducting interviews under pressure etc. Secondly, they need access to modern auditing tools – in particular computer-assisted audit techniques ("CAATs"). Unfortunately, most of the internal auditors who attend these sessions have neither. The role of auditors (both internal and external) in anti-fraud work is sometimes poorly understood and reliance on a traditional audit approach is often ineffective. This is discussed in detail later in the book.

- **"The board".** Although there is greater awareness today than there was in the 1990s of the responsibilities of the board of directors in preventing and detecting fraud, this answer has often to be teased out of delegates during discussions. This is more than a little surprising. The simple fact is that those individuals at the top of an organisation (whether directors, partners or a senior management team) are ultimately responsible for the risk management systems and internal controls operating in every business. Fraud falls firmly within this framework and yet this basic governance point does not seem to be widely understood.

- **"Management".** It is also surprising that this answer is not given more often. Management, in particular departmental heads and line managers, have prime responsibility for managing risk in business today. However, delegates often have to be prompted and reminded of this. This makes me question whether in practice managers are sufficiently "hands on" in dealing with risk. If not, this is a significant weakness, especially in an area like fraud. For example, it would be very dangerous for any organisation if its Head of Procurement was not well aware of fraud risks in the supply chain and buying processes of the business.

- **"The Risk Manager".** The perception of fraud as a business risk is increasing but unfortunately few delegates seem aware of one of the key principles of modern risk management, namely that "risk devolves to the line". In other words, effective management of risk is carried out by line managers and departmental heads, rather than by nominated individuals. The importance of the role of the Risk Manager has increased following the recent financial crisis, when an under-pricing of risk in financial services in particular was one of the factors in a number of large institutions either failing (e.g. Lehman Brothers) or being compelled to seek government help (e.g. the Royal Bank of Scotland). The role of the Risk Manager is one of engagement and influence, of coordination, of reporting – not of managing risk directly. The day-to-day management of risk has to be devolved to managers throughout the business if it is to be effective.

- **"Security".** A much rarer answer these days, other than by delegates from financial services and insurance institutions or from the public sector, where organisations typically employ teams of investigators and specialists to deal vigorously with the risks posed by organised crime gangs, benefit cheats and other external fraud threats.

There are never any right or wrong answers to questions around responsibility but what I would say is that most of the responses that I am given are incomplete. In fact I would go further and say that it is very rare indeed for a delegate to give me what I would regard as a complete answer to this question. The answer that I always look for, and try to steer the discussion towards, brings together three of the answers given above: first, the board and senior management team; secondly, managers – in particular departmental heads and line managers; and thirdly, everyone.

These elements combine to form the powerful "Responsibility Framework" which we will turn to shortly.

Before discussing the Responsibility Framework, there is one other important point that I want to make arising out of the discussions with delegates on the responsibility question. As mentioned above, by far the most common answer that I am given to this question is "everyone". It is of course encouraging that managers and staff seem very well aware of the importance of this inclusive concept, no doubt from other training they have received in areas like risk management. But perhaps because I hear it so often, I have grown concerned that this has become simply a default answer, a stock response without real meaning or reference to what is actually happening within businesses. To help explore what the answer "everyone" might mean in practice I often ask a supplemental question as follows:

> If I were to go to your offices, pick three people at random from your organisation (they could be the Chairman, the receptionist, middle managers, clerks - anyone) and ask them the question "who is responsible for preventing and detecting fraud in your organisation", are you confident that I would receive the same answer that you have just given me, namely "everyone"?

Amazingly, I have worked with very few delegates who have given a confident, unqualified "yes" to this supplemental question! It does happen, but it is rare. The implication of this is that the answer "everyone" is indeed a default option, an idealised response or a "best practice" solution. It is likely that many organisations are failing in practice to get all of their staff involved in the fight against fraud. Awareness of responsibility is a basic requirement for good risk management.

Consider the following. If a hypothetical fire (of whatever sort) were to go off in your business how would you want your people to react? Pretty obviously, you will want the first person who becomes aware of it to be the one who shouts "Fire!" You absolutely do not want that employee to leave it to someone else because the individual does not consider it to be his or her responsibility. This principle applies to fraud as it does to any other area of risk.

Poor awareness of responsibility is a serious weakness in any organisation. The answers to the first question of the Quiz that I have received over many years lead me to believe that, in the specific area of fraud risk management, it is a serious weakness that is widespread in business today. It needs to be addressed proactively through training and the quality of supervision by line managers, which in turn requires the commitment of time, resources and money by the board of directors. This brings us back to the Responsibility Framework.

Responsibility Framework

Introduction

The starting point of effective risk management (and fraud is of course a risk) for any organisation is to have a clear awareness throughout the organisation of responsibility at three levels: the board of directors and senior managers; line managers and departmental heads; and every individual member of staff. An overview of responsibility at each of the three levels is as follows:

• **The board and the senior management team.** The people at the top establish the values of an organisation and set policy. The collective body (we are calling it here for simplicity "the board")

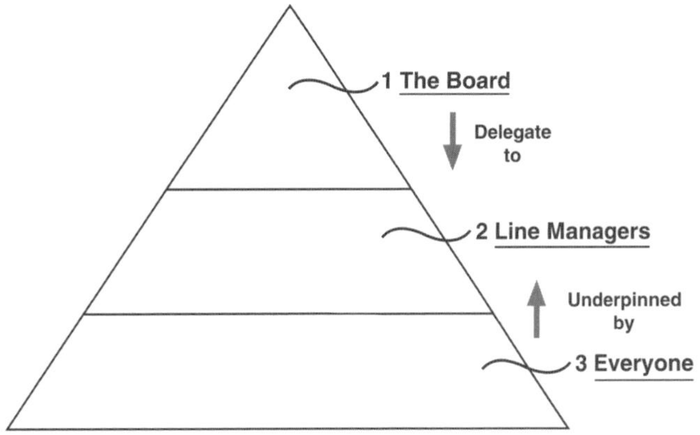

Diagram 1.1   Responsibility Framework

has ultimate responsibility for managing risk and for putting in place an appropriate system of internal controls to achieve this.

- **Line managers.** The board delegates to line managers. It is the role of managers to implement board policies on risk and control. So, managers should identify and evaluate the risks faced and design, operate and monitor a suitable system of internal control which implements the policies of the board.

- **Everyone.** All employees have some responsibility for risk management and internal control as part of their accountability for achieving their objectives. The participation of everyone underpins the framework.

I have coined the term "Responsibility Framework" for these roles and responsibilities. The framework can be represented diagrammatically as a triangle as shown in Diagram 1.1 above.

I always emphasise the importance of the Responsibility Framework to my delegates – both generally in terms of risk management and internal controls and of course specifically around managing fraud threats. I find the responsibility triangle diagram very useful for these purposes because it provides a simple visual picture of the framework.

International best practice

Both the concept of the Responsibility Framework and its representation as the triangle diagram are rooted in best practice corporate governance and risk and controls theory. I have based them directly on the report "Internal Control: Guidance for Directors on the Combined Code" ("the Turnbull Guidance") which was published in the UK in September 1999 and is at the time of writing being updated. The UK's Turnbull Guidance is one of the key internal control frameworks that have been developed around the world in recent years.

We need to look also at the US for ideas on responsibility within organisations. It has been the Americans who have led the way on this with two key control frameworks being developed in the US in the last 20 years. First, the "Internal Control – Integrated Framework" developed in 1992 by the Committee of Sponsoring Organisations of the Treadway Commission ("COSO"). This is currently being updated but it is still regarded as setting the standard for internal control frameworks around the world. The second key development affects those corporations with a listing in the US who need robust control frameworks in order to comply with the requirements of the Sarbanes-Oxley Act 2002 ("SOX").

All of these three frameworks are different but mutually compatible and each will be reviewed in some detail in Chapters 5 and 6 of the book.

Practical application

It is important to say, however, that whilst the Responsibility Framework is based upon international best practice, it is not simply a theoretical construction. It is to be found operating in practice day to day in those businesses with a strong controls and risk management culture all over the world.

As an example of this, the importance of the Responsibility Framework is understood absolutely by Sharon, the deputy CEO of a large financial institution in the Caribbean. Consider the following extract from my interview with her carried out for the purposes of this book. I started the interview by asking her the same question about the responsibility for preventing and detecting fraud that we have looked at as Question 1 in the Quiz. Here is Sharon's reply:

Steve, you would have to start off with something that is just so complicated! Well, I should say first the responsibility for ensuring that fraud is dealt with in a certain manner is vested in the executive and in the board. That's the way because obviously the leadership has to set the tone within the organisation and that is one of the things that is clear in our organisation. But then we say to our staff that everybody in the organisation is responsible for detecting fraud. You need this because it is only through your people in your branches saying if they see somebody doing this or doing that you are going to find out about fraud. You are not going to know sitting in a head office what somebody might be doing in a branch at the other end of the island! So therefore what does that mean for us? Firstly we have to develop the policies. We have determined in our organisation that there is to be zero tolerance for fraud. What that means is that it does not matter whether the fraudulent act results in the end in an actual loss to the organisation because the person carrying out the act simply does not remain with us any longer. And it does not matter how long they were with us – they have to go. That is easier said than done. It is difficult to do but once you say it then you have to live by it and people have to understand it that way, which is why it is so important to have buy-in at the more senior level and line-management level with respect to this.

And people in the organisation understand that now. So even when they think that somebody finds somebody who has done something fraudulently and they know it is fraudulent and even when they know the bank hasn't lost any money as a result, they also know the person can't remain in the organisation and we have set that awareness for ourselves. Another major thing for us is that we have to constantly train our people. You have to train people, let people understand what a fraudulent act is and then understand why it is important for us that we have zero tolerance. They need to understand what is so wrong about this, what did they do, how fraud at the end of the day can destroy an institution and if it destroys the institution then you yourself will not have a job and we need to keep connecting those dots all the time. So the thing we do, after we have the policies, is we do the training and it is very important in the training to keep showing the live example of what has happened, scenario-based training as you would call it.

And then of course what we do is we say to the managers of the branches and the business units that the cost of the fraud is to hit your bottom line, it does not come into head office. So you are very careful, you want to make sure managers understand their responsibility because they have to manage this, especially now with the way the market is. When there is pressure to make results you can't have all this fraud affecting your P & L. If there is fraud in one of our branches it's actually the branch itself that bears the cost, it's making clear to the branch manager that he's the point man on this, he's the guy who has to manage this. Those are the things that people need to learn and understand.

Sharon clearly "gets it" and so does her bank. She sets out here a very practical approach to fraud risk management and mentions two of the key ingredients that we will look at in detail later: the importance of culture (in the case of her bank it has a "zero tolerance" attitude to fraud) and the importance of getting the message conveyed to staff through training with senior staff members taking the lead.

The linkage between risk management and internal controls

Overview

We will look at both risk management and internal controls in detail in later Chapters of the book. It is useful at the outset, however, to set out some fundamental points regarding risk and controls and how the two inter-relate. Directors and managers need a good understanding of how this relationship works if their organisations are going to be able to manage fraud risk effectively. My discussions with delegates on the courses suggest that there may be some confusion as to how risk and controls actually relate to each other in practice, particularly for those who are not from a financial or an accounting background.

So, here are five key ideas that directors and managers should always bear in mind when looking at risk and controls:

- **Risk, broadly defined, means uncertainty.** In a business context risk equates to "uncertainty of outcome". If a company knew for certain what was going to happen in the future there would be no risk, but of course this is not possible. Consequently, risk must be managed.

- **Risk should be optimised, rather than minimised.** That is to say, every business should be looking to optimise the amount of risk it is prepared to accept in the pursuit of value, with the crucial reference point always being the risk appetite of each individual business. We consider the concept of risk appetite further in Chapter 4. Businesses will never be able to grow or achieve their corporate objectives simply by minimising risk. This is an important point and one that is not always readily apparent. As an example, I am often asked to speak about risk management at conferences and I sometimes find it an interesting exercise to ask delegates to raise their hands if they agree with the following statement: "We are looking to minimise risk in our business". There are always more hands raised than are not raised in answer.

- **Risk is dynamic, it changes all the time.** Internal controls are not dynamic, however. In many organisations, especially mature businesses, control systems and procedures have evolved slowly over time and may be characterised as being essentially historic, as remaining "anchored in the past". As a result, gaps often appear between risks (which are changing) and controls (which are slow to react to those changes). There is real danger for all businesses if these gaps are allowed to grow too wide.

- **Risk determines controls, not the other way around.** Internal controls exist for many reasons but fundamentally they are there to help to manage risk. It is simply not possible, therefore, for any organisation to have an effective and efficient system of internal controls in place unless it is based on a thorough, systematic and ongoing assessment of risk in the business.

- **Understand the essence of the control concept.** Key aspects of controls need to be understood also, in addition to the ideas on risk. Here, there are two crucial questions about control effectiveness. All directors and managers need to know what these questions are, they need to ask them regularly within their businesses and they need to understand the answers before they can properly conclude on the adequacy of their internal control systems. The first key question is: "are the controls effectively designed?" The key reference point here is risk and the basic equation is: the higher the risk, the stronger the controls. For a control to be properly designated as "strong" generally it will require the involvement of a senior manager or an experienced member of staff. As a matter of principle, high-risk areas should not be allocated to junior or inexperienced members of staff. The second key question is: "are the controls working effectively, in accordance with the control design?" Just because a control or procedure happens to be written down in a manual does not mean that it will be carried out in practice. From my experience, internal auditors often spend more time on the second question than on the first. They look in particular for evidence that controls are working rather than first considering whether the design of the control is appropriate. This is a mistake.

Control design linked to risk

Before moving on to look at the importance of evidence and the evidence-based approach, there is one point coming out of the above analysis that is worth emphasising. Controls need to be properly designed if they are to be effective. Good control design is impossible without good risk analysis. This is as true for fraud as it is for any other area of risk in business. One of the fundamental requirements for effective management of fraud is for an organisation to understand where the threats are in its own particular business model. This requires a thorough, systematic and informed assessment of fraud risk in the business. We will refer to this later as a "fraud risk profile". The great majority of delegates that I work with tell me that their own organisations do not have such a fraud risk profile. In reply I tell them that this is a serious weakness, so that this is often the first key action point for delegates arising on the day.

The importance of evidence

Introduction

Evidence is critical in discharging management responsibilities in business today. One of the big changes between how business was conducted in the 1990s and how it is conducted today as we move into the second decade of the new millennium is the emphasis now put on decisions and actions to be "evidence-based". In the previous century this was not so. Then, executives and managers would routinely act on decisions based on judgement calls arising out of discussions that were not written down or on information not retained or simply on "gut feel" – a phrase that, in the business context, usually refers to pattern-recognition, the instincts that make a manager good at his or her job. It would be both risky and unprofessional to take this approach today. Courts of law, regulators, auditors and other interested third parties look for evidence to support the decisions taken, especially where those decisions turn out, with hindsight, to have been sub-optimal – an executive euphemism for what are commonly known as mistakes! If there is no evidence to support the decision-making process and it turns out that mistakes have been made, then the directors and managers concerned are always vulnerable to accusations that they had not discharged their responsibilities properly and had therefore been negligent.

Examples

There are many examples today of the need for business decisions to be based firmly on evidence. Consider the following three examples that I use regularly in my training courses:

Example: external audit questioning. The first is from my own experience as an external auditor. I started work in 1979 as a trainee accountant in London. From time to time I would be required to ask questions of the Finance Director of the audit client that I was working on. Here my duties were very clear: I was to be fully briefed and prepared, arrange for a convenient time to meet the Finance Director, go in armed with my notebook and questions, ask the relevant questions, record faithfully the answers given and . . . nothing else. That was it! If the answers to any of the questions I raised were considered to be of fundamental importance to the audit opinion, the audit partner would include the question concerned in the firm's "Letter of Representation" addressed to the board of directors of the client company, who would be required to sign it before the audit opinion was signed off in order to provide formal written confirmation of key representations made to us during the course of the audit. If I was starting my audit career again today I would do everything as before (obviously my notebook would now be replaced by my netbook!) but with one crucial addition. On completion of my meeting with the Finance Director I would have to carry out work myself in order to obtain sufficient, reliable, independent corroborative evidence that what he or she told me was actually true. The whole catalogue of corporate scandals involving people at the top of major corporations in the intervening 30 years (BCCI, Enron, WorldCom, Tyco, Parmalat, Refco and many others) has destroyed forever the myth of self-evident senior management probity, honesty and integrity.

Example: anti-money laundering. My second example relates to the fight against financial crime in its broadest sense – that of anti-money laundering and counter-terrorist financing. The 21st century has seen a marked increase in the rigour with which the authorities around the world have attempted to combat money laundering and the financing of terror. The terrorist atrocities in the US on 11 September 2001 increased the momentum here because of the realisation that much of the money needed by Mohammed Attah and his co-terrorists from al-Qaeda to prepare for the attacks (to pay for food, accommodation, training courses to learn how to fly aeroplanes etc.) was sent to bank accounts they had set up in the US from banks in Germany and the Middle East using standard bank transfer mechanisms. One consequence is that terrorist financing since that time has been closely coupled with money laundering in terms of the law and regulations. Financial institutions are now required to have measures in place to prevent and deter money laundering and terrorist financing and to report any "suspicious transactions" promptly to the authorities. Legislation such as the USA PATRIOT Act 2001 and the Proceeds of Crime Act 2002 in the UK place significant personal responsibility on nominated officers (usually the Money Laundering Reporting Officers or "MLROs") in this regard. Potentially, these individuals could end up in jail if they are found to have been negligent in carrying out their duties. It is therefore imperative that MLROs document fully the reasons for all decisions taken. This applies in particular in situations where the MLRO has taken the decision that a transaction reported to him or her by a member of staff as being "suspicious" is not to be reported onto the authorities because their own investigation has shown it not in fact to be part of a money laundering or terrorist financing scheme. If subsequently this decision turns out to have been wrong, so that a money-launderer and/or a terrorist has indeed been allowed to take advantage of the system as a result, it is critical that the MLRO is able to point to the evidence of his or her notes showing that, in all the circumstances available at the time, the decision taken was reasonable. Without the evidence the court is likely to conclude that no work was carried out, with the result that the MLRO could well end up in jail for negligence.

Example: UK Bribery Act 2010. Another example can be found in the UK's Bribery Act 2010. We will look at the Act in detail later in the book – it is highly relevant because, in my view, bribery and corruption should properly be viewed as important component parts of corporate fraud, as will be demonstrated in the next Chapter. The key point to make on the Bribery Act at this stage is that the only defence to the new and far-reaching section 7 offence under the Act of the failure of a commercial organisation to prevent bribery is that, despite a particular case of bribery, the organisation in fact did have "adequate procedures" in place to prevent and deter bribery. Examples of what these procedures might be are provided in guidance issued by the Ministry of Justice and include such measures as a bribery risk assessment, a zero tolerance anti-bribery policy signed off by the board, appropriate policies on gifts and hospitality, and robust controls such as whistleblowing hotlines and staff training programmes. The essential feature though is that all of these measures and procedures must actually exist. For example, there must be evidence of the training being carried out, with a register showing the dates when the training took place and the names of those who attended.

Evidence of management of fraud risks

This focus on evidence has as much importance for fraud as it has for all other areas of risk management. As we have seen, it is necessary that awareness of responsibility for preventing and detecting fraud exists at all levels if an organisation is to have a solid foundation for the management of fraud risk. Equally important, however, is that the organisation is able to point to policies, procedures, controls and behaviours that demonstrate that the Responsibility Framework is real and that it exists in practice and not just in theory. Governance and anti-fraud controls are discussed in detail throughout the book but as examples of minimum standards here the following should apply:

- An anti-fraud policy statement. There should be a clear statement by the board, signed off by the Chairman or CEO, of the organisation's robust attitude towards fraud and the severe consequences for anyone attempting fraud against the organisation.

- Line managers should have their responsibility for managing risk in their departments set out clearly in their annual objectives. With this having been set, the appraisal process should pick up actual performance in this area. This provides managers with a clear incentive to perform in this area.

- All managers and staff should receive appropriate anti-fraud awareness training, both on induction and also re-enforced periodically thereafter. Without this it will be difficult indeed to be confident that everyone in an organisation is aware of his or her responsibilities in fraud prevention and detection.

If measures such as these ones (and others) are not in place, the board and senior management will have great difficulty in demonstrating that they have discharged their responsibilities to minimise fraud threats adequately. In the absence of any anti-fraud policy statement from the board, without risk management featuring in managers' targets and appraisals so that managers have an incentive to perform in this area, and with no anti-fraud training programmes in place it will be difficult indeed for any organisation to claim with credibility that it has taken all appropriate steps to manage its fraud risk effectively.

The role of audit in fraud prevention and detection

Overview

Audit is often thought to play a crucial role in reducing fraud risk. Indeed, if members of the public were to be canvassed at random and asked whether auditors were responsible for preventing and detecting fraud, I have no doubt that the answer would be a resounding "yes"! Much of this conviction might be to do with popular misconceptions about what auditors are actually there to do – there is little clear understanding of the roles of either internal auditors or external auditors outside of the respective auditing professions. However, in my experience, directors and managers also place too much reliance on traditional auditing to provide protection against fraud. Traditional auditing, as we shall see later in Chapter 6, will include a review of systems and controls in conjunction with a more detailed look at the documentary evidence for "samples" – a relatively small number of transactions, selected at random. The sample sizes will either be based on the laws of probability or on judgement. None of this should provide assurance to senior management that any frauds that are being committed in their organisation will be detected by the auditors.

Little training for auditors on fraud awareness

A big part of the problem is that auditors receive very little fraud awareness or investigation training. This was made absolutely clear to me by Teresa, an experienced internal auditor who has headed up internal audit departments in the past and is now a member of the audit committee of a local authority in the UK. This is what she told me during our interview about her own experiences of fraud and her training:

> I think in general, during my time as an internal auditor there was probably very little time spent on formal fraud training. Probably the only time I came across fraud was in one of the organisations I worked for and then purely by chance. I just happened to stumble across something which was relating to the very old fashioned pension incentive scheme payments, basically payments to move people out of housing into private, rented homes. You had to fulfil certain criteria and there were many letters on file and I have to admit, when I read them, I thought it can't possibly be a fraud because it's too well documented to be a fraud – but of course it was! Again, that was kind of I had to learn on the case if you know what I mean because other than technical training through the ACCA (the Association of Certified Chartered Accountants) I really knew very little about it. So I'd say on a day-to-day basis other than stumbling across something like that I probably would spend very little time on it. Other than maybe, if we were doing our own audit programme looking at the kind of fraud risk element within it, but again you know very little actual time would have been spent on fraud. I think that it probably wasn't until I became the head of an internal audit department when you sort of suddenly realise actually how these aspects link together in terms of internal audit, counter- fraud etc. and how you know one can feed into the other and you can become much more effective. Of course I was working in the local authority at that stage with a trained team of fraud investigators. I undertook my own training then as well so that I could understand what they were talking about and more about the risk of fraud within each organisation.

Teresa points to a lack of understanding and focus on fraud that is prevalent in many of the internal audit departments that I have worked with myself. Training for auditors is crucial, as Teresa's comments indicate.

Problems and remedies

In my view, traditional auditing simply does not "cut it" in terms of effective anti-fraud work. There is often a poor appreciation and awareness of fraud risk amongst an internal audit team. The small sample sizes used make it extremely unlikely that any fraudulent transactions that might be in the system will actually be selected for review during the audit process and often fraud as a business risk is never even discussed during the audit. External auditors are required by their standards to consider the issue of fraud in a financial statement audit but there remains considerable scepticism amongst the delegates on my courses about the effectiveness of external auditors in preventing and detecting fraud.

However, directors and managers need to know that there are a number of ways in which auditors can be highly effective in the fight against fraud. The use of "surprise audits", specific fraud audits carried out using a more informed assessment of risk, together with audit tools that enable data mining to take place, are all examples of how to improve audit effectiveness in this area. We will look at both the limitations of traditional auditing and more modern, alternative and effective audit approaches in more detail later in Chapter 6.

The strategic approach to managing fraud risk

Best practice guidance

In 2008, an important piece of anti-fraud guidance was published entitled "Managing the Business Risk of Fraud: A Practical Guide".[1] This work was sponsored jointly by: The Institute of Internal Auditors, the American Institute of Certified Public Accountants, and the Association of Certified Fraud Examiners. This guidance makes the key point that "diligent and on-going effort" is needed if an organisation is to protect itself against significant fraud threats. It sets out five key principles for proactive fraud risk management as follows:

- **Principle 1**: a fraud risk management programme should be in place, as part of the organisation's governance structure. This will include a written policy stating the expectations of the board of directors and senior management regarding managing fraud risk.

- **Principle 2**: there should be an assessment of fraud risk carried out by the organisation periodically to identify specific threats and changes to the risk profile that need to be controlled and mitigated.

- **Principle 3**: the organisation should have prevention controls and techniques in place to avoid potential key fraud risk events.

- **Principle 4**: the organisation should have detective controls and techniques available to uncover fraud events when preventative measures fail or unmitigated risks are realised.

- **Principle 5**: a reporting process should be in place, together with a coordinated approach to investigation and corrective action. This should help ensure that potential fraud is dealt with in an appropriate and timely manner.

This is powerful and best practice guidance. In my view it is essential that all organisations adopt this strategic approach in practice if the fraud threat is to be managed effectively. In fact, I have been emphasising these principles to my delegates for years in a slightly different format, one that I have termed the Fraud Risk Management Framework.

The Fraud Risk Management Framework

Introduction

This framework is a very simple and powerful way of demonstrating the key components of fraud risk management architecture. It is neatly summarised in Diagram 1.2. I like to take my delegates through the framework in the following way, always starting by pointing to the box at the bottom of the diagram headed "Investigation" and telling them a little of my early experiences as an international fraud investigator. There are five stages in my description to the delegates, as follows:

1. Overview of the framework

I first started working in the forensic and fraud auditing area in the early 1990s. At that time very few businesses in the UK had anything approximating to a fraud risk management programme. Most directors and managers that I spoke to at the time refused to admit that fraud was a problem at all, with a typical attitude being: there has never been any fraud in our business, our people are honest and we trust them. It was very frustrating at times. I remember when I was in forensics at Touche Ross trying to pitch an anti-fraud risk profiling product that we were working on to the Finance Director of a travel company and being told: "that's quite interesting, but what has it to do with us? We do not have any fraud in our business." Just as he was saying this, his secretary came in with a number of cheques for him to sign, which he duly did without even stopping to look at them. I remember thinking at the time that it was perhaps no coincidence that this business had never discovered any fraud!

2. Investigation

During the 1990s the attitude of business to fraud was fundamentally reactive. Essentially, directors and managers would hide behind the fiction that fraud "never happens here" and

Diagram 1.2   Fraud Risk Management Framework

keep their fingers crossed. Typically, on discovery of any form of financial crime, there would be an internal investigation but very rarely would this be reported to the police. So far as managing risk went, they would rely on some form of fidelity insurance cover if the crime was significant and look to that to reduce the financial impact of the fraud.

This reactive approach is still adopted by many businesses today but it is becoming less common. Now, directors and managers are looking more to investing resources in the so-called "upstream activities" of fraud prevention and deterrence. There are various reasons for this, most notably a greater realisation of the importance of reputation in business and the need always to protect the brand. Nothing torpedoes reputation more quickly than a fraud scandal. The other main reason is more pragmatic. The insurance industry is now much less inclined to pay out on a fraud claim without carrying out some review work first. Insurers expect their clients to have in place adequate measures to prevent fraud and, if this is not in fact the case, will seek to avoid paying out under the policy on the grounds that their client has been negligent in failing to put proper systems and controls in place and has therefore contributed to the fraud.

Of course it remains the case that fraud events need to be investigated thoroughly and professionally. All organisations need to have access to investigative expertise, either internally or by using an external source such as forensic accountants or the police. We will look at fraud investigations in detail in Chapter 9 of the book.

3. Prevention and deterrence
The modern approach to fraud focuses first of all on prevention – the policies, controls, training and communication that organisations use to try to stop fraud from occurring. There are a variety of anti-fraud prevention controls available, from generic controls like segregation of duties and delegation of authority through to specific measures such as mandatory vacations and fraud awareness training. Some are more effective than others, and all must be seen in the context of the particular circumstances and characteristics of each individual organisation. We will discuss anti-fraud prevention controls in detail in Chapter 7 of the book.

The bridge between the first box ("Prevention") and the second box ("Detection") is deterrence. Deterrence may be defined as the modification of behaviour through the threat of sanctions. Deterrence controls such as surprise audits have been shown to be highly effective in practice in reducing fraud, yet they are used only infrequently in business today. Fraud is, in essence, a people problem and controls that seek to influence behaviour through the perception of detection are very important. Deterrence mechanisms are often poorly understood by directors and managers and so are frequently under-utilised. We look at this whole area and in particular the importance of the "perception of detection" concept in more detail in Chapter 8 of the book.

4. Detection
The second box is labelled "Detection" and delegates are always very interested in this area of the fraud framework. This observation goes wider than delegates on my training courses however, as everyone that I have worked with in business in a forensic context has wanted to be able to detect fraud. Well, the first thing that I always say here is that fraud is in reality very difficult to detect! It is often carried out by individuals who are in senior positions or who have worked for an organisation for a long time and so have a detailed knowledge of the systems and of any control weaknesses. They are therefore in the ideal position to commit and conceal fraud. The purpose of detective controls is to reduce the exposure gap – the length of time from when a fraud starts to when the victim organisation finds out about it. The typical exposure gap in business will be around 18 months to two years. This often comes as quite a shock to delegates and it illustrates well

the practical difficulties in uncovering fraudulent schemes. This is an area we will return to at length later in Chapter 8.

5. Risk-Based Approach

I always suggest to my delegates that the most important part of the diagram is not the boxes at all but rather the background, which is denoted by the word "Risk". The "risk" framework provides the entire context within which fraud has to be managed. The delegates will broadly agree with me on this, which is always encouraging. However, when I ask how many of the organisations represented in the room have taken the time and effort to identify, analyse, assess and document their fraud risk exposure, very few of my delegates ever put their hands up. This remains true even today. It is disappointing and a little surprising given the greater awareness of the importance of risk management principles today. Risk is dynamic, it changes all the time. This is particularly true of a threat like fraud and yet most businesses seem not to be aware of the importance of a regular, systematic assessment of fraud risk in order for the mitigating controls and procedures to be periodically updated and therefore to remain adequate. Specific fraud risks change all the time. If anti-fraud controls remain the same, then over time there is a widening gap between risk and controls. There is danger for all organisations in this widening gap.

Risk principles underpin this book and we will return frequently to the risk-based approach in tackling fraud frequently in the coming Chapters.

Summary – Five Key Learning Points for Directors and Managers

This Chapter on responsibility provides the overall framework that will enable directors and managers to deal with the threats of fraud in an effective and proportionate way. Before looking at some of the detailed controls and procedures in later Chapters it is worth pausing a moment and looking at the key lessons learned. There are five key learning points as follows:

✓ Remember the Responsibility Framework and the associated triangle diagram. All risks and controls can be fitted into this framework. Ultimate responsibility for managing risk resides with the board and senior managers. This is devolved to departmental heads and line managers who become effectively the point men and women in your organisation in relation to risk and controls. To make the whole thing work, the framework is underpinned by everyone being aware of personal responsibility for risk and controls when carrying out their work.

✓ Carry out regular fraud risk assessment (or risk profiling) exercises. Risk must be assessed and prioritised if it is to be managed effectively. Without assessing risk it will be impossible to design proportionate controls to manage your fraud threats effectively.

✓ Make sure that everything done to manage fraud risk is evidence-based. This means that the fraud risk assessment must be documented and also that all policies, procedures, training programmes etc. must exist and be updated regularly.

✓ Do not over-rely on traditional audit techniques for fraud prevention and detection. Be realistic in terms of the focus of external audit work and try to improve internal audit capabilities through a combination of recruiting experts and investing in training programmes and/or modern detective tools.

✓ Take a strategic approach to the problem. Commit to a fraud risk management programme, be proactive and focus resources on the areas of prevention and deterrence. Have appropriate detective measures in place to reduce the exposure gap to a minimum and have access to investigation expertise, either external or in-house, to give assurance that potential future fraud events will be dealt with in an appropriate and timely manner.

2 Meaning

Fraud Awareness Quiz – Question 2

What is fraud and what percentage of annual turnover are losses from fraud estimated to cost a typical organisation each year? Give three practices or types of behaviour that you consider to be examples of fraud.

The hairs on the back of my neck

It is May 2000 and I am sitting in a conference room in the London head office of one of the largest companies in the UK. It has been a difficult meeting, one of those high pressure situations that come with the job from time to time. Sitting alongside me is the company's Director of Human Resources. Opposite us on the other side of the table is one of the company's area managers – or to be more precise, one of the company's ex-area managers, as the Director of Human Resources has just fired him. Before he did so I spent 30 minutes going through the results of my investigation into the ex-manager's activities following an anonymous tip-off: complaints of sexual harassment and inappropriate workplace behaviour; submitting inflated expense claims; the use of company property for private purposes; and alcohol misuse. Working with the company's internal auditors, I found evidence to substantiate most of these allegations – not all of them, but sufficient for these purposes. The man is no longer with the company.

I am confident that my approach and technique has been pure text book throughout. I have simply presented each piece of evidence that we found to the ex-manager during the course of the meeting, going through each component part in a calm, methodical, non-judgemental manner. After some initial objections, he has listened to what I have had to say and remained silent, by and large. At the end of my review, the Director of Human Resources has told him that in his opinion all this adds up to a track record of unacceptable behaviour that constitutes gross misconduct. A deal is quickly done, much to my frustration because I feel that we have more than enough evidence to justify a straight dismissal without the need for any negotiation. The ex-manager agrees to leave the company without recourse to any tribunal or legal process, in return for which he is to receive a sum of around £40,000 by way of a "compromise agreement" together with a "clean" reference.

The formal meeting is now over and I begin to clear away my papers. I start to become aware that the ex-manager is staring straight at me; he seems to be concentrating hard. Clearly he has something on his mind. He then begins to speak – he is not angry any more but speaks in flat, matter-of-fact tone of voice: "Steve, I have to tell you that I don't think that I've done anything terrible here and yet I've just lost my job. It's clear from everything that you have said that you think I've behaved very badly. Maybe I have. But all this talk about fraud and abuse – well, you don't know the half of it, old son. If you want to get serious about what goes on in this company I can tell you that you have been looking in the wrong place and at the wrong man. You should take a look at Mr "X" and what he and his gang have been up to in Northampton. Some of that stuff will make your eyes water. Then come back and talk to me about fraud and abuse."

ame Mr "X" means nothing to me; I have never heard him mentioned before. But there is just
thing about the way that the ex-manager says this, the way that he is looking at me that
makes the hairs on the back of my neck stand up. I have a strong gut feeling that there is real
substance to the ex-manager's allegation, that it is not simply a malicious reaction to his sacking.
I just know that there is some unfinished business here. I think to myself that it is very likely that
I will be spending quite a lot of time in Northampton in the near future.

Introduction

We will return to look further at Mr "X" and his activities in Chapter 9. In the meantime, this
incident is a good example of something that I have seen frequently throughout my career, namely
a fraudster expressing the view that he or she has done nothing wrong. The conduct of other staff
members is often used to justify this stance. Organisations need to be aware of this and to take the
time to define clearly what is meant by fraud and other corrupt business practices so that there can
be no confusion, genuine or fabricated, in the future.

Inconsistency renders the effective management of risk within an organisation impossible. This
general principle applies especially to the specific risk area of fraud. It is important that
organisations are precise in what they mean by the term fraud and that they always treat its
symptoms in the same way if they are to manage the threats it poses effectively. As noted, in my
experience such consistency is often lacking so that the word fraud can mean different things to
different people. Sometimes in the modern world of global business this is inevitable as it relates to
a jurisdictional point, where the law can provide precise definitions and throws up subtle cross-
border differences. These legal differences can prove to be harmful to the prospects of success in
cross-border fraud investigations. Sometimes however the differences can be traced back to
corporate culture and to behaviours within organisations. Inconsistencies here are not helpful
to effective fraud risk management. For example, the management of such areas as sickness levels,
expense claims or mutual hospitality with potential suppliers will vary from company to company
and also sometimes from manager to manager within an individual company. The board and
senior management need to establish a clear understanding of what constitutes fraud and what the
consequences of such action, if detected, will be.

This Chapter looks at what fraud actually is and what it is not. It reviews the constituent parts of
fraud from three angles: first, definitions of fraud and the implications arising from them; secondly
one of the classic and very important "fraud typologies" developed by the Association of Certified
Fraud Examiners ("ACFE"); and thirdly, a brief overview of some of the law in regard to fraud,
with particular reference to the position in the UK and in the US. It looks at some estimates of the
financial cost of fraud and considers the collateral damage that can be suffered by organisations
that are victims of fraud. The Chapter reaches a straightforward conclusion: the costs of fraud are
significant and they are likely to increase as the global economy continues to struggle

Before we look at what fraud is all about we need to return to the Quiz and to Question 2.

Answers to the Quiz

Fraud Awareness Quiz – Question 2

What is fraud and what percentage of annual turnover are losses from fraud estimated to
cost a typical organisation each year? Give three practices or types of behaviour that you
consider to be examples of fraud.

This question asks delegates to consider their own understanding of what the word fraud actually means in practice, as well as to share their perceptions of the extent of fraud in terms of the most straightforward and obvious measure of the risk, that of financial loss. The second part of the question has proved to be much easier for them to answer than the first and we will look at this aspect of the question now.

The people who come on my courses have consistently shown a very good awareness of the financial impact of fraud over the years. The majority of their answers fall within the range 2% to 5% of turnover. This is absolutely in line with much of the research on the extent of losses from fraud. As an example, the Association of Certified Fraud Examiners ("ACFE")[1] summarises one of the key findings of its 2010 Report to the Nations on Occupational Fraud and Abuse ("RTTNs") very succinctly as follows: "Survey participants estimated that the typical organisation loses 5% of its annual revenue to fraud." Occasionally, delegates will come up with different answers, almost always giving higher percentages rather than lower – 12% of turnover, sometimes as high as 15%. These estimates are simply too high and represent an exaggeration of fraud risk. Any organisation that loses 15% of its turnover to fraud is unlikely to survive very long as a going concern. For it must be remembered that losses from fraud will always come straight off the bottom line of an organisation's profit and loss account – that is to say, fraud losses reduce net profit after margins and overheads have been taken into account. It will take a much bigger increase in future turnover (the top line of the profit and loss account) to make up for these losses.

Delegates struggle much more with the first part of this question, of defining what fraud actually is. We will come back to this at the end of the Chapter when we are in the best position to assess the delegates' answers. Before we move on to look at the definitions, it is important to appreciate from the outset that fraud is complicated and is often looked at in different ways within organisations.

As an example of this, consider Jerry's response to a question that I asked him at the start of our interview for this book about his own perceptions of fraud and fraud threats. Jerry is a very experienced banker with over 20 years' experience of working in the retail network of one of the largest financial institutions in the UK. This is what he had to say.

I think there are three different types of fraud levels within the banking industry at the moment. I would say they start with basic and deliberate fraud as I call it. The banks are now hiring people from mobile phone companies and the like, you know fairly unethical people are coming in or else they might have links to organised crime. So, that's their sole purpose, to perpetrate fraud, to get third party finance i.e. they are debiting people's accounts or they are falsifying the opening of accounts, that sort of thing. So, criminal acts, that's one type of fraud as I see it.

The second level is internal fraud for personal gain i.e. manipulating the system to increase your own incentive payments. As an example there was a fairly widespread form of fraud that happened in our bank recently. Here the incentive was around account opening but you had actually to activate an account before you got paid for it. In other words, a £1 credit at least had to go through the account. So people were paying £1 into the account, taking it out, paying £1 into the next account, taking it out again and that was so that they got paid for opening these accounts. You got paid £x amount for one account a month, you got paid £y amount for three accounts, so they were manipulating the system for their own financial gain. But you could say that all they were doing was putting the £1 through the customer's account so the customer wasn't being disadvantaged at all. There was a perception that this was ok because it was seen as a "victimless fraud" as such.

The third one results from pressure of targets. This is not for financial gain but it's to ease the pressure of being put "on disciplinary" for not performing. As an example, the bank might set you a target for "switchers" i.e. customers or businesses moving from one bank to another. You might see a customer who is in fact a start-up customer (not a switcher at all) but he's going to fit your portfolio i.e. the level of your portfolio and what you are targeted on. All you need is a sort code and an account number so you might decide to make one up or use a sort code and account number from another switcher purely to hit a target, not for financial gain because you are not putting money in there to get paid for it. But this is how people act sometimes because otherwise the pressure of the huge targets that have been ramped up will be too much. These targets are often impossible to meet. I mean you could easily have targets that go up 100% every year, year on year and there comes a stage when you just can't hit that, it's impossible. So it is fraud, yes, but I would say that it is the least serious type if you will, because it's not for financial gain. Although I guess the flip side of it is that you could get incentives for it if you do well in always hitting your targets.

So that's the sort of three levels of fraud we see at the moment.

Jerry is painting quite a complicated picture here, but it reflects the reality of what is happening day to day in his bank. We will look at the motives for fraud in the next Chapter. As for pressure, this is one of the most important reasons why essentially good people can be driven to do bad things in the workplace and we will return to examine aspects of pressure at various places in the book. Before that, let us now look at some definitions and levels of fraud that have wide acceptance in the business world.

Fraud definitions

There are many definitions of fraud to be found in the anti-fraud laws and regulations of countries around the world. It is important to be clear right at the start that these legal definitions must always be referred to and followed when conducting fraud investigations. We will look at some of them at the end of this Chapter. However, legal definitions are not the most helpful sources when looking to put together a consistent framework that will enable directors and managers to deal with threats of internal fraud in business in the most effective way.

Whenever I work on training courses or speak at conferences I prefer to refer my delegates to a definition with a more worldwide application. As a chartered accountant I naturally look to what the international accounting and auditing standard setters have to say. In the case of fraud, the auditing standards both in the US and internationally provide very comprehensive and helpful definitions. I normally use the definition contained in International Standards on Auditing No.240: The Auditor's Responsibility to Consider Fraud in an Audit of Financial Statements ("ISA 240"),[2] although the definition in the Statement on Auditing Standards No.99: Consideration of Fraud in a Financial Statement Audit ("SAS 99")[3] in the US is very similar.

The ISA 240 definition of fraud is as follows:

> An intentional act by one or more individuals among management, those charged with governance, employees or third parties involving the use of deception to obtain an unjust or illegal advantage. *(ISA 240)*

This definition is at once simple and powerful and it is also extremely useful as a reference point. It is based around the Responsibility Framework that we discussed in Chapter 1, with the additional dimension of threats posed by third parties, those from outside the organisation. In the context of this book, which focuses on internal or occupational fraud, we address third party risk primarily in the context of corruption schemes which often involve insiders acting in collusion with third parties. The definition also addresses the very important question of the motives of the fraudster – the desire to obtain an unjust or illegal advantage. As we will see in the next Chapter, motives can be both financial (greed or a response to financial pressure of one kind or another) and non-financial (job dissatisfaction, ego, a sense of entitlement, the need to maintain a personal reputation etc.).

There are two words in the definition that I always take the time to highlight to my delegates because they are of fundamental importance. These key words are "deception" and "intentional" and it is crucial that their significance in the context of fraud risk management is properly understood. Each is looked at in turn below.

Key word – deception

It is an obvious thing to say that fraud is a hidden and concealed act or scheme. But this has one simple consequence that is often overlooked – fraud is almost always difficult to detect. It is often carried out by managers in senior positions or by employees who have worked in their organisations for many years. These individuals are likely to have extensive knowledge of the systems, controls and procedures of the organisation and will often be able to use this both to circumvent internal controls and also to conceal the subsequent fraud.

Whenever I work on consultancy projects, the directors and managers (and internal auditors!) of my clients are always very keen to know how they can better detect fraud. There are modern detective techniques, such as data mining, which can be very helpful here and we will discuss these in detail in Chapter 8. But I always preface any advice on fraud detection with a very important caveat – fraud is difficult to detect even for trained investigators so that it is always more effective for directors and managers to invest time and resources in strategies designed to prevent and deter fraud from happening in the first place.

The time element of fraud is sometimes referred to as the "exposure gap". The exposure gap is the length of time from when a fraudulent activity starts to when it is discovered. Recent research carried out by the ACFE concludes that the average "exposure gap" of a fraud scheme in an organisation is 18 months. In other words, a fraudster can expect to have 18 months to carry on his or her illicit activities before they are caught. It could of course be far longer than this. The case that I always use to illustrate the potential longevity of fraud is that of John Rusnak.

Example: Allied Irish Bank.[4] Mr Rusnak is the now infamous ex-currency trader who worked for Allied Irish Bank in the Baltimore offices of its US subsidiary, Allfirst Financial. He was regarded as a loyal and trusted employee and as a pillar of the local community.

However, he was also a strong and influential personality who was engaged in extensive and long-running fraud. Described in the subsequent investigation report into the fraud as being "unusually clever and devious", Mr Rusnak was found to have carried out numerous unauthorised and high value transactions (foreign exchange deals, commodities swaps and other trades) over a five-year period before his fraudulent trading was finally discovered in February 2002.

Key word – intentional

The second key word in the definition is "intentional". Fraud is not the same thing at all as an error or a mistake. Errors and mistakes happen from time to time in all organisations. Fraud is to be distinguished from them by looking at the intention behind the act. It is very important that this distinction is made because whether we like it or not, we all make mistakes. We are all human and human beings make mistakes.

I like to illustrate this point to my delegates by asking them who is the most successful manager in the history of the English Premier League – most people have an opinion on football! The answer will come back inevitably as Sir Alex Ferguson, the manager of Manchester United Football Club. However many trophies he has won with Manchester United, Sir Alex has made countless mistakes and errors in the transfer market when buying new players. As an example, he once paid £3.5 million for Eric Djemba-Djemba, the Cameroon international, as a replacement for Roy Keene in United's midfield, only to sell him some 18 months later to Aston Villa for £1.5 million after the player failed to establish himself at Old Trafford. This was perhaps not the best use of his shareholders' money!

It is important to be honest and realistic – we all make mistakes in our work. But of course that does not make us all fraudsters. As we will see in later Chapters, the attitude of some organisations towards errors and mistakes is both curious and harmful: errors are seen as badges of incompetence whilst mistakes are treated as unacceptable – any mistake that comes to light is treated as a career-limiting event. These attitudes serve only to promote one of the most corrosive components of culture that can exist in any organisation – that of blame. If a blame culture exists in an organisation (or even the perception of a blame culture, which is often closer to the truth) there will be various consequences, all of them harmful. The one that concerns us most here is the strong temptation for managers and employees working in an organisation which does have a blame culture to keep quiet about errors and mistakes, to seek to cover them up and to try to find some way to correct them before they are detected. That way, it is thought, nobody will be any the wiser and careers will be safeguarded as a result.

However, I continually emphasise to my delegates the danger of crossover into fraud territory here. If an error or mistake is incapable of being corrected quickly, then the individual concerned can very soon find himself or herself involved in an ongoing scheme of deception that could last for months or even years. In other words, there is a risk that mistakes that are covered up will turn into fraudulent deception over time. The risk is greatest of course in organisations that lack a culture of transparency and proper accountability. The best example of this is the story of Nick Leeson and the collapse of Barings Bank in the 1990s.

Example: Barings Bank and Nick Leeson.[5] Mr Leeson is the notorious "rogue trader" whose unauthorised and concealed trading activities in the early 1990s resulted in losses of over £860 million and brought down his employer, Barings Bank, at the time the oldest bank in the City of London. In his autobiography, *Rogue Trader*, Mr Leeson makes it clear that his unauthorised deals did not start out as fraud at all. Instead they had their origins in a series of errors and dealing losses incurred by staff in his department. Mr Leeson headed up the front office trading operations of the Barings' subsidiary based in Singapore. On one particular day staff in his department lost £20,000 on a foreign exchange transaction. A series of further errors brought total losses from mistakes alone to over £100,000. These losses would certainly be high-lighted by variance analysis of results carried out by the accounts team in London. Mr Leeson was convinced, because of his perception of the culture at Barings Bank, that the result would be dramatic – the individuals in his team who made the mistakes would no doubt be fired and he would be stripped of all his responsibilities. According to his version of events in the book, he could not simply stand idly by and watch any of his staff lose their jobs in this way. Instead he decided to take action. He took it upon himself to conceal the losses from head office by transferring them from the profit and loss account to a balance sheet suspense account – the infamous "88888 account" that he used for this purpose. Mr Leeson then went on to spend much of the next three years effectively trying to trade out of these losses, ultimately with a spectacular lack of success. So, it could be argued that losses that started out at just over £100,000 turned into a black hole of almost £1 billion that brought down Barings Bank. Mr Leeson was obviously engaged in fraudulent activities. What is often not realised or commented upon is that the Barings case provides a good example of the danger of crossover from incompetence (the mistakes made by staff in the Singapore office) to fraud via cover-up.

ACFE occupational fraud typology

The Association of Certified Fraud Examiners ("ACFE") describes itself as "the world's largest anti-fraud organisation and premier provider of anti-fraud training and education". Its aim is to reduce business fraud worldwide. Established in the US in 1988 by the renowned fraud expert Dr Joseph T. Wells, it is in my view the most important single source on internal fraud and the risks posed to business organisations of all types today. It is well-established as a professional body that awards the qualification of "certified fraud examiner" to individuals passing its accreditation process. It has over 55,000 members in more than 140 countries around the world.

The ACFE focuses its attention on internal or occupational fraud. It defines occupational fraud as:

The use of one's occupation for personal enrichment through the deliberate misuse or misapplication of the employing organisation's resources or assets.

The ACFE has carried out many studies and research projects on internal fraud. As a result of the research it has identified a number of key fraud characteristics, from which it has developed a typology for occupational fraud which the Association calls the "occupational fraud classification system". This divides occupational fraud into three primary categories that are used by individuals to defraud their employers:

- Fraudulent financial statements schemes;
- Asset misappropriation; and
- Corruption.

In my opinion, these three categories provide an excellent and very helpful framework for a thorough analysis of occupational fraud. The key components of each category are set out below.

1. Fraudulent financial statements schemes

Introduction

The ACFE has a very straightforward description of fraudulent financial statement schemes, namely the falsification of an organisation's financial statements in order to make it appear more or less profitable.

If an organisation's report and accounts, prepared and signed off by its directors and senior managers, are shown to be wrong and misleading, there can only be two possible causes: error or fraud. Modern accounting and reporting rules are certainly complicated and, despite all the checking that goes on in the financial reporting process and the extra assurance provided by an external audit, there have been many instances of accounts having to be revised subsequent to their publication in order to correct mistakes. However, there have also been many cases of financial statements being wrong because of fraud. As always, the critical difference is whether there was an intention to deceive on the part of those compiling the various connected but disparate numbers, information and descriptions that comprise the financial statements.

Involvement of directors and executives

Financial statements fraud is most often carried out by directors and senior managers looking to gain advantage from presenting the financial results of their organisations as better than they actually are. The reasons for doing this are various but are likely to include one of the following: the need to raise money from the markets; the desire to keep the company share price high; the need to maintain a high share price is often related to executives' own share-holding or to executives having personal loans either directly from the company or from a bank but secured against company stock; and the personal driver of hitting targets in order to secure a bonus. We will review a very obvious example of financial statements fraud in the case of the WorldCom scandal later on in this Chapter when looking at the phenomenon of financial engineering. Here, Mr Ebbers (the CEO) and Mr Sullivan (the CFO) attempted to mislead investors and the markets into thinking that their company was performing well and meeting its targets by manipulating the accounting rules. Mr Ebbers was convicted in 2005 of all the charges against him (fraud, conspiracy and filing false documents) and ordered to serve a 25-year prison sentence. This was the maximum sentence available to the courts and is a good indication of how seriously this crime is viewed in the US. In contrast, Mr Sullivan pleaded guilty to the same charges and agreed to testify against Mr Ebbers, which was critical to the success of the prosecution's case. Consequently, Mr Sullivan received a five-year sentence and was released in 2009 having served four years in prison.

Accounting standards

The basic framework for financial reporting was set out in Chapter 1: the directors and senior management are responsible for producing the financial statements which, in all but the smallest of organisations, are then subject to an external, independent audit, the end result of which is the audit report. The financial statements must be drawn up in accordance with the law but also crucially in accordance with generally accepted accounting standards or practices, often referred to by the acronym "GAAP". In the past, these GAAPs could vary significantly around the world – indeed each country would have its own set of generally accepted accounting standards. In recent years however there has been a drive by the accounting authorities to bring the standards closer together and much work has been done to compile a set of international accounting standards. These international standards have now gained widespread recognition, for example by the European Union and other countries. They have obvious advantages, especially for the global investor. Despite much having been achieved recently in terms of accounting convergence, at the time of writing in early 2012 the two largest economies in the world, the US and China, still retain their own national accounting standards.

A set of financial statements does not have to be accurate. Instead, it must be "fairly stated" and in accordance with the law – classically, it is required to be "true and fair". This introduces the concept of materiality. Also, the accounting standards themselves are sometimes open to interpretation, managers have a range of possible accounting policies to choose from when compiling the accounts (e.g. the depreciation policy – how fast or how slowly to write down the value of the fixed assets?) and some areas of the accounts cannot be completed by precise calculation but require estimates from management (e.g. the level of bad and doubtful debts in the ledgers that have to be provided against). All of this brings in a degree of subjectivity that provides opportunities for fraud.

Senior executives have not been averse to making use of these opportunities as is shown by the whole slew of financial statement fraud that was uncovered in major US corporates at the start of this century: in addition to the WorldCom case, the scandals involving Enron, Tyco and Q-West are all examples of financial statements fraud in listed American companies at the outset of the 21st century. They provoked a crisis in confidence amongst the investor community in the US concerning the quality (or otherwise) of controls surrounding the financial reporting process and the safeguards (or otherwise) provided by the external auditors. These concerns led directly to the passing of the Sarbanes-Oxley Act in 2002. We will return to look in more detail at the issues concerning weaknesses in corporate governance and external audit later in the book.

Manipulation of financial statements

The ACFE identifies a number of areas in the financial statements that are frequently targeted for abuse by senior management when committing fraud as follows:

- **Improper revenue recognition.** The top line figure in the profit and loss account is described variously as turnover, revenue or sales. However it is described, this is the number in the accounts that is most often abused by fraudsters. Methods vary but the one most frequently used is simply to bring forward sales that are genuine but are earned in the next financial year into the current year's results. In other words, sales income is recognised in the accounts prematurely, thereby fraudulently increasing profit. There are other methods too. Sales are sometimes simply inflated or else are bogus and reflect entirely fictitious transactions. The problem with these last two methods is that they carry more risk of detection for the fraudster. Because of the conventions of double-entry bookkeeping, if an inflated or a fictitious sale is created then a fictitious debtor will also have to be created to make the books balance. As will be appreciated, this increases the chance of detection significantly.

- **Concealed liabilities.** The failure to disclose in the report and accounts significant amounts that the company owes, or has committed to spending or might lose because of a pending legal claim, is another important way that executive fraudsters deceive investors into thinking that the prospects of the organisation are better (or less subject to risk) than they are in reality.

- **Inadequate disclosures.** Annual financial statements should provide their readers with all necessary information to form a judgement on the true state of play of the organisation. However, in reality accounting disclosure is often opaque, brief and unhelpful. One of the criticisms levelled at the senior executives of Enron was that the only reference in their financial statements to the extensive network of off-balance-sheet special purpose vehicles that they made use of was in a single, very detailed and opaque accounting note.

- **Improper asset valuations.** Boosting improperly the value of fixed assets (e.g. property, plant and machinery, computer equipment etc.) or current assets such as trade debtors is another way that a fraudster can mislead investors.

Example: Polly Peck. Polly Peck is not a financial statements fraud case but I include it here to illustrate the limits of the information contained in company annual reports and accounts, especially concerning business risk. It was the Polly Peck case that first brought this point home to me. Reading Polly Peck's accounts for the year ended 31 December 1989 (the last set published before the collapse) I was struck by how straightforward they seemed to be: those of a typical large, listed corporation, compiled to the standards of the time and including a clean audit report. Yet, I could see from my investigation work that the reality was different - Polly Peck was not a typical public company at all. Rather, it was an unusual conglomerate with a number of unique and high-risk features. First, much of its success was based on the profitability of the citrus fruit operations located in Turkey and in the TRNC, a self-declared state recognised by no country in the world other than Turkey. Cyprus was a partitioned island with embittered populations of Greeks and Turks on either side of the dividing "Green Line". This unstable environment led to uncertainties. As an example, consider this contingency: the citrus trees producing the fruit grew on land that was the subject of legal claims by the former owners, Greeks who had been removed by force after the Turkish invasion in 1974. The accounts contain typical upbeat statements about past successes and future prospects but are silent on the "Cyprus problem" and how it might impact the group. There was also a governance issue: the imbalance of power at the top, with Mr Nadir, the founder, still dominating despite the fact that Polly Peck was now a publicly listed company. The accounts disclose that he was both Chairman and Chief Executive, but they say nothing about the very significant control and influence that he wielded, for example his sole cheque signing powers. Mr Nadir's influence extended into the TRNC itself, where he had many personal business interests and apparently powerful political connections. Apart from one brief note, the accounts do not address the potential for conflicts of interest that existed here. So, there were various unusual and significant risks surrounding Polly Peck but these would not have been readily apparent to readers of the company's accounts (investors, lenders, suppliers) at the time.

In addition to these schemes identified by the ACFE, which mostly tend to have the effect of improving the results of an organisation, there is another important form of financial statement fraud, often known as "big bath provisioning". The "big bath" refers to situations where an organisation has enjoyed bumper results in a particular year, in fact the results are viewed as being too good by senior management, either because they attract too much by way of a tax charge or because they will raise unrealistic expectations of future performance. Consequently, management will make a provision in the accounts to reduce profit to a more "satisfactory" level. Although managers will seek to justify such provisions on the grounds of prudent accounting, if the adjustment is done to manipulate the figures in contravention of accounting standards, then it is indeed fraud. I should add that I came across the situation more often in the 1990s at the start of my career in forensic accounting – it is less of an issue in the years following the financial crisis when the results and profitability of many organisations are under extreme pressure.

2. Asset misappropriation

Introduction

The ACFE again takes a very straightforward view of asset misappropriation. It considers this to be any scheme that involves the theft or misuse of an organisation's assets.

Asset misappropriation is by far the most frequent type of internal fraud. The ACFE describes it as follows: "Asset misappropriation includes more than theft or embezzlement. It involves the misuse of any company asset for personal gain". This category involves many different types of fraud. The ACFE divides asset misappropriation into two basic sub-sets: cash schemes and schemes involving inventory and other assets.

Asset misappropriation – schemes involving inventory and other assets

Looking first at schemes involving inventory (stock) and other assets, here the fraudster obtains advantage from the use of company assets rather than from a direct cash conversion. One means of doing this is by theft (or larceny) and all businesses with high stock levels should be well aware of the importance of stringent warehouse procedures and regular stock counts to minimise the risk of losses here. The other means identified by the ACFE in this sub-set is fraud through asset misuse – in other words, employees using company property for personal purposes. Examples include: accessing the internet for personal use during work time (e.g. online shopping, booking holidays, viewing pornography – there are many different temptations!); downloading company documents and information for use elsewhere; and excessive personal calls on company telephones. We will return to this subject later in the book.

Asset misappropriation – cash schemes

The second and more important category of asset misappropriation is cash schemes. Here, the ACFE sub-divides cash schemes into three: cash larceny (the basic act of stealing money); skimming (a fraudulent activity often seen in the retail sector where a small amount of the sale receipt is skimmed off the top by the sales assistant or cash-till operator before it is recorded in the accounts and is diverted for his or her benefit); and fraudulent disbursements.

The most significant component of asset misappropriation frauds is fraudulent disbursements, which the ACFE defines as: "schemes where a distribution of funds is made from an account in an apparently normal manner". The ACFE identifies four key groups in this category, as follows:

- **Billing schemes.** These frauds involve the submission by the fraudster of bogus invoices (bills), typically in the name of a made-up supplier for non-existent goods or services. The fraudster ensures that these false invoices are then passed through the organisation's accounting system without detection, are correctly authorised for payment and finally result in cash being credited to an account controlled by the fraudster. As will be appreciated, these billing schemes are most often carried out by individuals working in the accounts depart, especially those who have direct experience in the areas of payments or on the purchase ledger. Billing schemes can be very difficult to detect once the false supplier has been set up on the system, so that controls over the authorisation of new suppliers are vital. Also, the payments system and the purchase ledger are areas where the use of detective techniques such as data mining can reduce losses significantly by picking up in a timely fashion not only fraudulent payments but also amounts paid away in error.

- **Payroll schemes.** These frauds involve either the creation of a bogus employee (or employees) or the misuse of information concerning a real life person (e.g. a previous employee who has left the company but whose details have remained on the system – with the exception of the person's bank account of course, the details of which the fraudster will definitely look to change). Either way, under a fraudulent scheme the result will be the payment of "salary" into accounts controlled by the fraudster. Normally these schemes are relatively minor, involving the creation of a small number of "ghosts" on the payroll by an individual working either directly in the payroll section or else as part of the team in the accounts department. However, sometimes payroll schemes can be carried out on an altogether different scale, as in the case of the Satyam fraud in India revealed in 2009. Here it is alleged that, as part of the scheme, senior executives created a scarcely-believable 13,000 bogus employees, and, it is said, the funds paid to these fictitious individuals as salaries were simply deposited into bank accounts controlled by the Chairman and his family. The root cause of the Satyam fraud would appear to be a wholesale failure of governance. We will look at this case in more detail in Chapter 5 when we address the corporate governance dimension to fraud directly.

- **Expense reimbursement schemes.** The submission of false and/or inflated claim forms by managers and staff in order to obtain reimbursement for expenditure they have allegedly incurred on behalf of the organisation is one of the most common forms of fraud. The claims can relate to a wide variety of items such as: travel expenses (mileage, train or aircraft fares), accommodation costs, subsistence costs (meals and overnight allowances), entertaining clients and many others. This is an area where factors such as corporate culture, tone at the top, the clarity of policies regarding the various types of expense claims and how rigorously and consistently these policies are applied in practice are critical if fraud risk is to be managed effectively. Certainly, this is an area in all small and medium-sized organisations where the vigilance and scrutiny of owners and senior managers can have a significant deterrence and detection effect, thereby reducing fraud risk.

- **Cheque tampering schemes.** Classically under these schemes, the payee on the cheque will be altered slightly so that the cheque is paid into an account set up and controlled by the fraudster. The amount on the cheque might also be altered. With the advent of BACS payment systems and online banking the risk of fraud through cheque tampering schemes is diminishing. However, if an organisation makes payments by cheque the risk remains and requires robust controls over the payment process to manage it. Of course, where online banking is used, the essential nature of the fraud risk remains (that is to say a scheme to divert payment from the legitimate payee to the fraudster) but the characteristics have changed and the focus of controls here should be on the safeguards surrounding the database that holds the payee details.

Asset misappropriation type frauds are timeless – they have always existed in business and no doubt will continue to do so in the future. There are many, many variations on the themes sketched out above.

Bernard, an experienced businessman and now the owner-manager of a successful manufacturing company based in London, gave me an interesting example of one such case of asset misappropriation during our interview. In addition to the facts of the case, another important feature of the extract from the interview set out below is that the fraud that Bernard describes was only discovered by accident when the fraudster was away from his office due to an unforeseen illness – another common theme that we will look at again in Chapter 8 on fraud detection.

I can remember a very simple story of a manager of a transport company who was taken ill with appendicitis. Obviously this was unexpected, he hadn't been away in over three or four years from his job and he was taken ill with appendicitis. He was rushed into hospital and he was going to be there for two or three weeks. While he was there a temporary manager, I think it was the area manager in fact, went down to cover the branch. While the area manager was there one day, this chap arrives and wants to see the original manager. The area manager explained that he was ill, and the chap says: "Oh well I've come to pay my rent." The area manager sort of looked at him a bit quaint and raised an eyebrow so the chap went on and said: "Well, you know I'm allowed to park my lorry in the yard and I pay rent for that." It turns out that this guy was paying £50 a week every week for parking his lorry. Now I'm going back 40 years or so when £50 was £50! I know it isn't that much today but the interesting thing is that he used to pay by cheque. Now, you have to ask, if he paid it by cheque just how exactly was the manager getting the money? The cheque was made out to the company so how was this rent for parking the lorry of £50 a week, every week going into the manager's back pocket? Well, what used to happen was that the company also had a cash business of handling transactions for cash from members of the public. People would come in and would want parcels sent out and delivered and they would pay cash for this. So what the fraudster would do was he would swap the cheque he got for the lorry rent for cash – he would simply take £50 cash, put the cash in his back pocket and substitute the cheque in its place. The cheque would clear, he'd have his £50 and all the books looked absolutely straight. It was a simple scheme but one that was very, very effective. Multiply that up and you've got a good case for fraud. Or, you might prefer to call it theft. It's just a question of under what banner you want to put it but fraud, all of this sort of thing, is pure theft at the end of the day, fraudsters are stealing and people do and will still continue to do it as we well know with recent events.

3. Corruption

Introduction
The third category of the ACFE's occupational fraud categorisation system addresses the very important and sometimes controversial area of corruption. For these purposes the ACFE considers corruption to be any scheme in which an employee uses his or her influence in a business transaction to obtain an unauthorised benefit contrary to that employee's duty to his or her employer.

The fact that the ACFE has defined corruption as a sub-set of fraud is both interesting and important in its own right because corruption is more usually seen as a stand-alone issue, or as a crime that stands side by side with fraud and not part of it. Certainly, I have run a number of in-house courses and workshops for organisations which have been badged by my clients as an "Anti-Fraud and Corruption Programme". Also, the relevant auditing standards (SAS 99 and ISA 240) set out the procedures auditors should follow in order to protect themselves against the risk of material misstatement in the report and accounts arising from either fraudulent financial statements or from asset misappropriation. The risks posed by corruption are not dealt with directly in these auditing standards.

Corruption around the world
Corruption is now a very topical and highly visible issue, especially from the political perspective, in many, many countries around the world. At the time of writing in early 2012 there have been widespread demonstrations and political turmoil in a number of Arab countries such as Tunisia, Egypt, Libya and Syria. These popular uprisings of the so-called "Arab Spring" have led to the fall from power of the political leaders and their associates in all these countries apart from Syria. Consider the example of Egypt. Here ex-President Mubarak had ruled as a dictator for over 30 years, a vast length of time. One of the first issues to be raised after his decision to stand down as President concerned the great wealth that Mr Mubarak and his family had allegedly accumulated during his time in power – how much had he "looted" from Egypt, where was it hidden around the world and what were the countries concerned going to do about it in terms of asset confiscation orders and restitution?

Of course, corruption has long been an issue in the corporate world too. However, it is only relatively recently that directors and executives have been compelled to view corruption as a high-risk issue (as opposed to low or medium risk) because of the combination of changes in the law and the increased legal penalties now attached to this crime. Developments in anti-corruption legislation provide the main driver for this. The practice of winning contracts through corruption, often involving the payment of bribes to public officials in developing countries where the projects are to be carried out, has been widespread. Anti-corruption legislation, with worldwide reach, began in the US in 1977 with the passing of the Foreign Corrupt Practices Act ("FCPA") and more recently has gained significant momentum. The United Nations Convention against Corruption fully entered into force in December 2005. The International Financial Institutions (for example the World Bank, the European Investment Bank and the European Bank of Reconstruction and Development) have now developed a consistent framework of tough anti-corruption programmes throughout their lending activities. As we have seen, the Bribery Act 2010 brings the UK firmly into line with the international anti-corruption agenda. Equally important has been the increasingly robust attitude of the authorities in using new legislation to prosecute companies that engage in bribery and corruption, as clearly shown by the Siemens corruption scandal. In 2008 this huge German conglomerate pleaded guilty to violating accounting provisions of the Foreign Corrupt Practices Act and had to pay $1.6 billion in fines to authorities in the US and in Germany. This is the largest ever settlement in a US foreign bribery case. In essence, this case was about Siemens using bribery of foreign public officials systematically and on a large scale to win contracts and retain business in Russia, China, Argentina and in many other countries around the world.

Corruption and occupational fraud

The ACFE of course looks at corruption purely in terms of its application to occupational fraud and divides the category into four sub-sections, as follows:

- **Conflicts of interest.** Conflicts of interest situations arise when a director, manager or employee has an undisclosed economic or personal interest in a transaction, contract or business venture. It is a fundamental principle of business, normally set out legally in every individual's contract of employment, that all employees owe their duties, loyalties and time to their employer, in return for which they receive remuneration in the form of salary, pension etc. There is always danger for any organisation when this principle is compromised. In practice this is likely to be a high-risk area as the conflicts in an organisation, if they exist, will very frequently involve directors and senior managers. There should be zero tolerance of conflicts of interest, with careful management and appropriate controls embedded through the business. A culture of transparency should be encouraged (e.g. through the use of such measures as annual declarations and gifts and hospitality registers) and controls to detect conflicts of interest should be in place. The most effective of these detective controls is a reporting mechanism such as a whistle-blowing hotline, with guaranteed confidentiality and protection against retaliation for those who make reports in good faith. This is an important area and we will look at it in detail in Chapter 8, both in terms of the risks and the controls involved.

- **Bribery.** The ACFE has a simple definition of bribery, which is the "offering, giving, receiving or soliciting of anything of value in order to influence". We will look at the legal definitions later in the book but at first sight this is straightforward: we all know what a bribe is and that it is illegal. However, we also know the reality, which is that bribery is a technique with widespread application in the business world, in developing countries in particular where it is used to win and retain business contracts in an increasingly competitive global market. The Siemens scandal provides a graphic example of precisely this. A combination of new laws, more rigorous prosecution of those laws by the authorities, and changing attitudes to bribery and corruption around the world are having an effect in terms of changing long-held customs and practices in this area. This will continue no doubt.

- **Illegal gratuities.** The ACFE views illegal gratuities as payments that are similar to bribes but without necessarily the intention to influence. They are generally small payments to officials in certain countries around the world to enable trade to take place – these are characterised as "facilitation payments" in the FCPA, under which a degree of latitude is shown by the authorities in the US regarding these payments. This is a controversial area, with some jurisdictions viewing all facilitation payments as bribes and therefore as being illegal. The UK's Bribery Act 2010 is a good example of such a zero tolerance approach.

- **Economic extortion.** Economic extortion occurs when an employee demands payment from a supplier in order to favour that supplier. This is a form of fraud that happens in particular in the procurement and supply chain environment, where sometimes a powerful individual in the buying company is able to determine the outcome of tenders for contracts by manipulating, circumventing or overriding his own organisation's tender process for personal gain.

The ACFE's "Report to the Nation"

Every two years the ACFE prepares a major report on occupational fraud and abuse based on data from actual fraud cases supplied to it by the certified fraud examiners who carried out the investigations. It titles these reports: Report to the Nation on Occupational Fraud and Abuse and these are referred to throughout this book by the acronym "RTTN". The first report was produced in 1996 and then a second in 2002, since then they have been updated every two years. In 2010, for the first time, this report included data from cases occurring outside the US to provide a global view of occupational fraud – this 2010 report is referred to as "RTTNs" in this book. As an example of the scale of the surveys undertaken to produce these reports, the 2010 RTTNs is based on an analysis of data compiled from 1,843 occupational fraud cases that occurred worldwide during 2008 and 2009 as submitted by the certified fraud examiners who investigated those cases. Each RTTN contains important findings on such issues as the size and frequency of fraud, the motives of fraudsters and which controls are the most effective in preventing, deterring and detecting fraud. In my view it is important that directors and managers are aware of the main results and conclusions contained in these reports and they are referred to at the appropriate points throughout this book.

Set out in Table 2.1 below are a number of unique factors compiled by the ACFE from an analysis of their survey work over the years which provides a very useful summary of the key points arising.

Table 2.1 ACFE Occupational Fraud Classification: Unique Factors

Descriptors	Fraudulent Statements	Asset Misappropriation	Corruption
Fraudster	Executive management	Employees	Two parties (one internal one external)
Size of Fraud	$1 m–$258 m	$93,000	$250,000
Frequency of Fraud*	7.9%	92.7%	30.1%
Motivation	Egocentric (stock prices, bonuses etc.)	Pressure, dissatisfaction	Economic (business drivers)
Beneficiaries	Company and fraudster	Fraudster (over company)	Fraudster
Size of Victim Company	Large	Small	Depends
Materiality	Likely	Unlikely	Depends

*Note: the sum of percentages in this chart exceeds 100% because fraud cases sometimes involve schemes from more than one category.

Fraud and the law

Introduction

Fraud is a crime in most jurisdictions around the world. It will also be a civil law violation. We look at the different aspects of the criminal law and the civil law as they relate to fraud in Chapter 9. It is vital of course that directors and managers understand the detailed legislation that applies in their own jurisdictions when considering measures to combat fraud and, in particular, when involved in fraud events leading to considerations of dismissing and prosecuting any staff members involved. Indeed, one of my priority points at the outset of any fraud investigation is to consult a suitably skilled and experienced lawyer.

However, the law is not the most helpful place to look when trying to explain to delegates or to clients the meaning of fraud. Generally, the law will define fraud around the terms of intentional deception that we saw when we looked at the auditing standards, and an action that is undertaken for personal gain or to damage another party. The specifics of the definition will vary from one legal jurisdiction to another, however, and the details can sometimes be difficult for the non-resident to grasp. As an example, the position in the US is complicated by the dual system of American federalism whereby the federal law (the supreme law of the land) is supplemented by state law which can, and often does, vary greatly from one state to the next.

The other relevant point about the law is that from time to time it changes. This is well illustrated by the Fraud Act 2006 which created for the first time in the UK the general offence of fraud – previously fraud cases had to be prosecuted under the old Theft Acts. Set out below are the major features of the Fraud Act, which serve as an example of how fraud is looked at in terms of legislation.

The Fraud Act 2006

The Fraud Act 2006 is an Act of the UK Parliament. It was designed by the legislators to simplify and modernise the law to make it fit for purpose in the 21st century and also to help in bringing under control the length and complexity of fraud trials. The Act creates a new general offence of fraud and provides a statutory definition, which falls into three parts as follows:

- **Fraud by false representation.** This is defined as where a person dishonestly makes a representation as to fact or law, expressly or implied, which they know to be false intending by so doing to make a gain or cause a loss to another party.

- **Fraud by failing to disclose information.** This is where a person dishonestly fails to disclose information to another which he or she is under a legal duty to disclose, intending thereby to make a gain or cause a loss to another party.

- **Fraud by abuse of position.** A person is in breach of this section if he or she occupies a position in which they are expected to safeguard, or not act against, the interests of another and they dishonestly abuse the position intending thereby to make a gain or cause a loss to another. A person may be regarded as having abused his or her position even though the conduct consisted of an omission rather than an overt act.

The Act makes dishonesty a prerequisite of fraud. This might seem self-evident but the two-stage test it sets out is helpful. The first stage is whether the behaviour in question would be regarded as dishonest by the ordinary standards of reasonable and honest people. The second stage is to consider whether the defendant was aware that his or her conduct would be regarded as dishonest.

The maximum custodial sentence under the Fraud Act 2006 is 10 years.

The Act also introduces new offences of obtaining services dishonestly and possessing, making or supplying equipment to commit fraud.

Commentary

This Act brings the law against fraud in the UK up to date and makes it fit for purpose in the business realities of the new millennium. It makes it easier for the authorities to prosecute both the maker of false credit cards and the author of false prospectuses alike. It shifts the legal focus to the intention of the perpetrators, rather than on the outcomes of the fraudulent actions. No victim is required.

Some examples of what the term "fraud" actually includes

We have already established the broad parameters of the subject: fraud is both a criminal and a civil offence in most jurisdictions and it represents a significant business risk to all organisations in the 21st century in terms of potential damage to their profits and their reputation. I like to spend some time early on with my delegates on training courses discussing a number of the key components of fraud. This is not to try to establish any sort of alternative typology to that of the ACFE but rather to build upon it and to establish some important points of principle and guidance up front. There are five aspects of fraud that I use for these purposes as follows:

- The abuse of systems and control procedures;

- The abuse of working practices;

- Financial engineering;

- Corruption; and

- Collusion.

Each is discussed in turn below.

1. Fraud as abuse of systems and control procedures

Every fraud represents an abuse of an organisation's systems and internal controls. This is a fairly obvious and self-evident statement yet it is important to emphasise the point at the outset. Controls and procedures are established to give assurance to the board and executives in many areas but their overarching purpose is to manage the various risks that every organisation faces. Controls matter and they should always be implemented and carried out efficiently by managers and staff at all levels within an organisation. Inconsistent application of internal controls and procedures is simply poor practice and is often indicative of weak management. It will certainly lead to a weak control environment and a corresponding increase in the risk of fraud (and other undesirable consequences) occurring – much more on this later.

2. Fraud as abuse of working practices

Abuse of working practices is a consequence of inappropriate controls and weak management. The essence of such abuse is often fraudulent behaviour even if it is rarely described as such. There is a basic workplace contract that covers most situations: managers and staff are paid to work a stipulated number of hours by their employers in order to carry out certain tasks and functions, the details of which are set out in contracts of employment. These arrangements are underpinned by the various codes of conduct, policies and procedures etc. established by the organisation's board or senior management team. Managers and staff are expected always to work in accordance with these. However, in reality there may be many activities and behaviours that fall outside company-approved working practices. They are very often tacitly condoned by management so that they become "custom and practice" in the workplace. They are only very rarely described as fraud. Examples of abuse of working practices are: using company equipment for private purposes; taking two hours for lunch rather than one; claiming overtime for hours not worked; drinking a bottle of wine at lunchtime; claiming excess mileage for business trips; phoning in as sick when there is in fact no illness; and many others no doubt.

Sickness and absenteeism can be a very difficult problem to manage in practice. In the UK people have a singular phrase they use to describe the bogus sickness issue. It is often used jokingly and it illustrates very well the curious attitude that managers and staff sometimes display in relation to this particular practice. The phrase is "throwing a sickie". When engaging in this practice, people will telephone a colleague at work, normally in the mornings on a Friday or a Monday to say that they are unable to come into work that day because they have a cold, or the "flu", or a bad stomach from a "dodgy curry" the night before – I am sure that everyone is familiar with this sort of thing. Amazingly, in the UK there is even a particular day (it happens to be the third Monday in January) when research has shown that more "sickies" are thrown than on any other day in the year. I remember listening to an interview on the radio as part of the BBC's "Today" programme on the third Monday in January one year when an eminent psychologist was the guest. I listened to his careful explanation of why throwing a sickie on this day was so common: January is a very depressing month for those of us who live in the UK; the weather is bad; the festivities of Christmas and New Year that brighten up our lives in the winter are over; many people who are self-employed have big tax bills to pay; the warm summer days seem a long way off, etc. etc. The psychologist was rationalising this type of behaviour, which was interesting but also, from my anti-fraud perspective, frustrating.

To stay with the "sickie" issue for a moment longer, let us be quite clear what we are talking about here. Individuals who "throw a sickie" are not really ill at all (genuine sickness has no part in this discussion), nor are they prepared to allocate the time that they spend away from work because of the "sickie" as part of their annual leave entitlement. Instead, they expect their work colleagues to cover for them and they expect to be paid as normal! What they are actually doing is "intentionally using deception in order to obtain an unjust or illegal advantage" as set out in ISA 240 above. In other words, they are committing fraud.

Sickness and absenteeism are often poorly handled by organisations and by managers. These issues are corrosive of morale and efficiency. At best, if they comprise isolated cases, they will create resentment, dissatisfaction and reduced productivity in the workplace. However, in extreme cases where sickness levels are high and absenteeism is widespread, they can also lead to significant pressures on business performance as the following example illustrates:

Example: British Airways plc.[6] In 2004 Rod Eddington, then the CEO of British Airways, wrote to his employees to complain of high levels of absenteeism. The average number of days taken off as sick by British Airways staff at that time was 15, twice the national average and this was estimated to cost the company some £58m a year. It is difficult to say how much of this was caused by genuine illnesses and how much was down to absenteeism. Certainly, the cabin crew, which represent a significant proportion of this company's staff, always work in extremely unusual conditions, spending much of their working life at over 30,000 feet up in the air! So they could be more susceptible to illness as a result. The cabin crew themselves were taking on average 22 days sick leave a year, but this still might be reasonable given their working conditions. However, this seems unlikely as the average number of days claimed as sick by pilots (who also spend most of their working lives in the air) was only seven in 2004. Mr Eddington's successor as CEO of British Airways, Willie Walsh, later commented on how much of crew absenteeism appeared to coincide with "Bank Holidays, sunny August days and major sporting events". In October 2005 the company agreed a new system with the unions which meant that cabin crew members were closely monitored if they clocked up a set number of sick days. As a result, sickness levels dropped to an average of 12 days a year at the company. For much of this period (and in subsequent years too) British Airways management was embroiled in a number of issues with the cabin crew unions, including pay and staffing levels in addition to sickness absence, so this issue has a lot to do with corporate culture and disagreements between the trades unions and management. As we will see, job dissatisfaction is a major cause of fraud in the workplace.

3. Fraud as financial engineering

We now turn to a different and often much more dangerous aspect of fraud. Financial engineering in the fraud context means the deliberate manipulation of figures in order to hit targets. The targets may be internally generated, most commonly associated with trigger points for the payment of bonuses. Targets can also be external in the sense that listed companies will make forecasts of performance (quarterly, half-yearly, annually) that their investors and the market generally will expect to be achieved when the actual results are announced. Failure to hit targets will almost always have negative consequences, for individuals in the case of internally generated targets and for both individuals and the organisation in the case of externally generated targets.

Fraud involving financial engineering is particularly dangerous for organisations both because of the sheer size of the numbers that could be involved and because it will often revolve around the conduct of individuals who hold senior or high profile positions within the organisation, thereby incurring increased risk of reputational damage in addition to financial loss. As examples of what I mean by this, set out below are aspects of two of the 21st century's highest profile corporate scandals: the first involves the activities of the trader at Société Générale bank, Jerome Kerviel and issues surrounding his personal bonus targets, whilst the second concerns the absolute determination of WorldCom's senior executives to satisfy market expectations on performance targets, no matter what had to be done to achieve this:

Example: Société Générale SA. Jerome Kerviel was employed by the very large French bank Société Générale in August 2000 on leaving university. Initially, he worked in the bank's backroom compliance department. In January 2005 he moved out of the back office and joined the prestigious Delta One derivatives desk as a front office market trader. At some later stage he started to trade beyond his authorised levels (and indeed even beyond the limits of the bank as a whole), using forged counterparty hedges. As noted in the Introduction, his unauthorised trading was discovered in January 2008 and resulted in losses to the bank of Euro 4.9 billion. Now there are many aspects to the Kerviel case, including the weak control environment and many internal control failings at the bank. However, it is most relevant here to note that in 2007 Monsieur Kerviel was paid less than Euro 100,000 per annum by the bank as his salary. This was a very reasonable annual salary of course but it was a relatively low wage in the financial world and perhaps it was not everything that a derivatives trader at one of France's largest banks would be looking for. However, there was a mechanism available to him to increase this salary significantly – the bank's bonus scheme. Monsieur Kerviel apparently told police after his arrest that he was guaranteed a bonus of Euro 300,000 for 2007 and that he was trying to negotiate for double that amount![7] At his trial the prosecution accused him of trying to deliver spectacular results to augment his bonus. In fact, the prosecutor was unable to present enough evidence to prove this to the court's satisfaction. It is clear from the trial reports that Monsieur Kerviel's motives for the fraud were varied and complicated. However, it is certainly arguable that there was a dangerous mis-match at play here between the salary level of Monsieur Kerviel and the size of the potential bonuses available to him, something which, it might be thought, could provide a powerful incentive to abuse the system. Monsieur Kerviel was convicted of forgery, breach of trust and unauthorised computer use in 2011 and sentenced to five years in jail (two of which were suspended). He is currently appealing against the sentence.

Sometimes when I work with companies and boards of directors in particular I try to stimulate fresh thinking by asking provocative questions. One of the questions I ask is: "Are you looking to incentivise fraudulent behaviour?" The methods used by organisations to reward individuals for outstanding performance, especially when they feature keen and aggressive bonus and commission structures, should form a key component of the fraud risk assessments that I recommend in Chapter 4. Put simply, bonus schemes that encourage excessive risk taking can produce unintended consequences (such as fraud) and need to be carefully monitored.

Example: WorldCom.[8] The collapse of WorldCom, at the time the second largest telecoms company in the US, into bankruptcy in 2002 is one of the most important corporate scandals of recent times. The key point to note here is the reaction of the company's CEO, Bernie Ebbers, to external events. In the year 2000 the telecoms market in the US experienced a severe downturn. Mr Ebbers refused to downgrade previous aggressive forecasts that the company had made to the market for continued growth and profitability, despite the tough trading conditions. He knew very well that the stock price would likely be hammered by the market if he downgraded the forecasts. Instead, he went to his CFO, Scott Sullivan, and effectively told him to "fix the numbers". Now, if you believe Mr Sullivan, he initially refused to do this. However, when informed by his CEO that if he did not do this he, Mr Ebbers, would simply find another CFO who would ensure that the targets were hit, Mr Sullivan decided to comply. The essence of a key part of the fraud was breathtakingly simple: by means of a series of post-trail balance journal adjustments over five consecutive reporting quarters Mr Sullivan moved a total of $3.9 billion of line-rental costs from the profit and loss account to the balance sheet, classifying them as long-term investments. This was done in contravention of US Generally Accepted Accounting Principles (US "GAAP"). Of course, these transfers did the job that Mr Ebbers and Mr Sullivan intended them to do. They smartened up the published results of WorldCom in a hurry, thereby enabling the company to hit its forecast targets and so keep investors and the market content and the stock price high. Now it is worth mentioning that, all outward appearances aside, neither Mr Ebbers nor Mr Sullivan were stupid. They knew that their fraudulent scheme was untenable in the long term. However, they were hoping against hope that the market would upturn sooner rather than later, which would produce genuine profits and so allow them to start reversing the journals. Over time the books would be returned back to normal and no-one would ever find out what had really happened. However, the hoped-for market upturn did not come quickly enough. The fraud was discovered by Cynthia Cooper and her internal audit team before the economic cycle turned upwards. After huge effort and application, Ms Cooper was in a position to blow the whistle to the authorities and the biggest example of financial engineering fraud in history was uncovered (see Cooper 2008).[9]

4. Fraud as corruption

Bribery and corruption comprise an important sub-set of fraud as we have seen when looking at the ACFE fraud typology. However, this is not always clearly understood within organisations. As an indicator of this, I cannot recall a single delegate who has included corruption in his or her answers to Question 2 of the Fraud Awareness Quiz. So I like to introduce the subject of corruption (and the related areas of bribery, kickbacks and conflicts of interest) at an early stage on all of my courses. We will be returning to it at various stages of the book and in particular in Chapter 5 on governance.

Also, bribery and corruption are often placed in a separate "silo", so that organisations try to deal with the risks independently of fraud risk. The current concern amongst the business community in the UK around the implications of The Bribery Act 2010 is a good example of this. There is a danger that bribery will be looked at in isolation when clearly it is an integral part of financial crime in general and a sub-set of fraud in particular. The Bribery Act 2010 necessitates a zero tolerance approach to bribery by commercial organisations. The related Government Guidance sets out a number of steps for compliance. Examples of what the government is looking for by way of "adequate procedures" are: an assessment of bribery risk; top-level commitment; policies for areas of high risk (e.g. gifts and hospitality, promotional expenses, political donations); due diligence procedures; awareness training for all managers and staff; and a monitoring and review process. All of these measures are perfectly aligned to the fraud risk management methodologies advocated throughout this book. As a matter of principle it is in my view a mistake to divide the components of financial crime into separate silos – money laundering, terrorist financing, fraud, tax evasion, insider dealing, collusion and coercion, bribery and corruption. A consistent, holistic approach to financial crime risk is more effective.

5. Fraud as collusion

Collusion is another important component of fraud especially as it undermines the most important generic anti-fraud control of all, that of segregation of duties. Collusion exists where two or more people act together to circumvent controls and procedures. This could be internal collusion, where the people concerned are all working for the organisation that is being defrauded, or alternatively it could have an external dimension where one or more insider(s) will work with people from outside the company to extract funds illicitly for mutual benefit. As a final point, collusion can either be active (as in the WorldCom scheme above) or passive. Passive collusion is sometimes referred to as "pseudo-collusion" and it works when one individual takes advantage of the negligence of another to by-pass controls. For example, imagine a manager who is an authorised cheque signatory but is known always to sign every cheque that is put in front of him almost on auto-pilot, never asking questions, never bothering to look at the details on the cheque or examine the supporting documentation. A fraudster may well be able to take advantage of this knowledge by supplying bogus or forged paperwork to support a cheque made out to accounts under his or her control, confident in the knowledge that there is low risk of the fraud being detected because the manager will neither ask any questions nor look at the supporting documentation with any degree of rigour at all.

Fraud costs – scale and direction of travel

When considering fraud risk it is both important and helpful to consider some of the indicators as to the scale and size of the threat that fraud poses to society in general and to businesses in particular. An important related point is to decide whether fraud is increasing or decreasing as we move into the second decade of the 21st century. We will start by looking at the costs of fraud.

1. Costs of fraud

Overview

Fraud used to be thought of as a victimless crime, with little visibility, awareness or sympathy from the general public. Not any longer. The actions of the authorities around the world in highlighting the issues combined with the consequences of the 2007–09 financial crisis have resulted in much greater awareness of the harm done to society as a whole by this kind of abuse. For example, the UK's National Fraud Authority published a report in 2010 estimating that the total cost of fraud in the UK is over £38 billion each year.[10] This huge total is made very relevant to each of us because the report highlights that this actually represents a real cost of £765 per annum to every adult in the UK. The report talks about an inexorable "rising tide" of economic crime, a large part of which relates to tax fraud. Given the current UK Coalition government's tough programme of public spending cuts and tax rises that it considers necessary for repairing the nation's finances, the reality of tax evasion by wealthy individuals and businesses alone costing the economy some £7 billion a year in lost revenue is now greeted with outrage by large sections of the public. Indeed, even those businesses looking to minimise their tax bills by utilising lawful tax avoidance measures are now targeted by protesters.

Fraud "iceberg effect"

Before looking at some figures for fraud losses and the related costs to business, there is an important caveat to make in relation to the numbers. The great majority of the statistics and figures given on fraud that do not relate simply to the losses arising from actual fraud cases should be treated with a degree of caution because they will be based to an extent on estimates and extrapolations. Fraud schemes are hidden, they are concealed and are notoriously difficult to detect. Fraud is therefore not something that can be measured with great accuracy. It should be straightforward to see why fraud figures need to be treated with caution therefore. On the one hand, it might be thought that there is a natural tendency for financial crime specialists to over-estimate the costs of fraud. So, the figures for fraud losses could be exaggerated. On the other hand, however, there has long been a legitimate concern around attrition rates and what is thought to be a chronic under-reporting of fraud to the authorities. This has produced what might be described as the fraud "iceberg effect" – what is visible (first to the prosecuting authorities and secondly to the victim organisations) is only a small part of the total fraud problem. We are looking at a three-part process as follows:

- Part one is based on actual cases. Official figures represent those frauds that are known about (i.e. they have been discovered) and are in the public domain (i.e. they have been reported to the authorities). At any point in time it is thought that this represents no more than 20% of all occupational fraud.

- The second part relates to fraud that is known about, but which has not been reported to the authorities. Many businesses wish to protect their reputation above all else and are therefore reluctant to go to the police with a fraud problem, preferring instead to deal with the matter in-house. It is thought that this might be typical of 40% of all occupational fraud.

- Part three is a very difficult area – the amount of fraud in business that is undetected at any point in time and is not known about therefore. I always ask my delegates during a course how much fraud they think might be going on in their respective businesses right now, the existence of which they are completely unaware of. It is impossible to answer this with any degree of accuracy of course, but all delegates agree that it is extremely unlikely that the answer in their organisation will be zero. It is thought that undetected fraud might represent as much as 40% of the total.

ACFE estimates

Traditionally, losses incurred by businesses from fraud have been put somewhere in the range of 2–5% of turnover. The ACFE supports this, though consistently putting its estimates at the higher end of the range. Using survey data supplied by its members, the ACFE states in its 2010 RTTNs that survey participants estimate that the typical organisation loses 5% of its annual revenue to fraud. The insurance industry puts losses slightly higher, at 6% of turnover, following the financial crisis.

These estimates are useful benchmarks. Less helpfully, the ACFE attempts to come up with a "global loss" figure for fraud in the 2010 RTTNs. Applying the 5% figure above to estimates of gross world product for 2009, it arrives at an extrapolation of $2.9 trillion as the total amount lost to businesses around the world from occupational fraud each year. This is a truly massive number but it is virtually impossible for people to digest and relate to. It is also based entirely on extrapolation and is therefore largely meaningless. Of far more relevance to directors and managers are the actual losses suffered by organisations from fraud. Here the ACFE is much more helpful. The median loss reported by the ACFE from the cases in the 2010 study was $160,000, with almost 25% of cases involving losses of more than $1million.

Fraud loss measurement exercises

There have been a number of fraud loss measurement exercises conducted recently that try to provide a more accurate understanding of the true cost of fraud. There is now more detailed recording and reporting of losses from fraud and error in the public sectors (especially in public expenditure on healthcare and social security) in many countries around the world, including the US and Canada, the UK and Continental Europe, and Australia and New Zealand. In 2009 132 of these exercises from around the world were collated and analysed in an important study called *The Financial Cost of Fraud* (Gee, Button and Brooks, 2009).[11] The report's conclusions confirm that fraud is a significant cost and possibly more serious than previously estimated: "Losses to fraud and error can be measured – and cost effectively. On the basis of the evidence it is likely that losses in any organisation and in any area of expenditure will be at least 3%, probably more than 4% and possibly as much as 9%."

Without getting obsessed with the numbers, the figures confirm that fraud represents a significant financial cost to all businesses. In addition, however, there are also important intangible costs of being a victim of occupational fraud in terms of lost reputation and damage to staff morale. This might be termed "collateral damage" and all organisations need to be aware of it because of the important practical implications. Some of the key consequences of collateral damage are set out below.

Collateral damage – reputation

The most important component of collateral damage is harm to the reputation of an organisation, either the tarnishing of the brand or, in extreme circumstances, threatening the continued existence of the business.

> **Example: Arthur Andersen**. The most hard-hitting example of reputational damage is the case of the accounting firm Arthur Andersen. Arthur Andersen was one of the "Big 5" global accounting firms yet it lost its entire accountancy business because of the extreme negative publicity that it received in the fallout from the Enron scandal. In particular, the fact that the firm was found guilty at first hearing at a criminal trial in Houston Texas in 2002 of obstructing the criminal investigation into the Enron case by shredding documents[12] resulted in the wholesale loss of its client base. Although this legal decision was subsequently reversed on appeal, the damage had been done – Arthur Andersen not only lost its capacity to carry out audits of publicly-listed companies in the US as a result of the criminal conviction, it also lost its reputation for professionalism and integrity. Why should clients spend millions of dollars on fees to Arthur Andersen when nobody believed what that firm was saying anymore? The verdict was subsequently overturned on appeal and we will return to look at the Andersen case in more detail later in the next chapter of the book.

Collateral damage – effect on staff morale

The discovery of fraud carried out by a manager or employee often has a significant adverse effect on the morale and culture within the organisation. The impact is likely to be especially severe on those who had strong personal ties to, or who worked closely with, the fraudster, perhaps over many years. Here, morale is likely to be torpedoed and for two reasons. First, there will be natural feelings of betrayal, of trust being abused. Secondly, those individuals who have worked closely with the fraudster (especially those in the same department) are likely to be very concerned about possible damage to their own personal reputations. Will others in the organisation (especially senior managers) think that they were negligent or incompetent in not being aware of what was going on? Or worse, will people think that they were in some way involved in the fraud and colluding with the fraudster? Are their careers likely to be damaged by association?

These are serious concerns and they often have lasting effects. Adrian, a very experienced manager who worked in compliance for many years with a major international bank, is in no doubt as to how serious the effects of internal fraud can be within an organisation. During our interview, he gave me some very pertinent observations on just this subject in reply to one of my questions. This is what he told me:

> Then again coming back to fraud it's the same thing, it's apathetic management behaviour which allows fraud to creep into the organisation. This allows a rotten apple to plant the seed and to worm his way generally and cause financial distress and human distress to an organisation. Because if you've been defrauded by somebody in the organisation it's like, you know, basically you've been, I don't know . . . rape is a strong word, but you feel you've been raped because you've put trust in somebody who has been completely deceiving you. I don't think there's a more ultimate betrayal than that. It comes back to relationships and, after all, business entirely is linked with human relationships because the way we do business is through human relationships. When we

are in business we sell the human relationship and that is what gets you more business regardless of whether you've got the right "USP", the right product or whatever, it is that connection. If that connection is broken in an organisation there's nothing more damning and damaging for an organisation as a whole. So once that's happened, a big internal fraud, how do you pick the pieces up, how do people move on? You can go for a classical U-shape recovery curve or whatever. But the question always comes, the finger pointing, you have a "blame culture". That's it . . . you're burnt, if you're a manager responsible for that, you're burnt."

Collateral damage – opportunities

Before moving on, it is important to say that the position following discovery of an internal fraud scheme need not be entirely negative. There are also opportunities to improve corporate culture and strengthen controls in the aftermath of the discovery of a fraud, providing that directors and managers are able to handle the situation appropriately. There are a number of crucial actions that must happen and be seen to happen if there is to be any possibility of a positive outcome: first, the fraudster must be dismissed; secondly, the fraudster must be prosecuted and finally there must be some communication of the basic facts to the workforce. If this is all done then it is likely that awareness of fraud, anti-fraud controls and fraud deterrence factors will all improve significantly within the organisation.

As an observation, I have carried out many fraud reviews for clients over the years in the immediate aftermath of a fraud being discovered. I have almost always found that the people that I work with in these situations (both managers and staff) are fully aware of the need to avoid any recurrence of the problem and are fully committed to doing whatever is required to achieve this. As a result, they tend always to buy into the idea of zero tolerance of abuse around the issues of fraud, bribery and corruption etc. and are always very receptive to any recommendations for improving controls.

Of course, if the situation is handled without rigour and the fraudster is allowed to leave the business with good references and with no charges brought, then it can be a very different story altogether.

2. Direction of travel

Surveys and trend analyses have pointed to a stubborn increase in fraud during most of the last 20 years. There are a variety of reasons for this, any one of which (or any combination) could be especially relevant for an individual organisation, depending on its unique set of circumstances. These include: the ever increasing pressures to hit targets; a lack of awareness of the risks of fraud; and an over-reliance on both employee honesty and on traditional audit techniques for preventing and detecting fraud. Each of these important issues is addressed at various points throughout the book.

However, there is one fundamental and overarching principle regarding the prevalence of fraud in the general economy that all directors and managers need to be aware of. It is quite simple: when the economy downturns, the risk of fraud increases. There is no doubt that since 2007 and the onset of the financial crises the economy has downturned for many countries around the world.

So, there should be no surprise that the evidence from the cases being prosecuted through the courts strongly suggests that fraud was increasing fast in 2010 and 2011. The most recent survey at the time of writing is KPMG's Fraud Barometer.[13] This shows the level of fraud in the UK, as recorded by the cases going to trial, reached an all-time high in 2011, amounting to more than £3.5 billion. This survey has studied fraud cases every year since 1987.

It is more than a little counter-intuitive, therefore, to note that the discussions with delegates on my courses in recent years provide strong evidence that most organisations appear not to be responding to the raised threat-level by increasing their controls or focus on fraud. On the contrary, there are indications that controls are being reduced in terms of redundancies of middle managers. As a result, the "gap" between fraud risk and the controls needed to manage the risk is almost certainly growing wider at this time. There is real danger for any organisation when this gap grows. A different approach, based on risk assessment and the use of targeted and efficient controls is needed and we will look at practical ways of doing this throughout the book.

The direction of travel, so far as fraud risk is concerned, is clear – it is increasing. The main reasons for the increases in fraud at this time are as follows.

Increase in fraud – reduced controls

The first thing to say is that, far from increasing controls, the commercial realities of a downturn tend to force organisations to look for ways to cut their costs. A consequence of this is that control effectiveness is often diminished. Many commercial companies will look to "reduce headcount", a euphemism for making redundancies, in order to save money. These redundancies often happen in back office functions and at middle manager level – exactly the people who provide the vital segregation of duties in many organisations and who are ordinarily responsible for many of the traditional internal checks and anti-fraud preventative controls that we will discuss in Chapters 6, 7 and 8. The position is often worse in the public sector at this time, in particular right across Europe, in countries from Greece to the UK, where the need to make significant cost savings forces management into savage job cuts. Of course, public sector job losses are less palatable when they affect the front line (teachers, nurses, social workers etc.) so again most jobs are lost in the areas of finance, administration and support services. With jobs being lost in these areas, both segregation of duties controls and the level of internal checking are seriously weakened. This reduction in control in a financial downturn is particularly dangerous because it coincides with increased pressures on managers and employees to perform, which will impact on their behaviour and so make it likely that the risk of occupational fraud will go up.

Increase in fraud – changes in behaviour

The way that people behave tends to correspond to changes in their environment. There are various aspects of changed behaviour in times of recession, as a response to the different pressures that economic hardship brings, that are important from the fraud perspective. The first and most obvious thing to say is that the fear of losing one's job increases markedly in these conditions, so that managers and employees are looking above all else to protect their positions. Transparency recedes in this environment and mistakes, problems and issues are more likely to be concealed. Secondly, as financial hardship bites and people become increasingly desperate for money we move into territory that has been characterised as "need not greed" fraud. Fiddling of expense claims becomes more prevalent in these conditions. Finally, there is evidence to suggest that people change their attitude to fraudulent and criminal behaviour in these conditions – they become more tolerant of it and are perhaps more prepared to commit it themselves. Famously, in 2009 an Anglican priest in the UK was quoted in the press as saying that he considered that it was acceptable for individuals to steal from supermarkets by shoplifting in certain circumstances (for example, providing this was shoplifting from the large, national chains and not from local stores!).[14] As competition for jobs increases, people have fewer scruples concerning lying about their qualifications and/or their experience on CV's and application forms.

Increase in fraud – increased visibility

The third major reason why fraud is increasing in the years immediately following the financial crisis (and in many ways the most important reason) is that fraud schemes are simply more visible inside organisations when those organisations are experiencing tough trading conditions. In fact, the rise in fraud cases noted above in no small part represents schemes that were first entered into during times of strong growth, but which were only detected and uncovered during the subsequent times of economic hardship.

Warren Buffett, the legendary investor, has a saying which is often quoted in this context:

It is only when the tide goes out that you can tell who has been swimming naked.

What Mr Buffett means by this is that the strength of controls within an organisation, the quality of its business ethics and its tone at the top are only truly revealed when trading conditions are tough. When the economy is booming business focus tends to be on sales and growth with less attention being given to costs and controls. Where a strong control environment does not exist, lax practices often creep in, thereby providing conditions that cultivate fraudulent behaviour. If an employee actually does commit fraud there are likely to be many opportunities to hide it, many areas of "fat" in the figures so that it goes unnoticed. When business downturns, however, costs are scrutinised more tightly and controls become of paramount importance. This is the situation today. After the greatest financial crisis since the Second World War there is simply nowhere to hide fraud in most businesses any longer.

Many of these points were picked up by Frazer, a senior manager with a particular interest and expertise in fraud risk management, during our interview. I asked him specifically whether he was aware of an increased risk of fraud in his own organisation, a large government department in the UK's public sector. This is his reply:

I do think so, yes. I think fraud is made up of the two aspects – the opportunity and the incentive. I think one of the incentives is around a whole series of issues, you know, people are about to lose their job or they are being told they won't have a pay rise for the next five years, an increase in pension contributions, the decrease in pension payments, ego, work pressure, you know all of those reasons are probably heightened in the current climate. But what we are trying to do is ask our managers as well to enforce and comply with the controls and processes, the preventative controls that are in place, which is another aspect. It's not just about having the controls, it's about having the managers complying with them and following them. And we are also trying to get them to think about that human side – frauds are committed by individuals, by people – and to start thinking about their staff situation. You know, if their people are put in a position whereby they may have an opportunity . . . So without creating a suspicious environment, it's a case of the managers just being slightly more aware of changing behaviours, so we are starting to do that. But I must say, the recent figures that came out by the NFA (National Fraud Authority), they quoted the public sector having hugely higher rates of internal fraud than the private sector. How many private sector organisations will honestly report the internal fraud they have? Whereas in the public sector, of course, we are required to be transparent so I think some messages like that, it's whipping time for the public sector. It frustrates me a bit because the public sector, on the whole, is made up of very hard working people who are public servants.

As Frazer says, frauds are committed by individuals, by people. We will look at the pressures, drivers and motives that cause individuals to commit fraud in the next Chapter. But before we do so we need to return again to the Quiz and look at the answers to the first part of Question 2.

Answers to the Quiz

Fraud Awareness Quiz – Question 2
What is fraud and what percentage of annual turnover are losses from fraud estimated to cost a typical organisation each year? Give three actions or practices that you consider to be examples of fraud.

We saw at the start of this Chapter that the delegates on my courses generally have a very good awareness of the size of fraud loss relative to an organisation's turnover – it is somewhere in the range 2–5% of turnover. Consequently, the second part of this question is usually answered very well.

The first part of Question 2 ("What is fraud?") looks simple enough and, having worked through this Chapter, hopefully everyone now has a good idea of what is meant by fraud. As a result no doubt all of us can probably think of a number of different examples of fraud in the workplace that we have come across at various times in our careers.

However, I have to say that the great majority of delegates that I work with on my courses really struggle with this part of the question. Now, it may be related to the fact that I always hand the Quiz out at the start of the day just after the introductions when everyone is settling in and are getting a "feel" for the other delegates in the room. Whatever the cause there is a general reticence in coming forward with answers to this question. I am well aware that the subject matter of the course – fraud and other related financial crime risks – can sometimes act as an inhibitor to general discussion. In order to try to combat this natural tendency, I always take the time to say at the outset of the course (and well before we start work on the Quiz!) that the day will be conducted in accordance with the "Chatham House Rule". Chatham House in London is the home of one of the world's leading international think-tanks on foreign affairs. In order to encourage and facilitate free speech and debate in meetings, it has constructed a "rule" whereby all such discussions are to be conducted confidentially and on the basis that comments made will be non-attributable. Generally, I have had a very positive response when bringing the Chatham House Rule into play and delegates are keen to contribute their experiences to the discussions thereafter. However, there is a specific exception and that is in trying to prompt debate around the first part of Question 2, using examples.

In short, the answers that I receive to this question are generally bland and superficial, lacking in insight. In particular, they tend to be short and muddled in terms of delegates attempting to set out what they think fraud actually is. There seems to be little awareness of key definitions (either set out in law or in one of the accounting or auditing standards). The central ideas for a good understanding of fraud – namely, of an intentional act involving deception to gain an advantage – normally have to be teased out of the delegates. The great majority of delegates have not heard of the ACFE either so that an analysis of occupational fraud is not something they have come across before.

In fact, probably the most noteworthy points arising out of the answers to this question is when the discussion progresses to the delegates giving their examples of fraud events. Almost without exception, these relate to fraud in only one of the three categories set out in the ACFE fraud tree – that of asset misappropriation. The most frequent example by far relates to employees fiddling their expenses, often in terms of fraudulent travel and subsistence claims. Schemes involving an employee submitting bogus or inflated invoices and ultimately obtaining payment as a result are also common. Abuse of company purchase cards is often mentioned, as are various types of external, third party fraud scams. However, there is very little mention at all of the other categories in the ACFE typology, fraudulent financial statements and corruption. Only a small number of delegates have pointed to examples of financial fraud and I cannot remember a single delegate who has mentioned bribery and corruption.

It is difficult to draw conclusions from this observation. On the one hand it may simply confirm the accuracy of the analysis made by the ACFE, namely that asset misappropriation is by some distance the category of fraud most likely to arise in organisations. On the other hand, however, the absence of references to examples of either financial statements fraud or, more particularly, to corruption (given its relatively frequent occurrence in the ACFE's breakdown of fraud cases) could indicate a lack of awareness amongst directors and managers in business organisations of where fraud threats actually lie. My own view is that the second of these possibilities is the more likely explanation for the poor answers I am given to Question 2 of the Quiz. If true, this is a situation that is very worrying as it indicates significant weaknesses in the fight against fraud.

Summary – Five Key Learning Points for Directors and Managers

It is important that directors and managers are clear about what constitutes fraud so that they can deal with it in a consistent way throughout their organisations. Before moving on to consider the motives of fraudsters in the next Chapter, there are five key learning points to take from the Chapter as follows:

✓ Use the definition of fraud in the auditing standards as a reference point. Be aware in particular of the most important parts of the definition: fraud is an intentional act (so distinguishing it from an error or a mistake) involving the use of deception to gain an illicit advantage (so it is a hidden scheme and is often therefore very difficult to detect).

✓ Remember that there are three components of occupational fraud: fraudulent financial statements; asset misappropriation; and corruption. Most people think of fraud in terms of one or more of the asset misappropriation schemes only and this is a mistake.

✓ Use the ACFE's website as a key resource for information on and analysis of fraud. Also, consider making the most of the work of the ACFE either by taking out corporate membership for your organisation or by recruiting a Certified Fraud Examiner to join your internal audit team (or another suitable department), thereby increasing the capability of your business to deal with internal fraud threats.

✓ Understand that fraud is a real cost to your business, both in terms of financial loss and also of collateral damage. Studies show that organisations lose on average somewhere between 2–5%, perhaps more, of their turnover each year to internal fraud. However, the potential damage is not only financial as it can result in significant reputational damage and can also torpedo morale amongst employees inside the organisation.

✓ An economic downturn brings an increased risk of fraud. Don't simply ignore it. Instead, make a commitment to using modern, smart, targeted controls to provide your business with reasonable assurance around the prevention and detection of occupational fraud.

3 People

Fraud Awareness Quiz – Question 3
What percentage of employees do you consider to be totally honest?

_____

Appearances can be deceptive

It is July 2011. I am standing outside a restaurant in Ulaanbaatar, the capital city of Mongolia. It is early evening and the pavements are crowded with people, the street is full of cars and the city is alive with the rush hour bustle which will be familiar to businessmen all over the world. I am with Temuujin, an executive from the Mongolian Stock Exchange, who has been assisting me throughout the training project here in Mongolia. At this moment, he is trying to find a place for us to eat and it is proving to be more difficult than he expected. He is very keen for me to experience some authentic Mongolian cuisine so, rather than going again to the "Irish Bar" to have western food and drink as we have done on the last two evenings, we are going somewhere more adventurous tonight. However, the restaurant he has in mind for this is actually full with locals and we are told that there will be at least a 20-minute wait before a table becomes free. This is too long for Temuujin and, rather than wait, we leave the restaurant. Hence we are standing by the side of the road trying to flag down a taxi to take us to another one of his favourite eating places which, he tells me, is not far away. I have only been in Mongolia for three days so far but this is long enough for me to know that walking to the restaurant is not a good option – Ulaanbaatar has the worst pavements of any large city that I have ever visited.

Temuujin is an impressive young man – intelligent, educated in business studies in the US, fluent in English and sharply dressed. Tonight he is wearing a very expensive-looking suit, with matching shirt and tie. He tells me not to worry – we will soon be enjoying some top quality Mongolian cooking! He is trying to attract the attention of a taxi driver to pull over for us. He seems to be struggling a little and I become aware that he is being distracted by something. Then I see that it is a little girl, nothing to worry about. The girl is maybe six or seven years old, she is nicely dressed in her traditional Mongolian outfit and looks very sweet. But she is clearly bothering Temuujin, she is talking very energetically to him, almost aggressively trying to persuade him to buy something from a basket that she is carrying. I glance at her basket. All the merchandise that she has for sale look to me like "tourist tat" – packets of sweets, key rings and pens, all with the ubiquitous "Genghis Khan" logo on them. I smile to myself. It is quite amusing, she has clearly targeted the wrong guy – I am the "tourist" here after all. Temuujin will have no interest in this and will soon send her on her way. Then, after another stream of words from the girl, something truly surprising happens. Temuujin is carrying his jacket over his shoulder. He now brings it slowly down in front of him, eyes focused on the girl all the time. He takes out his wallet from the inside pocket, opens it and hands her some notes. He then turns away, doesn't even bother to wait to receive his purchase from the girl and returns to the business of hailing a cab.

Five minutes later we are sitting in a taxi and I ask him what on earth happened back there. Temuujin says simply: "That girl is dangerous!" Apparently he felt that he had to get away from her fast. She had told him that she was holding a felt-tipped pen in her hand and that, if he didn't give her some money she would use it to mark his very smart business shirt! He believed her. He tells me that local crime gangs in Ulaanbaatar use young girls in this way to extort money from businessmen and tourists. Temuujin did not think that it was worth the hassle or the damage to his shirt, so he had given the girl the equivalent of a couple of dollars to go away.

As he is telling me this I remember reading somewhere that Benjamin "Bugsy" Siegel, the notorious American gangster, began committing petty crime on the streets of the Lower East Side of Manhattan around the time of the First World War at a similar age to the sweet-looking Mongolian girl/extortionist. Appearances can certainly be deceptive!

Introduction

People commit financial crime. This is an obvious truism and yet, apart from a vague awareness of the threats posed by organised crime gangs, it is entirely unclear whether most of us understand the implications of this as we go about our everyday lives. Certainly, there are many, many examples all over the world of individuals being defrauded of their money and sometimes even of their life savings because they failed to exercise an appropriate degree of caution when presented with seemingly fabulous opportunities. Warnings about the dangers of things being "too good to be true" are well known but are frequently ignored. It seems that, very often, basic greed prevails.

This failure to apply common sense happens regularly in the business world also. It seems incredible to think that people can be hired by organisations without their qualifications and experience being checked thoroughly (sometimes new hires are not checked out at all), or that financial institutions are prepared to lend money to individuals on the strength of self-certified statements of income or assets given by those same individuals. Yet this does indeed happen from time to time as was seen in the US in particular during the years leading up to the recent financial crisis. Just to be clear at this point: I am not about to advocate that people in business should never trust anybody but what I am going to emphasise, both throughout this Chapter and indeed throughout the book, is that people in business should not be naïve. A proper understanding of risk is one of the keys to success in business. In terms of dealing with the "people problem" (which may be summarised as the propensity of individuals to engage in a variety of counter-productive work behaviour that includes committing financial crime), an awareness of behavioural risk is critical to success. This chapter provides the essential pointers. Put simply, all businesses should operate in line with the old saying: trust but verify.

This Chapter addresses the people problem in three ways. First, we look at some of the key conclusions from the academic research into aspects of human behaviour in relation to fraud, including the important concept of the "Fraud Triangle" based on Dr Cressey's research in the 1950s, together with the results of more modern studies. We then look at precisely who commits fraud in the business world and their reasons and motives for doing so. Finally, included throughout the Chapter are extracts from several of the interviews that I carried out for this book, which provide a fascinating insight into how professional business managers view behaviour and motives connected with fraud, together with their advice on how to manage some of these threats in practice.

But before we get to this analysis, let us return to the Quiz and to the answers to Question 3.

Answers to the Quiz

Fraud Awareness Quiz – Question 3
What percentage of employees do you consider to be totally honest?

Question 3 invites delegates to explore their perceptions of the fundamental concept of honesty and to compare these perceptions with the brutal reality of how people actually behave in practice. And the answer is indeed brutal. Based upon the research, no more than 10% of employees (that is to say, the total workforce of directors, managers and staff) in any organisation may be relied upon to be totally honest.

There is always a lot of discussion and interest around this question on my courses and I have set out below the main points that have been raised by delegates over the years.

The first thing to say is that during the early stages of the discussion I am often asked by a delegate to clarify what I mean by the phrase "totally honest". This is a good question and I always give the same reply: we are looking here specifically at honesty in the context of the workplace. That is to say, we are looking at the framework provided by the employer/employee contract: each employee receives a salary or wage in return for working a stipulated number of hours for the employer, during which time he or she will perform certain agreed activities and tasks. This is the basic contract of employment that all people working for an organisation will be familiar with. Most organisations will underpin their contracts of employment with various internal rules and systems that the employer uses to manage the business (and also of course to manage the behaviour of its people): codes of conduct, value statements, ethics charters, policies, procedures etc. So, with this providing the essential framework I will simply repeat the question to my delegates: given the workplace context, what percentage of employees do you consider are totally honest?

This question is guaranteed to produce a lot of discussion and debate and so is ideal for my purposes. Generally, the group in the room on a particular day will divide into two distinct camps: there are those who answer with very low percentage scores (5% or less, sometimes people will even have 0% as an answer) whilst there are almost always a significant number of others who have answers that are diametrically opposite (answers as high as 80% or 90% are relatively common here). As an observation, it is actually very rare for delegates to give answers that are in the middle range.

Let us consider the answers of each of the groups in turn, because there are a number of important implications for businesses coming out of this discussion, before we look at the results of the academic research into honesty.

Answers with very low percentage scores for total honesty

The majority of delegates tend to be in the camp with the very low percentage scores. This might be indicative of a healthy degree of scepticism existing in business organisations so far as fraud is concerned. However, from many discussions over the years, it is clear to me that in fact it is the use of the phrase "totally honest" in the question that has the biggest impact on the delegates' answers.

Some delegates will justify very low percentage scores in their answers by saying that it is unrealistic to expect people to obey all of the rules all of the time. Most of their colleagues will agree with this. They also do not think that people should be punished or disciplined for minor indiscretions. In this context, the most frequent example given is that "everybody" takes office paper-clips, pens and other items of office stationery for personal use at some stage in their careers. Indeed, I have heard the "paper-clips" comment so many times on my courses that I can only conclude that the much heralded "paper-less" office remains an environmental aspiration rather than a business reality today! There are other examples given, of course, including use of the internet for personal purposes and various timekeeping issues. In fact this type of issue is rarely a problem in practice. Most organisations will deal with this situation by inserting the word "reasonable" in their codes and policies. Although this introduces a "grey area", which I generally am not in favour of, it is helpful here because most people expect to be treated as adults and in a professional manner.

It is interesting to consider these comments in the light of the relatively recent emergence of the phrase "zero tolerance" in a business context. During the 1990s politicians and police forces in the US and the UK liked to use this phrase to show that they were tough on crime and on criminals. In the last 10 years it has become a feature of the business world too. Many companies refer in their policies to "zero tolerance" of fraud and related activities. The UK's Bribery Act 2010 exhibits a zero tolerance attitude to all bribery, no matter how small the bribe. One consequence of this approach to bribery is that small facilitation or grease payments made to public officials in certain developing countries around the world (for example, payments to officials working in Indian ports or Nigerian airports) that have long been considered to be a routine part of doing business in those countries are now illegal under the Bribery Act 2010. This is one of the main points of difference between the Bribery Act and the FCPA in the US.

We will look at anti-corruption legislation in more detail in Chapter 5 but it is important to note at this stage that phrases like "zero tolerance" are easy to talk about but are much harder to put into practice both for politicians and for business leaders. As the debate around the honesty question in the Quiz has demonstrated to me time and time again, people working for organisations, especially professional people, don't like the zero tolerance concept. In particular, they resent the idea that it might be applied against themselves for small transgressions against organisational rules that everybody commits from time to time. Also, they simply do not think that it works.

Frazer, who is a manager in a large department in the UK's public sector, had some thoughtful observations on the concept of zero tolerance when I put this to him during our interview. This is what he had to say:

> Now that's interesting, I'm interested in that whole perception of fraud. We briefly spoke about this before. I've discussed this with some senior colleagues also. Now the Head of Internal Audit would obviously want to take a zero tolerance approach. However, some of our more regionally based directors would possibly be at the far other end so they would probably want to treat most things as disciplinary and not necessarily categorise them as fraud at all. There are all sorts of reasons for this, not least it doesn't necessarily look good if you've got a lot of fraud on your patch. I think it's at the margins where it becomes interesting. Here you may have a policy where you allow your staff to use their work equipment for non-work purposes, for example they might be able to look at Amazon during their lunch break, now that's accepted, it's tolerated. However if they start using it during core hours then that's not really accepted but how do you deal with that, do you log that as a fraud? As a public sector body we have to log and report all our frauds to our sponsoring department. Now we could potentially be inundated with those.
>
> Now, I think it's at those margins that we need to consider our approach carefully and I'm not sure that we do take a zero tolerance approach. I think it's sometimes quite difficult to prove fraud and I think the intent to deceive for a personal gain or to avoid an obligation (that's how we essentially define fraud) is sometimes difficult to establish. And I think it's in order to better handle those marginal cases that we have developed a new process now. Instead of allowing anybody in the organisation, any senior manager in the organisation, to decide if something is fraud or is not fraud we've now centralised the decision. All suspected frauds are now reported centrally to our Director of Finance and our Head of HR Strategy so we've got the two, we've got both a check and a balance so to speak, we've got both of them there.

We will return to fraud reporting processes in more detail later in the book.

Answers with very high percentage scores for total honesty

A significant minority of delegates will normally be in the camp with the high percentage scores. From the discussions it is clear that most base their answers on their own personal experiences – put simply, they enjoy working with their colleagues and they trust them. This is often accompanied by a very positive attitude towards the particular organisations that these delegates work for, all of which is evidence of a healthy corporate culture. There is only one problem with both these comments and the related answers of 80% or 90% of the workforce being totally honest – it does not correspond with reality. In fact, these answers demonstrate levels of naivety that could be dangerous if a fraudster is able to take advantage of them. The research studies carried out on honesty consistently produce results with significantly lower percentage scores than this.

Before looking at the research results themselves, there is an important point to make here about perceptions of honesty. When I started using the Fraud Awareness Quiz on my courses, I soon noticed that all the delegates with high expectations of honesty (as indicated by their Quiz answers) found the "facts" derived from the research, when I presented them, to be both hideous and difficult to believe. In order to try to overcome these perception barriers erected by a number of delegates I have introduced a supplemental question to the Quiz in recent years which I direct to those people who have the high honesty scores. This supplemental question is simple and direct as follows:

What percentage of CVs and job application forms do you think have a material misstatement in them?

Rather than looking at the general and fairly nebulous concept of honesty, this supplemental question asks delegates to focus on a particular aspect of dishonesty in business – the number of people who are prepared to lie in order to get a job. The answers are immediately very different. Without exception, the scores given by delegates to this question are always higher than 20%, often as high as 50% or even 60%. The delegates understand the risk in this context very well: those individuals who are prepared to fabricate or inflate their academic qualifications or else grossly exaggerate their previous experience in order to get a job. For example, many positions advertised in business today will have as a minimum academic requirement the stipulation that the applicant is "educated to degree level". What happens in practice is that companies will receive numerous applications, many from people who claim to have a degree but in fact have never achieved one – they want the job and are prepared to lie in order to get it.

Clearly, people on my courses are well aware that this sort of thing goes on. In fact, very often the same delegates who have a strong perception of honesty generally have an exaggerated view of the level of dishonesty that actually occurs in this particular area. The level of dishonesty on CVs and on job application forms is often given by professional bodies at around the 30% mark. For example, the Chartered Institute of Personnel and Development in the UK reported in 2008 that 25% of employers in the UK withdrew job offers after discovering that someone had lied or had otherwise misrepresented their application.[1] Its research also showed that 23% of employers dismissed someone who was already in post for the same offence. It gave no statistics on the number of applicants who did not get beyond the official screening stage, despite lying on their CVs. Also, it should be noted that there have been a number of high profile cases of very successful and long-standing senior executives who have been dismissed for discrepancies on their CVs. Amazingly, it appears that senior executives are not always subject to a rigorous staff vetting process before they are appointed. We will return to look at some examples of this later in this Chapter.

The supplemental question has proved very effective for my purposes over the years as those delegates concerned can see the inconsistency in their answers to the two questions straight away. It also provides the basis for a much more constructive review of the basic honesty question itself. More generally, it illustrates the important point that raising awareness of risk around issues that people often find difficult to face up to (such as dishonesty and deceit) is more likely to be successful when specific examples are used rather than relying on discussions of general propositions.

The results of the research into honesty

There has been much academic research into behaviour in the workplace. For our purposes, the most important are those that focus on counter-productive work behaviour ("CWB") and workplace deviance – the deliberate or intentional desire to cause harm to an organisation. There are two important studies that are particularly useful in this regard. First, in the 1980s Hollinger and Clarke surveyed over 9,000 employees in the workforce and found that nearly 90% of them engaged in some form of workplace deviance including sick-time abuses and not working stipulated hours.[2] They found also that 30% of employees had stolen money or merchandise on the job. The second is based on the work of the American criminologist Donald Cressey. Dr Cressey's work highlights the importance of financial pressure as a motive for occupational fraud. It forms the basis of the "Fraud Triangle" and we will look at this in more detail shortly in this Chapter.

Putting this research together, there is a critical conclusion that owners, directors, managers and anyone else involved in the fight against fraud should be aware of. All financial crime is the result of a combination of two factors: motive and opportunity.

The ACFE has come up with a workplace deviance model that provides the basis for the answer to the Quiz question – see Diagram 3.1 below. This model shows that at any point in time no more than 10% of employees (including managers and directors) can be relied upon to be "totally honest". In addition to this, as many as 10% of the workforce might be described as being "totally dishonest". That is to say, as many as 10% of employees are looking to take advantage of any and every opportunity to benefit themselves at the expense of the company. However, the most important feature of the model is that the behaviour of the vast majority of the workforce – under this particular model of course it is 80% – is capable of being influenced. This provides an

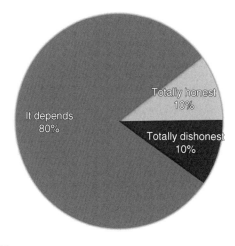

Diagram 3.1 Workplace Honesty

opportunity for directors and managers to reduce fraud risk because the biggest factor in influencing workplace behaviour is the strength of the internal controls within an organisation.

We will look at the drivers of behaviour around honesty in more detail later in this Chapter but the point I always emphasise to my delegates at this stage is that the honesty of the majority of the workforce is dependent on two factors: first, the personal circumstances of each individual employee; and secondly the culture, peer pressure and control environment of each individual business organisation. Most of the time, organisations will not be in a position to know very much about the crucial personal circumstances of their employees – their lifestyle, the state of their finances, their own health and also the health of their immediate family members. So, in practice, it is often difficult for managers to have an impact in this area (difficult but not impossible and we will examine the importance of being able to spot behavioural red flags later). However, managers can certainly influence the behaviour of their people and reduce the risk of internal fraud significantly by making sure that there is a strong culture in place, emphasising integrity, that the workforce is well motivated with skilled and engaged team leaders and, perhaps most importantly, that there is a robust system of internal controls and checks in place throughout the business. As we will see later in Chapter 8, strong internal controls will have a major deterrent effect on any individual who might be tempted to commit fraud. A key feature of this control framework should be well established segregation of duties – in order to reduce opportunity, it is important to divide responsibility.

The key strategic point coming out of this Quiz question is that it is well worth management investing time and money in developing strong control frameworks. After all, according to the research, around 90% of all employees are capable, in certain circumstances, of engaging in deviant workplace behaviour around breaking the rules, violating codes of conduct and committing financial crime.

The Fraud Triangle – the key behaviourial model

The classic model for understanding the basics of fraud and, in particular, why people commit fraud in the workplace remains the Fraud Triangle. The theory behind the model was developed in the 1950s by the renowned American criminologist and expert on the sociology of crime, Dr Donald Cressey. Dr Cressey was himself in the 1940s a student of another famous American criminologist and sociologist, Edwin Sutherland. Mr Sutherland was the man who first coined the phrase "white-collar crime" in 1939 to indicate "crime committed by a person of respectability and high social status in the course of his occupation".

Dr Cressey interviewed around 200 convicted fraudsters for his study. He described these individuals as "trust violators" because they had entered the workplace with no intention of stealing. Basically, these were ordinary people who ended up doing bad things. This is a very important observation. Dr Cressey's hypothesis provides a number of fundamental insights that go a long way to explaining why previously law abiding citizens like you and I can, in certain circumstances, be capable of committing occupational fraud. It is essential in my view that directors and managers are aware of the Fraud Triangle and understand the key messages contained within it if they are to manage fraud risk successfully.

Dr Cressey's research was published in 1953 in his work *Other People's Money: A Study in the Social Psychology of Embezzlement*.[3] His hypothesis was as follows:

> Trusted persons become trust violators when they conceive of themselves as having a financial problem which is non-sharable, are aware that this problem can be secretly

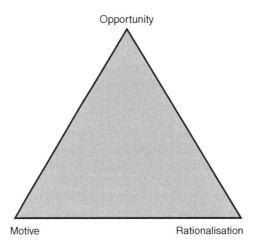

Diagram 3.2 The Fraud Triangle

resolved by violation of the position of financial trust and are able to apply to their own conduct in that situation verbalisations which enable them to adjust their conceptions of themselves as trusted persons with their conceptions of themselves as users of entrusted funds or property.

The key concept of the Fraud Triangle model (see Diagram 3.2) is based around this hypothesis. The most important conclusion from Dr Cressey's research is that there are three elements present in every fraud: motivation, opportunity and rationalisation.

Let us look at each of these three elements in turn.

Motivation

Motive (or pressure or incentive) provides the first leg of the Fraud Triangle. Dr Cressey believed that a person must always feel a pressure or a need to commit fraud. A key observation of his was that the great majority of fraudsters in his sample committed fraud in order to meet their financial obligations. So, he focused on this and defined fraud pressure as a "perceived non-sharable financial need". He highlighted problems that are usually personal to the individual and of which the individual is so ashamed that he or she is unwilling to share it with others. He found this to be particularly disturbing because often the fraudster would have received help from the organisation or colleagues if he or she had been prepared to talk about the problem with others. It is an important point.

Clearly, most of us have to deal with some form of financial pressure at some stage of our lives but most of us do not end up stealing from our employers. For Dr Cressey it is the "status deflating" feelings associated with that financial pressure – the embarrassment of not being able to pay bills, the shame associated with being evicted from the family home, the fear of exposure as an addict (whether to drugs, drink or sex) – that ultimately drive people along the first leg of the triangle. The concentration on financial pressure has been challenged by more recent studies (see below) but it remains one of the most important motives of fraud today.

Opportunity

The second leg of the Fraud Triangle is an opportunity that must exist within an organisation in order for a fraud to take place. The fraudsters in Dr Cressey's sample viewed such an opportunity as an open door for solving a non-sharable problem in secret by violating a trust. They also believed that they would not get caught. So, opportunity is both the ability to commit fraud and also the ability to conceal it. Some technical skill and knowledge of the systems and controls within an organisation is required to define such an opportunity and it is no coincidence that many fraudsters end up committing the crimes within their own job function. Also, a degree of autonomy is helpful and, as we will see later, one of the reasons why directors and managers represent a high fraud risk is because their rank in hierarchical organisations often gives them the ability to override controls.

It is important to recognise, however, that opportunities to commit fraud exist at all levels in many organisations because of the wide access that most employees have today to records, assets, valuables and information in the ordinary course of their jobs. The opportunities are greatest in organisations with weaknesses in their internal controls, especially where there are inadequate (or no) independent checks, segregation of duties, management approval and systems controls.

We will look at these areas again in much greater detail in Chapter 6 but the key point to understand here is that opportunity is the element of the Fraud Triangle over which business owners, directors and managers have the most control. The strength of the system of internal controls in an organisation is a critical factor in determining its vulnerability to fraud risk. Limiting opportunities for internal fraud is one very important way that organisations can reduce it.

Rationalisation

The third and final leg of the Fraud Triangle is the rationalisation process – the ability of the fraudster to convince himself or herself that the actions they are about to take are not really criminal at all. Dr Cressey indicated that a morally acceptable rationalisation is needed before the crime takes place – the fraudster needs this rationalisation process because he or she does not view themselves as a criminal. This represents a conscious decision by the perpetrator to place his or her needs above the needs of others. The rationalisation process enables the perpetrator to view illegal behaviour as acceptable, thereby preserving his or her self-image as a trustworthy person. Common rationalisations include: indulging in fraud to "even up the scorecard" because of, for example, a promotion that was not forthcoming or a pay rise that is perceived to be inadequate or an expected bonus that was not in fact received; taking money which is perceived as "just a loan" because the individual convinces himself or herself that they will pay it back shortly; thinking that it is acceptable to embezzle money because the company does not need the money and/or deserves to have it stolen because of "bad acts" against employees. Fraudsters will always try to rationalise away their crimes. To use a notorious example, consider the case of Nick Leeson below.

Example: Nick Leeson (Barings Bank). In his autobiography *Rogue Trader* Mr Leeson displays classic fraud rationalisation characteristics. It is clear throughout the book that he believes that he never received a penny from Barings Bank to which he was not entitled, despite that fact that his unauthorised trading ended up by destroying the bank. Mr Leeson has always maintained that he never benefited personally from his fraudulent activities and that all the money was simply lost. However, he did receive a bonus in February 1994 of £135,000 based entirely on the reported profits of his operation in the Barings Singapore office for 1993. These profits turned out to be bogus. His salary for that year was £50,000 so the bonus payment was highly significant.

The explanation Mr Leeson gives of this episode in his book is brief but is also very revealing of the mind-set of a fraudster – at once self-congratulatory and fearful, but throughout self-serving and displaying a great need always to justify his actions. Finally, there is the simple self-delusion that he will be able to resolve all the issues and then just walk away, free from it all. This is what he has to say:

> My operation, Barings Futures Singapore, had done well and the business was still soaring upwards. I'd recruited three more girls to help sort out the settlements in the back office and four more traders to handle the business on the dealing floor. My one problem was that the 88888 account was still in loss. I'd grown used to the size of the figures – it had a paper loss of over £30 million – but I couldn't get it to go away.

> I took the bonus. I felt I had no choice but to take it – because if I didn't, then my whole deceit would be discovered and we'd all collapse. I partially justified it to myself on account of the £90 million I had saved Barings in Jakarta, and the profits I had booked across to the accounts in Tokyo, but I knew that I was hiding a dangerous loss. I'd got it down to zero before, I'd just have to do it again. And then I'd never touch the 88888 account again. I'd leave Singapore and do something else. (Leeson, 1996, pp. 109 and 110)[4]

Motives of fraudsters – bringing the Fraud Triangle up to date

The Fraud Triangle remains the classic explanatory model for occupational fraud. Clearly, it cannot explain every situation but it does provide directors and managers with a methodology to enable them to understand and manage their fraud risks more effectively. The framework of the Fraud Triangle has gained widespread acclaim, for example it has been formally adopted by the auditing profession and has become an integral part of SAS 99 and IAS 240.

However, the Fraud Triangle is based upon Dr Cressey's research which is now over 50 years old. There have been many changes in society since then and many subsequent academic studies of bad attitudes at work, in particular why people engage in counter-productive work behaviours. It is the first leg of the Fraud Triangle – that of motivation – that needs some further comment and additions as a result of this more recent research.

I have summarised below the key conclusions from the later research that deals specifically with motives for occupational fraud – there are insights here that in certain respects go beyond the Fraud Triangle. However, there is little doubt that Dr Cressey's original conclusions on the other two legs of the Fraud Triangle remain as true today as they were in the 1950s: opportunity exists where fraudsters think they have the ability both to commit and to conceal the crime because of weaknesses in internal controls; and every fraudster that I have ever met or read about has tried to rationalise away his or her actions as being somehow non-criminal.

Let us now look briefly at the key findings from the modern research into motives for internal fraud.

Albrecht, Howe and Romney

Dr Cressey identified financial pressure as the key motive for committing fraud. This was broadly supported in the 1984 work *Deterring Fraud: The Internal Auditor's Perspective* (Albrecht, Howe and

Romney),[5] which was based on a review of over 200 fraud cases. The authors identified nine different types of motivators of individuals who commit internal fraud and abuse, classified as follows:

- Living beyond their means;

- An overwhelming desire for personal gain;

- High personal debt;

- A close association with customers;

- Feeling pay was not commensurate with responsibility;

- A wheeler-dealer attitude;

- Have a strong "beat the system" attitude;

- Excessive gambling habits; and

- Undue family or peer pressure

We will return to a number of these motivators of behaviour again when we look at indicators or red flags of fraud later in the book.

Hollinger and Clark

Another very important study into behaviour in the workplace was carried out in the 1980s by Richard Hollinger and John Clark, as mentioned above. Here, the authors conclude that, rather than financial pressure or greed, a different factor may well be the prime cause of employee fraud – that of job dissatisfaction.

Hollinger and Clark surveyed over 9,000 American workers thereby obtaining the data on which the conclusions for their work *Theft by Employees* are based. Their research closely correlated those employees who were dissatisfied with their jobs – across all age-groups but especially in younger workers who generally had been employed for shorter periods and therefore had lower levels of commitment to their organisation than the typical older worker – with those who are the most likely to engage in counter-productive workplace behaviour or criminality in order to redress a perceived unfairness or inequality. Just to be clear, this correlation does not mean that all employees who exhibit strong signs of being fed-up at work, who continually bad-mouth the company or its senior management, are also committing crimes like theft and fraud. However, it does mean that such employees represent an increased risk. This risk needs to be managed (and not simply ignored, as often happens in practice) if the organisation is to operate efficiently and losses from fraud are to be minimised.

Hollinger and Clark reached another interesting conclusion. They found that the same kinds of employees who engage in other forms of workplace deviance are also principally the ones who engage in employee theft. They found persuasive evidence that slow or sloppy workmanship, absenteeism, long coffee breaks, alcohol and substance misuse at work, coming in late and/or leaving early were more likely to be features of the job performance of the employee who was stealing.

Together, these conclusions form a powerful message for all directors and managers looking to minimise fraud risk in their organisations: a lowered prevalence of employee theft may be one valuable consequence of a management team that is responsive to the current perceptions and attitudes of its workforce. This is an important point and we will come back to it later in the book at both the strategic level (governance and tone at the top) and also the operational level (employee support programmes as key anti-fraud controls).

Ditton and others

More recent research has confirmed Hollinger and Clark's basic conclusion that the more dissatisfied the employee, the more likely he or she is to engage in workplace deviance, often including criminal behaviour and fraud. Studies in the US have shown that in some industry sectors (for example, among hotel employees and dock workers) it was firmly believed that pilferage was not theft but was somehow seen as a morally justified addition to wages. I have seen examples of this myself, when assisting client companies in the airline industry. There, some cabin crew would routinely leave the aircraft with bottles of gin or whisky in their kit bags. This was widely viewed as a perk of the job and not as theft. Indeed, it was "custom and practice", something handed down from senior cabin crew members to new recruits.

It has also been shown that theft is often perceived and justified by employees as a way of getting back at the boss or supervisor. One criminologist, Jason Ditton, has described this as "wages in kind" and identified three forms of "invisible wages": tips or fiddles from customers; pilferage and perks from employers.[6] There is a feeling of entitlement alongside resentment amongst some workers, the idea that they do not receive sufficient compensation for what they do from their contracted wages and salaries and that they are justified therefore in using other methods to provide them with a return that they consider is fair.

This same attitude was heard from some of the rioters in London during the disturbances in August 2011 by way of justification for their actions – the idea that breaking into a store and stealing a plasma TV was somehow acceptable because it was what they were "owed". Predictably perhaps, there has been a lot of outrage in the UK at this lack of moral compass displayed so obviously by the young people of today involved in the riots. Indeed, the widespread criminality and violence that happened on the streets of London and other cities in the UK at this time was truly shocking. But is it really anything new?

On the one hand, there have been riots from time to time involving looting in cities around the world throughout history and London is no exception to this. Also, there is nothing new in people using the idea that the system owes them something as a justification for actions that amount to basic theft. I stumbled by accident on a good example of this. Whilst working on this book I happened to be reading the classic novel *On the Road* by the American writer Jack Kerouac. The novel is set in the US in the late 1950s and has come to symbolise the attitudes of the "beat generation" at that time. Consider the following brief extracts in the context of the London riots and the justification for theft. Here, Mr Kerouac has the novel's narrator, Sol Paradise, ask Remi Boncoeur, his temporary travelling companion, in exasperation: "Why do you have to steal all the time?" The answer is very telling. Remi simply replies: "The world owes me a few things, that's all." Sol's reaction is to point out that, in that case, everybody in America is a natural born thief! (Kerouac, 1957, Part 1).[7]

On the other hand, there have of course been important changes in the workplace environment in the 25 years since the Hollinger and Clark study and two of these changes at least may have played a part in increasing fraud risk:

- The first concerns the erosion of loyalty felt by employees towards the organisations that employ them as a result of the restructuring of "work": practices such as downsizing, outsourcing, the use of short-term contractors and off-shoring have all combined to alienate the workforce and create an "every man for himself" type of culture. This should concentrate the minds of directors and managers towards the Hollinger and Clark conclusions because they have never seemed more relevant than they do today. One result of the new work practices, combined now with the economic downturn following the financial crisis of 2007–09, is that many employees in both the public and private sectors have already lost their jobs or are fearful of losing them in the near future. Of particular concern for fraud risk is that many of the jobs that have disappeared or which are under threat are in middle-management positions. The likely result is that people may no longer be carrying out the internal checks that I will be highlighting later in the book as an important part of control frameworks. So, in addition to increasing the sense of dis-enfranchisement amongst the workforce that remains, job cuts and staff lay-offs almost always undermine segregation of duties controls.

- The second change relates to the increased pressure that the remaining workers are put under. Skilled and talented people are given more and more responsibility but they do not always receive commensurate increases in their remuneration levels. This happens frequently in back office functions such as compliance and I see evidence of it all the time when talking to delegates on my courses. Take the role of Money Laundering Reporting Officer ("MLRO") for example.

Example: Role of MLROs and the lack of pay rises. When I run anti-money laundering training courses I will always ask those MLROs present in the room a direct question, which is: "What was the size of your pay increase when you were first made MLRO at your firm?" I do this not to be intrusive or to embarrass anyone but because I am pretty sure that I already know the answer – which turns out in most cases, as I expected, to be zero! In fact, I have only ever had one MLRO who replied differently to this question and said that he had received a modest pay rise on appointment. The MLROs generally feel that they have to take on the MLRO role and simply accept the situation or else they fear that they will be passed over in the future and their career prospects will be damaged. But they do not like it and there are clear indications from my discussions that some of them feel exploited and taken for granted. It is curious that firms choose to treat some of their most valuable employees in this way. They are saving money of course, but such actions are always likely to have unintended consequences attached to them – in this case it might provide another motive for fraud.

Wolfe and Hermanson

The research summarised above indicates that there are two important and different motives for internal fraud: first, some form of financial pressure and secondly a feeling of job dissatisfaction. These conclusions remain valid today and directors and managers certainly need to be aware of them if they are to be able to design effective control frameworks to prevent, deter and detect fraud. However, the 21st century has seen a spate of financial statements frauds, often for very high values and carried out over a long period of time, almost always committed by powerful individuals within the victim organisation. Sometimes the motives of these individuals seem egocentric, varied and difficult to classify.

In an attempt to improve fraud prevention and detection, David Wolfe and Dana Hermanson put forward the idea of a "Fraud Diamond" in 2004.[8] Under this model, in addition to addressing motive, opportunity and rationalisation, Wolfe and Hermanson suggest it is important also to consider a fourth element, namely an individual's capability to commit fraud. That is to say, there needs to be an awareness of those personal traits and abilities of the would-be fraudster that play a major role in whether fraud may actually occur even when the other three elements are all present. They identify in the Fraud Diamond study six of these factors, which they describe as "essential traits for committing fraud, especially over the long term". These are as follows:

- The person's position or function within the organisation, which may give that person the ability to create or exploit an opportunity not available to others. The CEO's position is particularly relevant here;

- The person being smart enough to understand and exploit accounting systems and internal control weaknesses;

- The person has a strong ego and great confidence that he or she will not be detected (or if detected, they will be able to talk themselves out of any difficulty);

- The person has a strong and very persuasive personality. Capable of abusing authority and very often a bully, he or she can convince others to commit or conceal fraud, or simply to look the other way;

- The person must also be an effective liar. This includes the ability to look people such as auditors in the eye and lie convincingly to them. They also must be able to keep track of the lies so that the overall story remains consistent; and

- Finally, to be a successful fraudster the person will be able to handle stress very well. For there is the constant risk of detection, with all its personal implications, as well as the need to conceal the fraud, often on a daily basis.

Classification of fraudsters

The great majority of fraudsters fall into one of the four categories set out below.

First-time offenders

It is very important that directors and managers understand that the great majority of internal fraudsters are first-time offenders. This was one of Dr Cressey's first observations back in the 1950s and most modern researchers confirm that it remains true today. For example, the ACFE in its first study of fraud cases worldwide, the 2010 RTTNs concludes that: "More than 85% of fraudsters in our study had never been previously charged or convicted for a fraud-related offence. This finding is consistent with our prior studies." This is a key observation.

People who have never been convicted of a crime in the past will be very concerned by the prospect of going to prison and so they are likely to assess the risks of being caught and prosecuted for their actions very carefully. Organisations with strong internal controls and a track record of prosecuting fraud can benefit from this because potential fraudsters are likely to be deterred from actually committing the crime as they will think that if they do so they will be caught, and, once caught, they will probably end up in jail. Without strong controls, this possibility is much reduced of course because the fear of being caught is simply not there. As Dr Cressey observed, once pressure or rationalisation factors exceed the fear of detection, individuals will actively look for opportunities to commit fraud and will seek out internal control weaknesses.

Recidivists

A different but related point is that recidivism rates (the repeated relapsing into criminal behaviour) for white-collar criminals are notoriously high. So, although the great majority of individuals join an organisation with no intention of stealing, it is important that the management of that organisation has reasonable assurance that none of their new hires has a track record of past convictions for fraud or other financial crime. For if a man or woman with such a track record is recruited then the risks of this employee re-offending will be significantly high. A check to the criminal records bureau (or equivalent) is therefore a very important control here. Of course, there might be very good business reasons to take on a particular applicant despite the fact that the individual has previous convictions for financial crime. The overarching point is that management needs to have a proper understanding of risk in order to make an informed decision.

Those who commit fraud to benefit the organisation

There is a third classification of internal fraudster, the individual who commits fraud for the perceived benefit of the organisation. Typically, this would be a CEO, a CFO or some other executive or board director who engages in financial statements fraud in order to hide trading difficulties and so mislead investors, creditors and the markets generally. For example, the disgraced former executives of WorldCom, Mr Ebbers and Mr Sullivan, said in their defence that everything they did in manipulating the accounts was done with a view to maintaining the share price and thereby ensuring the continued success of the company. As we have seen, this did not impress the court. It may also be thought to be disingenuous – from 2000, Mr Ebbers received approximately $375 million in loans from WorldCom to pay off his personal debts.

Outsiders

The final category comprises fraudsters who are external to the organisation. The most important components of external fraud are organised crime groups and here the key factor will be opportunity. In particular, these groups are looking to place their criminal associates within organisations and thereby gain advantage in terms of access to money, information or other assets. Banks and other financial services institutions are particularly at risk from this category of fraudster.

Although not the main focus of our interview, Martin, who has vast experience of retail banking in the UK, gave me an interesting perspective on this area of fraud risk when I met him. This is what he had to say:

> The other fear is external pressure on individuals. People can be quite vulnerable and in financial services organisations some people are targeted by people they know. Yes, friends, boyfriends or girlfriends or even somebody down the pub. Also, it could be, yes . . . the total third party organised crime gang. So that's there and I guess for the organisation then you go through the process of thinking how do you protect individuals from that. Organisations like this one will have helplines for staff, an 0800 number that employees can ring at any time to say confidentially: "This is happening, what the hell do I do?" It's so easy to get trapped. Years ago managers would be given an "ex- directory" number so that people couldn't get hold of their personal telephone numbers. I think in this day and age with your mobile number spread all over the marketing literature and dealer sheets, if you go out in the corridor everybody's telephone number is on a deal sheet or whatever you are very open to people. So, organisations like the banks tend to be

quite reserved around things like LinkedIn and other social networking sites because of the capacity for people to find out that little bit more about you. I mean I don't personally register with LinkedIn, I think it is something to avoid for me! Similarly, with Facebook, or anything else that puts your personal details into the public domain.

Profile of a fraudster

Introduction

So, who does commit internal fraud? The first thing to say is that there is no such thing as an identikit picture of a typical fraudster. Whether we like it or not, most of us, under certain conditions and pressures are capable of engaging in this form of criminal behaviour. However, there has been research and analysis work carried out looking specifically at those individuals who are responsible for internal fraud in an attempt to discern characteristics of those who commit fraud.

We look at fraud risk factors throughout this book, but it is worth setting out the main conclusions coming out of this analysis at this stage. Some might seem at first sight to be counter-intuitive and it is important that directors and managers are aware of them.

The greatest risk lies at the top

The first thing to say is that it is the people at the top of an organisation (the owners, directors and executives) that represent the greatest fraud risk in terms of potential loss. This might seem surprising but it actually makes perfect sense as they are the individuals with the greatest opportunity to commit fraud by overriding controls. In addition, they are likely to have the ability to conceal the fraud too. Messrs Skilling, Ebbers and Madoff are all good examples of this. Owners and executives commit a relatively small number of frauds compared with those carried out by the employees and managers in organisations but they tend to be high value crimes.

The ACFE concludes in the 2010 RTTNs that: "high-level perpetrators caused the greatest damage to their organisations. Frauds committed by owners/executives were more than three times as costly as frauds committed by managers and more than nine times as costly as employee fraud. Executive-level frauds also took much longer to detect." So, there is a strong correlation between the fraudster's position of authority and the losses resulting from the fraud. Also, the ACFE's research indicates that owners and executives commit the majority of financial statement frauds and are often involved in corruption schemes too.

The correlation between positions of authority and fraud loss has important implications for certain other characteristics of fraud risk in individuals, such as age, gender and education. The biggest fraud losses tend to result from the actions of well-educated, older males. If we look instead at the frequency of individual acts of fraud, rather than at the size of loss, then the age profile changes noticeably, with the majority of cases being committed by individuals between the ages of 31 and 45.

Tenure

The length of time someone has worked in an organisation is important as an indicator of fraud risk for three reasons: first, those working for a longer period of time tend to generate more trust from their managers and peers; secondly, they can develop a good understanding of the systems and procedures, thereby being in a position to spot weakness and evade internal controls; and finally they may reach higher levels of authority.

The ACFE's research has consistently found evidence to support this. In its 2010 RTTNs it reports that almost half of all the fraudsters in their study had been with the victim organisation for more than five years and that their frauds resulted in much more significant losses than those who had been employed for less than five years. 45% of the perpetrators had been with the victim organisation for between one and five years, so that new employees comprised a very small percentage of the fraudsters.

The squeezed middle

Fraud profiling exercises sometimes reveal different and unusual patterns that may reflect short-term factors in society or in the broader economy. The PricewaterhouseCoopers Global Economic Crime Survey of 2011[9] produced results that suggest that fraud risk in the UK might be changing (though not in other countries included in the survey). Their report found that middle managers are now responsible for as much as two-thirds of internal fraud at UK companies, a rise of 18 percentage points since 2009. Their data from countries elsewhere around the world was consistent with that of their previous crime surveys, namely that it is senior executives who represent the greatest internal fraud risk.

According to this crime survey, the typical internal fraudster in the UK is a male middle manager in his thirties who has been employed by the victim organisation for between three and five years. The survey suggests that one reason for this could be that the UK's poor economy is reducing the opportunities for promotion. Middle managers remain longer at that level than do their global counterparts and, if they cannot get promoted when they feel they deserve it, they might rationalise their subsequent committing of fraud accordingly.

This research points to an area of fraud risk that I have encountered before. It concerns highly-skilled technical managers who do not achieve promotion to senior management levels within organisations and are frustrated as a result. This may be combined with a lack of respect for the people who hold the senior positions because the middle manager perceives that his or her superior has an inadequate grasp of the technical detail. IT specialists can sometimes provide good examples of this risk.

Martin picked up on exactly this point during our interview. He made an interesting observation about the relationship dynamics at play in a large modern organisation, which can sometimes create the conditions for internal fraud. This is what he had to say:

> Most of the people who rise to the top in an organisation do so because they are good with people, they are leaders, they are not necessarily technicians. Technicians tend to get mired somewhere in the middle of the organisation. So you have leaders that are people out in front, usually sales orientated in its widest sense and the people who do the nuts and bolts are usually in the middle. That means that the leadership sometimes loses focus on what the technician is doing. If the technician is so inclined you've got a problem!

It is possible that the survey is highlighting that fact that technicians are indeed becoming much more inclined to fraud in the UK at this moment.

The fraudster's department

The part of the organisation that an individual works in (the department, area or function) will have an effect on the likelihood that he or she will commit fraud in terms of opportunity risk. These factors are considered in more detail elsewhere in the book. However, it is worth considering here that there are some obviously risky areas for a fraudster to be working in. This is highlighted by the ACFE in its 2010 RTTNs with the finding that 80% of all frauds in its study were committed by employees in one of six departments: accounting, operations, sales, customer service, purchasing and executive/upper management. This was a very similar result to that shown in the 2008 RTTN.

This finding is not surprising as the risk of some of the most important asset misappropriation schemes occurring is directly linked to the actions of people in certain departments because that is where the opportunity lies. Skimming and theft of cash are more likely in the customer service department than elsewhere in the organisation. Payroll fraud and cheque tampering schemes are more likely to occur in the accounts department, whereas the creation and payment of bogus invoices often comes out of the purchasing department. The type of department can also have an impact on corruption risk and many corruption schemes have their roots in either the purchasing department or within the sales team.

Of course, fraud risk is unique to each organisation. For financial services institutions, for example, it is those individuals working on the trading desks who probably represent the highest risk simply because of the size and speed of the fraud that can originate there. So, there are limitations to the ACFE's analysis here, as the main driver of fraud risk will always be the key characteristics of each individual organisation.

However, it is interesting to note that the ACFE has included the executive suite as one of the high-risk departments. I think that this is a very important observation and one that sometimes seems not to be recognised by the monitoring and review mechanisms that organisations have in place. For example, I am continually surprised at how often internal auditors do not consider the risks at board and senior management level. Internal auditors tend to look in great detail at the effectiveness of controls and procedures in place in every department in the organisation except the most important one of all – the board and senior management team. The implications of control breakdown here can be severe, as the ACFE highlights throughout its 2010 RTTNs and as I saw myself in the case of Asil Nadir and his abuse of his sole cheque signing powers at Polly Peck.

Much of the fraud risk in the executive suite centres on corruption schemes and fraudulent financial reporting, although interestingly the ACFE has found that billing fraud and expense reimbursement schemes are also very common. Again, I have seen this myself. In my experience, when an executive is committing fraud in a high value scheme, he or she is likely also to be engaged in low level scams too. In any proactive fraud detection work or in an investigation situation, it is always worth spending time checking the expense claims.

Motives of fraudsters – the business perspective

Many of the professionals that I have worked with in business or who have attended my courses are not aware of the specific conclusions coming out of the fraud research. However, both of these groups are generally very clear about what they consider to be the main cause of the problem. They feel strongly that pure, naked greed is the number one motive of internal fraud.

Bernard is a classic example of someone who holds this view. He is a very experienced business-man, an accountant by training but for many years now, following a management buyout, he has been the major shareholder and the Managing Director of a successful medium-sized manufacturing business in London. This was Bernard's reply when I asked him what he thought were the main causes of fraud:

> I think the main reason for fraud, always, is cash, it is money and I don't think it's changed. I think the methods of fraud have changed. I think people do different things in the way of getting money out of companies and out of businesses but basically, as the recent events with the Members of Parliament show, it is pure greed. People fiddle wherever they can, if they think they can get away with it money-wise they will. They might do it with time of course, people steal time. I know it's not fraud as such, but they are stealing, it's theft under any other guise. I don't think it's changed that much over the years. I think people are basically greedy and if they see a way to fiddle they will fiddle. People fiddling petty cash vouchers? It is fraud. They change amounts on them, they go out and spend £9, put a 1 in front of it and claim £19. They spend £1 and put a 2 behind it and claim £12. People will do silly things but I don't think it has changed. I think fraud has always been with us, always will be and I think the basic concept of fraud is still exactly the same as it always was. Pure greed and I think that is the basis of most fraud.

Greed is of course central to a number of the motivators identified by Albrecht et al above. Many of the discussions that I have with business people link a rise in fraud with perceptions of more greed in modern society. Putting this in the context of the Fraud Triangle, this perception suggests that people have lower levels of morals and integrity today than in the past and that this has led to people simply lacking the conscience necessary to overcome temptation. According to this analysis, more people are prepared to steal and commit fraud today than ever before. However, not everyone agrees. Bernard for example does not share this view, although, as he indicates in the extract above, he is well aware of the MPs expenses scandal in the UK that was exposed in 2009, which was a new low in terms of behaviour for our elected representatives.

Does greed really explain the significant increase in fraud costs since the start of the 21st century that we discussed in Chapter 2? As Bernard says, greed has been a recurring theme over the generations. As an example, Anthony Trollope's novel *The Way We Live Now* that I refer to in the Introduction details the activities of the "gigantic swindler" Augustus Melmotte in Victorian London (Trollope, 1875).[10] This novel was written by Trollope following his return to England in 1872 when he quickly became appalled by what he saw as declining standards in society and excessive greed everywhere. In fact, it was inspired by the financial scandals of the 1870s. Perhaps little has changed in 140 years!

Next, consider Martin's answer to the question "why do people commit fraud?" Martin is an experienced banker in the UK who has worked his way up to a senior management position in a large retail bank. These are his comments in the relevant extract from the interview I conducted with him.

> Although the most obvious reason is greed, there's another route that goes off into fear and that's another reason why we see fraud, you know, particularly in the banking environment. We'll go down the fear route because I think that's probably a little bit more interesting. One fear is that if somebody makes a mistake, their immediate thought is "how do I cover that up?" That then boils down to the type of characters

you are dealing with. Some people are so proud of what they do and are actually very, very conscientious, they could be tempted into doing something wrong because their record could be blemished. Whereas perhaps another character who is a little less worried about their performance and what somebody might think, actually might be less inclined under that scenario to commit fraud. Another reason for the fear is if they are behind on their budgets, so if they are financially under pressure in a financial services organisation that could be quite powerful. There is quite a lot of carrot in the financial services industry but there is also some stick and if people become sort of consistent "under-performers" there is a process in most organisations to move those people out. Their under-performance will be used as a very solid reason why they have been removed from the organisation, which may take years under other processes but here if you don't perform there is a sort of an accelerated process and you can follow that through.

Martin highlights the "fear factor" brought about by different forms of pressure in the banking industry. My next interviewee, Charles, picked up some of these themes but placed them in a broader context, referring to a number of different factors that influence individual behaviour, both in the workplace and outside. Charles is from a financial background originally but he then moved over to corporate planning and strategy and spent many years working at senior management levels for a large American company both in the US and in Europe. This is what he had to say when I asked him whether he thought that fraud is currently on the increase and, if so, why that might be:

My guess is that the risk is going up. I think there are a number of factors. The first is that the economy is pretty perilous at the moment and a lot of people are going to have money problems and therefore the temptation to fix them somehow is going to be there. The second thing is, as time goes on, we become more and more unequal as a society and so the resentments might very well be increasing and also of course more and more money is in the hands of fewer and fewer people so those people are going to be sort of targeted. I suppose the third factor would be people feel less loyalty to organisations. Organisations after all haven't shown employees very much loyalty over the past few decades and so the contract between employee and organisation is now very much more a sort of short term commercially interested one and that breaks down the loyalty and trust and is more likely to lead to fraudulent behaviour.

Charles would never pretend to be an expert in fraud but he does have a very good feel for the business environment. A lot of what he is saying here replicates a number of the key points in classic fraud theory from those of Dr Cressey and the Fraud Triangle to the conclusions of Hollinger and Clark.

Finally, consider the views of Adrian. Adrian is based in Gibraltar and now works in the professional services sector, but for many years he was the Compliance Officer of a major international bank. He too considers that the drivers of fraudulent behaviour are essentially personal and his views are actually very consistent with Dr Cressey's conclusions. This is what Adrian had to say by way of reply to my question asking what he thinks are the main causes of internal fraud:

The main reasons for internal fraud are personal circumstances, which could be either financial or psychological. I don't know, to be honest, the human mind is very complicated. I don't know what the motivators are but in any event it's got to be driven by personal circumstances, something might be happening at home, they require extra cash or whatever. Then again it could be a grievance but the majority of normal people who have a grievance, they go, they leave the company, they don't hang around and do any harm because ultimately it can get them into trouble. So, I don't necessarily think that the reasons why people commit fraud are all that complicated. It's probably some innate emotion that's driving it and causing that person to act. Unless that person is genuinely evil of course – you do get these kinds of people. Normal people I would say are driven by personal circumstances.

Summary – Five Key Learning Points for Directors and Managers

People commit fraud. In this Chapter we have seen how the motives behind fraudulent behaviour can vary and how frameworks such as the Fraud Triangle can help us to understand better the various drivers and pressure points at play here. There are a number of important learning points for directors and managers to take from the Chapter, as follows:

✓ Be aware of the two overarching principles of internal fraud, so far as managing the "people risk" component of it is concerned. First, the three legs of the Fraud Triangle are present in every fraud case: motive, opportunity and rationalisation. Secondly, the biggest risk in any organisation in terms of losses from fraud lies at the top with the owners, directors and executives.

✓ Understand that, although basic greed is often thought to be the main motive of fraud, the research indicates that the position is more complicated and nuanced in reality. Financial pressure and/or job dissatisfaction are in fact the two main drivers of much fraudulent behaviour.

✓ Recognise that there are two aspects to the opportunity factor. First, the fraudster must work in a suitable position or role within an organisation that will mean that it is possible for him or her to carry out the prospective fraud. The keys to this are authority and/or autonomy. Secondly, the perpetrator must also believe that they can conceal the fraud successfully in order to avoid detection.

✓ Commit to establishing a strong control framework. Most fraudsters are first-time offenders. This means that any individual who might be thinking of committing fraud in the future is likely never to have been convicted of a crime in the past. Therefore he or she is also likely to be very fearful of the prospect of being caught, convicted and sent to prison as a result of committing fraud. A strong control framework will always serve as a particularly powerful deterrent in this situation because it will increase the perception in the mind of the prospective fraudster that any crime committed in the organisation will be detected and that the perpetrator will go to prison as a result.

✓ Recognise that as a result of the difficult economic conditions in the US, Europe and elsewhere around the world, fraud risk has increased significantly in most public and private sector organisations. Look to install smarter controls. Targeted anti-fraud controls, linked to a good understanding of fraud risk, provide the most effective solution for directors and managers.

As we have already seen, risk drives controls, not the other way around. So, before we look at specific anti-fraud controls in detail we need to look to solid foundations first, which we will do in the next Chapter – Risk.

4 Risk

Fraud Awareness Quiz – Question 4
What percentage (by value) of internal fraud is committed by women?

We are all risk managers now

It is July 2004. I am standing at a lectern in the lecture hall of the Bahamas Institute of Financial Services in Nassau, the capital and commercial centre of the Commonwealth of the Bahamas. I am preparing to present a lecture to the directors, senior managers and other representatives of the financial services industry in the Bahamas at a "Breakfast Briefing". The room is packed, there are well over 100 people in attendance and I am feeling pretty nervous. This is my first "speech" in the Caribbean after all. I am giving the lecture to a large, high-powered audience of finance professionals. The title of the talk is "Basel II and Operational Risk",[1] not the easiest subject matter for anyone to digest over their bacon and eggs at 9.00 o'clock in the morning. Still, I take confidence from the fact that everyone seems to be enjoying their breakfast, I give myself a last pep talk (along the lines of: "Steve, don't screw it up!") and I begin.

I start by thanking my hosts at the Institute for inviting me to their beautiful island and then extend this thanks to everyone for making me feel so welcome on my first visit to the Bahamas. I say that I almost feel at home and give two examples. First, my taxi driver pointed out Sean Connery's villa on the drive from my hotel into Nassau this morning, and I say that it's always nice to hear news about old friends and to know that they are doing so well for themselves. Secondly, I tell them that I am staying on the beautiful Paradise Island nearby, which means that I am surrounded by sea and sand, all bathed in the most gorgeous sunshine. I say that this is all very similar to the views and weather conditions back home in London town! People laugh, they are obviously in a positive frame of mind and this breaks the ice. I have their attention now.

I then get down to business. I first take everyone through the background to the Basel Capital Accord, the new capital adequacy standard for financial institutions. We look at the rationale and meaning of the new "Three Pillars" approach, then pause briefly to go through the numbers and the capital ratios themselves. Then I come to the major section of the talk which is on the new risk-based approach and the improvements in risk management that Basel II is meant to bring about, using the management of financial crime, money laundering and fraud as my main examples.

The talk seems to go down well with the audience. I sense that most people in the room have remained interested and engaged throughout. My pace and timing are also good and I manage to hit my mark for the Question & Answer slot right on time. The conference chairman looks pleased.

So I am feeling pretty good when I say: "Thank you Ladies and Gentlemen. Does anyone have any questions?" There is a pause, a period of silence and I think for a moment that I will be able to close without having to field any questions at all. Not so lucky! After a brief delay a man at the back of the hall raises his hand and stands up. It is the first question so everyone turns round to look as he says the following: "Steve, I enjoyed the talk very much. But I am concerned that all this stuff you say about risk management, the assessment and documentation and the things we are expected to do now . . . I am concerned it will all take up too much of my time. I can see that this is going to stop me from doing my job. What do you have to say to that?"

I am stunned for a moment. This is not a promising question to be given first up, in fact it is much worse than that – it is awful, terrible even. It is clear that this gentleman has not bought into what I have been saying for the last hour at all. The talk has all been about how risk management is central to the new Basel II approach and that modern risk management is not an optional add-on, something to focus on haphazardly from time to time but is rather a continuous, ongoing process that needs to be embedded in the organisation's culture. The gentleman asking the question simply has not "got it". Risk management IS his job and it is an integral part of everything he does when at work. Or at least it should be.

I feel like walking away from the lectern and banging my head against the nearest wall.

Of course, I don't actually do this. Instead, I try to remain calm and professional while searching for an appropriate way to respond. I smile and after a few seconds (which seem like many minutes to me), I say by way of an answer: "Thank you Sir for the question. I understand your concerns, I really do. However, I have to tell you that business has changed in the 21st century and one of the biggest areas of change is in the management of risk. All of us in this room today simply have to find a way to deal with all this 'stuff' as you have described it. It is now essential that there are processes in place to manage risk and evidence to back up decisions taken. We may all have to change certain things about the way that we work and I know that no-one likes change. However, we are all in this together. All of us in this room are in the same position. We may all have different job titles, but essentially we all do the same job. Sir, we are all risk managers now."

That's all I say. I don't know whether the gentleman is satisfied with this answer but there are general murmurs of approval in the room and, now that the first question is out of the way, many more people have their hands up in the air wanting to ask questions. I breathe a sigh of relief – I am able to move the discussion on. I point to a lady sitting near the front. She stands up to ask her question, which is about how the risk of money laundering fits into the Basel II framework. This sounds like a more difficult question than the first one but in fact it is much easier. It is easier because I know exactly how to answer this one! "Thank you, Madam, another good question. Now, Basel II deals with money laundering threats in the following way . . ."

Introduction

The management of risk has always been of fundamental importance to all organisations. Yet risk management – the formalised processes used today to identify, assess, prioritise, manage, mitigate, communicate and report on risk – is a relatively new business discipline. As an example, it may well astonish some of the younger readers of this book to learn that there were no "risk registers" used in any of the clients in my last audit portfolio in1990. How times have changed!

Risk management, as an idea, developed steadily throughout the 20th century, out of a combination of wars, weather-related disasters, mathematical theories and business imperatives. The advantages of taking a disciplined approach to future uncertainties, based on probabilities rather than on luck or faith, became clear. The title of Chief Risk Officer was first used in 1993 by James Lam at GE Capital to describe a function that involved managing "all aspects of risk". Peter Bernstein, in his influential book *Against the Gods: The Remarkable Story of Risk*[2] published in 1996 summarised this changed attitude as follows: "If everything is a matter of luck, risk management is a meaningless exercise. Invoking luck obscures truth because it separates an event from its cause."

Developments in risk management theory were encouraged and adopted by businesses, driven notably by the insurance and financial services sectors in the US, so that by the end of the 1990s formalised processes were becoming the norm in many organisations. Risk management was embraced by private sector companies and the public sector alike around the twin goals of prudence and productivity, thereby enabling organisations to avoid unnecessary waste of resources but at the same time providing them with assurance that objectives would be met in areas such as financial planning and health and safety.

One of the central themes of this book is that fraud represents a significant risk to all businesses in the 21st century, both in terms of tangible risk to their profits and also intangible risk to their reputation. Given the continuing high profile coverage of fraud, at all levels, in the media and the periodic but recurring headline scandals involving senior figures in business organisations this should be pretty obvious. Yet many of the clients that I work with and the majority of the delegates who attend my courses do not seem to take a logical, disciplined, evidence-based approach to fraud or other areas of financial crime. Fraud risk is poorly analysed (if at all) and anti-fraud controls are poorly designed as a result. This failure to "take a risk-based approach" to fraud is truly surprising and is one of the main reasons for writing this book.

This Chapter provides a brief overview of risk management – a risk management primer if you will – based around counter-pointing best practice theory with my own practical experience from working with clients in this area over many years together with the ideas of the delegates who attend my courses. The important area of reputation risk is examined and we see how association with fraud can have serious implications for even the most well-respected of brands. We will look at strategic approaches to risk management and see how these have been recently adapted by the authorities in the anti-money laundering arena in particular to provide increased assurance that organised criminals and terrorists are not abusing the facilities offered by the global financial services industry for their illegal aims. The Chapter concludes with the key idea that every business needs to develop and keep updated its own individual fraud risk profile in order to ensure that high priority threats are identified and managed effectively.

But first we return to the Quiz and the answers to Question 4.

Answers to the Quiz

Fraud Awareness Quiz – Question 4
What percentage (by value) of internal fraud is committed by women?

This is in many ways the most eye-catching question in the Quiz. Certainly, it is a question that always manages to stimulate much interest, discussion and debate because of its focus on gender, even though it is set in a fraud context. Of course I have deliberately phrased the question in this way to engage the attention of my delegates and sometimes this has backfired on me rather by distracting attention from more important messages I want to convey. As an example, I remember giving a talk on various aspects of financial crime at a conference for business leaders in the financial services sector in Port of Spain, Trinidad and Tobago a number of years ago. During the course of this presentation I decided to take a chance and ask the audience this question, just to see what reaction it got. Well, the room was soon in uproar – everybody had a view on this and wanted to have their say. So after only a few minutes of discussion, I had to cut short the debate by answering the question myself in order that we could move onto the central message of the talk. However, if I thought that this was the end of the matter, then I was wrong. There were representatives of the Trinidad and Tobago press present at the conference and the next day newspapers in Port of Spain were reporting the whole conference under the banner headline: "Fraud Expert Says Men Commit More Fraud than Women"!

Actually, this is not really a question about gender differences – whether in terms of morals, honesty or behaviour – at all. It is a question about risk. The key to the correct answer is to be found in the phrase in brackets in the question – "by value". We will return to this shortly.

Some delegates are reluctant to put anything down in writing as an answer to this question, saying they have never thought about it before and are disinclined simply to guess. For the majority of delegates who do write something down, the answers to this question fall broadly into three categories as follows:

- **50%.** A significant minority of delegates have answered the question in this way over the years. It is a logical answer and indeed it is the answer that I myself may well have given before I understood more about the nature of fraud risk. As we will see later, all the research indicates that there is little difference between men and women in terms of honesty and their respective attitudes to fraud. However, there are still today significant differences in the workplace hierarchy between men and women, most importantly differences in the number of senior positions held by men and women within organisations. If we are to measure fraud risk by value, then the result is influenced most by the seniority of individuals within business. Despite gender equality laws, the simple fact remains that far more directors and senior executives are men than are women. This has a very important impact on fraud risk, not least because those statistics which are based upon the quantum of fraud are heavily skewed by the huge scandals that hit the headlines from time to time. To commit high value fraud an individual must have the opportunity to do so within an organisation and this almost always necessitates being in a position of high office (or one that carries with it control and a large measure of autonomy over a significant part of the business).

- **60% (or more).** A small number of delegates will say that women represent the greater fraud risk. Normally, this is because either they have real life experience of a fraud committed within their organisation by a woman, or they feel that most fraud is carried out in departments like accounts, cashiers or purchasing, where they may have noticed that a lot of women work. Of course it is absolutely true that women are capable of carrying out fraud. However, because of the fact that men occupy more senior positions in business the opportunities for women to carry out high-value fraud are very often restricted. When the opportunity does present itself, women are not averse to committing fraud, as the following example (mentioned by a number of delegates attending my training courses in the UK) shows:

Example: Joyti De-Laurey.[3] Mrs De-Laurey worked as the personal assistant to two senior executives at Goldman Sachs, the investment banking and securities firm, in London starting in 1998: Jennifer Moses and then later Scott Mead. The executives were both highly paid, especially Mr Mead who, because he was a partner in the firm, received a pay-out of approximately $50 million when Goldman Sachs went public in 1999. This was in addition to his annual salary and bonuses that amounted to millions of dollars a year. Mr Mead was obviously very successful and he was no doubt a very busy man too, so that it was Mrs De-Laurey who normally handled all his routine banking arrangements. One day in 2002, however, following delays by Mrs De-Laurey in producing some bank statements that he needed in a hurry, he decided to order them and review them himself. This was extraordinary, it was not part of his normal routine. Imagine Mr Mead's surprise when, going through the bank statements he started to find significant discrepancies in his accounts – for example, there was one transfer out of his account for over £2 million to someone named Schahhou! On enquiry, this turned out to be Mrs De-Laurey's mother and the police were called in. The investigation found that Mrs De-Laurey had stolen over £1 million from Ms Moses and over £3 million from Mr Mead using forged and genuine signatures sent by fax to "authorise" transfers. She was able to do this because the two executives trusted her and had given her full access to their account details. They were so busy that they did not have the time to check their affairs in detail and were so wealthy that they apparently did not notice very large amounts of money going missing from their accounts. Mrs De-Laurey spent the money on cars, jewellery, a powerboat and property both in Cyprus and in the UK. She was found guilty in April 2004 of stealing over £4.3 million and was sentenced to seven years in prison. At her trial the judge described her as someone for whom "lying was woven into the very fabric of your being".

- **10–40%.** The answers of the majority delegates on my courses reflect their views that women actually carry out less than half of all internal fraud by value. Some even come up with the "correct" answer of 20–30%. The reasons given for women committing less fraud than men are various. They range from the tongue-in-cheek views that women are smarter than men and so don't get caught or that women are able to persuade men to carry out the fraud on their behalf, to the observational views that delegates have seen cases of men committing fraud in their own organisations or that men have largely been responsible for almost all of the high profile corporate frauds that make the news headlines.

As mentioned above, the answer that is supported by the ACFE's research is "around 20–30%". Or to put it more fully, no more than 30% of fraud by value is committed by women. This finding reflects one of the key risk factors concerning fraud – simply that fraud depends critically on opportunity. Owners, senior managers, executives and directors have more opportunities to commit (and to conceal) fraud than do other employees. Although we have long been in the age of gender equality under the law, this is not reflected in the reality of most business organisations, especially when it comes to leadership. The representation of women on the governing bodies of listed companies in countries in Europe has plateaued during the last decade at around 11% only, leading to some countries introducing a quota system by law as a way of compelling gender diversity on the business community. This started in Norway. In 2003 the Norwegian Parliament decided to make a 40% gender quota mandatory for the boards of all of Norway's publically listed companies.

The position regarding gender diversity on boards of directors is similar in the US. A report in March 2011 from the Inter Organisational Network, a US body advancing the cause of greater gender diversity in the boardroom, found that in Fortune 500 companies women hold between 12% and 20% of board seats only.[4]

Things may be slowly changing for women in the workplace and in the world of fraud too. In its 2002 RTTN, the ACFE found that only 23% of fraud by value was committed by women. In the 2010 RTTNs this had increased to 30%.

Before moving on, there is one final point to make here coming out of the Quiz. The question asks about fraud in terms of value. If instead we were to look at the actual instances of internal fraud, so that each fraud case counts the same regardless of size and quantum of loss, then here the disparity between men and women becomes less marked. Research by the ACFE in previous years indicated that there is broadly a 60–40% split, with men again committing more fraud than women. The results of the 2010 RTTNs shows this gap widening, with two-thirds of the frauds being committed by males. The fact that men commit more frauds than women should not be surprising – there are more men than women in the workplace. The fraud statistics are simply a reflection of the realities of business life in both the public and the private sectors today.

Risk management primer

Introduction

Today risk management is an important part of the day-to-day operations of most organisations. In contrast to the mid-1990s, there are now a multitude of institutes, educational courses and books devoted to the subject. Risk management is not the core subject of this book so we do not need to examine the development of the theory in great detail here. However, in my view an under-standing of the fundamental principles of risk management is needed in order to manage fraud threats effectively. So, it is important to understand the basics.

We start with a definition. There are of course many definitions of risk management today. The earliest was set out in the first recognised Risk Management Standard published in 1995 following its development by a multi-disciplinary task force of Standards Australia/Standards New Zealand.[5] The Standard has been revised since but the power of the original definition remains and is sufficient for our purposes as follows:

> Risk management is a process to identify, assess, manage and control potential events or situations, to provide reasonable assurance regarding the achievement of the organisation's objectives.

The very important principle that risk management provides organisations with "reasonable assurance" regarding the achievement of objectives, and not with certainty, is set out here. Also, the framework for the management of risk in a business context is established around the achievement of the organisation's objectives. All businesses exist to achieve certain things. These objectives should be articulated by the board and senior management. Risk is anything and everything that could impact on the successful achievement of those business objectives.

Organisations need a structured, disciplined process to manage risk in the 21st century because the risk universe is now so complicated and inter-connected. A discussion on risk management in the 1990s would almost certainly have coalesced around just two types of risk – financial risks and the important area of health and safety. Today, there are a variety of different risk types that all have to be managed because each could have a significant effect on an organisation. Examples of modern risk types are: reputation; financial; health and safety; technological; ethical; environmental; geo-political; legal and regulatory; credit; operational; competition; liquidity and counter-party; staff-related; political; contractual and physical. Risk management professionals would no doubt point to others also.

Culture

We will look at reputation risk in more detail later in this Chapter, but before we move on it is important to note that the culture of an organisation is at least as important as the processes it uses in determining how successful the organisation will be at managing its risks. Organisational culture is hugely influenced by the directors and senior management – the "tone at the top" factor which we will examine in the next Chapter on governance.

One key issue for risk managers to assess is the extent to which there is a "blame culture" in the organisation. By that I mean does a culture exist in which mistakes and errors of judgement are viewed as career-limiting events? If the answer is essentially "yes", then the effect within the organisation is likely to be corrosive of transparency, with issues and problems tending to be swept under the carpet and kept hidden from senior management. We have seen already that this type of culture and behaviour can be very dangerous in a fraud context. It is also damaging to effective risk management generally, which should always embrace the idea of openness so that the key risks facing an organisation at any point in time are "put on the table", are communicated to everyone and are fully discussed and analysed with a view to managing them successfully in order to achieve stated business objectives.

The dangers of failing to be honest about risk in your business are illustrated in the following example, taken from my own experience. This project was with one of the largest housing associations in the UK and it involved working with them over many months at all levels to develop a new risk management process that was most appropriate to the organisation itself. The timing was right at the end of the 20th century, so the project was innovative for its time and it had the firm backing of the housing association's senior management team.

Example: Housing Association (UK). The project was split into various stages, the first of which was for me to carry out some initial research by interviewing managers and staff across the country. I used the information and feedback that I received from these interviews to inform my work on the later stages of the project, in particular raising the awareness of risk throughout the housing association by means of a series of presentations and workshops. I gave the first presentation to the association's senior management team and departmental managers from around the country. I allocated time in the presentation to address the issue of stress in the workplace and the various risks associated with it. I did this because many employees had raised their stress-related problems with me – they were working with largely disadvantaged client families, many with chaotic lifestyles involving drugs or alcohol-related addiction problems and doing so often under great time pressure to meet challenging targets. Many of them were generally defensive and unenthusiastic about the new risk management process because they saw it as adding to their problems through extra form-filling and bureaucracy. So, I spent a part of the presentation talking about stress. At the first coffee break I was confronted by the association's Human Resources Director who asked me pointedly: "Steve, what are you doing? Why are you spending so much time talking about stress?" I was slightly taken aback by this abrupt approach but replied that I was talking about stress because this had been raised with me by many of the association's managers and staff and it was clearly an important subject for them. She disagreed: "We do not have any stress in our organisation." I was very surprised to hear this as it was clearly contrary to everything I had heard from the employees. So, I simply asked her what she would say about the emotional state of the workforce, to which she replied: "We have a number of occupational health issues." With that, she abruptly turned round and walked away!

Risk soundings exercise

I have found over the years that the most effective way of making sure that the delegates on my fraud courses understand the fundamentals of risk management is to ask them a number of simple questions. I will then use their answers as the bridge to a discussion on fraud risk management specifically. I call these "soundings exercises". Set out below are five questions that I like to ask, together with the most typical replies from delegates.

1. What is risk?

This is a pretty straightforward question and yet it is one that most people struggle to answer either succinctly or well. The majority of my delegates will say that risk is a threat, something that can go wrong, an occurrence that can damage the organisation or its reputation. Probability is often mentioned, sometimes impact too. But they focus overwhelmingly on downside risk. It is really only those delegates who have had experience of working in a risk management department that respond differently. They bring a more balanced view into play by talking about the successful achievement of objectives through taking advantage of opportunities as well as minimising the threats.

The most succinct answer to the question: "What is risk?", and also the best starting point in terms of a discussion on risk, is provided by the phrase "uncertainty of outcome". In an uncertain world, two things can happen: there are indeed a huge number of threats, things that can go wrong in both our personal and our business lives; but there are also opportunities. Modern risk management is about managing both sides of this "risk tree" so that organisations can deal effectively with potential future events that create uncertainty. This means being able to respond in a manner that reduces the likelihood of downside outcomes and increases the upside.

These discussions around this first question illustrate what in my experience are a number of fairly widespread misconceptions about risk and about risk appetite. It seems to me that the difficulties in answering this question start with the modern connotations around the word "risk" which are almost wholly negative, to do with threats and danger. As we have seen, all organisations exist to achieve certain things, which are articulated as business objectives. Certain risks have to be taken if these business objectives are to be achieved. As mentioned in Chapter 1, it is unrealistic to think that risk should be minimised. Rather it has to be managed. I like to illustrate this key point on a training course by saying to my delegates that if I wanted to minimise my own risk on that particular day I would have stayed in bed, got up late, read the newspaper, maybe watched some sport on the television and generally enjoyed a nice, lazy day at home. I would thereby avoid the risks of travelling to the course and putting my professional reputation on the line by working with the delegates. Although I would certainly reduce my risk (whether I would even then succeed in minimising it is another question – think of the high proportion of accidents that happen in the home!), I would be faced with a big business problem – I would not get paid!

All organisations need to take certain risks if they are to achieve their objectives and deliver value for their stakeholders over the long term. The extent of the risks that each organisation is prepared to take will vary and will depend crucially on the risk appetite of the individual organisation concerned. Risk appetite, on a broad level, is the amount of risk an entity is willing to take in the pursuit of value. It is obvious that a hedge fund will have a greater appetite for risk than a public body like a local authority, but anyone thinking that a public body has no appetite for risk is seriously mistaken. For example, consider the millions of pounds of public money deposited by a number of local authorities in the UK (including my own!) in Icelandic banks at the time of the financial crisis. Here the local authorities concerned got the risk/reward equation badly wrong. They decided to chase very small increases in the interest rates offered on money placed on deposit by the Icelandic banks compared with other institutions in the UK at the time but in return they took on significantly increased risk! Of course, when the Icelandic banks failed, the money was not returned (at the time of writing the recovery of these deposits is still the subject of ongoing litigation, the indications being that the local authorities will indeed get their money back). This case illustrates the potential consequences of poor risk awareness and the related failure of organisations to spell out their appetite for risk.

2. It is considered best practice today that organisatons should have a comprehensive and robust system of risk management. What are the main reasons for investing in an effective risk management process?

As a starting point for the discussion on this question, I remind delegates that risk management is a relatively new area of business and that few organisations had formalised risk management processes at the start of the 1990s. Of course, this does not mean that the majority of organisations were not managing risk in 1990 – risk has always had to be managed for business success to be achieved – but rather that it was then done in a different, less structured and less evidential way than happens today.

I look for two broad reasons as answers in the discussions around this question. The first is to do with added value whilst the second is rooted in compliance practices. Delegates generally home in pretty quickly on the first reason, which is that a structured risk management process provides organisations with greater assurance that their business objectives will be achieved. Having a process and structure in place allows managers and staff a better prospect of identifying, prioritising, managing and mitigating risk in a thoughtful, methodical way, all of which adds value to their business. Interestingly, when I ask the delegates if they do this in respect of the specific risk of fraud very few of them reply in the affirmative. This weakness, and the benefits of correcting it, provides one of the recurring themes of this book.

The second reason is much less obvious to my delegates. It is that the risk management structures, procedures and reports provide the evidence that the board and senior management have discharged their responsibilities so far as managing risk is concerned. We have seen already that one of the important differences between business practices as conducted in the early 21st century and how they were carried at the end of the last century is that today everything must be evidence-based. If judgement calls made at the top of the organisation turn out subsequently to have been sub-optimal or just plain wrong, evidence of the decision-making process will be required by interested third parties (auditors, regulators, the court etc.) if the managers concerned are to protect themselves from negligence claims.

As has been stated, successful organisations have always managed risk well in the past but this was often done by intuition, by "gut-feel" or pattern recognition – good managers simply knew what to do! As an example of what I mean by this, I will often refer delegates to the career of one of my personal heroes, Admiral Horatio Nelson, probably the most successful naval officer in history (to explain, I am a historian by background and I studied Modern History at Oxford). Of course, Nelson was above all else a military genius. He was operating at a time when there were no impact and probability charts and he would have had absolutely no understanding of the term "risk manager". However, he was one of the great risk managers in history and I like to use elements of his Trafalgar campaign in 1805 to illustrate the point.

Example: Trafalgar Campaign 1805.[6] Nelson's strategy in the lead-up to the battle of Trafalgar, and his tactics during the battle, were driven by his acute understanding of risk. The greatest threat to England in 1805 was that of invasion by Napoleon's armies. To counter this, Nelson devised a strategy based on annihilation of the enemy fleet. He did not seek a traditional naval battle of the times, with the two warring fleets firing broadsides at one another from a distance, until one side disengaged and sailed away largely intact. Nelson's intention was to destroy the combined French and Spanish fleet and thereby take away any possibility of Napoleon being able to invade England – in modern risk management terms he was looking to terminate the risk of invasion. He knew that if he could bring about a pell-mell battle, he would enable superior English gunnery and superior English seamanship to be brought to bear. To do so, he planned to adopt shock tactics, first used by Admiral Rodney in the 18th century, and attack the enemy line in columns. How did he communicate these tactics to his captains? He did not have e-mail or text messaging facilities and there was not a BlackBerry in sight! Instead he used the now old-fashioned but always very effective means of face-to-face communication – he invited his captains to dine with him in the great cabin of his flagship, HMS Victory, on two consecutive evenings to celebrate his forty-seventh birthday. During the course of the meals, he drew out his battle plans on a napkin – the so-called "Nelson Touch". So energised were his captains by the genius of their admiral and the brilliance of his concept that they all went away convinced that they would win the battle. He thus achieved what we might describe today as "buy-in" for his plans. Of course, Nelson brought his plans off superbly and the Royal Navy won a crushing victory over the combined French and Spanish fleets at Trafalgar, a victory that not only ended the threat of invasion by Napoleon's armies but established Britain as the dominant world naval power for over a century. However, some people argue that Trafalgar was not a complete success because Nelson himself was killed during the battle. This is true, and indeed such was the love felt by the English captains for their admiral, that some would no doubt have preferred the battle to have been inconclusive and Nelson to have survived than to have the victory but at the cost of their admiral's death. But this was not Nelson's view at all. He did not go below decks when the fighting started, he did not remove his admiral's coat displaying all his medals as his captains repeatedly urged him to do. He chose to remain on deck to lead his men. Of course, by so doing he presented an obvious target to the French and Spanish sharpshooters positioned in their ships' rigging and in due course he was shot and fatally wounded. But for Nelson, this was an acceptable risk. Unacceptable risk would have been to allow the enemy fleet to sail away from the engagement largely intact, meaning that the threat of invasion of England would remain.

Nelson achieved hero status at Trafalgar. Yet it is sometimes forgotten that even he received severe criticism both from his superiors and in the English press at certain times during his career when his judgement and decision-making were thought to be suspect. Each of us makes mistakes from time to time. It is important today for managers to have evidence of their decisions and the reasons for taking them if they are to defend themselves against criticism and forensic review. Compliance has been the driver of many changes in business practices over the last 20 years and risk management is one of them.

3. Who is responsible for managing risk in your organisation?

The answers to this question involve revisiting the "Responsibility Framework" discussed in Chapter 1. This was presented there as the best way to manage fraud risk: where ultimate responsibility for fighting fraud resides with the board of directors, who delegate the responsibility primarily to line managers and where the whole structure is underpinned by everybody in the organisation being aware of his or her responsibilities. It is also the best framework for managing risk in general.

There are three points to make here in addition to those made in Chapter 1:

- First, a simple observation. Most of my delegates do not draw a triangle on their answer sheets or refer to the Responsibility Framework when answering this question, even though I usually ask it less than two hours after we have worked through the Fraud Awareness Quiz! As will be recalled, Question 1 of the Quiz asks about responsibility for preventing and detecting fraud and the Responsibility Framework is introduced as the most effective answer to this question. Instead of referring to this answer, most delegates tend to revert to the answer "everyone". Of course, sometimes this makes me question how effective my teaching methods are (or, alternatively, how awake my delegates are!). Mostly, however, I think it underlines just how much of an automatic response this answer is to questions about responsibility in modern business today. Once again, there is very little confidence from the delegates, in answer to the same supplemental question that I posed in the Fraud Awareness Quiz, that most managers and employees in their organisations would actually be aware of their individual responsibilities for risk management. There appears to be a general business weakness here, a fundamental disconnection between the theoretical understanding of managers and the practical realities of business life. Without a clear, ongoing commitment to risk management training, with the key points being reinforced by supervisors and team leaders on a day-to-day basis, there can be no assurance that a risk-aware culture exists in any organisation.

- Secondly, a significant minority of delegates will point to nominated individuals (e.g. the Chief Risk Officer) or specialist departments (e.g. the Risk Management Department) as being responsible for managing risk in their organisations. Whilst this might seem to be an obvious and correct answer, it is actually too simplistic and highlights a common misunderstanding about the role of risk management professionals within business. Risk management profes-sionals are increasingly seen, especially following the risk management failures in a number of banks and other institutions during the recent financial crisis, as providing essential expertise in this area. There is more recognition today that risk managers should be given high status within organisations and be independent of operating departments. This is entirely appropriate and certainly enhancing the status and independence of risk managers will serve to increase the credibility of control and risk frameworks within organisations in the future. However, risk managers do not and will not themselves manage risk day to day. The responsibilities of the Chief Risk Officer are primarily ones of coordination (to make sure that risk policies, methodol-ogies, controls and mitigating actions are being carried out throughout the organisation) and of reporting (to make sure that the board, the audit committee and senior management receive appropriate and timely information regarding the management of risk) rather than hands-on risk management. Responsibility for managing risk in reality will always reside with managers and employees at every level and in every department of the organisation.

- Thirdly, a number of delegates from the financial services industry have recently made reference to the so-called "Three Lines of Defence" model in their answers to this question. In this model the first line of defence for an organisation in terms of its risk management is said to be the business line management – exactly as referred to in the Responsibility Framework. The second line of defence is the risk management function, with the third line being an independent review and challenge process as might for example be provided by the internal audit department. Although not a new concept, the three lines of defence model has been given prominence by the Basel Committee on Banking Supervision in its consultation paper "Sound Practices for the Management and Supervision of Operational Risk" published in December 2010.[7] Clearly, this paper has made an impression on some delegates! In my view, the three lines of defence model is entirely consistent with the Responsibility Framework as it simply focuses on the line managers component and drills down into areas of specialism within that component.

4. How is risk measured?

This question is straightforward. It is crucial that organisations are able to prioritise the potential risks facing their businesses so that management attention and resources can be directed towards the high priority items. In order to do so, risk must be capable of being measured. The delegates on my courses have shown good understanding in this area over the years, with the great majority being aware of the two key metrics that are most commonly used as a measurement of risk: impact (or severity) and probability (or frequency). Impact is the measure of the severity of an event should it materialise. Probability is the likelihood of an event materialising during a certain period of time.

The actual risk measure used in business can be either quantitative or qualitative. The financial services industry in particular has pioneered a quantified approach, that is to say, an approach where risk is expressed in actual $ amounts. During the early 1990s the "quants" at JPMorgan in the US, working under the bank's then CEO Sir Dennis Weatherstone, developed its innovative risk model known as Value at Risk ("VaR"), which sought to express risk as a single number. Other financial institutions followed suit and by the late 1990s VaR had become the industry standard for risk models. Many other business sectors have preferred to express risk in a qualitative way, often using a simple, if subjective "high, medium, low" analysis of risk. Either approach is acceptable, depending on business requirements. For our purposes here the important point is that the objective remains the same under both approaches: to provide the business with a measure of risk to enable it to design a proportionate response that gives the organisation reasonable assurance that its corporate objectives will be achieved.

5. What are the key components of the risk management architecture in your organisation?

As might be imagined I get a variety of responses to this question. Many delegates point to awareness training programmes, others mention the risk department or the risk reporting process, some even refer to a risk management strategy, policy and guidelines document which is signed off by the board. For the great majority, however, the most important component of their risk management architecture is the risk register. The risk register is not yet universally used, however. A small number of delegates will say that their organisations do not use the risk register system and so they themselves are not familiar with either the concept or the contents. They are the exception, however, and I am always careful to take those who are unfamiliar with this through an example of a risk register during one of the breaks during the day. The risk register is the key document in most risk management systems today and it is worth spending a little time on this.

The modern risk register has a variety of possible formats but all are basically glorified Excel spreadsheets. Many appear with a "traffic light" component of red, amber and green representing high risk, medium risk and low risk respectively. This provides a common reference point. Best practice is for these risk registers to be "owned" by managers and staff throughout the business. They are often compiled after workshop sessions and should be updated regularly. Consequently, there may well be a network of risk registers throughout the organisation, with each main production, sales and service department being responsible for its own register. There should also be a high level, strategic risk register, showing the most significant risks of the organisation which is owned and regularly reviewed by the board.

The design of these registers is set out to enable three things to be evidenced clearly:

- First, the initial columns on the spreadsheet provide space for the identification of the various risks that the organisation faces and their measurement in terms of their impact and probability scores. This produces an inherent (or gross) risk score – a measure of risk BEFORE the application of whatever controls and mitigating procedures the organisation has put in place to manage the risks.

- Secondly, working across the spreadsheet, there are further columns used to set out the controls and monitoring procedures that the organisation has in place to manage the risks. These controls and procedures need to be assessed and graded broadly as strong, medium or weak. Based on the combination of the size of the gross risk and the strength (or otherwise) of the controls and monitoring procedures over the risk, a residual (or net) risk score is produced – a measure of risk AFTER the application of controls and procedures. This is the key reference point. The overall aim of the risk register is to ensure that the risk that an organisation is running with at a particular point in time is acceptable – that is to say that the residual risk score is within the corporate risk appetite. Risk registers highlight areas of high residual risk that need to be reduced by additional controls and/or mitigating procedures to bring them within the corporate risk appetite.

- Thirdly, the final columns of the spreadsheet are used to set out any action plans required to reduce the unacceptably high residual risk areas, together with the names of those individuals delegated to be responsible for implementing them and the relevant timelines.

The risk register is crucial because it both enables the management of risk at all levels in the business and also provides evidence of the risk management process – the identification and analysis of risk, the assessment of controls and action plans with responsibilities and timelines where needed.

Avoid the tick-box attitude

Before moving on to look at strategic risk management, there is one word of warning for all directors and managers in terms of putting in place comprehensive, detailed risk management systems, with policies, registers, regular reports etc. These are necessary but they will not enable business improvements to take place or value to be added to the business unless they are accompanied by intelligent review and analysis of what the detailed information is actually saying about the business and its risk profile. Sometimes I work with organisations that have become obsessed with the detail of the risk management process, where the focus is meeting deadlines in order to tick a box.

Adrian emphasised this point during my interview with him for this book. Adrian has a wealth of experience in compliance working for a large international bank and he has come across precisely this issue in the past. This is what he told me during our interview:

> I think the problem is that because of this tick-box attitude which most organisations have, I really have yet to see an organisation in my experience that really analyses and puts into practice the information that comes up from having such controls in place. I think that most organisations are just following the "rigmarole", following the policy requirement and there's a complete lack of understanding or appreciation to use that management information effectively to improve the organisation. So, no, I think I take the sceptical view that basically you need to have operational risk management or risk management meetings – yeah, it might flag up stuff, you might take action but really they are just doing it because they are obliged to by way of procedure. I don't think that people are really understanding or getting any real mileage about basically how using that information can positively improve the performance of the businesses. Ultimately, people just tend to look at the bottom line of profit and even then there is probably a complete misunderstanding of what that really means or how it's actually derived. It's still a very cost accounting view of how to generate business and most organisations are still doing it by costs.

Strategic risk management and the "4Ts" approach

Risk management cycle

There are many ways that organisations can choose to manage risk today and, as we saw in Chapter 1, the board and senior management are responsible for designing and implementing the method that is most appropriate for each organisation. Whatever specific methodology is chosen, most organisations operate around a broad five-stage risk management cycle: the strategy for managing risk is set by the board; there are then distinct processes both to identify and to prioritise risk; the existing controls and monitoring procedures are then assessed; and finally there must be a process to measure the residual risk position and to monitor progress going forward. The whole process should be dynamic and ongoing – it is important to remember that risk management is not a static event that happens quarterly or even once a year. Risk management is never "just for Christmas"!

The strategic risk management cycle is set out in Diagram 4.1.

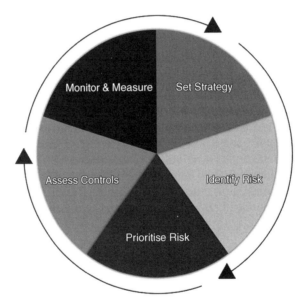

Diagram 4.1   The risk management cycle

The "4Ts" approach

When working with delegates on a course I like to make use of a particular risk management strategy known as the "4Ts" approach. This strategy, together with the exercise that we will come on to shortly, is particularly good at demonstrating the crucial linkage between risk and controls in business as well as providing delegates with an insight into the various options available to them for managing risk. The "4Ts" approach proposes that every risk exposure in an organisation can be managed according to one of four alternative methods, each one beginning with the letter T as follows:

- Tolerate – accept the risk; or

- Transfer – let someone else take part of the risk; or

- Terminate – eliminate the risk; or

- Treat – take cost-effective in-house actions to reduce the risk.

The "4Ts" approach – exercise

Having introduced the delegates to the "4Ts" approach, I then show them on a flipchart the simple Boston Matrix set out in Diagram 4.2, with four quadrants and the axes representing impact and probability, the measures of risk. By way of explanation, I work around the matrix describing the situation in each quadrant in turn: starting in the bottom left-hand quadrant there is a low probability of a low impact event occurring; moving to the bottom right-hand quadrant there is a high probability of a low impact event occurring; in the top right-hand quadrant there is a high probability of a high impact event occurring; and finally in the top left-hand quadrant there is a low probability of a high impact event occurring.

Having described the matrix, I then ask the delegates to carry out an exercise set out below on the "4Ts" approach. This exercise is the best way that I know of cementing (or raising) awareness of the crucial linkage between risk and controls. Risk drives controls, not the other way around, and this exercise serves to illustrate this point perfectly. It also enables delegates to see clearly that there are various distinct ways and methods available to them to manage risk. I normally give the delegates only a short amount of time to do this (two minutes is more than enough time for these purposes) before I take them through each quadrant of the matrix in turn, using the flipchart.

> EXERCISE: There are four quadrants in the Boston Matrix and four "Ts" in the "4Ts" approach. Each "T" belongs in one quadrant of the matrix and one quadrant only. Please place each "T" in the correct quadrant.

I thoroughly recommend this exercise. In case any reader wishes to try it out for themselves, the answers and the related discussion points are set out at the end of this Chapter.

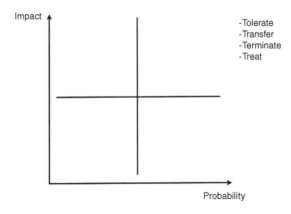

Diagram 4.2   The "4Ts" approach

The use of insurance

Before moving on, I want to emphasise at this stage one key point made in the answer to the exercise on the "4Ts" approach. This is that traditional internal control systems are designed to reduce probability risk – in other words, the likelihood that an event will materialise in a given timeframe. Traditional controls should not be relied upon to reduce the impact of an event, if that event should ever in fact come about. The potential extent or otherwise of the impact of an event is of course of critical importance to any organisation. So, in order to reduce impact risk it is vital that senior management understands the importance of contingency plans and risk transfer mechanisms. The most common use of contingency planning in business today is around the design, communication and testing of disaster recovery plans. This is a critical part of resiliency. Of equal importance to successful risk management is how effectively an organisation is able to utilise the most important risk transfer mechanism in business – insurance.

Insurance plays a very important part in the management of fraud risk too, especially fidelity insurance cover in the event of senior people acting dishonestly. As we have seen, the greatest risk to an organisation from fraud actually resides at the top of the organisation – from owners, directors, senior managers etc. These are the people who have the power within organisations to override controls and the ability to conceal fraud. So, for example, if a Finance Director decides to commit fraud, for whatever reason, it is always possible that the protection provided by the organisation's internal control system will prove to be an inadequate defence, at least in the short term. Large sums of money could be lost in this situation and, upon discovery, the reputation of the organisation may well be damaged too if the crime becomes public knowledge. Of course, fidelity insurance cover can do nothing to reduce the impact of reputational damage but it can go a long way towards limiting the financial impact of the fraud. Providing the terms of the policy have been adhered to, the organisation has the prospect of recovering from the insurance company concerned substantially all of its losses from the fraud. This is effective risk management.

So, it is very important that an organisation's insurance policies generally, and in the context of this book its fidelity insurance policy in particular, are adequate for the needs of the business and are kept up to date.

The importance of insurance as a means of recovering losses from fraud is well illustrated by the events discussed in the detailed fraud case study set out in Chapter 9.

The key risk – reputation

The threat of damage to reputation, whether personal or corporate, is one of the biggest risks of the 21st century. Reputation itself has various components which go beyond the essentials of technical skill and craftsmanship: consistency of performance is crucial as it is past performance that establishes an organisation's track record; the track record leads to the key concept of integrity, of doing the right thing first time, every time; integrity builds up trust, the "x-factor" which may be described as the residue of promises fulfilled, and includes the key management challenge of matching the behaviour of their people with the corporate values of the organisation; trust leads to respect and to positive public perception. All of these factors combine to bring the prospect of sustainability and long-term success. For a company these components provide the essential building blocks on which corporate branding and image can be built. For individuals, they provide the essence of our character, of our personal brand if you will.

There are many, many examples that illustrate the truth of the maxim that reputation takes years to build but only seconds to destroy. In terms of what can happen to individuals, the maxim is illustrated very well by the recent and dramatic fall from grace of the British fashion designer John Galliano. In 2011, following an anti-Semitic outburst at a nightclub that was widely reported in the press, Mr Galliano was quickly dismissed as the creative director of the Dior fashion house and was then dropped from his own fashion label despite a long and hitherto brilliant career in the fashion industry.[8]

Of course, corporations are also highly vulnerable to reputational damage. Although we are concerned principally with financial crime issues in this book, a brand can be damaged in other ways too. BP plc is one of the world's leading international oil and gas companies. What happened to the company in 2010 illustrates very well the reputational damage that can follow from health and safety failures and environmental damage.

> **Example: BP plc and the Deepwater Horizon tragedy.**[9] Following the disastrous fire at the Macondo oil well in the Gulf of Mexico in April 2010, which resulted in the deaths of 11 men working on the Deepwater Horizon oil rig, together with many more injuries and in massive oil spillage and environmental damage, BP's corporate reputation was shredded. The company share price halved in the months following the tragedy and at the time of writing over a year later it is still trading at a 33% discount compared to its peers. BP has incurred significant brand damage, most notably in its key market of the US, where trust and respect for BP there have been hugely reduced despite the corporation's efforts to be fair and even generous in its compensation payments to the many local businesses and individuals that have suffered financial loss as a result of the tragedy. The reputations of a number of key individuals have also suffered, most notably that of BP's ex-CEO, Tony Hayward who, following a number of ill-judged comments and poor performances in front of the media, became almost a "hate figure" in the US.

Death, human tragedy and environmental damage provide one of the two broad categories of events that can tarnish corporate reputation most quickly – the other is fraud and corruption. BP is not alone in that the damage to its reputation was caused by a health and safety scandal: Union Carbide (the Bhopal tragedy in India); Exxon (the" Exxon Valdez" disaster); and Occidental (the fire on the Piper Alpha rig) are other examples from the chemicals and energy sectors.

We are concerned in this book with the second broad area of threat to reputation – the issues of fraud, greed and financial crime. They can be just as corrosive to corporate brands as death and environmental tragedies and they can severely tarnish and even destroy corporate reputation very quickly. There are numerous examples of this which we discuss at various stages throughout the book: Barings, Enron, WorldCom, Parmalat, Galleon, Madoff and others.

However, I am going to use a different example here to illustrate the risks associated with reputational damage. I am a chartered accountant by training and profession and for me the most dramatic way that I can describe the consequences of reputational damage and the threat that this poses to any organisation is to relate the story of what happened to one of the world's leading accountancy firms at the start of the 21st century. At that time there were five global accounting firms, today there are only four. And I must say that if anyone had suggested to me in the year 2000 that, less than three years later, one of these firms would effectively have ceased to exist I would have thought that they were mad. This firm had over 100,000 highly trained professional staff working in offices all around the world and their clients included many of the world's largest and most sophisticated organisations. Yet this firm's brand was fatally damaged in quick time, it was holed below the water line and it very soon lost its core business clients. So, if anyone ever suggests to you that reputational risk is exaggerated, that it is not really all that serious an issue, just reply with two words – Arthur Andersen. This is what happened.

Reputation risk – the Arthur Andersen/Enron case[10]

Background
Arthur Andersen ("Andersen") founded the eponymous firm in 1913 in Chicago offering accounting, auditing and tax services. The firm quickly became known for an uncompromising adherence to accounting principles. It grew throughout the 20th century and in the year 2000 it was the biggest accountancy firm in the world. However, in 2002 Andersen was convicted of one count of obstruction of justice by a court in Houston, Texas. It therefore became the first accounting firm in history to be criminally convicted. On one level, this criminal conviction meant that the firm could no longer provide auditing services to publically quoted corporations. On another level, it meant that the firm had lost its reputation for integrity and professionalism. Unsurprisingly, it lost its clients too. How could this have happened to Andersen, a respected global professional services firm?

Relationship with Enron
Enron was an important client of Andersen. It was a relationship that embroiled Andersen in controversy when Enron collapsed and filed for bankruptcy protection in 2001. The firm acted as auditors and financial advisers to Enron for many years (it also audited the accounts of other major companies made notorious through fraud, for example WorldCom). Enron notoriously became bankrupt through corporate fraud.

Much has been made subsequently of the alleged conflicts of interest between Enron and Andersen, whereby Andersen was paid $25 million a year as the auditor of Enron and received almost the same amount, $25 million a year, for providing consultancy services to Enron. It has been said that these conflicts made it impossible for Andersen to do a proper audit. It is no doubt true that there were a number of close relationships amongst certain individuals at Enron's headquarters in Houston, Texas and the accountants in Andersen's local Houston office. This network of relationships has been highlighted by Bethany McLean and Peter Elkind in their authoritative book on the Enron scandal *The Smartest Guys in the Room*.[11] However, the situation of a company's auditors also acting as consultants to the same company was by no means extraordinary at the time. Rather, it was common practice and was indeed considered essential to the business models of the big accounting firms – audit fees alone were incapable of generating the required levels of profitability or revenue growth.

Guilty of a criminal offence
It is possible that Andersen might have been able to survive scrutiny of the competence of its audit work in the Enron and WorldCom cases. The specific problem that Andersen had, which it was unable to deal with, was that it was accused and then found guilty by a court in Houston, Texas in June 2002 of the criminal offence of obstructing justice by shredding documents relating to Enron. Of course, both the criminal charge and Andersen's by now controversial relationship with Enron were in the public domain and the firm had already lost much of its business by the time of the verdict. The Court's decision was to a large extent anticipated and only served to confirm that Andersen had lost its reputation for professionalism and its reputation for integrity. Soon after the verdict, Andersen announced that it would stop auditing publicly traded companies, thereby pre-empting an almost certain official ban. Shortly thereafter it started to lose its remaining clients too. After all, why spend millions of dollars a year to have Andersen sign off your accounts or to provide advice when nobody believed what Andersen was saying any more?

Verdict overturned

There is an irony in the ending of this story that is not often mentioned. Andersen appealed against the initial court judgement and the appeal was successful. In 2005 the conviction was overturned by the Supreme Court in a unanimous vote. The Supreme Court found that Anderson had in fact shredded documents in accordance with its own document-shredding policy rather than as part of a scheme to obstruct the authorities. So the firm could claim that it had acted professionally and properly throughout. However, the timing of the appeal hearing was far too late to save Andersen's reputation. The firm's brand was fatally damaged and it simply could not recover. As a result, five global accounting firms were reduced to four, a position that remains the same today.

There is one final misconception concerning Andersen. The firm never filed for bankruptcy. After the conviction, the audit, tax and consulting practices were separated and sold to various competitor firms. Andersen remains a business and it continues to operate a training facility for professionals in Illinois.

Reputation and ethics

It is of course difficult for any organisation to obtain complete confidence around the management of reputation risk. One ingredient that is absolutely essential however is good business ethics. Andersen certainly would claim to have had this. Whether Enron had ethical principles at the forefront of its culture is more debatable, however. Despite a number of innovative measures, for example its "Vision and Values Platform" and its Ethics Charter the culture of the organisation was overwhelmingly arrogant and aggressive. Much of this of course had to do with the tone at the top and it seems that good ethics was never a priority for Enron's senior executives. Take Mr Skilling for example. In 1997 he was promoted to President and Chief Operating Officer of Enron and was widely thought to be a most effective "Number 2" to the Chairman and CEO Ken Lay (Mr Skilling was promoted to CEO for a short time in 2001 before he famously resigned in August of that year, citing personal reasons). Everything that I have read about Mr Skilling indicates that he was focused throughout his career on maximising shareholder returns. All the evidence suggests that he was less concerned about the methods used by Enron to hit its targets and rather more about the fact that the targets themselves were indeed being achieved. As an example, it has been said that Mr Skilling never attended a single class on business ethics throughout his time at Harvard Business School. This would certainly not be a recommended course of action for an aspiring young executive today!

Corporate reputation is thoroughly rooted in the management of business ethics, a subject that we will turn to in the last Chapter of the book.

Taking a risk-based approach to financial crime

Introduction

The importance of taking a proportionate, risk-based approach to fraud is one of the recurring themes of this book. However, I am advocating this as a matter of best practice. I am unable to point to any law or set of regulations which compels an organisation to adopt a risk-based approach in the area of fraud. This may change in the near future but at the point of writing, in early 2012, it is not the case.

I say that there may be developments in the near future advisedly, because there are recent examples in other areas of financial crime management of the principle of risk assessment being enshrined in the law and/or in official guidance. Two such examples are set out below.

Approach to bribery and corruption

One such example of this is seen in the official guidance accompanying the Bribery Act 2010 in the UK. This Act requires a commercial organisation to have "adequate procedures" in place if it is to be able to defend itself against a charge under the new corporate offence of failing to prevent bribery. The UK's Ministry of Justice has published Guidance[12] on what it considers adequate procedures to be. This Guidance actually comprises a classic piece of risk management theory. The guidance notes are built around six guiding principles. The first of these is that a commercial organisation should adopt proportionate procedures, the key determinant of which is the degree of bribery risk that it faces. The third of these principles is stated to be "risk assessment" which is then described in the following terms: "the commercial organisation assesses the nature and extent of its exposure to potential external and internal risks of bribery. The assessment is periodic, informed and documented." So, we see here a recent piece of official guidance, incorporating the essential elements of the risk-based approach, being applied to one aspect of financial crime, that of bribery and corruption.

Approach to money laundering and terrorist financing

Another example of the official adoption of the risk-based approach when combatting financial crime is provided by the Third Money Laundering Directive,[13] which became law throughout the European Union in December 2007. One of its main provisions is to make mandatory a risk-based approach to anti-money laundering and counter-terrorist financing activities generally and to customer due diligence procedures in particular for all "relevant persons" falling under the ambit of the Directive. The highly influential Joint Money Laundering Steering Group ("JMLSG")[14] in the UK has responded to the Directive by issuing detailed guidance notes. It is worth spending a little time looking at these guidance notes because they illustrate again the official adoption of the risk-based approach for dealing with financial crime.

The key change in approach in the guidance notes is the move from the old "tick-box" regime to one based on judgement. Previously, financial institutions and other businesses that fell under the anti-money laundering regulations had been required to treat all customers in essentially the same way for identification purposes regardless of their circumstances, location, type of business etc. Now, obviously the vast majority of customers that a typical financial institution services are neither money launderers nor terrorists so the old approach represented an extremely inefficient use of resources – the controls and monitoring processes employed by the institution were spread evenly across all its customers regardless of the risk each one represented. The new risk-based approach requires regulated institutions to identify the riskier customers and to allocate their resources accordingly – i.e. to ensure that those individuals, companies, trusts etc. that are high risk receive a proportionately higher degree of due diligence checks than are given to the majority of low risk customers. So, the overall aim of the JMLSG approach is to enable regulated institutions to assess the most cost-effective and proportionate way to manage and mitigate the risks from money launderers and terrorists that they face. The JMLSG sets out a five-step process to achieve this whereby every institution should:

- Identify the money laundering and terrorist financing risks that are relevant to its particular circumstances;

- Assess the risks according to four factors: the customers themselves; the products offered by the institution; delivery channels through which the institution meets its customers (for example face-to-face, introductions from agents, online etc.); and geographical areas of operation;

- Design and implement proportionate controls to manage and mitigate the assessed risks;

- Monitor and improve the operation of these controls over time; and

- Document and record appropriately what has been done and the reasons for the actions taken.

There is one more important point to make about the new anti-money laundering regime. It does away with the pretence that it is possible for an institution to have certainty that its systems and procedures will never be breached or abused by a drugs dealer, a corrupt politician, a white-collar criminal or a terrorist in the future. The idea of certainty, the "comfort blanket" that prevention and deterrence measures will always work, is nice to have in theory but is simply impossible to achieve in practice. The new anti-money laundering regime adopts a more realistic approach. It recognises that at some stage in the future every institution is likely to be a target of organised criminals or terrorists and on very rare occasions these attacks will succeed. The new rules require institutions to design and implement measures that give them reasonable assurance that money laundering and terrorist financing activities are not being carried out by their customers. Crucially, the authorities have provided assurance to institutions that they will not be hammered should their systems be breached in a particular case of money laundering or terrorist financing providing they can demonstrate they took all reasonable prevention and deterrence measures. Hence the reason why it is so important for all institutions to ensure that their systems and controls are fully documented, and that full notes are available showing the thinking and reasoning behind all key decisions taken.

Taking a holistic approach to financial crime

My advice to organisations and delegates alike is always to take a holistic, risk-based approach to the management of financial crime. For far too long the individual components of financial crime have been dealt with separately. Anti-money laundering is perhaps the best example of this. Over the last 20 years there have developed separate controls and procedures, distinctive awareness training programmes, a specific nominated officer (the Money Laundering Reporting Officer) and even new jargon and phraseology to deal with money laundering and terrorist financing threats. For example, individuals in positions of political power are described in money laundering parlance as "PEPs", an acronym standing for politically exposed persons. PEPs are always categorised as high risk because of their potential to abuse their power to enrich themselves and their families illegally. As such, the regulations quite correctly require organisations that deal with PEPs to have stronger controls in place over these activities than over the activities of more standard (and therefore low risk) customers. However, these strong controls are not described as such, rather they are termed "enhanced due diligence procedures"!

Financial institutions have developed very thorough procedures to deal with money laundering and terrorist financing threats because they have been compelled to do so by the laws and regulations in place and by the threat of regulatory fines and/or criminal prosecution if they fail to do so. However, this rigour has often not been transferred to other related areas like internal fraud, where controls and awareness often remain relatively weak.

Contrast this approach with that taken by casinos. In my experience, those delegates attending my courses who work in the gaming industry are always very well aware of fraud threats and their organisations seem to have robust anti-fraud controls in place. They are less focused on money laundering threats (despite being part of the regulated sector).

There are benefits and efficiencies to be gained from taking a holistic view of the various financial crime threats: money laundering and terrorist financing; fraud; bribery and corruption; insider dealing; collusion, coercion and cartels. From talking to delegates recently, there are signs that organisations, in particular financial services institutions, are looking to develop such a holistic approach to financial crime generally. Certainly, in my opinion this would represent improved practices and would be in-line with the direction of travel of recent legislation and official guidance.

Taking a risk-based approach to fraud

Overview

Using risk-based principles to manage fraud threats should not be a theoretical box-ticking exercise but rather it should be an integral part of how directors and managers run their organisations. I was particularly impressed by the way that Sharon answered a question that I asked her about fraud risk during our interview. Sharon is deputy CEO of a large financial services group in the Caribbean. This is what she had to say on the subject of risk:

> Well you must remember we run a whole financial services group so when you talk about fraud risk it's complicated. You start with fraud from tellers in your retail network, a customer comes to deposit $5,000, they write him a transaction slip for $4,000 and then skim $1,000 and therefore what do you do? You need to put cameras and monitors of some sort in for that type of risk. Looking at the bigger picture, we have a risk-based system and it reports into an area of operational risk. They look at the risk in the environment. You have an audit department that does risk-based auditing and they look at the area of fraud and where your potential areas of risk are. Then based on that you have to put in place risk mitigation measures and then operational risk monitors to make sure that those measures are in place. The report goes to a senior management Risk Committee so it says: these are the potential areas of fraud, this is what is being done and then if there is in fact a fraud in a particular area this has happened. Because as soon as you get a fraud in a particular area you have to determine what do I put in place to make sure this does not happen again and somebody else has to monitor that it has actually been put in place. And then we also monitor the cost to us.
>
> We have fraud risk in the branch network, we have treasury, we have our traders – huge risk right there, I mean those things can happen. Then you have the corporate bank where people are dealing with fairly large transactions and so on and how they structure those transactions. You must make sure that everything is in place to ensure that people are not being able to take money on the side. Of course, the other area of risk in our organisation is procurement because we might be buying heavily at any point in time. As an example, if we take these netbooks, you go out at any point in time and you might buy 50–100 netbooks so therefore you have to have your procurement policies built a certain way and somebody monitoring the programme and then monitoring adherence to the pro-gramme on a very regular basis. You have to put all those processes in place so it is time consuming, it's human resource consuming. In certain areas you have to use the IT systems to be able to do it. But it is necessary to be able to do it because you need to protect the institution because one trigger, by the click of the button, could wipe you out. You might say that a teller is only taking $1,000 but if you have in your system 300 tellers

and they are all taking $1,000 and you don't realise this for six months you know your retail bank is practically bankrupt. So all of those things matter. And of course, the other thing is fraud breeds fraud so if people think they can get on like this in an environment it starts going into all areas and before you know it you end up in an organisation where it's just a complete disaster.

As I have highlighted already, it is in my view essential that every organisation should have a fraud risk profile. That is to say, it should periodically assess and prioritise the risk that fraud poses to its business formally and methodically. It should then use this risk assessment as the basis for designing and updating proportionate controls and monitoring procedures to mitigate the threats identified. We look at fraud risks throughout the book – threats from people, from failing controls, from different types of business transactions. Before moving onto these, there are two important areas to discuss at this stage: setting out the practical steps and processes needed for putting together the fraud risk profile itself and then summarising the overarching strategic framework which organisations should be working within by combining risk management theory with the day-to-day realities of fraud threats.

1. Fraud risk profile

The first thing to say about the fraud risk profile is that it should be entirely consistent in terms of template and methodology with whatever general risk management system that the organisation uses. There is no need for a special process for fraud. For example, companies in the regulated sector for anti-money laundering and counter-terrorist financing purposes should be able to add an anti-fraud component to their existing risk processes relatively easily. This would lead to a financial crime threat assessment which would be a powerful risk management tool for any financial institution. Most other organisations should be able to produce a fraud risk profile by following the steps below using their existing risk management systems. For anyone reading this whose organisation does not have a formalised, documented system, showing clearly how risk is identified, assessed, controlled and monitored, then my advice is very straightforward – you need to develop one! Even a small business needs a risk management system, but one that is proportionate and appropriate to its own particular needs. I suggest you talk to your auditors in the first instance as they should be able to give you advice in this area.

Many people, especially those who work for small or medium-sized organisations are initially put off the idea of creating a fraud risk profile by a perception that it will take an immense amount of time and effort. In fact, this need not be the case at all. There are three essential ingredients to producing a first cut of the fraud risk profile: the right people; the right equipment; and the right amount of time.

- In terms of getting together the right people, I always encourage a workshop approach. Here it is important to resist the temptation to have too many people involved. Studies show that the ideal size of a working group in terms of producing practical ideas and outcomes is actually only five people. So, a good representative group would include the "owner" of fraud risk management (this could be, for example, the Finance Director, or the head of internal audit or the Compliance Officer etc.) and perhaps four to seven other interested parties from some of the key departments involved in managing fraud risk, for example: accounts; procurement and supply chain; treasury; human resources; internal audit; security. The workshop will benefit from having a facilitator also. In my experience an outsider with good knowledge of fraud who can stimulate the discussion and is focused on achieving the objective of a completed first draft of the profile can be very helpful.

- In terms of the right equipment, you will need a laptop loaded with the risk management template together with a flipchart and/or a whiteboard. One of the workshop participants should be familiar with the template and have responsibility for updating and amending it as the discussion is taking place. I recommend that each participant is given a blank sheet of paper. A good starting point for the workshop would be for the facilitator to ask each person to write down the three most important fraud risks facing the organisation from their own particular point of view.

- Finally, in terms of the right amount of time, this is relatively straightforward. I would advocate that all the participants should be prepared to devote three hours of dedicated time to this workshop – have one break, no other interruptions, and certainly no BlackBerries!

Frazer's organisation, in the UK's public sector, has used a fraud risk register for a number of years now. Frazer and his colleagues are using it to raise awareness of the fraud threat throughout the organisation and to allocate responsibilities. This is what he told me about the register during our interview:

> The register has probably been in operation for over five years now. It was initially set up with help from a firm of accountants. Over the years, it's been refined. We review it every year and this year we've gone a bit further by having a workshop where we've tried to allocate ownership of those risks. This workshop was held recently with our most senior managers to make sure that they understand what we have in our fraud risk register, that they own it, that the current and the target scores are understandable and acceptable to them and that the mitigations in place would help them move from the current score to the target score and indeed that they are proportionate measures. It is starting to become a management tool, rather than just a register.
>
> Our top risks on the register reflect the current climate around the public sector. The first is to do with GPC cards, with potential misuse of GPC cards. These are basically government cards issued to individuals for purchasing certain, pre-agreed products and services within very strict levels and limits. Then there are a number of risks around procurement – there's always lots of opportunities, dis-aggregation and that sort of thing. There are risks around theft of equipment – we are a large organisation and we have a lot of assets, a lot of smallish but quite valuable assets that sometimes can go missing and they're not simply necessarily "lost". We are probably going to do a sweep at some stage of expenses also given the current economic climate. We are publicly funded and therefore we need to make sure that every £ of taxpayers' money, or the other sources of income that we get, is spent on the work that we are supposed to be spending it on, which is our core work. The other significant potential impact of internal fraud is on our reputation and it doesn't matter all the good work we've done over the years, one major internal fraud, particularly in the current climate with the attitude to the public sector, could undo all of that good work so we treat it very seriously.

2. Strategic approach to fraud risk

Looking again at the Boston Matrix that we used to work through the "4Ts" approach earlier in this Chapter, the specific risk of fraud risk may be placed firmly in this matrix in two distinct places: in the high probability, low impact quadrant; and in the low probability, high impact quadrant. As will be appreciated, these are two very different types of risk which should be managed in different ways. We examine each in turn below.

Fraud as high probability, low impact risk

First, fraud risk appears in the high probability, low impact quadrant. There are a whole series of specific fraud threats to an organisation that do not in themselves represent high impact risk but where the overall effect is likely to be corrosive. Examples are: submitting false invoices, fiddling expense claims, skimming cash, adding ghost employees to the payroll. There are many others and they are combined in the ACFE fraud typology under the category "asset misappropriation". The probability of these risks materialising in the absence of internal controls is high.

Organisations should look to a combination of traditional, generic controls and specific anti-fraud controls to reduce the probability of these risks actually happening to acceptable levels. Notice that I am not advocating the elimination of fraud here, rather a strategy of containment and mini-misation. Of course I would like to eliminate all fraud but I know from experience that it is simply impossible, it cannot be done. There is no system of control, no set of processes that are guaranteed to be fraud-proof. Also, it would in many ways be counter-productive for an organisation to attempt to eliminate fraud completely from its business as this would mean introducing layers of bureaucratic controls and intrusive questioning. Such an approach would not only be costly, it would serve ultimately to stifle value creation and to undermine the trust of customers, suppliers and other stakeholders.

To illustrate this point, I like to use an example based on a different type of business threat, one that is faced by retailers in particular, that of shoplifting. During the late 1990s I was working on a consulting assignment for a large retailer in the UK, based at its main store in Oxford Street, London. I was asked to join a project group which was looking at the problem of losses incurred through "shrinkage". The term shrinkage is used by retailers to include a variety of different types of day-to-day losses in a store, including for example, food wastage and breakages of stock. The most significant element of shrinkage, however, is almost always losses due to shoplifting. This is what happened on my project.

Example: UK retailer, late 1990s. In common with most other retailers, especially those operating in the West End of London where stores are often targeted by thieves, my client was experiencing problems with shoplifting. One day there was an idea floated in the project group that management should be taking a much more proactive stance against shoplifting, including robust actions designed to stop completely all of this type of theft. Actions discussed included: the hiring of many more security guards, installing CCTV cameras throughout the store and taking a much firmer line with people who were caught stealing. This last initiative would mean not only handing them over to the police (which was no deterrent for a "professional" shoplifter as the courts would simply give them a small fine with no jail term attached) but also taking them through the civil courts for repayment of losses that their actions had caused to the store. Interestingly, the security expert in the group supported this last idea but was not in favour of adopting a zero tolerance approach. She felt very strongly that most of these measures would be counter-productive: not only would the costs involved be significant but the huge increase in visible security that was being proposed might well harm the perception of the whole shopping experience for customers by turning the retailer's flagship store almost into an armed camp. After considerable discussion, the security expert's views prevailed and the idea of eliminating all shoplifting from the store was rejected. Instead, the retailer looked to manage the shrinkage problem in a more proportionate way. Measures were put in place so that the data on shrinkage would be collected more quickly and would be more closely analysed with a view to ensuring that losses were contained within the range of 1–2% of turnover – the "national average" for retail stores at the time. Extra controls would be targeted at any departments in the store where losses were increasing above this level. Intelligence on known shoplifters would be shared with other stores operating in Oxford Street with a view to identifying "problem individuals" quickly. People who were caught shoplifting would be vigorously pursued and the idea of using civil legal proceedings against them to recover losses was taken up. This approach made a lot of sense to me at the time. It was proportionate and risk based. Indeed, this is exactly the approach that I recommend that organisations should adopt in a fraud context throughout this book.

Fraud as low probability, high impact risk

Secondly, fraud risk appears in the low probability, high impact quadrant. This is another, quite distinct category of risk, where owners, senior managers or individuals in charge of high spending departments commit fraud that seriously damages the organisation. The ACFE categorises these situations under two headings: fraudulent financial statements and corruption. There is less probability of these types of fraud happening than with asset misappropriation, but if they do the consequences are likely to be much more serious. This is classic high impact, low probability risk.

All organisations need a different approach here and should adopt a strategy of risk avoidance. Fidelity insurance cover is essential in order to reduce the impact risk of such events. However, the fundamental requirements are for a robust governance structure to be in place, incorporating checks and balances at the top of the organisation together with strong business ethics. We look specifically at the governance dimension in the next Chapter.

Summary – Five Key Learning Points for Directors and Managers

Modern best practice is to take a risk-based approach to fraud and other areas of financial crime. Unfortunately, it is not always clear that everyone in business organisations understand what this phrase actually means in practice. This Chapter has attempted to provide a concise guide to the risk-based approach. Included are some important points for directors and managers regarding the management of fraud risk itself. These key points are summarised below:

✓ Remember that fraud risk is linked to positions of seniority and power in an organisation. Although it might seem counter-intuitive, the owners, directors and senior managers of a business represent the greatest fraud risks in that business.

✓ Adopt a twin-track approach, depending on the type of fraud risk: financial statement fraud and corruption issues are low probability, high impact risks and demand a strategy of avoidance; asset misappropriation schemes on the other hand represent high probability, low impact risks and should be managed using proportionate controls to contain threats to acceptable levels.

✓ Ensure that your insurance strategy is adequate and appropriate not only in terms of providing cover against potential losses from fraud but also that it is consistent with the overall business strategy of your organisation.

✓ Understand the importance of a documented process for managing risk in the 21st century. If your organisation does not have such a process, make a commitment to spend the necessary money and time to install a risk management system that is proportionate to your individual business needs as soon as possible – your auditors should be able to help with this.

✓ Make sure that a specific fraud risk assessment is prepared, documented and regularly updated. If possible, expand this to include any other areas of financial crime that are relevant to your business, so that the most powerful, holistic approach is taken to managing financial crime risks.

The "4Ts" approach – answer to the exercise

When I introduce the "4Ts" exercise on my courses I start with the blank Boston Matrix set out in Diagram 4.2 above and ask the delegates to complete it by inserting the appropriate "T" into each. Each "T" goes in one box only. During the subsequent discussion, we progress round the Matrix as described below, to arrive at the completed answer, shown in Diagram 4.3 below.

(a) Bottom left-hand quadrant = TOLERATE

We begin in the bottom left-hand corner of the matrix. Most of my delegates will have the correct answer for this quadrant, which is to tolerate risk. However, I always give them the following caveat at this point. Although it is relatively easy to see in the nice academic environment of the classroom that low probability, low impact risks should be tolerated and accepted by business, I would be very confident that if I were to spend time in any of the businesses represented in the room I would find examples of this not happening, of situations where the business spends valuable time, energy and resources trying to manage things that do not matter. There are practical challenges in this quadrant for all managers in terms of optimising the use of business resources – process re-engineering is often difficult because individuals and institutions are resistant to change. However, there are big opportunities in terms of increased efficiency if these challenges can be overcome. After all, if the only answer to the question: "Why are we doing this?" is the

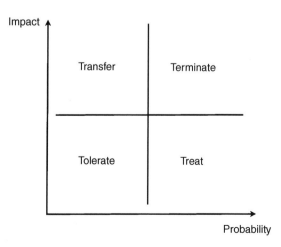

Diagram 4.3   The "4Ts" approach

response "Because we have always done it this way" then clearly there could be room for improvement.

(b) Top right-hand quadrant = TERMINATE

We then move diametrically across the matrix to the top right-hand corner. Again, most delegates will have the correct answer in this quadrant, which is to terminate risk. They will see that there are some things in business that are simply too risky to be taken on – wherever possible organisations should end operations in these areas or, better still, not enter into them in the first place. I usually have two comments to make at this stage. The first is that sometimes public sector bodies do not have the option of terminating certain extremely risky but also essential areas of their operations, for example providing care for adults with chronic drugs and/or alcohol issues. Secondly, I make the point that risk management theory is never prescriptive so that any activity, no matter how extreme, may be justified according to the individual situation – all actions in business depend crucially on the judgements made by managers according to the circum- stances. For example, there is the well-known maxim of risk and reward. Organisations sometimes are prepared to take on significant risks in the expectation of receiving significant returns should the deal succeed. All that traditional risk theory stipulates here is that very high risks should be matched by very strong controls. Of course the type of control will vary depending on the transaction but the common thread running through all controls deemed to be "strong" is that a senior and/or experienced manager is involved in the detail of a high-risk transaction. It would be a fundamental mistake for a business to delegate the management of a high-risk area to junior or inexperienced members of staff.

(c) Bottom right-hand quadrant = TREAT

We next turn to the bottom right-hand corner of the matrix. Here there is often some disagreement over the correct answer in this quadrant, which is to treat risk. Many delegates will say at first that risk should be transferred here. However, the "4Ts" approach stipulates that high probability low impact risk should be treated. In other words, it is here that the policies and procedures, the internal controls frameworks and manuals that most organisations have developed are brought into play. The reason is simple. Traditional internal controls exist primarily to reduce probability risk. They will not generally have any effect on the impact of an event should that event actually materialise. In order to reduce the impact of an event, contingency plans (e.g. disaster recovery plans) or risk transfer mechanisms (e.g. insurance) are required. Traditional systems, internal controls policies and procedures are designed to reduce the frequency of an event materialising.

(d) Top left-hand quadrant = TRANSFER

Finally we arrive at the top left-hand corner of the matrix, low probability high impact risk. The correct answer is transfer – it is the only "T" remaining now! Often in practice this will be the hardest area of risk for an organisation to deal with because nobody wishes to spend money on managing an event which, though theoretically possible, is very unlikely to happen in the first place! The most efficient way to manage these risks is to transfer a portion of them to another party. Although at first sight this might seem surprising, in practice risk transfer mechanisms are used all the time in business.

By far the most widely used risk transfer mechanism in business is insurance. The essence of insurance is the transfer of a portion of risk to a third party, the insurer, who will take on the risk in exchange for a fee. Insurance is therefore central to the risk management strategy of most businesses and yet, in my experience, it seldom features prominently on either risk registers or on the work schedules of the internal audit department. In my view this is a mistake and illustrates sometimes poor awareness of what risk management is really all about. Of course, there are other ways that risk can be transferred: financial services businesses are used to the idea of hedging foreign currency or interest rate exposures; many organisations have made use of outsourcing opportunities over the last 20 years (it should be noted that outsourcing is not a termination of risk, but is rather a transfer of risk, largely around processing functions, whilst still retaining ownership of the risk overall); and many local authorities in the UK have chosen to go into partnership with other service providers (e.g. police, health and education) in an attempt to leverage up the quality of the services they provide to residents whilst at the same time spreading the associated risks.

5 Governance

Fraud Awareness Quiz – Question 5

What are the first two words or phrases that come into your mind when you hear the term corporate governance?

_____

People disappear in Texas

I am sitting in my room at the Embassy Suites Hotel in San Antonio, Texas. It is a Thursday evening in July 1998. I am coming to the end of a telephone call with a corporate lawyer in Washington, giving her a progress report on my assignment. I am in the US working for a UK FTSE 100 company that had bought an American group a couple of years previously. Following changes in the board and the senior management team in the UK, I have been asked to review the activities of one of the American group's subsidiary companies that operates primarily in Texas but also all along the Mexican border through a series of retail outlets. This company had been a family-owned business in the past, with a reputation for being both profitable and also aggressive risk-takers. I am tasked with reporting back to the UK board at the end of the assignment.

I have been talking to the American lawyer for about 20 minutes now, updating her on progress. I tell her that the assignment is going well overall and that I am receiving most of the assistance that I need from the managers and staff. However, I do have concerns. It is already clear to me that the company is still dominated by the founding family and, from everything that I have heard, the family remain a powerful force all along the border. I say to the lawyer that it seems to me to be operating as a separate fiefdom, with little regard for its UK parent company. I mention my unease at some of the activities that are going on in the retail stores along the border and the lack of documentation and audit trail in many areas. The lawyer asks for examples. I tell her that I have particular worries at the extent of the cross-border trading activities that take place, often with apparently very rich individuals who seem to come out of the Mexican desert, buy widely and extravagantly in the stores, often paying in cash and then simply disappear. I feel the risk surrounding these activities is high, certainly way beyond the risk appetite of the parent company, which has the reputation of being one of the most conservative of all the major listed companies in the UK. I tell her about one major area of weakness. There is minimal documentation and records kept on file concerning the identity of these big-spending Mexican customers, contrary to the requirements of the US anti-money laundering legislation. Much of what I have been shown by way of copy passports and signatures looks like poor forgeries to me. My big concern is that if the tax authorities (the Internal Revenue Service) or one of the other US regulatory authorities become aware of this they could shut the whole operation down.

The lawyer is now clearly worried too. She asks me if I have raised these points with the family as yet. I say no, I have not had the chance to speak to any of them directly on this so far. I have mentioned one or two concerns in passing to the operational managers, without getting much of a response. I intend to raise this with the family next week.

The conversation is now drawing to a close. This is my first time in Texas and, as a matter of courtesy, the lawyer asks me what I am planning to do with my time in San Antonio over the weekend. I say that actually I have a rather exciting time planned for me, all courtesy of the client. I have been invited to spend the whole of Saturday touring the family ranch deep in up-country Texas and to have dinner there with the heads of the family that evening – the famous father and mother team that I have heard so much about but have not yet met. The plan is that I will stay the night at the ranch and return to San Antonio on the following Sunday afternoon. I say that there might be an opportunity to talk some business with the family heads too. Then . . . silence. The line suddenly goes very quiet. Finally, the lawyer starts talking again, but she is back to using her business voice now. She says to me: "Steve, I want you to listen to me. You are not to go to the ranch under any circumstances this weekend, do you understand? You must think of an excuse and give your apologies to the family. Tell them that London wants an urgent progress report or that something has come up at the last minute. You are not to go to that ranch. Do you understand?" I reply: "Of course I understand, but why don't you want me to go to the ranch? What is the problem here?" and she gives me the following chilling reply: "It's simple, Steve. People disappear in Texas. All it takes is just one wrong word . . . "

Introduction

"Where was the board?" This is a question frequently asked by shareholders, stakeholders and media commentators alike when an organisation is hit by scandal, crisis or business failure. There have been many such examples of headline corporate scandals in recent years. Set out below, by way of illustration, are 20 infamous cases, listed in no particular order:

Lehman Brothers; Enron; Siemens; Parmalat; BP; Galleon; Bernard L Madoff Investment Securities; Polly Peck; Barings; Yukos; Northern Rock; Refco; Royal Bank of Scotland; Satyam; WorldCom; Société Générale; Tyco; Arthur Andersen; Hollinger; and Allied Irish Banks.

Each case is different. Some are examples of business failure with weaknesses in the decision-making process or poor risk management, or health and safety issues. Others are more to do with the issues that concern us directly in this book; corporate fraud, bribery and corruption, greed and shortfalls in business ethics. In some of these latter examples, a number of main board directors have been found guilty of committing criminal offences. What these scandals all have in common however is that each one demonstrates shortfalls in governance right at the top of corporations.

The UK Code of Corporate Governance[1] describes the importance of corporate governance in its very first paragraph:

> The purpose of corporate governance is to facilitate effective, entrepreneurial and prudent management that can deliver the long-term success of the company.

The Code then sets out what it considers corporate governance to mean in paragraph 3, as follows:

> Corporate governance is what the board of a company does and how it sets the values of a company and is to be distinguished from the day-to-day operational management of a company by full time executives.

Good governance at the top of an organisation is vital for its success. This governance dimension is a crucial component of the anti-fraud controls framework also. There are two main reasons for this.

- First, directors and senior managers need to be actively engaged in the fight against financial crime if it is to have any real traction throughout an organisation. As we have seen, it is they who have ultimate responsibility for preventing and detecting fraud in their organisations. To discharge this responsibility they need to establish appropriate systems and controls to give them reasonable assurance that fraud risk is being managed. They also need to set the right ethical tone for the organisation and make it clear to their employees what values and behaviours are expected and will be rewarded. The allocation of responsibility for managing fraud risk to a specific member of the board or senior management team is now regarded as best practice.

- Secondly, it is the actions and behaviours of directors and senior managers themselves that are often the problem. A number of the examples listed above resulted in main board directors being found guilty of financial crime and receiving prison sentences as a result: Enron, Parmalat, Bernard L Madoff Investment Securities, WorldCom, Hollinger, Yukos and Galleon (at the time of writing, the Satyam case is still going through the legal process in India). These are all scandals involving large listed corporations. As we have seen from the ACFE's research, the risks of fraud involving owners, directors and senior managers are high in small and medium-sized organisations also. So, scandal has often been the result of fraud committed at the very top of organisations. It is clearly important, therefore, that appropriate checks and balances exist at this level too. This is where governance controls come into play. There is always a need for good corporate governance both in a fraud context as well as in a general business context.

This Chapter examines those aspects of corporate governance that are fundamental to a proper understanding of fraud risks and sets out the key governance controls required to manage them. It includes an overview of the UK governance code and also the SOX in the US. It examines the key attributes of an effective board of directors around competency and behaviour and counter-points these with the threats posed by potential conflicts of interest and corruption at the top of business. Two of the most important examples of corporate governance failures are looked at in detail: the Enron case in the US and then the ongoing Satyam scandal in India. Finally, the corruption component of fraud is examined in the light of current legislation and regulation and the risks these bring to individuals and organisations alike.

First we need to return to the Quiz and find out what the term "corporate governance" actually means to the people who work in business organisations today.

Answers to the Quiz

Fraud Awareness Quiz – Question 5
What are the first two words or phrases that come into your mind when you hear the term corporate governance?

Background

This is a different type of question to most of the others in the Quiz as there are no right and wrong answers to it. I use it on fraud courses to stimulate a discussion on what corporate governance is all about. This provides important background for my delegates before we go on to look at the critical governance dimension of the fraud problem. So, I have tried to replicate the main points coming out of these discussions below. They lead to, if not a "correct" description of corporate governance, then hopefully a better understanding of what corporate governance is all about.

Corporate governance means different things to different people. I know this very well from working with and teaching business professionals around the world. Consequently, every delegate has a different answer to the question and none are unequivocally right or wrong.

My own personal view is that corporate governance is all about how companies are run at the top. It has two fundamental components: board compliance and board performance. But when I am teaching about fraud I need to know what the delegates who are attending the course on a particular day think about this and their answers to this question give me a very good indication.

Governance as compliance

The first thing to say is that, over the years, a big majority of delegates have approached this question entirely from a business compliance viewpoint. The exact words and phrases used have differed from delegate to delegate of course, but most of them show a direct linkage between corporate governance and business compliance. Typical answers include the following: operating within the law of the land; adhering to stock exchange listing rules (for those companies whose shares are publically listed); or complying with all the relevant regulations and standards in place in a particular business sector. There are a number of particular words and phrases that I hear repeated time and time again as answers to this question: internal controls; policies; systems and procedures; rules and regulations; supervision; monitoring of management; transparency; and accountability. Words that I hear less often, but which are still firmly associated with compliance are: integrity; responsibility; codes; even box-ticking.

The performance element

From time to time some delegates have answered the question in a different way. They use words and phrases that go beyond the compliance component – they relate more to the other essential feature of corporate governance, the performance element. The words and phrases include: strategy setting; managing risk; setting values; and developing business ethics. I am encouraged whenever I hear them.

However, I have to say that one of the most surprising observations from the Quiz is that no one, not a single delegate that I have ever taught has used the words "leadership" or "entrepreneurship" when answering this question. I think that this is remarkable. Take the traditional corporate environment for example – what is the board of directors there to do if not to lead the company?

In order to emphasise the importance of the board performance component of corporate governance, I will often ask the delegates a supplemental question at this point, as follows:

> What are corporations and business entities trying to achieve in the world today, why do they exist?

Most delegates answer this supplemental question in a very traditional way – businesses exist to make profits! In fact this answer has its origins in the 1970s and in the theories of Milton Friedman and the Chicago School of Economics. It's a good answer because profitability remains a prerequisite for success and indeed for survival in a market economy today. I tell them that nothing I am about to say contradicts the fundamental point that all businesses in the private sector need to be profitable. The concept of "profit" is not really relevant to the public sector, however. As my delegates are often executives from a mixture of public sector and private sector organisations, I encourage them to think not so much in terms of profit but more of "value" as the benchmark of success. Also I stress the importance of thinking long term rather than focusing always on short-term results.

In this way, we arrive at a powerful answer to the supplemental question above which is: all organisations exist to maximise value over the long term. In order to achieve this, the delegates can see that those people at the top of organisations need to make a positive contribution by leading the business and by taking informed decisions in such areas as strategy and risk. These are the actions that will lead to added value in the long term. For example, directors and executives absolutely must contribute to and endorse the organisation's strategic plan – in many ways judgements made around the positioning of a company in changing markets are the most important decisions that a board of directors can ever take.

To illustrate the importance of strategic planning, I like to take two minutes to tell the delegates a very simple story, as follows:

Imagine two old-fashioned British explorers in the jungle – hobnail boots, baggy shorts, knobbly knees etc. etc. They are having a successful expedition until one day when they come to a clearing in the jungle and see right in front of them the biggest tiger in India. The tiger is looking straight at them and is less than 100 yards away. How do the two explorers react? Well, they react in very different ways. The first one starts to panic, he holds his head in his hands and says repeatedly: "We are going to die! We are going to die!". His colleague behaves very differently. He remains calm and composed. He walks over to the nearest rock and sits down. He takes his rucksack off his back, opens it and takes out of it a very modern pair of running shoes. He then proceeds to take off his hobnail boots and to put on the running shoes. The first explorer looks at him in disbelief and says: "What do you think you are doing? You must be mad! You will never be able to out-run that tiger". His colleague looks up at him, smiles, shakes his head and replies: "You just don't get it do you my friend? I don't need to out-run the tiger. I just need to out-run you!"

Although a little predictable perhaps, this story always goes down well with my delegates – it is amusing and they quickly see its relevance to the modern business world. After all, since 2007 all organisations in the West have come face to face with the tiger in the form of the global economic downturn. Many organisations will survive the downturn of course, a smaller number will even come out of it stronger but a significant minority will make the wrong choices – they will go out of business as a result. How well a business fares in difficult and changing market conditions depends crucially on decisions made by its board of directors and senior executives.

Board conformance and board performance

Having used the supplemental question to develop ideas, I will now return to the main question and give the delegates my own answer which is: "board conformance and board performance". There are two points that I always emphasise here.

- The first concerns the role of the board. As we saw in the introduction, corporate governance is about what the board of an organisation does and is to be distinguished from the day-to-day operational management of the business by executives.

- The second provides the overarching governance framework. There are certain things that are absolutely necessary in order for any organisation to achieve good corporate governance: compliance with the law and regulations; accountability and transparency to shareholders; and integrity. These are the characteristics that I am looking for when I talk about board conformance and unless a business can demonstrate that it has them, it will never get to first base in terms of good corporate governance in my view. However, although these qualities are absolutely necessary, they are not in themselves sufficient for good corporate governance. Compliance alone is not sufficient to get a business to where it wants to go, which should be to maximise its value over the long term for the benefit of shareholders and stakeholders. In order to achieve this, the board must perform.

These ideas are adapted from the work of the corporate governance expert, Professor Bob Garratt. In 1996 Professor Garratt wrote the highly influential book The Fish Rots from the Head.[2] This book is about what he saw as a crisis in the boardroom and how to address this by developing the skills and competencies of directors. From my own perspective at the time, working as a forensic accountant on large fraud and corruption cases, I could see very well the validity of his central point that major problems in business start at the top. Professor Garratt updated his ideas in his later work Thin on Top,[3] published in 2003. In Thin on Top he sets out what he sees as the fundamental dilemma for directors: how to "dynamically balance board performance with board conformance".

The governance concerns that Professor Garratt raises are as relevant for the managing of fraud risk as they are for managing the business as a whole. This is well illustrated by perhaps the most famous fraud case of recent times, that of Enron Corporation in the US.

Enron – a failure of corporate governance

Introduction

The Enron scandal[4] has come to symbolise for some observers all that is bad about big business: fraud, greed, arrogance and deceit. Others see the failure more in terms of poor business models leading ultimately to a crisis in investor confidence: for all their claims to be "smart", Enron executives often struggled to turn their clever ideas and innovative accounting practices into long-term sustainable growth. For me, Enron seems to have been more illusion than substance and its collapse was ultimately brought about by a failure of corporate governance.

Corporate governance often appears to be a dry and dusty subject with little practical application to the performance of business organisations. From the discussion on the Quiz question, it will be clear that this is not a viewpoint to which I subscribe. I like to use the Enron case to illustrate the fundamental importance of governance to business success or failure. There are a number of studies and surveys of the attitudes of investors towards governance (e.g. by McKinsey & Co.[5]) that attempt to prove the link between good governance and good business, leading to an increase in shareholder value. These are interesting pieces of research but personally I prefer always to stand this governance equation on its head. For me, the key point is that the absence of good governance will destroy shareholder value. I have seen this many times before and the Enron case provides the perfect example.

Company history

Enron Corporation was a US energy, commodities and services company based in Houston, Texas. In just 15 years it grew from a small base to being one of America's largest corporations, employing some 21,000 staff in more than 40 countries. Enron's Chairman and CEO throughout this period was Ken Lay and he was supported by the ex-McKinsey consultant, Jeff Skilling, who joined the Enron payroll in 1990. The company received widespread recognition for its transition from an old-line energy company with pipelines and power plants into a high-technology global enterprise that traded energy contracts like commodities, launched into new industries like broadband communications and oversaw a multi-billion dollar international investment portfolio.

In August 2000, Enron's stock price hit its highest value of $90 per share. The company was unable to sustain its success thereafter, however. A steady decline in share price during 2001 became a crisis of investor confidence from October of that year and, amid allegations of widespread accounting fraud, Enron filed for bankruptcy protection in December 2001. It has become perhaps the most notorious example of corporate fraud and corruption of recent years.

Consequences of scandal

The consequences of the scandal were wide-ranging. The bankruptcy brought misery and loss to the company's stakeholders (its employees, creditors and shareholders) and led directly to the passing of the SOX in 2002. The leading individuals in the saga were prosecuted and found guilty. Mr Skilling was found guilty at his trial in 2006 of 19 charges of conspiracy to commit securities and wire fraud and of making false statements to auditors. He was sentenced to just over 24 years in prison and fined $45 million. Mr Lay was found guilty on all counts of securities fraud, wire fraud and making false and misleading statements. He died of a heart attack before the appeals process was exhausted so that his conviction was abated. Andy Fastow, Enron's CFO, cooperated with the prosecution, pleaded guilty to two counts of wire and securities fraud and received a reduced sentence of six years in jail followed by two years on probation. He was required to forfeit $23 million of family assets. Over 20 other Enron executives and accounting officers either pleaded guilty or were found guilty of crimes committed at Enron. Also, JP Morgan Chase and Citigroup paid over $250 million between them to settle allegations from the Securities and Exchange Commission that they helped Enron manipulate its financial statements and mislead investors without admitting any wrongdoing.

There are many ways of approaching the Enron scandal. To my mind it has always been primarily a failure of governance.

Governance failure

The first finding of the Report on the role of the board of directors in Enron's collapse published in July 2002 by the US Senate Subcommittee on Investigations[6] makes clear the extent of the governance breakdown at the company. The Enron directors attending the Subcommittee hearings made much of the fact that they cannot be held accountable for misconduct of management that was concealed from them. The Subcommittee disagreed and its conclusions on the fiduciary failure of the Enron board are set out below.

> **Fiduciary Failure.** The Enron Board of Directors failed to safeguard Enron shareholders and contributed to the collapse of the seventh largest public company in the United States by allowing Enron to engage in high risk accounting, inappropriate conflict of interest transactions, extensive undisclosed off-the-books activities and excessive executive compensation. The Board witnessed numerous indications of questionable practices by Enron management over several years but chose to ignore them to the detriment of Enron shareholders, employees and business associates.

When focusing on the circumstances of that company which led to fraud, I like to take my delegates through a series of individual examples of what happened which build into a powerful lesson about the importance of having governance structures that work in practice, rather than simply looking good in theory. In many ways, Enron was the ultimate corporate governance illusion. It ticked every box in terms of best practice at the time. The following analysis explores some of the issues (others are addressed elsewhere in the book). I call it "Enron by the numbers" and as this title suggests, the analysis is based around some of the key numbers that have emerged from the Enron saga. We will look at this in two aspects, the general governance failures here below and then the specific issues with the Enron audit and compliance committee, which we will return to in Chapter 6.

Enron by the numbers – part 1

- **101 billion.** Enron was a seriously large corporation, at one point being ranked as the seventh largest company in the US. 101 billion is the amount (in US dollars) of turnover earned in 2000, as disclosed in its Annual Report and Accounts for that year, before the share price collapsed. Because it was such a large company, with importance to the whole of the US economy, it was of course the subject of scrutiny from a variety of reputable external third parties, in addition to its own internal control mechanisms. These third parties included: auditors, lawyers, bankers, brokers and analysts, fund managers, credit reference agencies, regulators and others. When the share price dramatically collapsed and Enron was forced to file for bankruptcy at the end of 2001, there was huge outrage and concern amongst corporate investors about how this could possibly have happened. The traditional safeguards surrounding an American listed company had all proved to be ineffective. Concerns were directed in particular at what appeared to be serious shortcomings in the controls and assurance mechanisms surrounding the financial reporting process. These concerns led directly to the passing of the SOX in 2002.

- **27 billion.** This is the total amount (in US dollars) of poor-performing businesses, doubtful debts and other tarnished assets that Enron moved off its consolidated balance sheet and placed in special purpose vehicles created specifically to do this. This was almost half of the company's asset total! The Senate Committee report described these as "unconsolidated affiliates". Only a single, if detailed, accounting note in the Annual Report and Accounts described to investors and other interested parties what had happened. It is important to say that what Enron was doing here was not illegal or in contravention of accounting standards under US GAAP at the time. But the effect was to improve the appearance of Enron's balance sheet significantly with no more than minimal transparency concerning the unconsolidated affiliates – the relevant accounting note was opaque to say the least. The initiative around these off-balance sheet items was driven by Mr Fastow, the CFO, who was an expert in securitisation and therefore ideally placed to set up and oversee the special purpose vehicles structures. This is one example of high-risk accounting practices at Enron. Another, particularly favoured by Mr Skilling, was the aggressive use of mark-to-market accounting to enable profits on certain projects to be brought forward and booked early in the accounting records, rather than be spread evenly over the life of the project as would happen under the traditional historical cost accounting. Again, this practice was permitted by the accounting standards of the day and was signed off by Andersen, the auditor. So, we see a pattern of aggressive, rather than illegal, accounting at Enron all with the objective of presenting the best possible results for the company, thereby maximising shareholder value. And they succeeded – at least in the short term!

- **4,300.** This figure relates to the total number of special purpose vehicles that Mr Fastow and his team created to enable the off-balance sheet transactions described above to take place. This is a vast network of companies. One truly astonishing aspect of this is that not a single one of these deals represented a true commercial business transaction. They were all accounting manoeuvres. It has always seemed significant to me that, in the admittedly different context of a money laundering review, the artificial nature of the transactions would have been sufficient to categorise them as "suspicious" and so requiring independent investigation. Once again, Andersen, the auditor, was content to approve these transactions, so long as they were each, as individual entities, properly constituted. In October 2001, following an accounting oversight relating to one of the off-balance sheet partnerships, Andersen insisted that Enron make disclosures and adjustments resulting in a $1.2 billion reduction in shareholder equity. This contributed to investor concerns that continued to drive Enron's share price down.

- **265,000,000.** This is the amount of money (in US dollars) that Lou Pi, a director of one of the main Enron subsidiary companies, received when he legitimately cashed in his share options on leaving the company in 2000. Mr Pi was a controversial figure for much of his time at Enron and although a close associate of Mr Skilling he was not thought to be a star executive performer by any means. Yet this is a colossal amount of money that he was able to take out of the company as executive compensation. Mr Pi subsequently invested it in land, becoming in the process the second-largest property owner in Arizona. I like to ask the delegates on my courses a key question when we get to this point: who were the executives of Enron running the business for, the share-holders or themselves?

- **15 and 2.** Enron had a board of directors that appeared to be perfectly constituted according to the corporate governance standards of the time. In reality, there were a number of significant weaknesses in Enron's governance structure. The number 15 relates to the number of non-executive directors that Enron had on its board in the year 2000, all of them widely respected figures from the business, academic or political worlds. The number 2 relates to the number of executives on the board: Mr Lay and Mr Skilling. It is sometimes said that having both Messrs Lay and Skilling on the board provided Enron with a measure of balance and division of responsibilities at the top. There may be something in this, although it should not be overstated. For much of the time Mr Lay was both Chairman and CEO, with Mr Skilling in the post of COO (Chief Operating Officer). Mr Skilling was promoted to CEO only in the year 2001 and he remained in that post for around six months before controversially resigning. Following Mr Skilling's resignation, Mr Lay took back the CEO position. So, although Mr Skilling is often put forward as the driving force at Enron, in fact he was very much the number two for most of the time – Mr Lay had the real power in the corporation. As for the non-executive directors, it might be thought that by having so many of them on the board, they would constitute a real balance to the executives and ensure that executive plans were subject to a robust challenge and scrutiny process. This did not in fact happen, and the non-executives proved to be ineffective in this respect for various reasons: they lacked a clear leader; they were well paid, with a number receiving consultancy fees or financial support for their academic or medical charities in addition to their directors' fees; the chairmen of the executive, finance, compensation and audit committees had all served on the Enron board for over 15 years. It seems that, collectively, they were not prepared to rock the hitherto very successful Enron boat. The Senate Subcommittee

Report describes the board relationships as harmonious, with board votes being generally unanimous and only two instances over many years involving dissenting votes. Warren Buffett has described this type of non-executive performance as: "providing an illusion of competent independence". It is an important observation and much of the governance reform in the US and in the UK following the Enron bankruptcy was designed to beef up the role of the non-executive directors.

- **3.** This relates to the three waivers of its own code of conduct made by the board with little debate or independent inquiry that enabled Mr Fastow to establish and operate off-the-books three private equity funds in 1999 and 2000. These funds (named LJM 1, LJM 2 and LJM 3 after the initials of Mr Fastow's wife and children) were designed specifically to transact business with Enron. The Senate Subcommittee made the following comments in its report: "This arrangement allowed inappropriate conflict of interest transactions as well as accounting and related party disclosure problems due to the dual role of Mr Fastow as a senior officer at Enron and an equity holder and general manager of the new entities." These entities paid Mr Fastow over $30 million in fees for acting in this management capacity, far more than his Enron salary. This is a good example of a failure to apply standards consistently right at the top of the organisation. It is also an example of weak leadership, allowing short-term considerations of maximising profit to outweigh the long-term implications and risk of authorising such an obvious conflict of interest situation.

We will return to examine other aspects of the Enron scandal in the next Chapter.

Governance overview – relationships and agency risk

Background

The regulation of corporate governance has long been an important part of company law. The importance of the shareholders of a business (the owners or investors) being able to hold their directors and managers to account was a key part of the design of the original joint stock companies. Company law has always provided for various aspects of this accountability relationship: companies must hold general meetings each year and provide their shareholders with certain minimum information, most importantly, the annual report and accounts. Proper financial accounting to shareholders is a critical part of good corporate governance. In most countries today this is underpinned by company law and international accounting standards, the correct application of which is independently verified by the external auditors.

The last 20 years have seen a developing interest in corporate governance in many countries around the world. In particular, there have been efforts to improve the governance standards of companies that seek to raise money from outside investors by being listed on a stock exchange. There have been various initiatives to do so, generally in one of two ways: either by drafting tougher laws and/or by developing codes of best practice. To illustrate this from personal experience, when I started to investigate the situation surrounding the collapse of the public company Polly Peck in 1990 there was not a single corporate governance code setting out best practices of behaviour for directors like Mr Nadir anywhere in the world. Today, such codes exist in over 60 countries. These developments have been essentially reactive to a number of corporate scandals and abuses, occurring at various times in various countries, often involving fraud and always destroying shareholder value. They have been driven by investors and their market place – the stock exchange. This is particularly true in the UK, with the development of, and subsequent amendments to, a code of corporate governance and in the US with the passing of the SOX in 2002. We look at each of these later in the Chapter.

The key governance players

Sir Adrian Cadbury's Committee described corporate governance as: "the system by which organisations are directed and controlled" (Cadbury Committee, paragraph 2.5, 1992).[7] Today, as we have seen in the answers to Question 5 of the Quiz, corporate governance is thought of in more dynamic terms, as something that facilitates effective, entrepreneurial and prudent management that can deliver the long-term success of the company. It involves complying with all applicable laws, regulations and rules, but it also involves performance and effectiveness in the relationships between the key governance players: shareholders, directors, managers, company secretariat, the company itself and the company's stakeholders. There are two key points to make here:

- First, the company itself is a separate legal entity. The directors owe their prime duty, not to the shareholders or the stakeholders, but to the company itself. From running many corporate governance workshops, I have to say that people in the corporate world are not always aware of this fundamental principle – even experienced directors are sometimes unclear on this point.

- Secondly, the stakeholder concept has gained much traction over the last 15 years or so. The term "stakeholder" includes any group or individual who can affect, or is affected by, the achievement of the organisation's objectives. It therefore has wide application and encompasses: employees, customers, suppliers, regulators, the government and the general public.

Although all stakeholders are important, the key corporate governance relationships and interactions take place between the three groups shown in Diagrams 5.1 and 5.2 below: shareholders, managers and directors. In classic corporate governance theory, it is the shareholders who hold the power in any corporation: they are the owners of the company and have the ability to elect and dismiss directors and to hire and fire managers. There is no doubt that shareholders were able to exercise effective control in the 19th and early 20th centuries, especially when those same owners were also the managers in their business. Today however the share register of a large publically-listed corporation will typically show thousands of owners at any one time, with the result that the collective power of shareholders has been splintered and diluted.

Agency risk and the role of independent non-executive directors

The shareholders of a corporation today will appoint professionals to manage their business for them – the executives that comprise an organisation's senior management team. These managers work full-time in the business and are effectively the agents of the shareholders. Included in their ranks are the Chief Executive Officer and the Chief Finance Officer, both of whom would typically also sit on the board of directors as executive directors. Of course, senior managers should act always in the interests of the company for the benefit of the shareholders as a whole. However, the dubious decision-making of executives in high profile fraud scandals combined with the huge total remuneration packages that top business people can earn today (comprising salary, pension contributions, bonuses and share incentive schemes), makes it sometimes appear that these individuals are acting primarily in their own interests and not in the interest of the shareholders. This is exactly the sort of concern that we looked at above when reviewing the Enron case.

Shareholders ←Report to / Provide capital to→ Management

Diagram 5.1 Agency risk

Agency Risk

Directors

Elect and dismiss

Update

Account to

Manage
Agency Risk

Monitor

Report to   Provide capital to

Shareholders ←——————————————→ Management

Diagram 5.2   The management of agency risk

The technical term for this is agency risk. Much of the work going into the codes of governance and the development of company legislation in the last 20 years has been carried out for the purpose of managing agency risk. To do so, code writers and law makers are increasingly looking to the directors, and in particular to independent non-executive directors, to strengthen corporate governance frameworks. Non-executive directors are individuals who work on a part-time basis and are paid a fee for doing this. They are said to be "independent" if they have no other connection with the company, its shareholders or its management. The crucial role of independent non-executive directors in modern corporate governance theory is to act as the fulcrum between shareholders and managers. They provide the essential balance and assurance between the prime interests of the shareholders who provide capital for the business and those of professional managers who spend that capital to add value to the company.

The relationships around agency risk are summarised in the two schematics in the diagrams above. In the first, Diagram 5.1 we see the old-fashioned model of shareholders dealing directly with their agents, the technical managers who ran the business day-to-day. The most senior of these managers would comprise the executives on the board, who would traditionally be much more powerful than the non-executive directors. Shareholders provided capital to managers, who in turn report back to shareholders.

In the second schematic, shown in Diagram 5.2 above, we have now added the crucial element of directors to the mix, to represent a modern, balanced board as created by the development of governance codes and legislation over the last 20 years. Here power is shared much more equally between executive and non-executive directors. Directors are accountable to their shareholders. It is the directors, especially the independent non-executive directors, who act as the fulcrum in the continuing relationship between shareholders and managers, so that there is greater assurance that the executives are always promoting the interests of the shareholders. In other words, it is the importance and responsibilities now given to the independent non-executive directors that enable agency risk to be managed with reasonable assurance.

The development of corporate governance codes and legislation
Rules-based and principles-based governance regimes

Corporate governance regimes have developed in different ways around the world. History, culture and tradition have played a big part in the way that governance has developed in each country. There is one fundamental difference in the way that governance has developed and that is between those regimes that are based on rules and those that are based on principles.

- Some governance systems are based firmly on the law. That is to say, compliance with the system is underpinned by legislation. Codes with legal enforceability are rules and so these are known as "rules-based" regimes. The most important example of this is the US where compliance with the SOX for example is a legal requirement for listed companies and their directors.

- Others are based on governance codes of best practice where compliance is voluntary rather than a legal requirement. These are known as "principles-based" regimes. The first such code emerged in the UK out of the work of the Cadbury Committee in 1992. Here the findings of the Committee were not incorporated into company law as many at the time expected to happen. The Committee took the view that informality would be more powerful than legal rules: "At the heart of the Committee's recommendations is a Code of Best Practice designed to achieve the necessary high standards of corporate behaviour" (Cadbury Committee, paragraph 1.3, 1992).[8] The requirement to comply with the code was contained within the listing rules for publicly-traded companies. The key principle of "comply or explain" emerged: companies listed on the London Stock Exchange are expected to comply with the code but, if they choose not to do so they are required to explain the reasons for such non-compliance in their annual reports and accounts. There are no legal implications, no law has been broken. So, this is a self-regulatory system and is much more flexible than one based on rules. Since Cadbury, many countries around the world have chosen to adopt the principles-based approach.

Whatever type of system is chosen, whether it is rules-based or principles-based, the overriding aim of improved corporate governance is always the same: stronger corporate governance leads to increased investor confidence which in turn enables access to broader-based and cheaper capital. This aspiration applies at both the individual company level and also for developing nation states. I have personal experience of this latter point, from my work in Mauritius.

Example: the development of corporate governance in Mauritius. I was fortunate enough to carry out two projects on the beautiful island of Mauritius in 2005 and 2006. I facilitated a series of workshops for executives and senior managers in the financial services industry on corporate governance and risk management on behalf of the country's banking association. This was part of a concerted drive by the government of Mauritius to improve corporate governance in the country and, of equal importance, to improve the perception of corporate governance by potential foreign investors. The Taylor Committee had been set up in 2001 and it produced a draft "Code of Corporate Governance for Mauritius" in 2003. This was ratified in 2004. The Taylor Code as it became known is aimed in particular at impressing and influencing investors in the rapidly expanding Indian capital markets. By raising the overall standards of governance, board behaviour and ethics, it was hoped that Indian investors would feel more confident in placing their money in Mauritius; the island would then attract a greater proportion of Indian capital placed offshore, the majority of which had hitherto been invested in South Africa and Dubai.

The US and the UK governance regimes

Let us now look briefly at the corporate governance regimes in the UK and in the US. We will use an overview of the SOX and the Corporate Governance Code to illustrate the main features of the principles-based and the rules-based systems respectively. Each has played a very important role in the development of the modern system of active and informed engagement by the board of directors in the oversight and governance of their corporations.

However, it is fair to say that neither model was able to prevent the high-profile corporate failures arising out of the financial crisis of 2007–09 such as Lehman Brothers in the US and the Royal Bank of Scotland in the UK. As a result, both the US and the UK governance regimes have been altered in response to the fresh thinking that the crisis provoked. In the UK, this has resulted in significant changes to its governance code. In the US recourse has been made to further legislation. The widespread calls for more rigour in financial regulation and consumer protection coming out of the crisis led to the passing of another major piece of legislation by Congress, this time the Dodd-Frank Wall Street Reform and Consumer Protection Act 2010. Before that, the Fraud Enforcement and Recovery Act of 2009 signalled a more aggressive approach by the US authorities against fraud generally and against mortgage fraud in particular.

We look at both systems below, beginning with corporate governance in the US.

1. The Sarbanes-Oxley Act 2002

Introduction
The Sarbanes-Oxley Act ("SOX") was passed by the US Congress in July 2002. It introduced major changes to the regulation of corporate governance and financial practice for all companies listed on one of the US exchanges and therefore regulated by the Securities and Exchange Commission ("SEC"), wherever situated around the world. It is named after Senator Paul Sarbanes and Representative Michael Oxley, who were its main architects.

The law was passed as a direct response to concerns in the investor community following the bankruptcies of Enron in particular in December 2001, but also those of Global Crossing in January 2002 and WorldCom in July 2002. These were all very large listed US corporations whose collapses were associated with major fraud, conflicts of interest and accounting scandals. How could this happen? The resulting investigations and media publicity highlighted many shortcomings, but in particular the failings around financial reporting, internal controls and auditing standards caused dismay to investors. The SOX sets out to address these shortcomings directly. It imposes new duties and significant penalties for non-compliance on public companies and their executives, directors, auditors, lawyers and securities analysts. Its primary purpose was to bolster confidence in US capital markets.

The SOX is a comprehensive piece of legislation, arranged into 11 "titles" or sections. Compliance with it is, of course, mandatory. The most important aspects of the Act for our purposes are summarised below.

Public Company Accounting Oversight Board
The SOX established this independent five-person board, overseen by the SEC designed to strengthen the assurance provided to investors by the audit process. All accounting firms wishing to audit US listed companies are now required to register with the board. The board has powers to:

- Oversee the audit of public companies;

- Establish auditing reporting standards and rules; and

- Inspect, investigate and enforce compliance on the part of registered public accounting firms and those associated with those firms.

Auditor independence

The independence of the external auditor is fundamental to the audit process and to good corporate governance. There was a general perception that the independence of Arthur Andersen from its client Enron had been compromised by long-standing personal relationships and by consulting fees – Andersen was famously paid the same amount in fees each year both to act as consultants to Enron and to act as auditors (around $25 million, in each case). The SOX set out to strengthen auditor independence through the following measures:

- Prohibiting an auditor from undertaking certain specified non-audit services at the same time as performing the audit. These services include: bookkeeping; internal audit; and the design and implementation of financial information systems. Other work, such as tax services, may be carried out for an audit client, providing the audit committee has approved it in advance.

- Introducing an element of auditor rotation by prohibiting an audit partner from being the lead or reviewing auditor for more than five consecutive years.

- Placing a one-year prohibition on an audit firm from performing the audit if one of the company's senior executives had been employed by the same firm and had participated in the audit of the company during the previous year.

- Requiring that audit firms report more fully to the audit committee on contentious matters, for example critical accounting policies, alternative treatments and their implications under US GAAP.

Independence and responsibility

The SOX gives the audit committee responsibility for appointing, setting the fees and overseeing the work of the external auditors. Also, there is a new requirement that every member of the audit committee should be an independent non-executive director.

The CEO and the CFO are given significant extra personal responsibility under the SOX. They are required to certify personally in financial reports that the reports do not contain material misstatements, that the financial statements are fairly stated, that they have received all necessary information and that the internal controls have been reviewed for effectiveness within 90 days of the report. As a result, the CEO and CFO have to take ownership of their financial statements in a meaningful way.

Enhanced financial disclosures

Perhaps the most notorious and costly of all the extra requirements on listed companies under the SOX are the Section 404 provisions concerning management's assessment of the internal controls surrounding the financial reporting process. The reason is simple: it was precisely because of poor controls in this area that senior executives of Enron were able to mislead investors about the state of health and future prospects of the company.

Section 404 requires companies to publish an internal control report as part of their annual report, concerning the scope and adequacy of the internal control structure and procedures for financial reporting. This internal control report must also assess the effectiveness of such controls and procedures. In addition, an external accounting firm must attest to, and report on, the company's assessment of the effectiveness of the internal control structure and procedures for financial reporting (the so-called attestation report).

In addition, companies are required to publish financial statements that reflect all material correcting adjustments and disclose all material off-balance sheet transactions.

The SOX prohibits most personal loans to directors and executives by a corporation.

There is also a requirement for the company to disclose whether it has adopted a code of ethics for its senior financial officers and whether its audit committee consists of at least one member who is a financial expert.

Corporate and criminal fraud accountability and penalties
The SOX has very significant deterrence provisions for the would-be white-collar criminal built into it, including the following:

- Establishes criminal penalties of fines and/or up to 20 years' imprisonment for knowingly altering, destroying, mutilating, concealing or falsifying records with the intention to obstruct, impede or influence either a Federal investigation or a matter of bankruptcy.

- Establishes criminal penalties of fines and/or imprisonment of up to 10 years on any accountant who knowingly and wilfully violates the requirement to maintain all audit or review papers for a period of five years.

- Subjects to fine or imprisonment of up to 25 years any person who knowingly defrauds shareholders of publicly traded companies.

- Provides protection for whistle-blowers by prohibiting a publicly traded company from retaliating against an employee because of any lawful act by the employee to assist in a fraud investigation.

- Provides increased penalties for mail and wire fraud from five to 20 years in prison.

- Provides increased penalties for violations of the Employee Retirement Income Security Act 1974 of up to $500,000 and/or 10 years in prison.

- Establishes criminal liability for the failure of corporate officers to certify reports, including a maximum imprisonment of 10 years for knowing that the report does not comply with the Act, or 20 years for wilfully certifying a statement knowing it does not comply with the Act.

Commentary on the SOX
The SOX has had a very considerable impact on governance standards. It largely achieved its main objective of restoring investor confidence, especially with regard to both the production and the auditing of the financial statements. The responsibility on board members for good governance has increased also. Under the SOX, board members are expected to be informed and engaged and their role in the oversight of the financial reporting in particular is now very important.

The SOX has not been without its critics, however. The extra liabilities and penalties on directors for non-conformance are seen by some as a disincentive to entrepreneurship, whilst the costs on companies of complying with the Act have been high. Compliance costs are particularly burdensome in the area of reporting on the effectiveness of the internal controls over the financial reporting process. One of the ironies of the SOX is that the audit profession has benefited hugely from this aspect of the Act, certainly in terms of the extra fees that the accounting firms have earned as a result of Section 404 compliance, despite the fact that perceived weaknesses in external auditing was one of its main drivers in the first place.

The SOX and the financial crisis

The provisions of the SOX are specifically designed to address the risk posed to investors by senior executive fraud, accounting irregularities and poor auditing. They are not designed to provide protection against the combination of circumstances that brought about the financial crisis of 2007–09. As the report of the Financial Crisis Inquiry Commission, set up by Congress in 2009 to determine the causes, makes clear this crisis was brought about by a combination of factors including: the relaxation of credit standards in US mortgage lending and the collapse of the subsequent housing bubble; the drying up of credit markets following the panic brought about by the failure of Lehman Brothers; failures in financial regulations and supervision; excessive borrowing and risky investments; and failures of risk management. However, it is the headline conclusion of the Inquiry that is most relevant for our purposes here:

> **We conclude that this financial crisis was avoidable**. The crisis was the result of human action and inaction, not of Mother Nature or computer models gone haywire. The captains of finance and the public stewards of our financial system ignored warnings and failed to question, understand and manage evolving risks within a system essential to the well-being of the American public. (Financial Crisis Inquiry Report, p.xvii, 2011)[9]

So, the financial crisis has much to do with poor judgements and decision-making by those at the top of business. It was not primarily brought about by the malfeasance of corporate executives as was the case in the headline scandals of the late 1990s. However, although malpractice is not the primary factor, it nevertheless still had a part to play in the actions of the authorities and the thinking of the public following this crisis. For example, the SEC has charged a number of financial institutions (e.g. Citigroup, Goldman Sachs and JP Morgan Securities) with misleading investors and improper pricing in complex mortgage securities transactions relating to the packaging and promotion of collateralised debt obligations. The regulator reached settlements with the firms concerned whereby they agreed to pay penalties of hundreds of millions of dollars and did not admit liability.

More generally, there has been great concern in the US at what was seen as widespread mis-selling of mortgages to ordinary American citizens. The US government sought to address this concern directly by passing another piece of legislation, the Fraud Enforcement and Recovery Act 2009.

The Fraud Enforcement and Recovery Act 2009

One of the government's goals in passing the Fraud Enforcement and Recovery Act 2009 ("FERA") is the increased prosecution of fraud at a time when it had just succeeded in passing a trillion-dollar stimulus package for the US economy. So, there was increased risk of fraud against taxpayer funds at that time and calls for better oversight of government contractors. FERA is also an attack on mortgage fraud and related wrongdoing, which was seen as widely prevalent. The Senate Judiciary Committee had revealed that in 2008 there were more than 65,000 suspicious activity reports filed with the Treasury Department alleging mortgage fraud compared with only 4,700 in 2001, nearly 13 times as many.

There are three main provisions of the FERA as follows:

- It expands the Department of Justice's authority to prosecute mortgage fraud, commodities fraud and fraud involving the public funds allocated to stimulate the economy under the Troubled Asset Relief Program ("TARP") and the Recovery Act;

- It authorises almost $500 million in additional resources for government fraud investigations, prosecutions and civil proceedings; and

- It establishes the Financial Crisis Inquiry Commission to investigate the causes of the financial crisis, as mentioned above.

The Dodd-Frank Wall Street Reform and Consumer Protection Act 2010

The main purpose of the Dodd-Frank Act is to make a repeat of the recent financial crisis less likely through regulatory reform of the financial services industry. It makes financial institutions more accountable for their actions and enhances oversight of the industry to detect and prevent systemic risk before it reaches crisis level. The introductory description contained in the Act gives a good idea of its breadth and scope. It describes itself as: "An Act to promote the financial stability of the United States by improving accountability and transparency in the financial system, to end 'too big to fail', to protect the American taxpayer by ending bailouts, to protect consumers from abusive financial services practices, and for other purposes."

The Dodd-Frank Act makes a variety of changes specific to the US regulatory framework, including: the creation of a consumer financial protection watchdog for retail financial products and services; the creation of the Financial Stability Oversight Council to monitor and reduce systemic risks; provisions to limit large, complex financial companies and end "too big to fail" bailouts (including the Volcker rule which prohibits banks from proprietary trading, owning hedge funds etc.); the reallocation of authority among the federal regulators; the regulation of the derivatives market and hedge funds; and the introduction of new requirements and oversight for credit ratings agencies.

There are also a number of important reforms to executive compensation and corporate governance in the Act that are of relevance to us because they show that the American legislators are trying to influence the behaviour of people at the top of large corporations. In particular, there was a concern that short-term targets and the need always to maximise shareholder value were dominating corporate decision-making, rather than a focus on longer term sustainability. The scale and structure of many executive incentive schemes in the US, together with their lack of transparency, seemed designed to encourage greed and risky behaviour. The Dodd-Frank Act tries to address these concerns through a number of measures that give shareholders a "say on pay" and create greater accountability as follows:

- Shareholders are given the right to a non-binding vote on executive pay and golden parachutes. This gives shareholders the opportunity to voice their disapproval of excessive or misguided incentive schemes and hold their executives accountable. It is similar to the procedure that was introduced in the UK in 2002 whereby listed companies are required to submit an executive remuneration report to a non-binding shareholder vote at the annual general meeting. It is arguable how effective this requirement has been in curbing executive pay awards in the UK as, at the time of writing, concerns over payments that seem to reward poor corporate performance persist. However, the requirement has raised sensitivities and certainly, the Chairman and the board would view any situation where the votes cast against the report were in excess of 20% of the total extremely seriously.

- The Act gives the SEC the authority to grant shareholders proxy access to nominate directors. This measure is designed to help shift executive focus from short-term profits to long-term growth and stability.

- The listing rules in the US will be altered so that compensation committees that set the pay levels for executives will in future comprise independent non-executive directors only. This is in line with the best practice principle that no one who works in a public listed company should be able to set their own pay. The compensation committees will have the authority to hire compensation consultants in order to strengthen their independence from the executives.

- The Act requires that public companies set policies to take back executive compensation if it was based on inaccurate financial statements.

This section has provided a brief overview of the most important recent developments in US corporate governance. These have been enacted in legislation and are mandatory as a result. We will look now at the alternative system of governance, based around non-binding principles set out in codes of best practice. We will use the system in the UK as the example.

2. The UK Corporate Governance Code

History
A series of corporate scandals in the UK in the early 1990s (e.g. Polly Peck, BCCI, Maxwell, Guinness, Barlow Clowes) provides the essential background to the development of the UK's corporate governance code. What was noticeable about these particular scandals was that they were all caused by the actions of directors and senior management who were directly involved in irregular and/or criminal conduct. Alarmingly for investors, this conduct was not picked up by either the external auditors or by the regulators. The Cadbury Committee, under the Chairmanship of Sir Adrian Cadbury was set up in 1991 against the background of corporate scandal.

The Cadbury Report in 1992 provided for the first time anywhere in the world a written framework for corporate governance. As we have seen, it recommended a principles-based approach. Consequently, self-regulation has become the basis for the governance of companies listed on the London Stock Exchange ever since. UK-listed companies effectively govern themselves, with the crucial reference point being the market. The theory underpinning the comply or explain principle is that if the market does not like what a company is doing in areas of non-compliance as disclosed in the report and accounts it will "punish" the company by selling the shares.

The original Cadbury Code has been updated a number of times since 1992. It is regularly reviewed in consultation with companies and investors, most recently in 2010. The influence of the developing UK codes on corporate governance thinking has been widespread around the world. In the UK it is widely regarded as an indicator of best practice in governance not only for publically-listed companies but also for private companies and for organisations in the public sector. It has also been influential in the development of other governance codes around the world, for example, in the thinking of the King Commission in South Africa.

The post-financial crisis position
The UK Corporate Governance Code ("the Code"),[10] which replaced the old "Combined Code" in 2010, was developed in the aftermath of the financial crisis of 2007–09 and some of its new provisions attempt to address the weaknesses of leadership and judgement shown by the boards of directors of some large companies in the UK at the time. It should be noted that the high profile failures of listed companies in the UK such as Northern Rock, HBOS, Lloyds and the Royal Bank of Scotland during the crisis are not associated with misconduct but rather with poor decision-making and with inappropriate boardroom behaviours. As discussed above, the position is more complicated in the US.

As we have seen, the Code is not a rigid set of rules, nor a "one-size fits all" template that all listed companies, regardless of size and business model must follow. One of its strengths lies in its flexibility. It consists of Code Principles (main and supporting) and more detailed Code Provisions built around five key sections: leadership; effectiveness; accountability; remuneration; and relations with shareholders.

Key aspects of UK corporate governance

The key aspects of the UK's corporate governance regime are summarised by the Financial Reporting Council (the UK's independent governance regulator) in a paper published in 2010.[11] These are set out below:

- A single, unitary board, comprising both executive and non-executive directors, collectively responsible for the sustainable success of the company.

- A series of important checks and balances right at the top of the company including:

  - Different individuals holding the key offices of Chief Executive Officer and Chairman (the thinking here is simple: the CEO runs the business but the Chairman runs the board and thereby provides crucial division of power at the top of the organisation);

  - Balance around the boardroom table (at least 50% of the board, excluding the Chairman, should be independent non-executive directors);

  - Strong, independent audit and remuneration committees (comprising independent non-executive directors only); and

  - Annual evaluation by the board of its own performance (a very important introduction into the Code in 2003, this has moved from being a very contentious provision, resisted by many directors, into an accepted part of the structures needed to improve performance).

- Transparency on the appointment and remuneration of directors.

- Effective rights for shareholders, who are encouraged to engage with the companies in which they invest.

- The fundamental principle of comply or explain on which the Code is based.

The importance of checks and balances at the top

Controls are crucial to managing fraud risk. This is an obvious point to make yet I continue to be surprised whenever I work with UK companies or run courses for executives in the UK at how little awareness there is of the need for assurance mechanisms to provide evidence that the governance controls outlined above actually do work in practice. For example, internal auditors will spend a lot of time looking at the effectiveness of controls in every major part of the business except one – the controls around the behaviour of the board and senior executives. As we have seen, fraud risk is inherently high for senior executives. However, it is not only in areas like fraud that this failure to gain assurance on the workings of the board should be of concern. The board comprises the most important group of people in the entire business and yet the way that it operates, its composition, skill sets and performance levels are rarely scrutinised in a traditional way. Professor Garratt and others have long advocated more formal "governance audits" and a move in this direction would be beneficial and perhaps result in significantly strengthened control frameworks.

The importance of respecting the comply or explain principle

The hallmark of UK corporate governance is the "comply or explain" principle. As we have seen, this principle allows companies a degree of flexibility in how they put into practice the provisions of the Code. This flexibility has proved to be attractive to corporations around the world. Many companies have chosen to list their shares in London rather than in New York or elsewhere because of it. However, the principle of comply or explain is designed to operate in a certain way. The UK Listing Rules require that companies do adopt the main principles set out in the Code and report to shareholders on how they have done so. These main principles largely address aspects of board behaviour and are the core of the Code. The flexibility in the system is directed towards the extent of compliance with the more detailed Code provisions. It is recognised that an alternative to the practice recommended by a Code provision may be justified in the particular circumstances facing an individual company if a better governance solution for that company can be achieved by other means. So if a board of directors considers that an alternative treatment to that set out in the Code provisions is more appropriate to the particular circumstances of the company, then the board is free to follow the alternative. A condition of doing so is that the reasons for the alternative treatment should be explained clearly and carefully to shareholders, so that the market can react on an informed basis.

Sometimes, however, the directors of listed companies act in ways that test the flexibility of the Code to its limits, thereby increasing risk and causing concern in the investor community. One of the best examples of this in recent times was the case of Marks and Spencer Group plc and the board decision to appoint Sir Stuart Rose as both Chairman and Chief Executive, thereby apparently flying in the face of the (then) Combined Code. This is a summary of what happened.

Example: Marks and Spencer Group plc.[12] In 2008 the board of the iconic British retailer Marks and Spencer Group plc ("M&S") promoted its then Chief Executive, Sir Stuart Rose, to the position of Executive Chairman for a period of up to three years. This seemed to go against the spirit of one of the most high profile principles of the Combined Code, namely that there should be a clear division of responsibilities at the head of a company. It was certainly contrary to the related code provision calling for different individuals to exercise the roles of Chairman and Chief Executive. This division of responsibilities is sometimes referred to as the cornerstone of UK corporate governance. Of course, M&S had later to explain its reasons for doing this in its report and accounts. The immediate consequence of this decision was considerable disquiet amongst investors, fund managers, businessmen and those with an interest in corporate governance. I can personally attest to this because I happened to be running a corporate governance workshop at the London Stock Exchange on the very day that M&S announced to the media that Sir Stuart Rose was to be the Executive Chairman on Monday 10 March 2008. This announcement torpedoed my carefully worked out programme for the day as the only subject the delegates wanted to talk about was "what on earth is going on at M&S?" There were two areas of criticism of the M&S board expressed in the discussions on the day, both of which I think are perceptive. First, there was a strong feeling in the room that the company should have communicated better with its shareholders. Secondly, there was the view that fundamentally this was a failure of succession planning by the M&S board. In the aftermath, there were no obvious consequences of the decision in operational terms as M&S continued to perform reasonably well. However, the suspicion remained that M&S shares continued to trade at a "governance discount" throughout the time that Sir Stuart remained as Executive Chairman and certainly there was much speculation about who would replace him. In the event, he was replaced as Chief Executive by Marc Bolland on 1 May 2010, since when M&S has reverted to a conventional structure at the top of its business.

Competency and behaviour – the key drivers of board performance

Corporate scandals short-circuit very quickly to the actions and decisions taken by those at the top. The way in which directors conduct themselves (in terms of their behaviours) and the skills that they bring to the role (in terms of their competencies) are crucial to how an organisation performs. Shortcomings in either area will lead to problems: competency issues are generally associated with poor performance, whilst poor behaviours are generally thought to lead to integrity failings, including fraud. The two are not mutually exclusive however and we examine some of the main issues of both below in terms of their impact on fraud risk.

1. The competency of directors

Introduction

An effective board selection process is a critical prerequisite of success. Directors should be appointed only after a thorough selection process, which makes use of outside agencies (headhunters, recruitment consultants etc.) to access the best available candidates. The aim should be to move away from the old-fashioned passive or "country-club" type of situation where the Chairman and CEO would nominate friends and associates to be the non-executive directors. We saw something similar to this when looking at the Enron case. The Code stipulates that the selection of new directors onto the board should be as a result of "a formal, rigorous and transparent" procedure. Listed companies will usually make use of a Nominations Committee (or equivalent) to lead this process.

So, the selection process should provide greater assurance around the competency of directors. How effective is this in practice? I like to explore this with the delegates on my courses by asking them two direct questions:

- First, are the directors of your organisation competent?

- Secondly, are you sure that they have the mix of technical skills, business acumen and experience of the organisation and/or its business sector to discharge their responsibilities effectively and promote the long-term success of your business?

Often when I ask delegates these questions they are surprised – they simply assume (and hope!) that the answer to both questions is "yes". These are important and not merely rhetorical questions, however. After all, there are no tests or examinations that individuals have to pass before they are eligible to be a director, so there is very little by way of an objective measure of competency here (the Institute of Directors in the UK has introduced a professional qualification for people to become a Chartered Director in recent years, which is a step forward, but of course it is not mandatory).

I am keen to explore this aspect of governance because there have been a number of examples of competency shortfalls over the last 20 years that have had severe implications for the performance of the company concerned and also, sometimes, on its exposure to fraud risk. As an example, Mr Lesson makes it clear throughout his book *Rogue Trader* that he had nothing but contempt for the senior managers and directors of Barings Bank because they did not know anything about the technical aspects of his foreign exchange arbitrage transactions and so were unable to ask the right questions of him which would have uncovered the fraud sooner. More recently, there has been widespread criticism of the poor awareness of risk, in the form of complex derivative products, carried on their balance sheets, exhibited by many directors of financial services institutions during the financial crisis of 2007–09. By and large this lack of awareness led to a huge under-pricing of risk in the financial system and so contributed directly to the financial crisis itself. It did not result in fraud, however.

Let us look at a number of these competency issues and their implications at various levels around the boardroom table.

The CEO

If the Chief Executive Officer of an organisation is not up to the job and/or is the subject of personal criticism in the media, the results may suffer and the brand may be damaged as a result. Ultimately in such a case the Chairman will have to ask the CEO to stand down. Sometimes this becomes clear during normal trading conditions and at other times it only becomes clear during a crisis. The implications of the latter can be severe.

Consider the example of Tony Hayward, the ex-CEO of BP. He was forced to resign from his position during the investigation into the circumstances surrounding the Deepwater Horizon oil rig tragedy. Everything that I have read about Mr Hayward suggests that he has high competency in the technical aspects of the oil industry. However, his position was fatally undermined by a number of ill-judged and insensitive comments reported by the press and subsequently highlighted in the US by politicians and the media generally. To take one example, during a tour of the stricken Gulf area Mr Hayward famously said "I want my life back".[13] In view of the fact that there were 11 people killed as a result of the explosion on the oil rig, this appeared as a singularly inappropriate comment. So, was this simply bad luck? Well, I have never met Mr Hayward so I cannot comment directly. However, I have met a number of executives and managers on my courses that have either known him or have worked with him in the past. They all told me that based on their memories of him it was not a complete surprise to them that Mr Hayward had made these comments. Mr Hayward was certainly a technically competent manager and he was clearly frustrated at times by his difficulties. Speaking to the BBC in November 2010 he said that if he had "a degree in acting from RADA rather than a degree in geology I may have done better" in handling the fallout from the Deepwater Horizon disaster. Sometimes technical proficiency is not sufficient, however. The skill-set required of a modern CEO of a global multinational corporation is very broad and, in my view, it absolutely must include poise and professionalism when dealing with the media.

Are all CEOs as technically proficient in their particular industry sectors as Mr Hayward is in his? Does it matter? Well, it can look extremely odd if the CEO is unable to demonstrate competence. It can also make an organisation more vulnerable in difficult times because the CEO has no personal craftsmanship on which to draw and therefore may lack credibility in leading the board discussions to find an optimal solution to the problems. As an example, I set out below a question and answer story that has been circulating in the UK ever since the financial crisis. It is amusing but the basic facts are true and I have used it on several occasions to illustrate the competency issue on my courses. The question is as follows:

> Who is the odd man out amongst the following four people and why: Fred Goodwin (ex-CEO of the Royal Bank of Scotland Group plc); Adam Applegarth (ex-CEO of Northern Rock plc); Andy Hornby (ex-CEO of HBOS plc); and Sir Terry Wogan (veteran Irish disc jockey, television broadcaster and famous UK personality).

The delegates (even those not from the UK) normally have little trouble in correctly nominating Sir Terry Wogan as the odd man out. However, very rarely am I given the "correct" reason why this is the case (there have been many who have pointed to the obviously different career paths, but they all know that this is not what I am looking for). I normally pause for a second before giving them the punch-line: Sir Terry Wogan is the only one out of the four named individuals who has a banking qualification!

The Chairman

The Chairman is the leader of the board, setting the board agenda, its working tone and ethos in order to promote effective decision-making and constructive debate. So the capability of the Chairman in this role will be of the utmost importance in determining the success or otherwise of the board. Personal qualities are more important than technical expertise here. Characteristics such as personal credibility and stature, being an effective communicator who is able to listen and at the same time has the ability to clarify viewpoints and summarise positions impartially are vital in this role.

However, part of the Chairman's credibility is vested in him or her being able to make constructive contributions and, at times, challenges to the plans and strategies of the executives. To do so effectively the Chairman needs to be either highly experienced in the business world generally or to have expertise in the industry sector of the organisation concerned. Sometimes this is not obviously the case, even in the largest of companies. Consider the example of Northern Rock plc and its ex-chairman Matt Ridley.

Example: Northern Rock plc ("Northern Rock"). Northern Rock used to be listed as one of the FTSE top 100 companies in the UK. It is the bank that infamously had to be nationalised by the UK government in 2008 following the onset of the credit crunch. Northern Rock developed severe liquidity problems that forced it to approach the Bank of England for emergency financial support in September 2007. News of this triggered panic demands by depositors (often ordinary men and women concerned about their life savings) for their money back, thereby causing a run on the bank. The non-executive Chairman of Northern Rock at the time was Matt Ridley, whose background may well be considered unusual for a man holding the chairmanship of a large UK-listed bank. He is a scientist, journalist and author, holding a zoology PhD from the University of Oxford and working at The Economist magazine as science editor before going on to become the author of a number of popular science books. He was appointed a non-executive director of Northern Rock in 1994. Dr Ridley's father, Viscount Ridley, had been a director of the company for 30 years and had served as Chairman from 1987 to 1992. Dr Ridley himself became the Chairman in 2004 and remained in that role until his resignation in October 2007. Although clearly a highly intelligent man and no doubt committed and hard-working, Dr Ridley's experience of business and of the banking industry in the years leading up to the crisis in 2007 appears somewhat limited: in addition to his non-executive roles at Northern Rock, he was the non-executive chairman of a venture capital trust and the founding chairman of a local science village. Two of the conclusions of the Treasury Select Committee's report into the collapse are relevant here: first, Northern Rock's failure is attributed primarily to the board, with the non-executives criticised for not restraining the high-risk strategy of the executives; and secondly, concern is expressed at the lack of relevant financial qualifications of both the Chairman (Dr Ridley) and the Chief Executive (Mr Applegarth).

The Chief Financial Officer

The CFO will serve the board in a technical capacity, providing advice, guidance and assurance over the financial affairs of the organisation. Financial competence and craftsmanship, normally underpinned by an accounting qualification and bolstered by years of relevant experience, is considered to be a prerequisite of this senior executive position in most organisations. It is not necessarily always the case, however. In recent years the promotion of people with "talent" above all other qualities has become fashionable. The idea is that the most intelligent and resourceful employees can deliver extraordinary results if they are given opportunities. This philosophy is sometimes taken to extremes, as illustrated in the following two cases. Both companies concerned famously went into bankruptcy in the US. Finance is certainly one area in business that normally benefits from experts taking the leading roles.

- The first example refers again to the Enron case. Mr Fastow was appointed Chief Financial Officer of Enron in 1998 at the age of 36. Although not a main board position it is still remarkable that he was made CFO at such a young age, especially as this was without him having any accounting qualifications. His expertise was in corporate finance and asset-backed securities and as a result he did not have the knowledge and experience of a traditional Finance Director. Mr Fastow no doubt proved very useful to Mr Skilling and the Enron board in the short term when constructing the network of special purpose vehicles that fuelled the company's spectacular results. However, he had neither the broad accounting knowledge nor the business acumen and wisdom to enable him to promote success at Enron over the long term. The drivers of short-term success at Enron involved aggressive accounting practices. Mr Fastow seemed to have little time for the time-honoured accounting concept of prudence.

- The second example is a later case and concerns the US investment bank Lehman Brothers during the period of difficult trading conditions leading up to the financial crisis. The appointment of Erin Callan as Chief Financial Officer of Lehman Brothers in December 2007 made a big and positive impression in the media at the time, at least in the short term: she was young, female, charismatic and an altogether innovative choice. However, Ms Callan's appointment carried with it a degree of risk also, something that should have been appreciated by the board: she was made CFO without an accounting degree or relevant financial qualification and with little detailed knowledge of the firm's treasury operations. Ms Callan was a tax lawyer before she joined Lehman Brothers in 1995 and then worked in investment banking. She lasted only six months as CFO before resigning in June 2008 after losing the confidence of Mr Fuld, Lehman's CEO, and the markets. It is clear that Ms Callan was promoted to CFO at a particularly dangerous time in the history of the firm. It seems likely that her lack of financial experience and craftsmanship may well have been less than helpful when carrying out her new, very demanding job day-to-day.

2. The behaviour of directors

Introduction
The Financial Reporting Council concluded in its review of the UK governance regime following the financial crisis that the quality of corporate governance ultimately depends on behaviour not process (Financial Reporting Council, 2009, paragraph 2.1).[14] Positive behaviours and attitudes on the part of the board of directors as a whole include the following: an independent and challenging approach, putting the proposals of executives through a proper scrutiny process; effective delegation; setting the strategy and structure for the business; transparency throughout; and being accountable to shareholders and responsive to stakeholders. The most important qualities for directors as individuals include: integrity; providing vision and values; being committed to the success of the organisation; being able to listen and communicate well at all levels of the organisation; and being seen to participate in challenges and so inspire others to succeed.

The reality of the business world is sometimes very different from this of course. Corporate scandals and failures of the recent past, whether to do with poor judgement or with poor ethics, point clearly to a number of behaviours that directors are susceptible to, whether collectively and/or individually, which have contributed significantly to the problems. These are discussed below.

Domineering CEOs

The character and behaviour of an organisation's CEO is an important factor in business. They often have dominant personalities – many CEOs are extrovert, charismatic individuals who naturally dominate a room and who are able to drive and inspire their organisations to achieve long-term success. However, all directors and managers need to be aware that sometimes the effect can be very different and much less positive. Those CEOs who try to manage by creating fear in their subordinates and stifling all discussion and debate are, in my view, at best poor managers. Sometimes this behaviour can lead to real danger for an organisation in terms of CEOs seeking to use bullying tactics either to drive their own personal agendas through at the boardroom level, or else to force acquiescence amongst the workforce in their criminal behaviour.

This is not a theoretical concern – it does happen in business with reasonable frequency. For example, some of the CEOs who have been convicted of criminality were forceful personalities, not immune from using bullying tactics to push through their plans: Bernie Ebbers (at WorldCom); Ken Lay and Jeff Skilling (each in their different ways at Enron). An aggressive and abrasive management style is not the preserve of executives who are fraudsters of course and there have been many examples of successful Chief Executives with these characteristics. Sometimes these executives have been unable to deliver success over the long term and their methods and capabilities have been questioned as a result. Fred Goodwin, the ex-CEO (and ex-knight of the realm!) is perhaps the most notorious example of this in the UK at the time of writing.

The domineering CEO is a significant area of risk for all businesses. In Chapter 4 we classified senior executive fraud as high impact and low probability risk. The possibility of a CEO pushing through his or her personal agenda without adequate scrutiny and challenge comes in the same category, if less extreme because there is no criminality involved. In each case, organisations should adopt the strategy of risk avoidance through strong controls. This is where the governance controls set out in codes and legislation are particularly important. In particular, there is a need for: separate individuals to take the key positions of Chairman and CEO in order to provide a division of power at the top; effective scrutiny and challenge process from the board, especially the non-executive directors; balance around the boardroom table with a strong group of independent non-executive directors; and oversight at all stages of the financial reporting process.

Short-term focus

The tensions implicit in the business timespan between short and long-term objectives create one of the biggest practical challenges for directors of publicly listed companies. In theory, the position is straightforward: the board should always act in the best long-term interests of the company. In practice, the position is complicated in particular by the relentless pressure from investors and the markets for companies to perform, for them to hit their targets in the next quarterly report. Failure to achieve these targets will inevitably result in falls in the share price and yet more pressure to perform in the next quarter.

Often it is this relentless pressure on results that leads to poor decision-making around the boardroom table. We explore the connection between short-term incentives and greed in Chapter 10 on ethics. It is important to say here, however, that a focus on the share price and on the competition, without the anchor of the long-term view, can lead to mistakes and, with hindsight, to accusations of poor, weak or corrupt leadership. The recent financial crisis provides the background to a classic example of this. At the time, many comments in the media from politicians, economists and businessmen made it seem as if this crisis came out of a clear blue sky, that there were no warning signs and that it was simply no one's fault. In fact the reality was rather different. Some business leaders did indeed see the storm coming; they were simply unable to do anything about it for a variety of reasons. One of these reasons was the perceived requirement to continue with practices that were highly profitable in the short term and so satisfied their shareholders and the market generally. This is made quite clear by Charles Prince, then the CEO of Citigroup, during an interview he gave to the *Financial Times* in July 2007. This is an extract from the interview:

When the music stops in terms of liquidity, things will be complicated. But as long as the music is playing you've got to get up and dance. We're still dancing.[15]

Passive board – a lack of scrutiny and challenge

As we have seen, non-executive directors should provide an essential governance control by acting as a fulcrum that balances the interests of shareholders and executives. They should enable agency risk to be managed effectively. If they fail to challenge the executives or to subject management to robust scrutiny, then the control fails. There are many examples of this type of control failure throughout the book.

One notable example of a passive board is provided once again by the Enron case. The Powers Committee was set up to report to the Enron board of directors on the related party transactions between Enron and the investment partnerships created and managed by Mr Fastow. In its report of February 2002, the Committee stated that the Enron board of directors had "failed, in our judgement, in its oversight duties". It went on to conclude that:

while the primary responsibility for the financial reporting abuses lies with management, those abuses could and should have been prevented or detected at an earlier time had the board been more aggressive and vigilant. (Powers Committee, 2002, p.24)[16]

The recent corporate governance changes that we have looked at in the US and in the UK are designed to make such a control failure less likely in the future. It is to be hoped that they succeed. Warren Buffet's criticism of poor non-executives remains highly pertinent: "they provide an illusion of competent independence". Many frauds of the past have been predicated upon this illusion.

Conflicts of Interest

Any conflicts of interest at the top of an organisation are almost always corrosive. We saw a famous example of this at Enron when the board authorised Mr Fastow, the CFO, to be the manager of a number of the special purpose vehicles that he had set up, resulting in him being paid some $30 million in fees for doing so. There were provisions in Enron's code of ethics preventing conflicts of interest, but the board was prepared to waive these in order to secure Mr Fastow's full participation in the special purpose vehicle arrangements. Directors and officers are required by law to exercise a degree of skill, care and diligence and always to act in the interests of the company. This will not always be possible when they have an economic or personal interest in the other side of a transaction.

An important and related area of concern is around issues of insider dealing. One of the most important recent cases of insider dealing is the Galleon hedge fund scandal in the US. It is also a case that concerns conflicts of interest. Not only did this case highlight for the first time some very aggressive and innovative techniques used by the authorities to secure convictions but it also revealed that a number of senior business figures in the US were prepared to compromise their integrity in return for money.

Example: the Galleon Group case.[17] The Galleon Group family of hedge funds was founded in the US by the Sri Lankan businessman, Raj Rajaratnam in 1997. It proved to be highly successful, becoming one of the 10 largest hedge funds in the world with over $7 billion of funds under its management. However, in 2009 the US authorities investigated Mr Rajaratnam and many of his business associates and company insiders, analysts and traders, in a widespread crackdown against insider trading on Wall Street. The core of the allegations made was that Mr Rajaratnam was passed secret information which enabled him to make significant profits on future trades. An important development was the aggressive use of wire-taps by the authorities to obtain incriminating evidence – these tactics had previously been associated with action against drugs dealers and organised criminals, rather than to combat white-collar crime. The tactics were successful. Criminal charges were brought against over 50 of Mr Rajaratnam's informants, the majority of whom at the time of writing had either pleaded guilty or had been convicted at trial. As an indication of how significant this case is, one of the outstanding indictments is against Rajat Gupta, a former board member of Goldman Sachs and Procter & Gamble and the ex-head of the McKinsey consultancy, who is charged with insider trading. It is alleged that he shared secret information that he learnt as a board member of Goldman Sachs and Procter & Gamble with Mr Rajaratnam, his friend and business associate. Mr Gupta denies the charges but if he is convicted this has the potential to be hugely damaging to the reputations of Goldmans and McKinseys in particular, each of which claims to treat client information with the utmost confidence. Anil Kumar, another former McKinsey director, has pleaded guilty to passing information he learnt about clients to Mr Rajaratnam. There are major conflicts of interest issues attached to this case and the prosecution evidence from wire-taps has made these conflicts very obvious to the wider public. For example, one of the eye-catching allegations against Mr Gupta concerns Galleon's trading in Goldman's stock. Phone records apparently show that in September 2008 Mr Gupta called Mr Rajaratnam a mere 16 seconds after he had hung up from the Goldman board meeting (held via conference call) at which he learned the top secret and highly price-sensitive news that the bank was about to receive a $5 billion investment from Warren Buffet's Berkshire Hathaway. Very shortly thereafter it is alleged that Galleon began placing orders to buy Goldman shares. Mr Gupta denies all charges against him and his trial is due to be held in 2012. Mr Rajaratnam himself was found guilty in July 2011 and sentenced to 11 years in prison, the longest term ever for insider trading. He has filed a notice of appeal against his conviction.

The corruption component of fraud

Introduction

The Galleon scandal is usually portrayed as an insider trading and conflicts of interest case, which of course it is. However, it is also a case that has exposed business corruption on Wall Street. Those involved have been prosecuted through the criminal courts and, where found guilty, have received tough sentences. In this sense the case is part of a much wider crackdown on corrupt practices generally. This includes various robust pieces of legislation and regulations against economic crime, money laundering and the financing of terrorist movements around the world. Our focus here is on corruption, but all companies in the financial services industry in particular will be familiar with the far-reaching requirements of anti-money laundering legislation such as the USA PATRIOT Act and the Proceeds of Crime Act in the UK.

Often the global anti-corruption movement is thought to be focused primarily on politicians, and with good reason. It has long been known that political leaders in developing countries have been able to abuse their power to enrich themselves, their families, cronies and associates by embezzling public funds and stealing state assets. The Suharto, Marcos and Abacha regimes in Indonesia, the

Philippines and Nigeria respectively are three of the most notorious examples of this, but there are many others. It is not only corruption by political leaders that causes outrage, but also the widespread "graft" payments that have to be made to local public officials by ordinary citizens every day that can provoke anger. Take the recent mass demonstrations in India, for example. 2011 saw the development of a widespread anti-corruption movement throughout India, led by the activist Anna Hazare, with the aim of alleviating endemic corruption in public life through forcing the Indian parliament to enact tougher legislation.

The fight against political corruption around the world has been led by Transparency International ("TI")[18] since its formation in 1993. TI is the global civil-society pressure group, based in Berlin, whose mission is to create change towards a world free of corruption. It defines corruption as: "the abuse of entrusted power for private gain." Together with organisations like the World Bank it has drawn attention to the devastating impact of bribery and corruption, especially on the poor and vulnerable people in developing countries where incomes are depressed and child mortality rates increase as a result. Every year TI produces a Corruption Perceptions Index ("CPI") which measures the level of public sector corruption perceived to exist in the great majority of countries around the world and ranks them against each other. The CPI draws on the results of 13 independent surveys and looks at 178 countries. In 2010 the CPI ranked Denmark, New Zealand and Singapore as the least corrupt countries in the world and Somalia, Afghanistan and Myanmar (Burma) as the most corrupt.

To give some idea of scale here, the World Bank has estimated the global cost of bribery to be $1 trillion each year.[19] This excludes the worldwide costs of corruption such as the extent of embezzlement of public funds (from central or local budgets) or from theft (or misuse) of public assets. So, this is an enormous and very serious problem around the world.

Corrupt business practices

Concerns are not only centred on corrupt politicians, of course, and they have long extended into the corporate world. Fraud and corruption are very closely linked and indeed we saw in Chapter 2 that the ACFE classes corruption as one of the three component parts of its occupational fraud typology.

All individual cases will differ, but there are normally a number of common elements in business corruption schemes. The first thing to say is that they will always be secret arrangements involving two or more people. This is obvious, of course, but it does have an important consequence – a corruption scheme will be very difficult to detect, so that specific controls such as whistleblowing hotlines (which we discuss in Chapter 8) will be required to uncover them. Secondly, they will often involve paying out a financial inducement from company funds, say to a public official, in return for the award of a contract. One consequence of this will likely be false accounting carried out in the books of the company paying the bribes. The payment will have to be recorded somewhere and it will have to be mis-described to avoid instant detection – I have spent many years as an accountant and have seen many nominal ledgers in my time, but I have yet to come across a "bribery and corruption" account! There is often an overseas element involved as businesses chase contracts all over the world in a highly competitive market place – a payment to a foreign public official may be required to win or retain a lucrative business deal (or that is the perception anyway). These payments could be made direct but they often involve a third party agent, somebody who is based in the country where the work will take place. Finally, the payments themselves are often circuitous, being routed through various companies or bank accounts in different jurisdictions before they reach the recipient– the aim here being to disguise the audit trail surrounding these transactions.

There have been a number of headline corporate corruption scandals over the last 20 years. Two of the most famous are the BAE Systems case in the UK (involving allegations of bribes paid to secure lucrative arms contracts with the Saudi Arabian government) and the Siemens case (referred to earlier in the book). These cases have certainly served to highlight the issue, both for the media and for citizens alike.

However, it is the gradually strengthening laws and conventions around the world against business corruption, started in the US in the 1970s, that has made the compliance requirements in this area so important for commercial organisations today. Set out below is a brief overview of the key pieces of anti-corruption legislation and convention, set out in chronological order. Directors and managers need to be aware of the key points because they have significantly increased risk for individuals and commercial organisations alike that break the law in this area.

The US position – the Foreign Corrupt Practices Act

The Foreign Corrupt Practices Act ("FCPA") was passed in the US as far back as 1977 and it was a ground-breaking piece of legislation at the time. It has influenced the UK Bribery Act as we will see below. The overriding purpose of the FCPA is to crackdown on the bribery of foreign officials by corporations. There are a number of key aspects, summarised below.

- **The anti-bribery provisions.** The FCPA prohibits US companies and citizens, foreign companies listed on a US stock exchange, or any person acting while in the United States from corruptly paying or offering to pay, directly or indirectly, money or anything of value to a foreign official to obtain or retain business.

- **The books and records and internal control provisions.** The FCPA requires any companies (including foreign companies) with securities traded on a US exchange (or required to file reports with the Securities and Exchange Commission) to keep books and records that accurately reflect business transactions and to maintain effective internal controls.

- **Fines and penalties.** Violations of the FCPA can result in significant fines against individuals and corporations, as well as the imprisonment of those implicated (including company executives) for up to five years. In addition, there are harsh collateral sanctions available, including termination of government licences and debarment from government contracts.

- **Extra-territorial jurisdiction.** The reach of the FCPA is extensive. No US territorial nexus is required for the FCPA to be implicated against US companies and citizens. FCPA violations can, and often do, occur even if the prohibited activity takes place entirely outside of the United States. The activities of foreign companies listed on a US exchange are also covered by the Act as are any activities taking place in the United States.

- **Exceptions.** The one significant exception under the FCPA is if the payment to the foreign official is to expedite or secure the performance of a routine governmental action. These are facilitation payments, sometimes known as "grease" payments. The exception has limited application and generally only applies to non-discretionary actions by a foreign official such as processing paperwork, and providing routine government services such as allowing entry into the country for passengers with valid travel documents and permitting cargo to be unloaded from ships to a port.

The United Nations position – the UN Convention against Corruption Act 2005

The UN Convention against Corruption 2005 ("UNCAC") is the first legally binding international anti-corruption instrument. It has been signed by over 140 countries. The UNCAC is the culmination of series of developments in which experts and politicians have tried to establish effective measures against corruption at both the domestic and the international level. The Inter-American Convention against Corruption (1996), the OECD Anti-Bribery Convention (1997), and the African Union Convention on Preventing and Combatting Corruption (2003) are all examples of efforts made by organisations around the world under this drive. Following extensive negotiations, the text of the UN Convention was presented for approval by the United Nations General Assembly in 2003 and come into force in December 2005. With the passing of the UNCAC, international action against corruption has finally progressed from general considerations and declarative statements to legally binding agreements.

The UNCAC obliges all signatory countries to implement a wide and detailed range of anti-corruption measures affecting their laws, institutions and practices. These measures aim to promote the prevention, detection and sanctioning of corruption, as well as international cooperation between signatory powers on these matters. Some of the most important and far-reaching features of the UNCAC are as follows:

- It includes offences relating both to public sector corruption, including a broad definition of the term public official, and private sector (private-to-private) corruption.

- It provides an international cooperation framework that should improve mutual law enforcement assistance, notably in extradition and investigations.

- It sets out, for the first time, an asset recovery framework on a global basis covering countries in both the northern and the southern hemispheres.

The UK position – the Bribery Act 2010

The UK Bribery Act 2010 ("UKBA") came into force in July 2011. It is rooted firmly in the principles that underpin both the FCPA and in the UNCAC but it has attracted much controversy and not a little adverse comment in the UK. This is primarily for two reasons. First, it is widely regarded as the toughest piece of anti-corruption legislation anywhere in the world, going further than the FCPA in a number of important respects. Secondly, and connected to this, the UKBA takes an extremely robust view towards private sector corruption and places the onus on commercial organisations to prevent bribery. It is felt by some of the directors and managers that I work with that this will place an unfair burden on UK companies, especially those looking to compete for business overseas, and that it will lead to both the loss of some existing contracts and the failure to win new ones, at least in the short term.

For many years, the FCPA led the way in terms of international anti-corruption enforcement. The UKBA is part of the more recent and broader international trend exemplified by the UNCAC. There are a number of similarities between the FCPA and the UKBA: both laws have extensive extra-territorial application; both have provisions making it an offence to bribe foreign officials; and both have severe sanctions, though the UKBA is even tougher here with unlimited fines and/or a maximum of 10 years imprisonment for anyone found guilty of bribery. However, there are a number of important differences also:

- The FCPA deals with bribing foreign officials, not with private-to-private bribery;

- The FCPA only covers active bribery, that is to say the offering or paying of a bribe. The UKBA prohibits both active and passive bribery, where passive bribery is the flip-side of active bribery – agreeing to be bribed, taking the money;

- The FCPA creates an exception for facilitation payments. There are no such exemptions or exceptions in the UKBA – it is truly a "zero tolerance" piece of legislation. This means that all facilitation payments are deemed to be bribes, although the UK authorities have indicated that there will be discretion exercised in deciding whether to prosecute in these cases; and

- The UKBA creates the new corporate offence of failing to prevent bribery, which does not appear under the FCPA. In addition, the UKBA offence extends to acts of "associated persons" which means anyone who performs services for or on behalf of the commercial organisation. So, this would obviously include all employees, but it extends to agents, brokers, subsidiary companies and main contracting counterparties.

Directors and managers of all commercial organisations that carry on a business, or a part of a business in the UK need to be aware of the corporate offence under the UKBA of failing to prevent bribery in their organisations. This is a strict liability offence and, if an associate has been found to have paid a bribe intending thereby to obtain or retain business or a business advantage for the commercial organisation, then that organisation will be guilty of the corporate offence unless it can show that it had put in place "adequate procedures" designed to stop bribery from taking place. This is actually a piece of risk management theory applied to the legal process! We have already seen that controls cannot be guaranteed to work, they provide reasonable assurance only. This is exactly the point that the lawmakers have included in the UKBA. It means that a commercial organisation will have a full defence if it can show that, despite a particular case of bribery, it nevertheless had adequate procedures in place to prevent persons associated with it from bribing.

Guidance from the UK government[20] on what actually constitutes adequate procedures is formulated around six guiding principles. They are actually absolutely aligned to the best practice risk management and internal controls framework for financial crime that has been set out throughout this book. The guiding principles are as follows:

- **Proportionate procedures.** This is the overarching principle. It states that procedures to prevent bribery should be proportionate to the bribery risks the organisation faces and to the nature, scale and complexity of its activities. The procedures should be clear, practical, accessible, effectively implemented and enforced.

- **Top level commitment.** The top level management of the organisation should be committed to preventing bribery. Directors and managers should foster a culture in which bribery is never acceptable.

- **Risk assessment.** The organisation should assess the nature and extent of its exposure to potential external and internal risks of bribery. The assessment should be periodic, informed and documented.

- **Due diligence.** The organisation should apply due diligence procedures, taking a proportionate and risk-based approach, in respect of persons who perform or will perform services for or on behalf of the organisation, in order to mitigate identified bribery risks.

- **Communication (including training).** The organisation should seek to ensure that its bribery prevention policies are embedded and understood throughout the organisation through internal and external communication, including training, that are proportionate to the risks it faces.

- **Monitoring and review.** The organisation should monitor and review procedures designed to prevent bribery and make improvements where necessary.

The key controls (or adequate procedures) referred to in the government guidance include the following: a statement of zero tolerance of bribery, signed by the Chairman or CEO; regular and documented risk assessments; policies coming down from the board in high-risk areas such as gifts and entertainment, political donations and tendering processes; whistleblowing hotlines (or, as they are referred to in the official guidance, "speak-up procedures"); comprehensive training for all relevant staff that is mandatory, continuous and monitored; due diligence processes for agents and other third parties; and reference to the organisation's zero tolerance of bribery in its contractual terms and conditions.

We conclude the Chapter with a review of the second key fraud case that illustrates the extent of the problems that organisations can encounter if the controls at the top break down. This catastrophic failure of corporate governance happened in one of the most successful listed companies in India, Satyam.

The Satyam fraud

Introduction

On 7 January 2009 Ramalinga Raju, the founder and Chairman of Satyam Computer Services ("Satyam"), the fourth-largest computer outsourcing company in India, wrote a letter to the Satyam board that caused shock and disbelief to investors in India and around the world. He was in fact publicly announcing his involvement in a massive and long-standing accounting fraud. The letter began:

It is with deep regret and tremendous burden that I am carrying on my conscience, that I would like to bring the following facts to your notice:

1. The balance sheet carries as of September 30 2008:

   a. Inflated (non-existent) cash and bank balances of Rs 5,040 crore (as against Rs 5,361 crore reflected in the books);

   b. An accrued interest of Rs 376 crore, which is non-existent;

   c. An understated liability of Rs 1,230 crore on account of funds arranged by me;

   d. An overstated debtors position of Rs 490 crore (as against Rs 2,651 reflected in the books).

2. For the September quarter (Q2) we reported a revenue of Rs 2,700 crore and an operating margin of Rs 649 crore (24% of revenue) as against the actual revenues of Rs 2112 crore and an actual operating margin of Rs 61 crore (3% of revenues). This has resulted in artificial cash and bank balances going up by Rs 588 crore in Q2 alone.

The gap in the balance sheet has arisen purely on account of inflated profits over several years (limited only to Satyam standalone, books of subsidiaries reflecting true performance). What started as a marginal gap between actual operating profit and the one reflected in the books of accounts continued to grow over the years.

The letter continues over five pages in which Mr Raju says that he never benefited from the fraud personally and that no one else on the board was aware of it. At the end of the letter he tenders his resignation as Chairman of Satyam.[21]

For ease of understanding, the figures in Mr Raju's letter are expressed in Indian rupees, with a crore being a unit in the Indian number system equal to ten million. As to scale, the non-existent cash figure that he refers to as being included in the accounts is the equivalent of approximately $1 billion. This is the extent of the cash hole in the company's balance sheet.

Satyam has been dubbed the "Indian Enron" and with good reason. What Mr Raju admitted to in the letter is accounting fraud on a barely imaginable scale. Cash balances were overstated by $1 billion whilst the operating margin was inflated to 24% of revenue, when the actual figure was only 3%. The deception had been continued over a number of years. The credibility of all parts of the corporate governance system in India was immediately shaken: the board of directors; senior management; the audit process; and the regulators. It had a wider impact too because Satyam shares were also listed in New York and Amsterdam

The following paragraphs provide first some background information on the case and then move to an analysis and commentary on the Satyam scandal.

Background

Satyam was founded by Mr Raju and other members of his family as a private company in 1987 (ironically, the word "satyam" means "truth" in Sanskrit). Mr Raju obtained an MBA in the United States and came to be well regarded in India as a business pioneer and philanthropist. Satyam is an information technology services group offering consulting and outsourcing services primarily for export, with clients in many countries and business sectors around the world. It is based in the southern Indian city of Hyderabad. The company experienced rapid growth, especially in the computer outsourcing sector. It was listed first on the Bombay Stock Exchange in 1991 and then 10 years later it also listed in New York. In 2008 it obtained a secondary listing in Amsterdam, becoming the first non-European company to do so.

The strength of corporate governance practices in India has often been questioned because the biggest companies there have historically been dominated by powerful family dynasties and these individuals are seen in turn to hobnob with politicians. The "promoter phenomenon" as it is known, with its dominant family shareholdings and family friends sitting on company boards, is very prominent in India.

Satyam seemed to be different, however. There were six independent directors on the Satyam board in January 2009 and they were amongst the most respected figures in India covering key political, academic and corporate roles. Mr Raju himself referred often to his company's meticulous processes and highest standards of governance. In fact, it seemed that others agreed with him. In 2008, just four months before Mr Raju's letter to the board, Satyam was awarded the prestigious Golden Peacock Global Award for excellence in corporate governance by the UK-based World Council for Corporate Governance!

Satyam's accounting fraud

The case was originally investigated by the Serious Fraud Investigation Office ("SFIO") in India. Their reports are filed with the courts and are not available to the public but set out below are the key allegations (the trial process is not completed) drawn from a synthesis of the newspaper coverage and analysis in India.

- The falsification of the accounts apparently started in around 2001 as an attempt to keep the share price high. Business was coming under pressure at that time and the company had just listed on the New York Stock Exchange. The Satyam promoters, including Mr Raju offloaded their shareholdings in the market and used the proceeds to buy land.

- This appears to have been fraud on an industrial scale involving a dual set of accounting books. Mr Raju and other senior managers engineered a scheme that created more than 6,000 forged invoices to be used in Satyam's general ledger and financial statements. Satyam employees created dozens of fake bank statements to reflect fictional receipts for the sham invoices. This resulted in more than $1 billion in fictitious cash balances, representing almost half the company's total assets. The aim of the scheme was to inflate earnings and to create a perception that the company was carrying out huge volumes of business in order to attract potential customers and investors.

- The allegations indicate that the deception extended to the creation of a large number of fictitious company employees. According to the accounts and the payroll, the company employed some 53,000 people. In reality, only around 40,000 employees worked for Satyam, which means that almost 25% of the payroll was simply made up. Monthly salaries were paid to these 13,000 "ghost" employees, but the payments were made into accounts controlled by Mr Raju, who promptly siphoned off the money for his own purposes.

- The fraud was revealed by a whistle-blower who sent an anonymous email to one of the company's independent directors in December 2008. The trigger for this action was an abortive $1.6 billion bid by Satyam for two firms, Maytas Infra Limited and Maytas Properties Limited, both of which were owned by Mr Raju's sons. This was meant to provide a cover for the fraud but it led instead to a revolt by Satyam's independent shareholders, who had not been consulted, with the result that the bid had to be abandoned.

- Satyam's auditors were two partners in the local affiliate firm of Pricewaterhou- seCoopers ("PwC"). They received certificates from Satyam's banks showing cash balances that were in great variance with the figures for cash provided to them by management. This should have been an enormous red flag concerning the integrity of the Satyam accounting records but the PwC partners signed off the accounts with a clean audit opinion! Apparently, they were persuaded to do so by senior manage- ment at Satyam in return for receiving an exorbitant audit fee, several times the going market rate.

Consequences and commentary

Shortly after the fraud came to light, the India government seized control of the company by dissolving Satyam's board of directors and appointing new government-nominated directors. The new board then removed the former top managers of the company and oversaw a bidding process to select a new controlling shareholder in Satyam. At the same time the authorities were taking action against those responsible for the fraud.

India's Central Bureaux of Investigation has brought criminal charges against 10 individuals for falsification of accounts, criminal breach of trust, cheating and forgery. The defendants are: Mr Raju; two of Mr Raju's brothers (who were also on the Satyam board); the former CFO; three former executives; the former chief internal auditor; and the two former partners of PwC who were Satyam's auditors. The trial process is ongoing at the time of writing. Civil action is also pending in India.

In addition to these charges, Satyam's new leadership agreed to pay a $10 million penalty to settle charges of financial fraud brought by the Securities and Exchange Commission in the US. This was done without Satyam admitting wrongdoing.

The Satyam case seems to confirm the troubled reputation that Indian corporate governance has acquired for nepotism and a lack of transparency. Certainly, the limitations of the Satyam independent non-executive directors are highlighted. There was a lack of scrutiny and challenge throughout. The non-executives gave Satyam an impressive veneer of good governance, but in reality this turned out to be an illusion – an illusion of competent independence. They did not provide any effective governance control and massive accounting fraud committed by the executives was the result.

Satyam also highlights continuing concerns over the safeguards provided by the external auditors. First, there are obvious conflicts of interest and corruption issues here in the reported actions of the two audit partners themselves. But the concerns go wider than the conduct of these two individuals. There are important issues here for PwC and for the other big accounting firms. The Satyam case clearly shows the difficulty that the global accounting firms have in providing a consistent quality of service around the world. This problem is caused by the patchwork nature of the big auditing firms' global networks, which are essentially a collection of national partnerships under a thin global umbrella organisation. The Satyam scandal has proved damaging to PwC in two regards. First, the cost of the fines: the PwC India affiliates agreed to settle the Securities and Exchange Commission's charges of fraud and paid a $6 million fine, the largest ever by a foreign-based accounting firm in an SEC enforcement action. But in addition to financial cost, the firm has suffered damage to its reputation. The SEC's overall conclusion and censure of the firm are both straightforward and telling: it found that the audit failures by the PwC India affiliates were not limited to Satyam but represented a quality control failure throughout PwC India.

Summary – Five Key Learning Points for Directors and Managers

The Enron and Satyam examples demonstrate very well the extent of the problems that can arise when corporate governance is ineffective. Directors and senior managers represent significant fraud risk in the "high impact, low probability" category that we discussed in Chapter 4. It is critical therefore that the governance controls at the top of the organisation are strong enough to provide reasonable assurance that this risk will not materialise, in particular in the areas of fraudulent financial reporting and corruption.

This Chapter contains a number of important messages for directors and managers, as set out below.

✓ Remember always that the prime duty of a director is to the company itself – not to the shareholders and certainly not to the stakeholders. This is a legal obligation and stems from the fact that a limited liability company is a separate legal entity.

✓ Put in place a formal review of the effectiveness of governance processes every year. This should comprise two elements: a self-assessment by the board of its own perform- ance combined with an independent review to be carried out by either an internal function (ideally by internal audit) or by an external third party.

✓ Ensure that there are strong controls in place surrounding the financial reporting process. The SOX has been the driver of an extremely robust control framework over financial reporting for companies listed in the US. But the many examples of accounting fraud carried out by directors and senior managers clearly show that no organisation can afford to be complacent in this area.

✓ Encourage debate, scrutiny and challenge around the boardroom table. It is vital, both for good business performance and for the effective management of risk (including fraud risk) that the directors operate as a high-performing team. Avoid the four bad habits of poor performing boards: passivity; cronyism; bullying; and ignorance.

✓ Be aware of the increased risks attached to bribery and corruption in the private sector as a result of new legislation and convention, underpinned by robust action by the authorities. Commit to a zero tolerance approach and make sure that adequate procedures are in place to prevent bribery anywhere in your business operations.

6 Controls

Fraud Awareness Quiz – Question 6
When assessing controls there are two fundamental questions that you should always ask. What are they?

_____

Getting run over by a bus

I am sitting in an elegant room in an old mansion house in Luxembourg City in the Grand Duchy of Luxembourg. It is April 1995. The house has been used in the past as a private residence but now it operates as the main office of a large European private banking group. I am here as part of a team from Touche Ross assigned to review the effectiveness of the bank's anti-money laundering controls and to make any recommendations for improvements that we think are needed in order for the bank to meet best international practices. We have been in Luxembourg for over two weeks now. I am coming to the end of a very frustrating meeting with three of the bank's account managers. In fact there is only one more question that I need to ask them.

The meeting has been set up to go through a number of queries that we have arising from our review of client files. There seem to be a number of significant weaknesses in the bank's controls and procedures. Specifically, we have come across a series of client files that contain minimal information only – there is little documentation to support either the identity of the customer concerned or the source of the funds that the customer has placed with the bank to invest on his or her behalf. These are both critical controls, required by the authorities for compliance with the anti-money laundering regulations and so are matters of major importance for our report. The bank should have strong due diligence controls in place over customer identity and source of funds. Put simply, we need to know what the business relationships represented by these files are all about and to see the supporting evidence.

The account managers are, as usual, showing themselves to be most charming and delightful fellows. I have got to know them quite well on the assignment so far: each is from a different country (France, Spain and Italy), all are well educated, knowledgeable about the business of private banking and effortlessly multi-lingual. Of course, this meeting has to be conducted in English as I myself, being born, brought up and educated in the UK, have no foreign language skills of note whatsoever. The account managers listen to my concerns and assure me that they will do everything they can to assist.

During the meeting they take me through the general story behind these customers and files that are giving me and my colleagues concern, but there are no specifics. The client files all relate to individuals who are apparently wealthy South Americans, from Brazil mostly, though some are from Argentina. The money placed by them with the bank is effectively "flight capital". They explain what they mean by this. Brazil in particular has a recent history of kidnappings of family members of the rich and famous by organised criminal gangs, with subsequent demands for huge ransoms. These demands are always made against the background of threats of extreme violence against the kidnapped victim in the event that the ransom is not paid. The customers have an urgent need to be very discreet about their wealth in their own countries, therefore. More than this, they have chosen to move a proportion of their wealth offshore in an attempt to reduce the kidnap and ransom risk. This is an interesting narrative (my immediate thought is "tax evasion" although I make sure to keep this thought to myself for the time being) but I emphasise to the account managers throughout that I will need some evidence, some documentation to support what they are telling me.

And this is core of the problem – they seem to have no evidence to show me at all. To every detailed question that I ask about a customer or the source of the funds going into an account I am given the same answer: "Ellie knows". I should say at this point that Ellie is the bank's General Manager, a very busy man who I have met only sporadically and briefly so far on the assignment. I notice that a number of the files that I want to discuss have the same name typed on the cover, designated as the account manager – "Trinnie". I am interested in this and ask if I can speak to Trinnie, can she join us in the meeting perhaps? However, they inform me that Trinnie is in fact one of the bank's young secretaries and she would certainly not be able to help me on the issues of customer identity and source of funds. It is simply a mistake that her name has been typed on the files – she is not a manager at all. So, if Trinnie cannot provide me with information on these particular customers, who can I ask? I know what the account managers will say almost as soon as I ask the question. Sure enough, the answer comes straight back, the same as always: "Ellie knows".

The meeting is closing. I make a formal request to set up a meeting with Ellie in the near future to go through two issues. First, the operation of the bank's due diligence controls on customer identification and source of funds in general. Secondly, I need to see some evidence relating to the customers from South America that we have discussed today. It is likely to be a long meeting and I ask for a one-hour slot in Ellie's diary. The account managers are sceptical about this, about whether he will be able to spare this amount of time, but they agree to ask him to do so for me. As always, they say that they want to help and are very courteous.

Before leaving, I look at the account managers and ask them my final question. It is very simple: "Gentlemen, thank you for your time today. I have one last question and I wonder if you can help me with it. Can you explain to me what will happen to the bank if Ellie is run over by a bus tomorrow?"

Introduction

The story I relate above is a good example of a number of assignments that I have worked on where it proved to be difficult to gain assurance that key controls in an organisation were actually working effectively. The reasons for this varied: sometimes it was caused by a lack of awareness by workers either of the control itself or, often, of the reasons why they should spend time carrying out a task simply because it was written down in a manual but which seemed unimportant to them; at other times it was because the checks were not being carried out due to time pressure; and again on occasion it was down to the fact that there was simply no available evidence to show that a control had in fact been carried out. Generally all of these situations have as their root cause a poor understanding by employees of the purpose of controls and a lack of respect for those controls as a result. Where this happens there is what may be termed poor control consciousness throughout an organisation. This was certainly something that was very apparent to me and my colleagues during the Luxembourg project described above.

Effective controls are of course essential if an organisation is to be able to manage its fraud risk successfully. We look at control theory and practice in detail in this Chapter and, in particular, at the steps that directors and managers can take in order to gain the assurance that their controls are indeed working effectively. We begin by going back to first principles and looking at some of the key characteristics of controls. The difficult area of "custom and practice" is considered – that is to say, those aspects of behaviour within organisations that develop from time to time outside of, and separate from, the authorised policies and procedures. Two examples are used to illustrate the problems that can arise as a result of this from my own experience. We then move on to look at a number of very important controls frameworks that have been developed in the last 20 years which now have wide application around the world. The benefit of using one of these frameworks is that it will promote controls consciousness throughout the organisation and provide the directors and managers with the assurance they need around the operation of their controls.

The Chapter ends with a review of two controls that directors and managers often rely heavily on to prevent and detect fraud: auditing and the work of the audit committee. In fact it could be said that the external audit process is the most widely used control of all in the fight against fraud as most commercial organisations and public sector bodies are required to have an independent audit of their financial statements each year. However, as the Chapter shows, traditional auditing methods (whether by external auditors or internal auditors) and passive audit committees have proved to be largely ineffectual controls in practice. A proactive, risk-focused approach is required from both the auditors and the audit committee members if they are to have real impact against fraud.

Before we look at controls theory and practice, we need to return to the Quiz and the answers to Question 6.

Answers to the Quiz

Fraud Awareness Quiz – Question 6
When assessing controls there are two fundamental questions that you should always ask. What are they?

I include this general question in the Quiz because I want to know what my delegates think is the real function and purpose of controls in their organisations. In particular, I want to see whether the key controls concepts are familiar to those executives and managers who are from a non-financial and a non-auditing background. In my view, it is very important that all directors and managers, not only finance people and auditors, understand these concepts because controls play a crucial role in managing risk. Clearly they are central to preventing and detecting fraud. So what does the controls concept mean to the men and women who manage businesses today?

The two-part answer to the question is given in detail at the end of this section. In brief, the first part is to do with the design effectiveness of the controls, whilst the second part is to do with their operating efficiency.

When I first introduced this question into the Quiz I suspected that the quality of the answers that I was given would depend largely on the make-up of the delegates on any particular day. I thought that those delegates with some financial training or who came from an auditing background would be well equipped to answer the question, whilst those without any experience of audit or financial and accounting theory might struggle with it. In fact, my suspicion has turned out to be largely correct! Almost all the auditors and financial managers that I work with on the courses, whether currently in this role or with previous experience, seem to get the question at least half right – they are all aware of the need for controls to operate efficiently. Interestingly, not all of them address the importance of design effectiveness in their answers.

Of the delegates from a more general business background, many are also aware of what the answer to the second fundamental question is, although some of them struggle to express this knowledge succinctly because they are not familiar with the language and jargon typically used in controls theory. However, almost none of them have answers that include the design effectiveness point. This lack of awareness is perhaps understandable, but it is also potentially dangerous. There is an important skills gap for many people in business here, because a lack of knowledge of basic controls and risk management theory will undermine the effectiveness of the management review process, which is so important if risks such as fraud and financial crime threats generally are to be minimised.

The two fundamental questions that should always be asked when assessing a control are:

- **First, is the control effectively designed?** This question addresses design effectiveness directly. Here the key reference point is always risk. Risk drives controls, not the other way round, and controls should always be proportionate to risk. There is a very simple and powerful rule of thumb here – the bigger the risk the stronger the controls over that risk need to be. This is the question that many of my delegates apparently are not asking when they are working as managers in their businesses. It is an important omission because, as we have seen, risk is dynamic so that it changes all the time. Controls on the other hand are not so dynamic, they tend to be static and anchored in the past. All organisations develop their own patterns and ways of working and their employees become comfortable with these routines. I have worked with many clients where their controls, systems and procedures have remained essentially unchanged year on year, whilst the risks in their business might have altered significantly. This creates control gaps and there is danger for all organisations in these gaps. One of the challenges for directors and managers is to make sure that their business is run efficiently and effectively. To achieve this, the resources of the organisation, the time and effort of the workforce have to be directed to those areas of the business that matter most. In other words, a proportionate approach is needed. This cannot be achieved unless the question about control design is asked frequently and in a systematic way. It is very important.

- **Secondly, is the control working efficiently?** This question points to operating efficiency. In other words, directors and managers need assurance that the control is actually operating in practice in exactly the same way that it is meant to operate in theory, that is to say, in accordance with the control design. It is important to understand that just because controls and procedures are written down in a manual it does not necessarily follow that the written instructions are always adhered to in full (or even at all) by employees. As we have seen, almost all delegates on my courses are aware of the importance of this question, but do they actually ask the question in practice? Well, I have my doubts sometimes because not all organisations have internal audit departments and internal auditors are the people who are most likely to be carrying out this type of work. Of course, internal audit is not the only means by which assurance that controls are actually working in practice can be gained – management review is very important here, especially in smaller organisations. But some checking is certainly required, controls cannot simply be assumed to be working efficiently. Also, to be meaningful, the checks should be carried out by people who are independent of the process under scrutiny. So, whilst it is encouraging to know that most managers and directors are aware of this question, ongoing monitoring and review work throughout the organisation is always going to be required in order to be able to answer it positively.

I have seen many examples in practice of control systems being poorly designed or not working properly – sometimes both. When control breakdowns are not detected quickly, there are very often serious consequences for the business, whether fraud-related or not.

As an example, consider the findings on the following assignment that I worked on a number of years ago at an airline company in the UK. There were a number of different aspects to this project and I deal with it in two parts, first immediately below and then again later on in this Chapter. The first part of the case shows the problems that can arise when operational situations change, but the controls over that part of the operation remain the same.

Controls Case Study – Part 1

Introduction

I was part of a team commissioned by a British charter airline to look at the reasons for poor profitability from the bars in the in-flight sales division. That is to say, we were retained to analyse the results from one area of the business, the sales made by the cabin crews out of the bars on the aircraft – the containers holding the stock of perfumes, alcohol, tobacco and gifts, the products that were sold to passengers in the air during each flight. Profit margins on these sales should have been high, in the 60–70% range. In fact, they were consistently much lower than this, with some flights even recording losses. Clearly, something was going badly wrong.

The airline operated from airports or bases all around the UK. We found that the management information was poor and the analysis of that information was virtually non-existent. For example, there was no analysis showing the profitability of these sales by base. There were a number of possible causes of the problem and, in the absence of any meaningful information, we had to construct working hypotheses of what might be happening.

Concerns over stock control

One area of concern was over stock control. The airline had its own bonded warehouses at the airports and used a third party transport company to deliver the bars from the warehouses to the aircraft prior to take-off. The profitability from the in-flight sales on many flights was so low that I was concerned that these bars might be delivered "short" – that is to say, short of valuable stock items that the airline would still be paying for.

Going through the procedures manual for in-flight sales, I identified one control in particular that should have prevented this possibility by identifying any short deliveries. This was a stock count. Every time a bar was delivered to an aircraft, the procedures manual stated that it had to be counted in full by the cabin crew before take-off, with the crew member carrying out the count then signing a docket and giving it to the transporters to confirm that the bar had indeed been delivered complete.

Testing the controls

I needed to test the operation of this control. To do so, rather than sitting at a desk and looking at documents I decided that I wanted to see these in-flight controls in action, including the stock count. Accordingly, I hitched a ride. I arranged something special with the airline management. I was to be the first person to board one of their aircraft flying to Spain (before the crew and the cleaners even!) so that I could observe everything that went on, from the pre-flight routines, through what happened on the flight itself, to the handling of the cash collected from in-flight sales by the crew after the aircraft had landed.

To my great surprise, I found that the key control of the stock count did not work at all. I observed the bar being delivered and I saw that it was stored in the galley at the back of the aircraft. However, no stock count took place. Instead, just before take-off, I saw one of the cabin crew members sign the docket thereby confirming that the bar had been completely and accurately delivered! But there had been no counting of the stock in the bar at all.

Analysing the problem

So, the first question I had for the crew in the post-flight de-briefing was very simple – what happened to the bar stock count? The crew members all looked at me as if I was mad. I was told that no-one carried out these stock counts anymore, not on any flights and for a very simple reason. Eighteen months previously, the airline had made a number of operational changes to try to improve efficiency, one of which resulted in the aircraft spending shorter periods of time on the ground between flights. As a consequence, the crew told me, they no longer had the time to carry out a full stock count of the bar. Everyone knew that it takes at least 30 minutes to count the bar in full and they no longer had this time available.

So no stock counts were now done at all, ever, not by any crew on any flight so far as they were aware. I pointed out that the docket had been signed, even though there was no count. The crew replied that they had to do this otherwise the delivery agents would never leave the plane before take-off! Although I did not mention it at the time, I knew very well that this last point meant that my client, the airline company, could have no possible recourse to the third party transporters in terms of short deliveries as the transporters would have files of signed-off dockets "proving" that the bars were always delivered as "complete".

Recommendations

It proved to be a relatively simple matter to fix this particular control design weakness. Our analysis showed that around 80% of the value of the bar was made up of a relatively small number of products – the watches and a number of high value perfumes. So, "Pareto's Principle" (the 80:20 rule) could be applied here to introduce an efficient control. Rather than count all the stock in the bar, if the crew members were to count the expensive products only (the watches and perfumes), they would cover the majority of the value in the bar very quickly. The crew agreed that it could be done before take-off.

This was a good, practical recommendation and it was subsequently adopted by the airline, with increased assurance and efficiency as a result. It was not the end of the airline's problems over poor profitability, however, and we will return to another aspect of this case later in the Chapter.

Internal controls overview

Background

Internal control is the term used to describe the various plans, methods and procedures that an organisation uses in order to meet its declared business objectives. For the purpose of this book, it is important to note that internal control is often viewed as the first line of defence for safeguarding assets and preventing and detecting fraud, errors, waste, abuse and mismanagement. However, management will use it to achieve various other essential objectives too: to bring order and efficiency; to ensure that the policies of the board are followed; to ensure the completeness and accuracy of records; and to ensure compliance with the law and all relevant regulations.

Above all, internal control helps an organisation to manage its risks. Every control should be designed in a way that is proportionate to the risk in question. One of the problems for mature organisations, those companies or public sector bodies that have existed for decades, is that their internal control systems will often pre-date their adoption of formalised risk management procedures of the type we discussed in Chapter 4. So individual controls, methods of working and customs and practices may well have evolved without using risk as a reference point at all. Controls against fraud risk are a classic example of this and they often appear to be haphazard and ineffective as a result.

Control characteristics

There are many different types of controls that organisations use. Examples are: policies and procedures; authorisation levels; segregation of duties; reconciliations; key performance indicators; physical security and systems access; recruitment and exit processes; internal audit; management review; training and development; ethics charters and codes of conduct; and many others. Some of them serve different purposes and many operate in different ways, so it is helpful to look at a number of key control characteristics.

Preventative and detective controls

Internal controls can be categorised into two broad types: preventative controls and detective controls. Each has different characteristics and each has a key role to play in the fight against fraud. The major features of each are as follows:

- **Preventative controls.** The aim of a preventative control is to stop an event from occurring or a risk from materialising in the first place. Robust staff recruitment procedures used by an organisation when hiring new employees are a good example of this. Their overall aim is to ensure that the organisation hires the best available people but an important by-product of the vetting process is that any undesirable or unsuitable applicants should be prevented from working in the business from the outset.

- **Detective controls.** Here the objective is different, it is to highlight or flag up or otherwise indicate to management that something has gone wrong – that is to say, when a risk, a problem or a fault in the system has occurred. Exception reporting, whereby parameters are used to highlight those transactions falling outside of the acceptable criteria, is a good example of a detective control. It is seen in many standard business processes today, for example in credit control where debtors outstanding for more than (say) 90 days are often listed in a separate report for management attention. It is also a vital component of anti-money laundering procedures for a financial institution, where very large individual transactions of greater than (say) $10 million will be highlighted, again for management review.

Manual and automated controls

Another important distinction to be made when assessing a control is whether the control is manual or is automated. A manual control exists where somebody (an individual) has actually got to do something, where he or she becomes physically involved in the process. For automated controls, however, this is not required because here they are programmed or inherent in the system being used – they are embedded in the system.

Automated controls are generally considered to be more efficient and cost-effective than manual controls. For example, each of the two detective controls noted above for credit control and anti-money laundering purposes could be carried out either by hand or by using a computer programme. Clearly it will be much quicker if the exception reports are prepared by computer rather than manually. The difficulty that smaller organisations face is in the initial cost of purchasing and installing the programmes required, which is often prohibitively high. So, whilst the large retail banks will rely on sophisticated computer-based transaction monitoring systems to detect suspicious transactions for anti-money laundering purposes, many small financial institutions still rely on their staff going through all transactions and flagging up manually those that they consider to be suspicious. In each situation, the exception reports will still need to be reviewed by management, but clearly the automated control is more efficient than the manual one here.

Hard controls and soft controls

A third way of looking at controls is to classify them as either "hard controls" or "soft controls".

Typically, hard controls are tangible and are often easier to audit as a result. Examples are:

- Documented policies, procedures and systems notes;

- Approvals and signatures;

- Reconciliations;

- Segregation of duties; and

- Physical controls.

Soft controls are more difficult to quantify and evaluate, but they are also very important to an organisation as they help to provide overall assurance and contribute to a strong control environment (we will discuss the important concept of the control environment later). Soft controls include:

- Organisational culture and values;

- Business ethics;

- Employee support programmes;

- Training and development; and

- Accountability and management oversight.

Internal control structure

Overview

Often when I am working on a consulting assignment, I become aware that a number of the non-financial managers that I am talking to are unclear about their organisation's internal control structure. Sometimes, even financial managers seem to have the wrong perspective on internal controls. This can create problems especially if it is indicative of a low control-consciousness throughout the organisation. If this is indeed the case then many risks will increase as a result, including fraud risks.

There are two important messages that I like to convey both to the directors and managers that I work with on consulting assignments and also to my course delegates regarding the internal control structure, as follows.

Broad perspective

The first message is to stress the importance of taking a broad perspective of the internal control structure. The control concept is not something that is confined to the organisation's controls manual, or to the documented sets of systems notes and controls or to the written down policies and procedures. Internal control has its origin in the cultural characteristics of an organisation and it is these that provide the entire context and setting for the manuals and policies. It is important that directors and managers are aware of this and are able to assess the key aspects of organisational culture from the controls perspective. The three areas of questioning set out below should always be considered when assessing whether internal controls are likely to be effective:

- First, what is the commitment of the organisation to competence, to training and developing its people? Do the managers and employees have the appropriate skills and training to do their jobs well?

- Secondly, what is the quality of supervision like throughout the organisation? To what extent are the departmental heads, team leaders and line managers able to manage, motivate and control their people?

- Thirdly, to what extent is the organisation committed to managing the behaviours of its employees so that they match the values of the business? Is the importance of always acting in accordance with the code of conduct and/or the ethics charter made clear to everyone who works in the organisation?

Avoid negative attitudes

My second important message is to encourage directors and managers to take action to dispel any negativity that their employees might have towards controls. For example, I sometimes hear the view expressed that controls are essentially bureaucratic, or that they "get in the way" or that they "stop me from doing my job". This is unhelpful and misleading. Most people working in either the public or the private sectors perform controls and interact with the control structure every day, often without even realising it.

Consider the hypothetical example of a woman working in the supply chain of a retail operation. At the start of the day she will use her password to log on to her computer; at some stage in the morning she will refer to the list of authorised suppliers to source goods and services when looking at a new order; she will attend various meetings with colleagues, for example to go through a list of prospective new suppliers to check whether or not they meet the criteria to be put on the authorised suppliers list; she will sign off invoices at various stages during the day; she will send the higher-value invoices to her boss for signature as these are outside of her authorisation limits; and at the end of the day she will tidy her desk as usual before turning off her computer and going home. All of these tasks are both part of her daily routine and also internal control activities.

So, I always try to emphasise the importance of maintaining a positive attitude towards controls, especially so when I am working with people who do not have a financial or auditing background. An internal control structure is simply a different way of viewing the business, a perspective that focuses on doing the right things in the right way.

Making the commitment

Controls are an important part of business and some are more important in the management of fraud risk than others as we will see in the remainder of this book. They require investment in order to be effective and not just an investment of money but also of committed action on the part of everyone in the organisation to make them work, starting at the top.

Adrian made a number of interesting observations along these lines when I interviewed him. He is from a compliance background and has a lot of experience of working with international businesses. I asked him at one point: "What are the most effective anti-fraud controls?" He gave me a powerful answer, even if it was not the one that I was expecting:

> You need total transparency and a good organisational set-up, where things are done as a matter of course, managers don't have to ask to get them done and nobody questions why it's being done. You need to create a culture whereby people understand that if you ask them things it's for a particular purpose, not because you may be distrusting them or anything like that. Once that acceptance is there then people start to follow and it becomes part of their behaviour. So the most effective control you can have is changing people's behaviour. In particular, avoid a blame culture – it doesn't serve anything, a blame culture.
>
> No matter how much money you put into this sort of thing, unless you actually believe in what you are doing it's not going to have any effect. You've got to really believe and again this comes from the top. If they really want an understanding, if they have an understanding of what the risks are and how they want me to respond, then it's a question of investment. It's not just in controls. You need to have the right people, they need to be suitably motivated, rewarded so it's not down to physical procedural issues because procedures are as good as the people who follow them so you need to go beyond that and look at everything. It doesn't work if you don't have the right people, things aren't going to be followed and if you don't convey that strength of feeling, that conviction from the top then nothing happens. Well I mean we are talking about inspirational management and it's impossible to have that when you are talking about big organisations. But what you can do is to make sure you have the right people who keep pressing the right buttons and then you start to have, you create this cultural awareness. Once that culture is in place then things eventually will start to follow and that is when you need to invest time and money in building up your "belt and braces" controls. These could be software or they could be, you know, procedural steps for people in certain gate-keeping positions to ensure that fraud and that sort of thing doesn't happen, making sure there's independence in function and things like that. It's more than just money, it's an emotional investment.

Adrian's point around the need for people in organisations, especially those at the top, to have the emotional commitment, the will if you like, to create a positive, disciplined culture is very astute and it is something that all directors and managers should be aware of.

Custom and practice

The importance of having respect for good practice and procedures, of having a controls consciousness that permeates the entire organisation, can be shown to best effect by counter-pointing, by considering some of the poor workplace behaviours that can develop without it. Often these behaviours are described as "custom and practice", the sorts of things that have developed over time, they are not written down anywhere as official procedures and they are certainly not policies that are signed off by the board. However, management have allowed them to continue so that over time they become accepted practices, customs that are handed down to new recruits over the years. They become "perks of the job" so to speak.

Some of these practices are very difficult to understand objectively and they can lead to behaviour which is questionable and potentially fraudulent. I set out below two examples of this, one from my own experience, the other a situation recounted to me by Teresa during our interview for this book. They are very different situations but they each illustrate the problems that can arise if management does not promote consistently good practice and respect for internal controls.

Teresa has wide experience of working in internal audit in the UK's public sector. The incident she describes is quite funny but also potentially very serious. It occurred when she was Head of Internal Audit at a large local authority in London. Many people in her organisation clearly knew what was going on in the situation she describes, but did nothing about it. The auditors, when they were told about it, were not interested because the potential financial impact looked small. The case concerned an aspect of the car parking scheme that the local authority was running, in particular the controls surrounding the cash paid into the parking meters by people wishing to park their cars legally on the streets in the borough. This is what Teresa had to say:

> The problem concerned a "custom and practice" thing that was allowed to develop. It sounds really stupid, but this came to my attention when a filing cabinet had fallen over in an office because of the sheer weight of the money that had been stored in there. We're talking coins and things, which had been collected from various car park meters. I mean that shows how old fashioned the system was anyway. The custom and practice was . . . well, they were still getting to the root of the problem after I'd left, but they were talking about an issue to do with the design of the machines that sort the coins. Once the machine gets too full, anything caught in the "funnelly bit" at the top isn't actually counted. So what we were being told, whether it's correct or not I don't know, is that the money that then hadn't been counted in the audit trail that these machines would give at the end of the day was put in a separate bag and taken to the office. Hence this filing cabinet that fell down was full of these coins. But you can imagine how, you know, in a borough of that size, how many coins were in there. I think that on the day the auditors noticed it there was probably £3,000 in there which is not that much money but you don't know how long it's been going on for, it's not gone through any accounts. And everybody knew about it, the contractors that were emptying the machines brought it in as custom and practice and it was put in this cabinet. The staff knew it was there, the manager knew it was there and you just think why hasn't anybody ever mentioned it? It's like there is an overall £2 million unreconciled difference on the account at the time and you've got a cabinet falling over because it's full of coins that you can't tell neither hide nor hair of where they've come from!

For my own example I return to the project, introduced earlier in the Chapter, that I carried out some years ago for a charter airline in the UK that was suffering from poor profitability in its in-flight sales division. As previously mentioned, this project had various aspects to it, one of which concerned an aspect of custom and practice that had been allowed to develop amongst the cabin crew with detrimental effects to the business. This is what we found.

Controls Case Study – Part 2

A second problem area

When analysing the results of the in-flight sales from the numerous flights made by the airline all over the world, my colleagues and I noticed an interesting pattern. The profitability of the bars from flights to long-haul destinations (e.g. Sydney and Los Angeles) was consistently low, with these bars always appearing in the bottom quartile of our charts. This seemed counter-intuitive to us as the crews would surely have more time to sell their products to customers on these flights, so they were likely to have more sales rather than less and more profits as a result rather than less.

Analysis and cause

So, we decided to raise this seeming anomaly with the cabin crew members during the various ongoing interviews and workshops that we held throughout the project to get their thoughts on what might be the cause of the low profitability of in-flight sales on long-haul flights. A number of factors emerged from these discussions, one of which was both truly surprising and very worrying. It was disclosed entirely voluntarily by the crew members.

Apparently, the airline rosters on long-haul flights were such that the same crew members would work in the cabin of the aircraft the whole way to its destination, after which they would have three to four days off to relax, all paid for, before working again in the cabin as the aircraft was flown back to the UK. Crew members told us that on every long-haul flight they and their colleagues would routinely take bottles of their favourite alcoholic drink (e.g. whiskey or gin) off the aircraft in their kit bags to enjoy at parties in the hotel during their down time. It was clear from what they were telling us that this had become firmly established custom and practice by crews working for the airline, seen as a "perk" of the job, something that was literally being handed down from one generation of cabin crew members to the next.

What concerned me and my colleagues, however, was that this practice was completely unofficial. There was nothing written down authorising crew members to take products from the bar without paying for them at all. Another area of concern was that it was also costing the company a lot of money. I made a quick calculation that put the costs at around £500,000 per annum. To outsiders like me and my colleagues this seemed to be nothing other than theft and theft on a large scale at that.

Recommendations

We raised this issue very quickly with senior management because it was clearly going to be difficult to handle and resolve satisfactorily. It was obvious from the workshops that the cabin crew members did not think they were doing anything wrong here. Also, the crews were generally very enthusiastic and dedicated employees. After discussion with management, we decided to try to change behaviours going forward by focusing not on issues of theft and criminality but on the amount that this practice was costing the company and that this was no longer tenable.

This message had a big impact. The cost to the company seemed genuinely to shock the crew members when we told them – they clearly had never thought of their perk in these terms at all. We informed them that the company could not afford it and that the practice had to stop in future. Management had hit upon a way to make this change easier for crew members to accept by revising the crew bonus scheme. In future this was to be based on both the amount of the sales made by each individual crew member as before but with an additional element according to the profitability of each flight as a whole. The aim was not only to incentivise high sales but also good stock control and cash handling too.

This proved a successful strategy. The cabin crews even agreed to our additional recommendation of spot searches of their kit bags at the end of a flight. Unfortunately, this further control was never in fact implemented because of opposition from another source – not the cabin crews but the flight crews (that is to say, the pilots).

Modern internal controls frameworks

We will turn now to a number of powerful models developed in recent years which each set out different ways for an organisation to order the various individual controls into an effective internal control framework. Directors and managers need to be aware of these models and should look to use the one most applicable to their own particular business in order to gain increased assurance over the management of risk, including of course fraud risk.

Overview

Set out below is a brief review of five major control frameworks developed since the early 1990s in the US, Canada and the UK. There have been others developed during this period, of course. For example, in response to the growing importance of the application of information technology ("IT") to the strategy and business processes of most organisations, an IT governance framework "Control Objectives for Information and Related Technology" ("COBIT") was developed in 1996 in the US as a reference for developing and managing internal controls and appropriate levels of security in IT. But the five models outlined below provide the key overarching controls frameworks that directors and managers need to be aware of and then to decide which of them is most appropriate for application in their own particular organisations. Each of the frameworks has been updated in response to changing circumstances and recommendations for improvement from time to time.

The majority of these five frameworks take a business-wide approach to internal controls. They broadly favour a principles based, risk-focused methodology, where the internal control system sits within a risk management framework. In these models, internal control works best when it is embedded within the organisation, with employees informed as to how it impacts on their roles and their responsibilities in terms of monitoring and reporting. Getting the culture, ethical framework and "tone at the top" right is recognised in all of the frameworks as being critically important and essential to the successful implementation of any internal control system. We will come back to this in the last Chapter of the book.

The exception that does not take the principles based, risk-focused approach is the Sarbanes Oxley Act of 2002 ("SOX") in the US and, in particular, the Section 404 provisions. As we have seen in Chapter 5, because this Act originates out of US legislation, it takes a different, rules-based approach. The SOX requirements are prescriptive and mandatory, focusing on compliance and accountability. They are very detailed but also narrowly focused as they concentrate on one aspect of internal controls, namely controls over the financial reporting process. The compliance requirements are costly.

It was thought by many at the time that standards around the world would change to become more aligned to the SOX regime. Of course, the SOX continues to have worldwide impact because every company that is listed on the US stock markets must comply with its provisions. However, other countries have not in fact chosen to change their existing internal control frameworks to be more closely aligned to the SOX model.

1. The COSO Framework – 1992

Introduction

The Committee of Sponsoring Organisations of the Treadway Commission ("COSO") was originally organised in the US in 1985 to sponsor the National Commission on Fraudulent Financial Reporting. It is a voluntary private sector organisation dedicated to improving organisational performance and governance through effective internal control, enterprise risk management and fraud deterrence. COSO is jointly sponsored by five major professional associations based in the US: the American Accounting Association ("AAA"), the American Institute of Certified Public Accountants ("AICPA"), Financial Executives International ("FEI"), the Institute of Management Accountants ("IMA") and the Institute of Internal Auditors ("IIA"). COSO has remained in existence since 1985, with representatives of the five sponsoring organisations coming together periodically to work on specific projects.

One of the main conclusions of the "Report of the National Commission on Fraudulent Financial Reporting", published in 1987, was to say that fraud resulted from poor internal controls. This was not a surprising conclusion. However, COSO then set about dealing with its implications directly. It commissioned the accountancy firm Coopers & Lybrand to study the issues raised in the report further and to prepare a report addressing internal control weaknesses.

The result was the truly ground-breaking publication titled: "Internal Control – Integrated Framework" ("the Framework").[1] The report was published in September 1992 and provides principles-based guidance for designing and implementing effective internal controls. It aims to provide a standard against which businesses and other entities – large or small, in the public or private sector, for-profit or not – can assess their control systems and determine how to improve them. The Framework has become the most widely used internal control framework in the US and has been adopted or adapted by numerous organisations in countries all around the world.

COSO definition of internal control

The Framework starts with an important definition which is broad-based and serves the needs of different parties. Internal control as defined by COSO is:

> A process, affected by an entity's board of directors, management and other personnel designed to provide reasonable assurance regarding the achievement of objectives in the following categories:

- Reliability of financial reporting;

- Effectiveness and efficiency of operations; and
- Compliance with applicable laws and regulations.

The Framework

The Framework itself consists of five inter-related components: control environment; risk assessment; control activities; information and communication; and monitoring. Although these components apply to all entities, COSO recognises that small or medium-sized organisations will no doubt implement them differently than will larger ones. A small company can still have effective internal control even though the controls themselves are less formal and structured.

COSO chooses to illustrate the Framework by way of a three-dimensional cube as set out in Diagram 6.1 below. Notice that the three distinct categories included in the definition of internal control above appear across the top of the cube – they are distinct but overlapping categories. Also, down the side of the cube are the various business units (unit A, unit B) and activities (activity 1, activity 2). The overarching principle of the Framework is one of consistency of controls across the organisation as a whole. Finally, the five components of the Framework are set out on the face of the cube. These five components interrelate and it is important to note that, in order for a control to be operating effectively in any of the three categories of the definition, COSO stipulates that all five of the components must be in place.

The five components

COSO describes the five components of the Framework as follows:

- **Control environment.** The control environment sets the tone of an organisation, influencing the control consciousness of its people. It is the foundation for all the other components of internal control, providing discipline and structure. Control environment factors include the integrity, ethical values and competence of the entity's people; management's philosophy and operating style; the way management assigns authority and responsibility, and organizes and develops its people; and the attention and direction provided by the board of directors

- **Risk assessment.** Every entity faces a variety of risks from external and internal sources that must be assessed. A pre-condition to risk assessment is the establishment of objectives, linked at

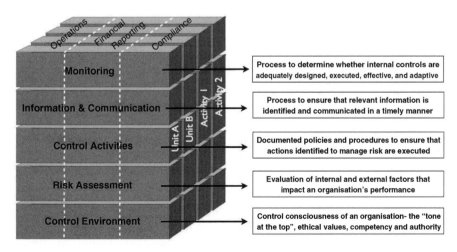

Diagram 6.1 The COSO Control Framework
(*Source*: COSO)

different levels and internally consistent. Risk assessment is the identification and analysis of relevant risks to the achievement of business objectives, forming a basis for determining how the risks should be managed. Because economic, industry, regulatory and operating conditions will continue to change, mechanisms are needed to identify and deal with the special risks associated with change.

• **Control activities.** Control activities are the policies and procedures that help ensure management directives are carried out. They help to make sure that necessary actions are taken to address risks to the achievement of the entity's objectives. Control activities occur throughout the organisation, at all levels and in all functions. They include a range of activities as diverse as approvals, authorisations, verifications, reconciliations, reviews of operating performance, security of assets and segregation of duties.

• **Information and Communication.** Pertinent information must be identified, captured and communicated in a form and timeframe that enable people to carry out their responsibilities. Information systems produce reports, containing operational, financial and compliance-related information, that make it possible to run and control the business. They deal not only with internally generated data, but also information about external events, activities and conditions necessary to informed business decision-making and external reporting. Effective communication must also occur in a broader sense, flowing down, across and up the organisation. All personnel must receive a clear message from top management that control responsibilities must be taken seriously. They must understand their own role in the internal control system, as well as how individual activities relate to the work of others. They must have a means of communicating significant information upstream. There also needs to be effective communication with external parties, such as customers, suppliers, regulators and shareholders.

• **Monitoring.** Internal control systems need to be monitored – a process that assesses the quality of the system's performance over time. This is accomplished through ongoing monitoring activities, separate evaluations or a combination of the two. Ongoing monitoring occurs in the course of operations. It includes regular management and supervisory activities, and other actions personnel take in performing their duties. The scope and frequency of separate evaluations will depend primarily on an assessment of risks and the effectiveness of ongoing monitoring procedures. Internal control deficiencies should be reported upstream, with serious matters reported to top management and the board.

Commentary

The Framework remains just as relevant today as when it was first published. For example, it has become the de facto standard for controls over financial reporting as organisations have adapted it to focus on the components that relate directly to Section 404 compliance following the passing of the SOX in 2002.

COSO announced in November 2010 that it was starting a new project to review and update the Framework, with a target publication date for an updated internal control framework of 2012 – the 20th anniversary of the original Framework. The review is likely to target in particular the various control evaluation tools that were included in the original report in order to make them more relevant in the increasingly complex business environment of the 21st century. As David Landsittel, the COSO Chairman, stated in the press release to launch this project: "Organisations can continue to apply the current Framework, inasmuch as its basic components are timeless, but the more detailed guidance and examples are somewhat dated."

2. The COCO Framework – 1995

Introduction
The COSO model above is an extremely robust internal controls framework. It has its limitations of course, not least because any internal controls system can be undermined by collusion among employees or overridden by coercion of senior management. We discuss these and other methods the fraudster might use to negate internal controls throughout this book. However, another potential area of limitation in the COSO model is that, by concentrating on systems, processes and documentation, it gives insufficient attention to the human element. Internal control involves human action which introduces the possibility of errors in processing or judgement. This human element is placed at the centre of a report issued by the Criteria of Control Board in Canada in 1995 under the aegis of the Canadian Institute of Chartered Accountants.

Definition
The report by the Criteria of Control Board (since renamed the Risk Management and Governance Board) was titled "Guidance on Control" and has come to be known as the CoCo Framework.[2] It defines control as comprising:

> those elements of an organisation (including its resources, systems, processes, culture and tasks) that, taken together, support people in the achievement of the organisation's objectives.

Framework
Control is seen as encompassing the entire organisation, starting with its smallest unit, the individual person. Controls over organisational activities are ultimately controls over the activities and behaviours of individual people. Under the CoCo Framework the essence of control is four connected high-level processes: purpose, commitment, capability, and monitoring and learning as follows.

- **Purpose** groups criteria that provide a sense of the organisation's direction. They address objectives including mission; vision and strategy; risks and opportunities; policies; planning; and performance targets and indicators.

- **Commitment** groups criteria that provide a sense of the organisation's identity and values. They address ethical values, including integrity; human resource policies; authority, responsibility and accountability; and mutual trust.

- **Capability** groups criteria that provide a sense of the organisation's competence. They address knowledge, skills and tools; communication processes; information; coordination; and control activities.

- **Monitoring and learning** groups criteria that provide a sense of the organisation's evolution. They address monitoring internal and external environments; monitoring performance; challenging assumptions; reassessing information needs and information systems; follow-up procedures; and assessing the effectiveness of control.

These processes are linked together in Diagram 6.2.

The Control Board summarises this framework as follows:

> A person performs a task, guided by an understanding of its purpose (the objective to be achieved) and supported by capability (information, resources, supplies and skills). The

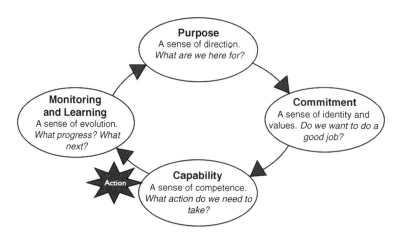

Diagram 6.2 The CoCo Control Framework
(*Source*: CoCo)

person will need a sense of commitment to perform the task well over time. The person will monitor his or her performance and the external environment to learn about how to do the task better and about changes to be made. The same is true of any team or work group. In any organization of people, the essence of control is purpose, commitment, capability, and monitoring and learning.

Commentary

The CoCo Framework was brought out only a few years after its COSO predecessor. It suffered by comparison. I have worked with no organisations where the CoCo Framework has been adopted formally. However, I have to say that the ideas behind it, in particular its emphasis on the drivers of positive behaviour and actions, have much resonance with some of the modern management philosophies, such as the business benefits that accrue to those organisations that are able to engage their employees passion and commitment to their work.

3. The Turnbull Guidance – 1999

Introduction

The original Cadbury Report in the UK left a significant piece of unfinished business. It contained a recommendation that the boards of listed companies should report on the effectiveness of their systems of internal control and that the auditors should report on this statement. This requirement was controversial because neither company boards nor auditors were willing to take responsibility for expressing an opinion on internal control effectiveness. A working party chaired by Nigel Turnbull, then Finance Director of Rank Group plc was established at the request of the London Stock Exchange to address this and other internal control requirements of the Combined Code. The subsequent report "Internal Control: Guidance for Directors on the Combined Code" ("the Turnbull Guidance")[3] was published in September 1999.

The Turnbull Guidance sets out best practice on internal control for UK listed companies and assists them in applying the UK Corporate Governance Code. The guidance requires companies to report annually on whether the board has reviewed the system of internal control. It encourages but does not require the board to express an opinion on the effectiveness of the system. There is no requirement for the auditors to do any additional work in this area.

The Turnbull Guidance was remarkable for promoting two cutting-edge ideas at that time. First, it introduced a close coupling of risk management and internal controls: it integrated risk management into internal control assessment and reporting and it stressed the responsibility of the board for both. Secondly it extended the review and reporting obligation to cover all areas of control (operational, financial and compliance) not just internal financial control as earlier reports in the UK had required.

The Turnbull Framework

Of particular importance for our purposes, the Turnbull Guidance introduces a four-stage framework for risk and controls that is both simple and powerful. It forms the basis of the Responsibility Framework set out in Chapter 1. As I mentioned in that Chapter, it is absolutely essential in my view that the Responsibility Framework is applied consistently throughout an organisation if it is to be in a position to manage its fraud risk effectively.

The four-stage framework as set out by Turnbull Guidance is as follows:

- **Stage 1. Identify and assess risks** by looking at aspects such as completeness of risks assessed, the impact and probability of a risk materialising together with timeframes;

- **Stage 2. Design appropriate controls over the risks.** Controls should be embedded in systems, should include both preventative and detective measures and be cost-effective and proportionate;

- **Stage 3. Test that the controls are working.** Here the aim is to be able to state positively that the controls are operating in practice in accordance with their design; and

- **Stage 4. Conclude on the effectiveness of the internal control system.** This should be carried out annually by the board, as stipulated in the framework.

Commentary

The Turnbull Guidance is regarded as best practice so far as internal controls and risk management is concerned in the UK. It provides a simple but effective and powerful framework that will benefit most organisations, not only the listed companies at which it is directly aimed. It has also achieved international recognition. For example, the US Securities and Exchange Commission has identified the Turnbull Guidance as a suitable framework for complying with US requirements to report on internal controls over financial reporting, as detailed in Section 404 of the SOX and related SEC rules (see below).

Whenever I work with directors and managers in the UK, they will often start by saying that their organisation does indeed comply with the Turnbull Guidance. However, when we look at how they manage a particular area of risk in practice – in this case fraud risk – it quickly becomes apparent that the Turnbull Guidance is not being followed. For example, even in 2011 very few managers told me that their companies had identified and assessed their fraud risk in a formal way so that they were able to provide a "fraud risk profile". In other words, Stage 1 of the framework above had not been carried out. As stated previously, it is important for directors and managers to realise that risk drives controls, not the other way round. Without a structured process to draw up a fraud risk profile it is very unlikely that the controls in place within a business will be adequate to prevent and detect fraud effectively. This is a fundamental weakness and it is one of the main reasons why organisations remain vulnerable to fraud threats today.

In 2004 the Financial Reporting Council ("FRC") set up a review group under the chairmanship of Douglas Flint (then the Group Finance Director of HSBC Holdings plc). The group strongly endorsed retention of the flexible, principles-based approach of the original guidance and made only a small number of changes to it.

The Turnbull Guidance is currently under scrutiny again. The FRC has announced that it will be conducting a limited review in 2012 following the recent changes to the UK Corporate Governance Code.

4. The SOX – 2002

Introduction

As we have seen, the US Congress passed the SOX in an effort to reduce public concern and restore investor confidence following a series of failures of large public corporations in the US brought about by accounting fraud. In addition to its many other requirements, the SOX introduces important new rules regarding evaluations of internal controls over the financial reporting process – the Section 404 provisions. These provisions apply to all companies registered with the Securities and Exchange Commission and are mandatory for these companies.

So the SOX has become a very important controls framework in its own right.

Section 404 requirements

Section 404(a): Management Assessment of Internal Controls requires that each annual report of a company registered with the Securities and Exchange Commission contains an internal control report which:

- States the responsibility of management for establishing and maintaining an adequate internal control structure and procedures for financial reporting; and

- Contains an assessment of the internal control structure and of the procedures for financial reporting.

Section 404(b): Internal Control and Financial Reporting requires that the company's auditor shall "attest to and report on the assessment made by management" in respect of the internal control assessment. This so-called attestation report must be made in accordance with standards issued by the Public Company Accounting Oversight Board.

In June 2004 the PCAOB issued Auditing Standard Number 2: "An Audit of Internal Control over Financial Reporting Performed in Conjunction with an Audit of Financial Statements." This was superseded in 2007 by Auditing Standard Number 5, which states that the audit of internal control over financial reporting should be integrated with the audit of the financial statements, despite the objectives of both not being identical. The standard says that if one or more material weaknesses exist, the company's internal control over financial reporting cannot be considered effective.

Commentary

The SOX has had a widespread impact in the US and beyond on perceptions of controls as discussed earlier in Chapter 5. It takes an extremely robust and detailed approach, but the focus is a narrow one in that it focuses on the controls surrounding the financial reporting process only. The SOX has proved controversial, in particular in respect of the costs incurred to comply with the Section 404 provisions, which many business people feel are disproportionate to the benefits achieved. However, others take the view that the improvements to, and greater assurance over, both the financial reporting and the auditing processes make the costs worthwhile. Those companies that are not required to be SOX-compliant should take on board the message that strong controls in these areas are essential and make the commitment to strengthening them if need be.

5. ERM Framework – 2004

Introduction

The Enterprise Risk Management Framework ("ERM")[4] was issued by COSO in 2004. This is COSO's second highly influential model and it was brought out 12 years after the first one, the integrated controls framework discussed above. In this more recent work, internal control is seen as an integral part of risk management. So, in the time since 1992 the focus of the committee's attention has shifted from internal control to the broader concept of enterprise risk management. As its name implies, ERM is concerned with each business enterprise as a whole and is looking for a consistent approach across all of the component parts of an enterprise – subsidiaries, business units and the entity level itself. The ERM framework stresses the importance of assessing risk when strategy setting – effective enterprise risk management starts at the top of the organisation and supports its mission and objectives.

Definition

COSO defines enterprise risk management as follows:

> Enterprise risk management is a process, effected by an entity's board of directors, management and other personnel, applied in strategy setting and across the enterprise, designed to identify potential events that may affect the entity, and manage risk to be within its risk appetite, to provide reasonable assurance regarding the achievement of entity objectives.

Commentary

The ERM framework is a major work on strategic risk management and we do not need to consider it in detail here. It is concerned with the wider external and internal risks relevant to the determination of the organisation's strategy to reach its objectives. It sees internal control as part of that process, so that internal control structures and procedures are instrumental in ensuring that these objectives are achieved. The ERM framework promotes a risk-based approach to internal control and to any internal assessment of its effectiveness. It takes a broad view of internal control and does not follow the SOX path of concentration on the controls surrounding the financial reporting process.

The role of audit in fraud prevention and detection

Introduction

Broadly, an audit is an evaluation process. There are many different types of audit today, including quality audits, energy audits and regulatory audits. We consider here the two that are most important from an anti-fraud perspective: external auditing and internal auditing. Later on in the Chapter we will look at the role of the audit committee, the mechanism by which many organisations look to provide oversight of the audit process and ensure that it delivers effective work in line with auditing standards.

Audit is often thought by non-specialists to look particularly for fraud and therefore to play a crucial role in reducing fraud risk. It is certainly true that well-directed fraud auditing has a very important part to play, especially in deterring people from committing fraud and in uncovering fraudulent schemes that are operating within organisations. In my view, however, directors and managers sometimes place too much reliance on traditional audit work to manage their fraud risk. By traditional auditing I mean in particular work based on the selection of a small sample of items for testing out of a much larger population of transactions, so that each item in the population has an equal chance of being selected. This is often carried out by auditors who have little understanding of fraud risk factors, no specialist fraud awareness or any investigation training and no appropriate audit tools. I believe that traditional auditing in these terms, whether carried out by external auditors or internal auditors, simply does not "cut it" in terms of effective anti-fraud work.

External auditing and internal auditing are different professions, each with separate and distinct responsibilities. The position of each in terms of the fight against fraud is, according to their respective governing bodies, rather different but each profession is some way removed from the popular perception of auditing as being essentially an "anti-fraud" activity.

We look at some of the limitations of traditional auditing as a control to prevent and detect fraud in this section, before moving on to consider the more proactive approach required under the new auditing standards. Before doing so we review the popular view of auditors' responsibilities in the fight against fraud and compare it with the realities of the work that they carry out in practice.

Perception and realities

It is important to be clear about the responsibilities of auditors in the prevention and detection of fraud because of three inter-connected factors that often confuse understanding in this area.

- The first factor is public perception. Ask a sample of individuals you meet in the street if they expect auditors to prevent and detect fraud and the answer will almost certainly be an overwhelming "yes". Most people think that one of the main reasons for having audits is to uncover fraud. As we will see below, this is very different to the perception of the governing bodies representing external and internal auditors.

- The second factor, perhaps influenced by the first, is that many people within organisations also think that auditors should be engaged in fighting fraud – not only in theory but also in practice. Further, senior managers often believe this too and so place undue reliance on audits to uncover fraud. Not only is this unrealistic but it can also be dangerous in the sense that managers may not realise that budgets based around traditional audit plans will actually have little time devoted to anti-fraud work. The auditors are unlikely to spend much time on fraud prevention and detection work unless specifically instructed to do so.

- Finally, most auditors are ill-equipped to tackle fraud. They lack the training, the mind-set and the methodology to be effective in either preventing or, in particular, detecting fraud. We discuss this further below. One consequence of this, when combined with the second factor noted above, is that I have worked with some internal auditors who are prepared to assume responsibility for fighting fraud even though they have no real understanding of what constitutes a fraud audit. They feel it is expected of them and so may carry out anti-fraud assignments but they often do so in an inefficient and ineffective way. Work of this sort is clearly not good value for money but it could also be dangerous if it encourages directors and managers to place unwarranted faith in such audits being able to prevent and detect fraud. It is a fundamental point that reliance should not be placed on traditional auditing to manage fraud risk – a different approach is needed as set out in the new auditing standards discussed below.

The external audit

Introduction

An external audit, often referred to as a statutory audit, is required by law in many countries for all but the smallest of companies. In the US and the EU it will be carried out by a Registered Auditor (normally a third party accounting firm that is independent of the auditee organisation) who provides a report to the owners of the company, printed as part of the company's annual financial statements showing the auditor's opinion on whether those financial statements are broadly "true and fair". The external audit is therefore an essential governance control. As we saw in Chapter 5, it is a central component of good corporate governance.

Set out below are some of the key features of the external audit.

Definitions

When I was working for Touche Ross in the audit department in London in the 1980s, my accountancy institute (the Institute of Chartered Accountants in England and Wales) had a very simple definition of an external audit as follows:

> The independent examination of, and expression of an opinion on, the financial statements of an enterprise.

There have been many changes in the auditing world since then. The Auditing Practices Board now sets standards and best practices in the UK. It gives the following statement, very relevant to the fraud question, as part of its overview of the Scope of an Audit of Financial Statements of Private Sector Entities issued in December 2010:

> An audit involves obtaining evidence about the amounts and disclosures in the financial statements sufficient to give reasonable assurance that the financial statements are free from material misstatement, whether caused by fraud or error. This includes an assessment of whether the accounting policies are appropriate to the entity's circumstances and have been consistently applied and adequately disclosed; the reasonableness of significant accounting estimates made by the directors; and the overall presentation of the financial statements.[5]

External audit essentials

The definitions are important and point to the essence of what external auditing is all about. Set out below are a number of key characteristics of an external audit that all directors and managers need to be aware of in order to assess how effective such an audit might be in preventing and detecting fraud in their organisations:

- It is a legal requirement in many jurisdictions that all but the smallest companies (and most public sector bodies too) should be subject to an external audit every year.

- External audits are normally carried out by people from professional services firms, so they are in that very obvious way seen to be independent of the organisation they are auditing.

- External auditing is now a highly regulated activity and in order to carry out audits a firm needs to gain accreditation and be recognised as a "Registered Auditor" in the relevant jurisdiction.

- External audits have a relatively narrow focus. They concentrate on the financial statements (meaning the annual report and accounts) of an organisation, on the controls surrounding the financial reporting process and on whether or not the information shown in the report and accounts is disclosed in accordance with applicable accounting standards and relevant company law.

- External auditors are independent. In particular, they are independent from the directors and management of the organisation being audited and this is crucial in terms of good corporate governance. The board and management are responsible for producing the report and accounts of their company each year, not the auditors. The auditors are responsible for their audit opinion.

- All external audits result in an audit report. The auditor's report is required to contain a clear expression of opinion on the financial statements taken as a whole. It is not therefore a statement of fact but is rather an opinion, based on the evidence collected during the audit. The report is addressed to the owners of the organisation being audited (in the case of a company it will be to the shareholders) and it is to the owners that the auditors owe a duty of care in terms of the standards of their work.

- The audit report does not refer to the financial statements as being "correct" or "accurate", but in the UK and other jurisdictions using this framework, the phrase used will be "true and fair". The distinction is important and is based on the key concept of materiality.

- The definition of external auditing does not refer to the prevention and detection of fraud. Rather, the definition emphasises that the auditors need to plan and perform their work in order to identify with "reasonable assurance" (we will come back to this phrase in a moment) material misstatements in the financial statements. Materiality is an important auditing concept. In the context of the financial statements, it means that there is nothing included in the financial statements (either through fraud or error), or excluded from them (again, either through fraud or error) which, if corrected, would alter the reader's perception of the picture given of the organisation by the financial statements as a whole.

- Audit work is carried out to provide "reasonable assurance" that the financial statements are free from material misstatement, it does not provide certainty. There are rarely any guarantees in business. We have already seen the importance of the phrase reasonable assurance in the control frameworks produced by COSO for example.

Should external auditors discover fraud?

Fraud is a controversial area for external auditors. Traditionally, they have been able to take a largely passive approach to auditor responsibility for fraud detection as a result of various Court judgements. The classic case in this regard is the 1896 Kingston Cotton Mill Case[6] in the UK, when Lord Justice Lopes ruled that:

> An auditor is not bound to be a detective, or to approach his work with suspicion, or with a foregone conclusion that there is something wrong. He is a watchdog, not a bloodhound.

Although 1896 may seem a very long time ago, the phrase "watchdog not bloodhound" was certainly used when I was sitting my accountancy examinations in the early 1980s to describe the auditor's responsibility.

This passive position has changed somewhat now as a result of the widespread criticism of the failure of the external auditors to detect fraud in the headline accounting scandals of 2001, notably the Enron and WorldCom scandals in the US. The same accounting firm audited both of these companies, that firm being Arthur Andersen. We have already seen the severe consequences for Arthur Andersen in terms of the destruction of its business model as a result of the reputational damage it suffered following the criminal conviction coupled with perceived shortfalls in its performance in these cases. New auditing standards were issued in the US and internationally in response to the wider criticism of the accounting profession as a whole resulting from these cases. These new standards are discussed later in this Chapter.

For the purposes of my fraud awareness training courses, the answer that I give to delegates to the question raised here (namely should external auditors discover fraud) is "it all depends". External audits should be planned and performed to obtain reasonable assurance that the financial statements are free from material misstatements, whether from error or from fraud. As we have seen in Chapter 2, the distinction between fraud and error depends crucially on whether there is any intention to deceive. Whether a properly planned and performed audit will actually discover fraud if it exists depends absolutely on two factors that are linked to the overriding caveat of materiality: first, the size of the fraud and secondly the size of the company being audited.

Small, low level frauds would normally only ever be detected during a standard external audit by chance, luck or coincidence – if, for example, the sample of items chosen at random by the auditor for detailed examination and audit testing should happen to include one of the fraudulent transactions.

There are no assurances that even large frauds will be uncovered by external audit work. Consider as an example a hypothetical fraud of $10 million. It seems obvious that external audit work should detect misstatements in the report and accounts of this size but this is by no means always the case. If the fraudulent scheme was carried out somewhere in the operations of a huge commercial group such as BP which regularly makes profits of $billions each quarter (unless it is faced with extraordinary costs arising from an extreme disaster such as the Gulf of Mexico oil spill) it is extremely unlikely that the fraud would be found by the external auditors. In this case, providing the standards of the work were satisfactory, the auditors would probably escape any censure for failing to detect the untoward transactions because the $10 million fraud would almost certainly be deemed to be immaterial to the results of the BP group. However, contrast this with a much smaller company, the hypothetical ABC Ltd, which has an annual turnover of $20 million and makes profits of $5 million a year. In this case a $10 million fraud is clearly material to ABC Ltd's report and accounts and the external auditors would most certainly be expected to uncover it. Failure to do so in these circumstances could well result in legal action against the auditors for negligence.

The external auditor's use of materiality to guide the work carried out is understandable – it would be impossible to do the job in the modern business world otherwise. However, it can lead to frustration on the part of senior managers of the audit clients who wish to take a robust approach to fraud in their business. Very often it must seem to them that the external auditors are not interested in any problems that come in below the audit materiality threshold.

An example of this was shown to me by Teresa during our interview. Teresa is a very experienced internal auditor in the UK public sector who has been committed to taking a zero tolerance approach to fraud in all the organisations in which she has worked. She made the following comments during our interview for this book in response to a question I asked her about whether the external auditors, even today, are really focusing upon fraud and fraud risk in its broadest element:

> I would probably say that in my last two organisations it's been very minimal. Probably they had more focus when I was working for the local authority although the extent of their interest there was more on the national fraud initiative and the data matching exercise undertaken. They wanted to make sure that, you know, we were doing our matches and we'd kind of signed and sealed the paperwork because they were in charge of it. But really they weren't that interested in the nitty-gritty of the frauds and on any

aspects of it in fact, unless the fraud was over their materiality limit which, I think, was about £10,000 then. Now, some of the frauds we were looking at were over this level but others . . . well, you couldn't quantify them because of course there were hardly any records but you know things like parking services, for example, I'm sure you could have been talking about hundreds of thousands of pounds potentially there. But because you couldn't substantiate it, you knew they really weren't that interested. I think it's very similar in the healthcare organisation that I'm in now. I think the external auditors now are not really interested . . . I'd say they're not interested at all in the fraud side.

Reasonable assurance

There is one final point to make before we look at internal auditing. External audits should be planned and performed to provide "reasonable assurance" only that the financial statements as a whole are free from material misstatements. There is no guarantee that a clean audit report means that there has been no fraud in an organisation during the time period that has been the subject of the audit. Even a well planned and executed audit might miss something, both major and minor. This is an important caveat when looking at an issue such as fraud which, as we have seen, is often carried out by directors and managers, those at the top in business, or else by staff who have worked for many years in the organisation – managers and staff in other words who know very well how the systems and controls work and so can conceal the fraud and mislead the auditors. Fraud is hidden and it is difficult to detect. In my experience, trying to bring a successful negligence claim against an external audit firm for failing to uncover fraud is seldom easy.

Internal auditing

Introduction

Internal auditing involves very different responsibilities, reporting lines and scope of work to those discussed above relating to the external audit. An internal audit is carried out to assist management and add value to the business by improving the performance of controls, risk management and governance processes across the organisation.

The key aspects of internal auditing are set out below, again from a fraud perspective.

Definitions

The Institute of Internal Auditors ("IIA")[7] defines an internal audit as:

> An independent, objective assurance and consulting activity designed to add value and improve an organisation's operations. It helps an organisation accomplish its objectives by bringing a systematic, disciplined approach to evaluate and improve the effectiveness of risk management, control and governance processes.

The IIA goes on to set out the responsibilities of internal auditors so far as fraud is concerned as follows:

> Internal auditors should have sufficient knowledge to identify indicators of fraud but they are not expected to have the expertise of a person whose prime responsibility is preventing and detecting fraud.

The IIA implemented a new standard in 2009 that requires internal auditors to consider fraud formally when planning their work, as follows:

Internal auditors must consider the probability of significant errors, fraud, non-compliance, and other exposures when developing the engagement objectives.

Internal audit essentials

Once again the definitions give a flavour of what internal auditing is all about. They point to a number of the key characteristics of internal auditing that are important in understanding how effective such an audit might be in preventing and detecting fraud. These are discussed below.

- There is no legal requirement in most jurisdictions for commercial organisations to have a dedicated internal audit function.

- Most internal auditors are employed by the same organisation that they are auditing (this is not always the case, however, and organisations may choose to outsource some or all of their internal audit requirements to third party accountancy firms). Because of this it is sometimes difficult for internal auditors to demonstrate their independence from operational managers and executives such as the CEO and the CFO. The independence of the internal audit function should be clearly set out in the Audit Charter and in reporting lines to the audit committee – see below.

- In contrast to the external audit, the scope of internal auditing is very broad. The definition hints at this by referring to work done in the areas of risk management, control and governance. Also, internal auditors are able to carry out internal consulting assignments in addition to basic assurance work. In fact, all areas of the business are within their scope of work. As an example, modern "operational" auditing would look to include in the planning process all activities associated with the main commercial markets of the operation (production, sales, after-sales support, service provision etc.) together with the major support departments that contribute to the well-being of the organisation as a whole (procurement, human resources, information technology etc.).

- The internal audit department needs to be independent if it is to achieve its objectives and add value to the business, just as we saw for the external audit. In particular, the internal auditors need to be independent of executive management and departmental heads within the organisation. There are two ways of achieving this. First, the reporting lines of internal audit should be to the audit committee, a committee which according to governance best practice should comprise independent non-executive directors only. Crucially, neither the CEO nor the CFO should be members of the audit committee. Secondly, the independence of the internal audit function should be set out in the Audit Charter, which is then signed off by the audit committee. The Audit Charter should set out in writing the key principle that internal auditors can look at anything and everything in the organisation and that it is for the Head of Internal Audit to determine the audit plan and scope of work. The Charter should provide direction as to the extent of the fraud prevention and detection work that is expected of the internal audit department and the resources that are to be allocated to this area of work.

- Internal audits, like external audit, result in reports which are opinions based upon the evidence found during the course of the audit work. Unlike the external audit report, these are for internal consumption – they will go typically to the department that was the subject of the audit, to executive management and to the audit committee.

Should internal auditors discover fraud?

There is an assumption in many of the organisations that I have worked in and which do possess an internal audit function, that the internal auditors will uncover fraud if it is there. This is a dangerous assumption. Certainly, as the definition from the IIA makes clear, it is not the prime responsibility of internal auditors to prevent and detect fraud. Fraud is hidden and is therefore difficult to detect. Without carrying out specific anti-fraud audits it is extremely unlikely that routine internal audit work will uncover any of the fraud schemes that might exist in an organisation.

From time to time in my career I have worked on projects jointly with members of the internal audit department of the organisation that has engaged me. Some of these have been fraud investigation assignments, some more general business consultancy work. Whenever I work with internal auditors, I am keen to find out if their responsibilities as set out in the Audit Charter extend to specific anti-fraud work. If they do, then my view is that the Head of Internal Audit needs to have three things in place to enable his or her department to discharge these responsibilities:

- First, a budget that includes some proactive fraud auditing assignments – that is to say, specific time set aside in the internal audit plan during which the auditors will look to uncover fraud in high-risk areas of the business if it is there;

- Secondly, some specialist training in fraud detection and investigation for the internal audit team in order to make them aware of the "indicators of fraud"; and

- Thirdly, access to modern fraud detection tools – computer-assisted audit techniques or so-called "data mining" software in particular. We will come back to this in Chapter 8 when looking at fraud deterrence and detection.

One way of increasing anti-fraud expertise in the internal audit department as a whole is to recruit a specialist. Financial services institutions and public sector bodies in the UK often do this in order to enable them to respond better to external fraud threats from organised crime gangs or benefit cheats. They will take on experienced investigators, sometimes ex-police officers or otherwise former Inland Revenue tax inspectors.

An increasingly popular alternative is to recruit a Certified Fraud Examiner – the ACFE provides an accredited course with an examination and the resulting qualification is highly respected both in the US and around the world. The advantage of recruiting a Certified Fraud Examiner is that he or she will have expertise particularly in indicators of internal fraud.

If the Audit Charter does not specifically include fraud-related work in its remit, then the directors and managers need to understand the limitations of traditional audit techniques in fighting fraud. We will look briefly at what these are before turning to a different, more modern approach to fraud that has been developed and set out in the auditing standards. These standards contain requirements for external auditors but in my view they can be adopted with benefit by internal auditors also as we will see.

Limitations of traditional audit techniques

Many companies place too much reliance on audit as a key control against fraud. Directors and managers need to appreciate that traditional audit techniques are of limited effectiveness in preventing and detecting fraud. There are two main reasons for this, discussed below.

Poor understanding of fraud risk

The first reason is quite simple and relates to the basic fraud equation. As we have seen, fraud results from a combination of motive and opportunity. Traditional auditing looks at half of this equation only, whilst largely ignoring the other half. Opportunity is certainly examined through audit review, analysis and testing of internal controls. However, in most audits the possible motives of fraudsters are simply not focused on at all. This is a serious weakness and it means that behavioural "red flags" and other warning signs that might point to the existence of fraud will often be missed as a result.

Internal auditors certainly need to be aware of the various pressures and motives that can lead to fraud. As we have seen, the IIA specifically states that they should have sufficient knowledge to identify indicators of fraud. As we saw in Chapter 3, there are many reasons why people commit fraud but the research of criminologists like Dr Cressey conclude that some of these are more important than others. It is essential that auditors are aware of the Fraud Triangle and other key pieces of research that are set out in that Chapter in order to be capable of detecting fraud. Situations vary of course but it is the behavioural "red flags" that are of real importance here. These are general indicators arising from the actions and attitudes of an individual that suggest, not that he or she is a fraudster, but that he or she is a high fraud risk. The auditor will then need to spend time looking at the particular circumstances involved. To summarise, the key behavioural red flags arising out of the research of criminologists and the work carried out by the ACFE are as follows:

- An individual who is living beyond their means;

- Someone who is experiencing financial difficulties;

- An individual that exhibits sudden and noticeable changes in behaviour or lifestyle patterns; and

- Someone who continually bad-mouths the company and its management and is showing obvious signs of being dissatisfied with his or her job.

Audit testing based on small sample sizes

The second reason why traditional auditing has proved to be largely ineffectual in preventing and detecting fraud relates to the methodology that auditors use to test controls. There are a number of factors here. First, auditors often test controls in what might be described as a limited and static way. More audit time is allocated to looking at how controls are working in practice rather than to considering the adequacy of the design of the controls in terms of managing risk. Then there is often a low awareness of fraud risk amongst audit teams. Also, as we have seen, controls can be overridden by management or circumvented by collusion. Finally and most importantly, audit testing of the effectiveness of controls is based upon samples.

The use of samples is an operational necessity for all audit teams because of the sheer volume of transactions in most businesses today. It is impossible to look at them all so auditors will pick a number of items out of the whole population that is under review. This is known as sampling. The sample sizes are invariably small (often being less than 5% of the number of items in the population under review). Although the laws of probability enable auditors using statistical sampling methods to extrapolate their conclusions from work on samples over the whole population with a nominated confidence level, the assurance that can be given on fraud risk from such a testing methodology is extremely limited. For example, consider an audit of expense claims. There may well be thousands of such claims made in a year in a reasonably large organisation and yet the audit sample selected for testing is likely to be less than one hundred of the actual expense claims made. In such circumstances, it becomes purely a matter of chance, of coincidence, if a fraudulent expense claim is included in the sample.

There are alternative audit approaches. Think of how much more effective the audit of expense claims would be from a fraud perspective if data mining software was used. We discuss data mining in Chapter 8. Its great advantage from a fraud audit perspective is that data mining software enables every expense claim made during the period under review to be interrogated against pre-determined risk criteria. This immediately brings greater assurance either that fraudulent claims will be discovered or else that there are indeed no such fraudulent expense claims submitted in the year. Directors and managers should be aware that data mining is a much more powerful method of detecting fraud than is placing reliance on traditional, sample-based testing.

The use of tailored fraud detection methods in high-risk areas forms part of a powerful alternative approach to fraud auditing, pioneered by the auditing authorities in the US in 2002 in the wake of the Enron and WorldCom scandals in particular and taken up also in the international accounting standards. We look at this new approach below.

SAS 99: Considerations of Fraud in a Financial Statement Audit

Introduction

Statement on Auditing Standards No.99: Consideration of Fraud in a Financial Statement Audit ("SAS 99")[8] is an auditing statement issued by the Auditing Standards Board of the American Institute of Certified Public Accountants ("AICPA") in October 2002. It was issued partly in response to the series of high-profile fraud scandals around the turn of the century involving large US corporates: Enron, WorldCom, Adelphia and Tyco. These were essentially accounting frauds, involving manipulation of the financial statements by senior executives within these large corporations. There was great concern in the investor community in the US that these frauds had not been uncovered by external audit.

SAS 99 puts significant new requirements on the work of external auditors regarding fraud and it increases the emphasis that should be placed on fraud risk during an audit, as follows:

> In planning and performing the audit to reduce audit risk to an acceptably low level, the auditor should consider the risks of material misstatements in the financial statements due to fraud.

It is important to say that there has been no change in the auditor's responsibilities as a result. The auditor still does not have responsibility for detecting fraud. The audit responsibility remains to plan and perform the work so that there is a reasonable chance that material misstatements in the financial statements will be uncovered.

SAS 99 has become extremely influential for external auditors elsewhere in the world too. The International Standard on Auditing 240: The Auditor's Responsibility to Consider Fraud in an Audit of Financial Statements ("ISA 240")[9] was first published as an exposure draft in 2003 and essentially adopts the same approach as that developed in the US under SAS 99.

What SAS 99 and ISA 240 say about fraud auditing

These are very important standards in terms of best practices for auditors to follow in order to have reasonable prospects of success in preventing and detecting fraud. They are external auditing standards and they impose requirements on all external auditors in terms of how they carry out their work. However, in my view the key steps in these standards, which are set out below, combine into an effective framework that can be adapted by internal auditors also.

The standards set out a powerful five-stage approach for auditors in planning and performing their work to ensure that fraud risk is adequately addressed. The five components have wide application as best practices to manage fraud risk and they are addressed at various stages of this book. They are summarised here below:

- An increased emphasis on professional scepticism throughout. This means in particular the auditor adopting a thorough, questioning approach, refusing to be fobbed off with incomplete explanations and always being willing to ask the difficult questions if they need to be asked.

- The audit team should brainstorm how fraud could occur in their clients' business. In other words the external auditors are required to construct a fraud risk profile, something that I encourage every organisation to do internally as a matter of best practice.

- The auditors should discuss fraud risk with the management and the departmental heads of their clients. It is important that fraud risk is addressed openly rather than being swept under the carpet if the deterrence factor that was introduced at the start of the book in context of the Fraud Risk Management Framework is to be maximised. This is discussed further in Chapter 8.

- Tailored fraud detection measures (e.g. data mining software) should be used in those areas of the audit where the risk of fraud is considered to be high. Again, data mining is addressed in detail in Chapter 8.

- The auditors should recognise that the risk of management override of controls exists in all companies. This is a truism but it is important always to realise that often the greatest fraud risk in any organisation resides at the top with the directors and senior managers.

Commentary

These key ideas incorporated in SAS 99 and ISA 240 provide a powerful framework for auditors to fight fraud effectively. The standards are designed for external auditors and must be followed by them. They provide assurance to directors and managers that the external auditors are taking the fraud issues seriously in their work.

However, I believe that each of the five principles set out above can be adapted for internal audit purposes also with much benefit. As an example, the brainstorming of fraud risk by external auditors is no doubt useful but it is very likely that a more informed risk profile would come out of a brainstorming session from within the organisation and involving the internal auditors. After all, the people who should have the best knowledge of the practical risks in a business are always the managers and staff who work day to day in that business, rather than outsiders however well informed.

The role of the audit committee

Introduction

The concept of the audit committee is now well established in many countries around the world as a crucial component of good corporate governance. Most codes of governance devote significant attention to the role of the audit committee, including the UK's Corporate Governance Code. The SOX significantly enhanced its importance in US companies and the 8th Directive on company law introduced a statutory requirement in 2006 that all listed companies in the EU must have audit committees.

There are now many similarities in the role and composition of the audit committee in listed companies. First, the audit committee is a committee of the board to which responsibilities are delegated, which are normally set out in a charter. Also, the committee should now comprise independent non-executive directors only, at least one of whom should either be a financial expert or should have recent and relevant financial experience. This means that executives such as the CFO and CEO should not be members of the audit committee. The numbers on the audit committee normally range from three to six. Finally and crucially for good corporate governance, both the external and the internal auditors will have reporting lines into the audit committee.

The precise responsibilities of an audit committee may vary from jurisdiction to jurisdiction, but there are now many similarities about the role. Generally, audit committee responsibilities will include the monitoring, review and oversight of the following:

* the integrity of the financial statements;

* the financial reporting process;

* the effectiveness of the company's internal control and risk management systems;

* the performance of the internal audit function;

* the hiring, performance and independence of the external auditors;

* any arrangements for the auditor to supply non-audit services; and

* the whistle-blowing arrangements.

Role of the audit committee in the fight against fraud

The audit committee has two roles when it comes to fraud prevention and detection, one general the other more specific.

To take the specific role first, the audit committee (or the board or senior management team where no audit committee exists) is an important component of the organisation's Fraud Risk Management Framework and it should be committed to a proactive approach. There are different aspects to this. First, the committee must understand what management is doing to prevent, deter and detect fraud. It should evaluate management's measures to fight fraud: the identification of fraud risks; the implementation of the anti-fraud measures identified; and the creation of the appropriate tone at the top. Active oversight by the committee helps to reinforce a zero tolerance approach to fraud. It can also serve as a deterrent to any member of the senior management team who might be thinking of engaging in fraudulent activity. It is vital that the committee receives regular reports on the status of reported or alleged frauds. Secondly, the audit committee should understand how internal and external strategies address fraud risk. The committee should make use of internal auditors or other designated personnel to monitor fraud risks. It will also discuss with the external auditor the auditor's planned approach to fraud detection as part of the financial statement audit. Relations between the audit committee and the external auditors should always be conducted on a frank, open and honest basis.

Now turning to the general role, we need to look first at the broad context. The responsibilities set out above together comprise a tough and wide-ranging remit for the audit committee. In order to succeed, it is first absolutely necessary that the audit committee is properly constituted according to the requirements of the particular jurisdiction concerned. Independence and competence are prerequisites here. However, compliance with the law and regulations might make the audit committee look good on paper but it will be no guarantee that the committee will operate in practice as a meaningful mechanism to promote good governance. In order to be effective the audit committee must exercise proper scrutiny and oversight in the areas listed above. This means, first of all, that the committee members are prepared to ask tough, probing and relevant questions. Secondly, the committee should be focused on playing a proactive role and not simply always reacting to what is brought to them by either management or auditors, external and internal.

Examples of poor performance by audit committees

Introduction
The audit committee is a very important governance control. To be a strong control, there are three essential requirements that the audit committee must have in order to be able to discharge properly its oversight role: strong leadership; independence from the executives; and reliable information. Like any control, audit committees do not always operate effectively in practice. There have been a number of high profile corporate scandals where the performance of the audit committee has been shown to be sub-optimal to say the least. We look at two of the most famous examples of audit committee failures below: the cases of Hollinger International and Enron. These examples clearly show that when one or more of the three requirements set out above are missing, the risk of senior executive fraud increases because the audit committee is unable to carry out its job properly.

Example 1 – Hollinger International
First, let us look at the case of Hollinger International, the Chicago-based publishing company that used to be headed, as Chairman and CEO, by the media mogul Conrad Black.

In 2007 Mr Black and two former executive officers of Hollinger International, together with the company's former corporate counsel, were convicted for their roles in the multi-million dollar fraud against investors in Hollinger International (another former executive, David Radler, pleaded guilty to one count of mail fraud in return for testimony against Mr Black and the others). Mr Black was found guilty of three counts of mail fraud and one count of obstruction of justice and acquitted of nine other charges. He was sentenced to serve six and a half years in prison. The case centred on conflicts of interest. The prosecution alleged that Mr Black and the other executives accused improperly diverted some $60 million from transactions concerning the sales of various group publications in the 1990s to themselves by dressing them up as "non-compete payments". The prosecution asserted that this money should properly have gone to Hollinger International and the shareholders.

Hollinger International's audit committee appears to have exercised poor oversight of the related-party transactions at the heart of the case which is surprising given how strong the committee looked on paper. It comprised three independent non-executive directors, all of whom were seasoned business leaders with experience of serving on the boards of major US corporations. The committee met several times each year. However, the trial testimony, together with the investigation report commissioned by the Hollinger Board[10] revealed a number of problems in the way that the committee functioned. First, it came out at the trial that although all three audit committee members were financially literate, no committee member was considered to be an audit committee financial expert. Secondly, the committee meetings were poorly organised: agendas were not always prepared and if they were, they were prepared by management; one audit committee member testified that members did not always receive papers or information before a meeting. Finally, the audit committee chair testified that he "trusted" management and that he relied "on the members of management who dealt with the Audit Committee to advise us of anything that should be brought to our attention". When the crucial related party transactions were raised by the executives the evidence at trial was that they were dealt with quickly by the committee, with little questioning and no requests for supporting documentation or further information.

Mr Black has always denied the fraud charges and at the time of writing he has successfully overturned on appeal two of the three mail fraud counts. The whole affair has been very damaging to Hollinger International and to the individuals concerned. It appears that a number of weaknesses of process together with a lack of rigorous challenge and scrutiny of the actions of the executives meant that Hollinger's audit committee proved to be an ineffective control. As a result, a key component of governance oversight was largely absent in this case.

Example 2 – Enron

Secondly, let us return to the Enron example. In Chapter 5 we looked at some of the key aspects of the scandal in a review that I described as "Enron by the numbers". We will repeat the exercise here but this time looking specifically at the role of Enron's audit and compliance committee ("audit committee"). We focus on some numbers that help to reveal that the Enron audit committee provides another very good example of the "illusion of competent independence" that Mr Buffett has cautioned against. The consequence for Enron was that it was the passivity of its audit committee which enabled the executives to continue their risky accounting policies.

Enron by the numbers - Part 2

- **6 and 2.** Each of Enron's main board committees looked strong on paper and this applies particularly to the audit committee. The number six refers to the number of audit committee members in 2001. All were independent non-executive directors and three were non-US residents. The Enron audit committee also looked strong in terms of competence as it possessed more financial expertise than many corporate audit committees at the time. The number 2 refers to the fact that two of its members had formal accounting training and professional experience: one was a former accounting professor and the other was a qualified accountant. What could possibly go wrong with the Enron accounting, auditing, internal controls and risk management processes with this strong audit committee in place? With the benefit of hindsight, this seems to be a question loaded with irony. It is important not to ignore the practical difficulties of outside directors who are always forced to rely extensively on information from management. Certainly, in testimony at the various hearings and trials it is clear that the non-executives felt that they had been misled by management and that the controls they put in place broke down. Nevertheless, there were warning signs about the performance of the Enron audit committee if anyone had thought to look harder. In a number of key respects the committee's performance only served to add to the Enron corporate governance illusion.

- **16.** This number relates to the length of time that the Chairman of the audit committee had served the Enron board in this capacity – from 1985, a total of 16 years. Although a widely respected former accounting professor, it might be thought that this is simply too long for the same individual to be in that role and that his independence might have been compromised as a result. As an indicator, the benchmark for "independence" in the UK Corporate Governance Code is nine years. Although there was no such guidance in the US at this time, it is always good practice to freshen up committees from time to time by bringing in new faces and replacing the Chairman periodically, as it is likely to instil new methods and fresh thinking. Enron certainly might have benefitted from this.

- **0.** This relates to the number of times that the audit committee ever challenged the executives after being briefed on a number of occasions by the auditors, Andersen, that Enron was using high-risk accounting policies. This is, in my view, truly remarkable. No committee member objected to the high-risk policies, or requested a second opinion or demanded a more prudent approach. Despite his long tenure the Chairman rarely had any contact with Andersen outside of official committee or board meetings. Clearly, the audit committee and the board relied upon Andersen, who provided a clean audit report year after year. But the committee and indeed all of the directors had been put on notice by Andersen that Enron was engaged in complex transactions, operating at times right at the edge in terms of its treatment of a number of highly significant accounting issues (such as the valuation methodologies and the off-balance sheet structures that we looked at in Chapter 5). As the Senate Subcommittee looking into the role of Enron's board of directors in the company's collapse has concluded:

  > But a failure by Andersen to object does not preclude our finding that the Enron board, with Andersen's concurrence, knowingly allowed Enron to use high risk accounting and failed in its fiduciary duty to ensure the company engaged in responsible financial reporting. (Permanent Subcommittee on Investigations, 2002, p. 24)[11]

- **0.** Nowhere is the passivity of the Enron audit committee members (and of the other board directors too for that matter) better illustrated than in their reaction to a seven-page letter addressed to Mr Lay in August 2001, setting out in detail a number of alleged irregularities in the company's accounting practices. The letter famously began by asking the question: "Has Enron become a risky place to work?"[12] Although written anonymously, the author of the letter subsequently made herself known to Mr Lay. She was Sherron Watkins, a certified public accountant who worked as a Vice President of Corporate Development at Enron. Ms Watkins has since become the most famous whistle-blower in the Enron case. She wrote her letter to Mr Lay in the immediate aftermath of Mr Skilling's resignation and departure from the company. Ms Watkins subsequently met Mr Lay face-to-face in his office to take him through the concerns set out in her letter which centred firmly on the company's accounting problems and what she saw as its very aggressive accounting. She warned Mr Lay in the letter of her concerns that Enron "will implode in a wave of accounting scandals" and that "the business world will consider past successes as nothing but an elaborate accounting hoax". Typically, Mr Lay did nothing. What is more surprising is that the Enron board did nothing either. The letter was brought to the outside directors' attention in October 2001 during presentations by Enron's outside legal counsel, Vinson & Elkins, first during an audit committee meeting and then during the full board meeting. Although the lawyers down-played the significance of the letter, indicating that their preliminary investigation of the employee's concerns had found nothing worth further investigation, the passivity of the board's reaction is noteworthy. The final number, again a zero, relates to the fact that not a single director (and certainly none of the audit committee members) was concerned enough to enquire of the lawyers who the author was or to ask to see a copy of the letter itself.

Summary – Five Key Learning Points for Directors and Managers

Controls are an essential component of the fight against fraud. In the next two Chapters we will look in detail at the various specific anti-fraud prevention and detection controls that are available to manage the risks. But before we do so there are a number of important lessons here for directors and managers in terms of establishing a robust control framework throughout their organisations.

✓ Make the commitment to create a transparent, controls-conscious organisation. This will require both money and resources but also, if it is to succeed, the emotional investment of those at the top.

✓ Always be vigilant and aware of what is happening in the workplace and of the customs and practices that may have built up over time. If this includes conduct that is inappropriate and/or detrimental to the success of the organisation, then take steps to stop the practices concerned and change the behaviour of employees.

✓ Make sure that controls are designed and updated so that they remain proportionate to the changing risks in the business. Also, have monitoring and review systems in place to confirm that the controls are actually operating in accordance with how they were designed.

✓ Be aware of the five control frameworks developed in the last 20 years. Choose to adopt the one that is most appropriate to the needs of your business or, in the case of small or medium-sized businesses, the parts of one of the frameworks that can be taken up with benefit by the business.

✓ Do not place undue reliance on traditional audits to prevent and detect fraud. Instead be aware of the more proactive approach required by the new auditing standards. Make sure that the external auditors are complying with these requirements and consider incorporating this new approach into the internal audit charter also. Ensure that the audit committee is both competent and independent but also that it is well led, proactive and is prepared to scrutinise and challenge the actions of executives when required.

7 Prevention

Fraud Awareness Quiz – Question 7
What anti-fraud controls and techniques does your organisation currently use to prevent fraud from occurring?

A question of black or white

I am sitting in a meeting room at the headquarters of one of the largest retailing groups in the UK, which is situated in the West End of London. It is October 1996. I have been working here for two weeks now, so this is just about the mid-point of my assignment. I am here to review the group's purchasing and payments systems on behalf of Touche Ross forensic services and the Finance Director has set us a challenge. He believes that the controls over these systems are very tight and he has commissioned us to test them out. In particular, he does not think that there are any weaknesses in them from a fraud perspective. So, this is our challenge – as forensic accountants and fraud experts, can we find any faults with his "fraud-proof systems"? Actually, it is a challenge that I have taken up personally because I have already told the Finance Director that he is wrong – there is no such thing as an internal control system that is guaranteed to be fraud-proof. We shall see – there is a pint of beer resting on the outcome. I have to report back to the Finance Director with my findings and recommendations by the end of the month. Not long at all.

I am coming to the end of a meeting with two of the key managers that I need to speak to on this project: the group's financial controller and the team leader of the cashiers and payments section in accounts. It has been a good meeting and I have learnt more about the company's systems as a result. However, there is one nagging issue from my personal point of view that is starting to concern me. The Finance Director's confidence in the strength of the controls over purchases and payments seems to be well-placed. Could this really be the first company I have ever seen with fraud-proof systems?

The meeting has served to confirm what my own tests have already shown, namely that company systems are well designed and are being operated effectively. There are strong internal control frameworks in place over both purchasing and payments with the following all contributing to reducing fraud risk: an accurate and up-to-date systems and procedures manual; well established and respected segregation of duties; authorisation levels that are understood and followed by all relevant staff; a strong supplier approval process; a modern purchase ordering system; a regular bank reconciliation procedure; strong physical controls over cheque books, petty cash etc.; and proper training for all staff.

The meeting is drawing to a close and I begin to summarise the main points arising. I always do this by asking a number of leading questions, designed to make sure that I have understood correctly what has been said to me in the meeting. During the course of these questions, I ask the team leader of the payments section to confirm my understanding of how the authorised cheque signing process works. Like many large organisations, this company operates with dual cheque signatory controls: a category A list of signatures and a category B list of signatures. The category A list comprises all the directors and senior executives of the company, whilst the category B list is made up of the various departmental heads and team leaders. Smaller cheques (that is to say, amounts below £10,000 in value in the case of this company) only require the signature of one individual on the B list by way of approval. However any cheque payments of £10,000 or more have to be counter-signed by someone on the A list also. The B list signatory would always sign the cheque first, thereby showing that they have satisfied themselves that everything is in order.

My question to the team leader is designed to make sure that I have understood the cheque payments system correctly: "So, as I understand it, having received the appropriate signatures from individuals on the category B list for all of the large cheques to go out on a particular day, you then take the cheques to one of the approved directors and senior executives for the second signature. And the cheques could be given to any of the individuals on the category A list for this purpose. Is this correct?" The answer is as follows: "Yes that's right . . . apart from those cheques that have to be signed on a Friday afternoon of course." I am genuinely surprised at this and ask what is so special about Friday afternoons? "Well, with the weekend coming up we always make sure everything is ready so that we can leave right on time on a Friday. So, we would never ask Mr White to sign a cheque on a Friday afternoon because he always has some sort of query, asking to see supporting documentation or questioning the amount or something. No, we would always give the cheques to be signed on Friday afternoons to Mr Black if he was around." "And why would you do that?" I ask. The answer comes back: "Because everybody knows that Mr Black never asks any questions at all – he is always happy to sign the cheques we give him straight away. And that is just what you want on a Friday afternoon."

So, not an earth-shattering revelation, not a "game-changer" so far as the group and its controls are concerned. I don't leap up and punch the air. But I do smile quietly to myself. I am starting to feel a little better now because this discussion has confirmed that the group systems are not fraud-proof. I will have something interesting and important to write about in the report after all – about how even well designed anti-fraud prevention controls can be undermined by a lack of awareness of risk at all levels in the organisation. The threat of pseudo-collusion is a very real one in this situation. It is apparently well known that Mr Black will sign any cheque that is put in front of him and a fraudster might be able to take advantage of this. So, the group will benefit from the report. And, I will enjoy that pint of beer from the Finance Director also.

Introduction

When working with Touche Ross in the early 1990s, my colleagues and I used to describe ourselves not so much as forensic accountants but as international fraud investigators. That is what we were paid to do, to go into organisations and investigate what had gone wrong with a view to helping our clients to recover the money that they had lost because of the fraud. It was fundamentally a reactive business at the time – analytical, "identify the culprit", litigation and recovery focused, involving intensive and detailed work with long hours always guaranteed, success never guaranteed! It was absolutely the best job in the world.

Times change and the example above relates to one of the first anti-fraud control reviews that I carried out, looking to assess the strengths and vulnerabilities of the system to fraud threats. I have done many more since. Fraud still happens of course and when it does it will be investigated. However, many more organisations today understand that it is better for their reputations and their bank balances to take a more proactive stance against fraud. Consequently, corporate attention has focused in recent years more on the "upstream" areas of prevention and deterrence in the Fraud Framework that we saw in Chapter 1. Of course, forensic accountants are very pleased to assist in this area too. We always were in fact, it was simply that back in the 1990s very few organisations thought that fraud would ever happen to them and so they were not prepared to pay accountancy firms large fees for advice on how to stop a problem that would never materialise. The retailer I refer to in the story above was exceptional for the time in that they asked us to review their systems specifically with a view to identifying any fraud weaknesses. But they displayed a touch of arrogance too. The Finance Director really did think that his systems were so good that it was impossible for fraud to happen in the company!

This Chapter takes a forensic approach to the critical area of fraud prevention. We pick up the key control concepts reviewed in the last Chapter and examine them here from two distinct perspectives. First, we look at the broad framework, the generic controls such as segregation of duties that provide the essential foundations for an effective fraud risk management strategy. As part of this we look at the main methods that fraudsters use to get around generic controls and try to conceal their crimes. Then we focus specifically on those controls that are designed with the purpose of preventing fraud from occurring. There is in fact a "menu" of such controls. It is important that directors and managers are aware of the menu so that they can select from it the most appropriate controls for their own particular situation. An important consideration in these decisions is always a cost/benefit analysis. Controls cost time, effort and money to implement. We make use of the ACFE's extensive surveys and analysis work carried out for the 2008 RTTN[1] and the 2010 RTTNs[2] seeking to demonstrate which controls actually work most effectively in practice. The results are used to inform the discussion throughout. The Chapter ends with my own 5-Point Fraud Prevention Plan, something that I always recommend to delegates on my courses as a low-cost, cogent and proportionate approach that will benefit most organisations. So, there is much essential information here for directors and managers who are looking to develop an effective control framework in their organisations.

Before we look at the controls in detail, we should return to the Quiz question and see how the delegates answered it in terms of the controls that they use in practice to prevent fraud from happening.

Answers to the Quiz

Fraud Awareness Quiz – Question 7
What anti-fraud controls and techniques does your organisation currently use to prevent fraud from occurring?

This question in the Quiz asks the delegates to consider the specific anti-fraud prevention controls that their own organisation uses. It is an opportunity for them to showcase the good practices that they have developed. I have to say that the question is almost always answered poorly. Sometimes it is answered very poorly indeed.

The answers that I receive at the start of the discussion, those that are written down by delegates, almost always refer to a number of well-known preventative controls in business: segregation of duties, authorisation limits, management review and access controls. These answers are in no sense wrong – they all refer to controls that play an important part in the fight against fraud. But they are disappointing nevertheless. These are generic controls that serve a number of broad business purposes and are not fraud-specific. If the organisations represented in the room relied only on these controls to prevent fraud, then they would in all likelihood be at considerable risk.

Also, these answers seem to me to be routine, almost standard responses to the question. As such they serve to confirm something that I have mentioned earlier, namely that fraud is a risk that often does not receive the detailed analysis and evaluation that it properly merits. Certainly, there has been very little awareness shown by delegates on my courses of the wide range of specific anti-fraud controls that are available to help directors and managers to deal with the threats. They appear to think that fraud risk is covered adequately by the generic controls. This is a dangerous assumption.

It is only when I press the delegates a little, encouraging them to be more specific, that I begin to see evidence that some of them at least are aware of a number of the specific measures available to reduce fraud risk. One observation coming out of the discussions is that a number of the key controls mentioned appear to be business-sector specific and are not used by organisations generally. Directors and managers need to be aware of the anti-fraud controls that have been shown to work in practice, perhaps in business sectors different from their own, so that they can look to make use of them in their own businesses. Specific anti-fraud controls that are mentioned in these discussions are:

- **Mandatory vacations.** Delegates from financial services firms in particular are well aware of the added assurance provided when organisations make it a requirement that employees, especially those in high-risk positions, not only take all of their holiday entitlement every year but must spend at least 10 consecutive working days on vacation each year. Other business sectors are noticeably less aware of this control.

- **Staff vetting.** Staff vetting is mentioned frequently as a control, although I have an important caveat to make here. From the discussions, I can only observe that many of the checks that are carried out in practice by businesses on prospective new members of staff lack rigour from an anti-fraud perspective. I say this because around half of the organisations represented on my courses carry out neither criminal record checks nor credit reference checks on potential new hires. These are the most important checks if fraud risk is to be minimised. My conclusion from the discussions is that these key checks are largely confined in practice to financial services firms and other regulated entities and are not used in other business sectors.

- **Audit committees.** These are frequently mentioned in discussions as an anti-fraud control, mainly by delegates from larger companies or from the public sector.

- **Internal audit.** Internal audit features often in these detailed discussions. However, again I have an important caveat to make here. I have seen little evidence on my courses of an understanding, even amongst auditors, of how to target the audit work so that it has a meaningful fraud focus.

- **Employee support programmes.** From time to time, delegates refer to the importance of an organisation having programmes in place to support those employees who experience problems with their finances, or develop addictions to alcohol or drugs etc., or have other difficulties which might affect their performance at work. This is an important and perceptive observation, showing good awareness of key aspects of behaviour in the light of the Fraud Triangle and the results of research into the motives of fraudsters that we saw in Chapter 3.

Each of these controls is examined in more detail later.

However, the most significant observation coming out of these discussions is that the really important anti-fraud controls, those that have been shown to be the most effective in practice in terms of reducing losses, are hardly ever mentioned by delegates. There seems to be a lack of awareness of what works here! At this stage, I always point out to delegates that I am surprised that they have not mentioned three controls in particular.

- **Training programmes.** First, I ask the delegates to consider the importance of training. My initial observation is that no one has ever mentioned in the subsequent discussion the broader context of business ethics here. There seems to be very little if any awareness of the relevance of ethical training programmes in a fraud context. Specific anti-fraud awareness training is different of course. Although it is rarely given as an answer to the question, it is clear from the discussions that many delegates are aware of its importance – indeed, some organisations even seem to be carrying it out! Raising fraud awareness throughout an organisation is critical if fraud threats are to be minimised and training is essential for this to happen. It is also more than a little surprising that training does not feature more strongly in the answers given that, at the time of taking the Quiz, the delegates are themselves benefiting from this control! As a final observation here, I would say that over the years my delegates have shown little awareness of the importance of culture and of cultural change in preventing fraud. We will examine this further later in the book in Chapter 10 on ethics.

- **Whistle-blowing hotlines.** Next, I ask the delegates to consider the critical area of fraud reporting channels, often described as "whistle-blowing hotlines". This is one of the most important anti-fraud controls, yet the reaction I have had from delegates over the years to the whistle-blowing concept has been mixed at best. One important factor is geography. The Americans that I have worked with, whether those based in the US or attending courses elsewhere, are generally both aware of the importance of whistle-blowing hotlines as an anti-fraud control and very supportive of them. Elsewhere, the reaction has been less favourable. Take the Caribbean for example. Here, I have found delegates to be both sceptical and suspicious of whistle-blowing mechanisms. This no doubt has much to do with the fact that the places that I have worked out there (Trinidad and Tobago and the Bahamas) are essentially small societies. I was very aware whilst working in the Caribbean of the feeling amongst delegates that "everybody knows everybody else" and that it is somehow not right to report on a friend or neighbour. I receive the same sort of reaction from delegates when I work in Gibraltar, again a small society. However, the most negative reactions are almost always from delegates in the UK and from Continental Europe. Many of these delegates don't seem to trust the whistle-blower programmes that their organisations run, whilst most of them think that they don't work anyway! We will discuss whistle-blowing hotlines in detail in the next Chapter but, to return to this question in the Quiz, I think it is very significant that these hotlines feature so infrequently in the answers.

- **Surprise audits.** Finally, no delegate has ever given as an answer to this question the control that has been consistently rated by the ACFE, along with whistle-blowing hotlines, as the most effective type of anti-fraud measure – the "surprise audit". I think that this is remarkable. It could be of course that the delegates consider this to be more of a detective control (or at least a deterrent) than a preventative control and so choose to ignore it for that reason. Certainly, this is arguable and indeed we will look at surprise audits in detail in the next Chapter on detection rather than in this one on prevention. However, I do not think this is the case with my delegates. Rather, I think that it is more a reflection of just how little surprise audits are used in practice by organisations today (with the exception of those in the financial services industry). There is an important lesson for all directors and managers here – surprise audits are an effective but under-used tool in the fight against fraud.

Fraud prevention controls

Introduction

Most organisations rely on a variety of controls and procedures to manage their fraud risks. Very often this is not the result of careful, structured planning, rather it is simply the way that controls within the organisation have evolved and developed over time. This of course comes back to one of the central themes of this book, which is that, for the most effective fraud risk management, organisations should focus first on developing a proper understanding of risk and only then on designing controls that are proportionate and appropriate to the risks.

Sometimes, however, for certain organisations, it is the combination of generic controls and specific anti-fraud measures that can work best, especially when they are well-suited to the corporate culture of the business.

Charles gave me a good illustration of this during our interview. He is not a fraud expert and I spent some time in the interview encouraging him to think of the various ways that the very large US organisation that he used to work for in the 1990s as head of their European Strategy Team actually managed its fraud risk. Once prompted, he came up with a very cogent explanation that serves as a good introduction to the themes of this Chapter. This is what he told me:

> Well, there are good disciplines aren't there? Segregation of duties being an obvious one and I remember clearly that there was a lot of attention on this. We worked very closely with our external auditors to ensure not just that the accounts were true and fair and so forth but that all of our internal procedures were beyond reproach. We did take a lot of note of anything the auditors came up with or suggested. We did have staff officers responsible for finance who would immediately get involved if there was any suspicion or evidence of fraud. Would I say that we had a pro-active programme to avoid fraud in the first place and then detect it and so forth? Probably not, in all honesty. One of the things that I really think, I suspect, helps a lot with the prevention and detection of fraud, prevention particularly, is having a good, strong collegiate type of culture and being very careful about who you hire. That certainly applied in the UK and I think it applied probably in most other locations around the world too. So, I'm told, fraud happened from time to time in that organisation as it probably happens in most organisations but there was I think, certainly in the 1990s when I first joined, there was a real feeling, a real collegiate feeling around the business and I think that is as important as anything. Nobody really felt like an outsider there.

Note the combination of generic controls (segregation of duties) and specific controls (staff vetting) here, but the collegiate culture is the most striking thing. We will return to the key area of culture in Chapter 10 on ethics.

The concept of the control environment

We have seen that the COSO Framework highlights the control environment as being the foundation of all internal control systems. The control environment sets the overall framework of an organisation, providing discipline and structure. Crucially for the issues in this Chapter, it influences the control consciousness of all employees in the workplace. Control environment factors include the integrity, ethical values and competence of the entity's people; management's philosophy and operating style; the way management assigns authority and responsibility, and organises and develops its people; and the attention and direction provided by the board of directors. These factors all combine into the phrase "tone at the top" and it is important to get this right if fraud risk is to be minimised.

Looking at the specific area of fraud risk management, there are a number of overarching factors that an organisation needs to give attention to if it is to succeed in minimising risk. The various controls and techniques to prevent, deter and detect fraud that are set out in this and the next

Chapter will have limited impact unless they are developed within an overall framework of best practice for this particular risk.

Control environment factors from a fraud perspective include: a robust risk management process, with appropriate insurance and fidelity cover; an IT governance framework with, in particular, appropriate levels of security built into it; an internal monitoring system, whether an internal audit function or some form of structured management review, to provide assurance that controls are working as intended; a professional Human Resources function that is respected throughout the organisation; some formal codification of the values, ethics and conduct expected of all people working for the organisation, together with effective communication of this; and a culture that encourages both transparency and accountability.

Key aspects of prevention – generic controls

Overview

The first thing to say here is to repeat a basic but fundamental point, namely that a robust system of internal controls is an essential prerequisite to preventing and deterring fraud successfully in any organisation. There are other important factors also, such as appropriate remuneration and incentive schemes for managers and staff, but strong internal controls are the basic building blocks for an effective anti-fraud framework.

Before examining the specific anti-fraud controls, let us look at some of the broader, more generic controls that businesses rely on every day. Three of the most effective of these generic anti-fraud controls are discussed below before we move on to review some of the main methods the fraudster uses to conceal or otherwise to circumvent these generic controls. In order to have assurance that fraud risk is being well managed, directors and managers need confidence that these three key generic controls are working both efficiently and effectively.

The three most important generic anti-fraud controls are: segregation of duties; authorisation limits; and physical controls over assets and records.

(a) Segregation of duties

Introduction
Segregation of duties is both a key concept of internal control and is itself the most important generic anti-fraud control because it is vital to an organisation's system of checks and balances. Accountants are very familiar with this concept, which traditionally means the separation in each business process of the following responsibilities: custody of assets; record keeping; authorisation; and reconciliation. Ideally, no one person should handle more than one of these responsibilities in a business process. Smaller businesses often find this difficult because of low staff numbers, but it is possible to compensate by including an independent supervisor or manager in the process.

The essential principle behind the segregation of duties concept is that no one person should have absolute autonomy or unfettered powers of decision-making in any area of business. This principle applies of course to day-to-day business transactions. For example, consider the purchasing function. Here, no single employee should have complete control over the ordering of goods, the collection of those goods from the supplier, the subsequent storage of the goods, making payment for those goods, finally organising their despatch from the warehouse and reconciling the accounts. The opportunities for theft and fraud should a manager or employee have autonomy over a number of stages in the purchasing cycle are of course very high.

Segregation at the top too

The importance of segregation of duties in the various business processes is clear to most managers and certainly to auditors. Less well understood is the need for a system of checks and balances right at the top of business also. As we have seen, the need for proper segregation of duties applies equally around the boardroom table as it does in every other working unit in an organisation. Indeed, it plays an important part in modern governance structures. It is why the separation of the offices of Chairman and CEO has always featured so prominently in the UK governance codes. It is why most governance codes and legislation around the world now stress the importance of having independent non-executive directors on the board and on the key board committees (e.g. the audit committee and the remuneration committee) in order to provide a balance to the views of the executives. As with every other aspect of controls, such checks and balances at the governance level provide reasonable assurance only that things will not go wrong around the boardroom table. There is never any certainty in business. As we have seen, Enron had a governance structure that appeared to be perfectly aligned with best governance practices at the time. Although Mr Lay had combined the offices of Chairman and CEO at Enron for over 15 years, he stood down as CEO in February 2001 to allow Mr Skilling, the dynamic executive and long-standing COO at Enron, to be promoted to CEO. It appeared as if corporate governance had in 2001 got even better at Enron. However, Mr Skilling resigned after six months in the job and by the end of the year the company had filed for bankruptcy protection. Once again, we see that appearances can sometimes be deceptive!

Personal fiefdoms

Finally, it is always important to be aware of the dangers associated with "personal fiefdoms" in business. The phrase personal fiefdom is used to describe a situation where a certain individual has attained such a position of power, influence and autonomy in a business unit, or a subsidiary company or a division, either through outstanding results or through force of personality (or a combination of the two), that he or she is able to do pretty well as they please without being subject to even routine checking.

It is interesting to consider the roots of this phrase. The idea of a personal fiefdom refers back to periods in medieval English history when there were great tensions between the King and members of the aristocracy. Typically, certain nobles and barons would try to exercise as much power and control on their own lands and spheres of influence as the King would allow them to. Ultimately of course if the King proved to be weak his authority would be undermined by the actions of these "over-mighty subjects". This is exactly what happened in the fifteenth century in England during the reign of King Henry VI. Henry VI's general weakness as a king was compounded with periods of insanity. This proved to be a disastrous combination for the country as it emboldened certain nobles and led directly to the Wars of the Roses – a 30-year period of sporadic violence over disputed claims to the throne by the aristocratic houses of York and Lancaster. It was also bad news for King Henry VI himself as he lost first his crown and then his life. However, as the influential historian K. B. McFarlane famously said: "It is only under-mighty kings that have over-mighty subjects" (McFarlane, 1973, p.179)[3].

A personal fiefdom was contrary to the normal order of medieval society, which is frequently referred to as "feudal" which was built upon the principle of "servitium debitum" — service owed. Indeed, historians have characterised such fiefdoms by the descriptive phrase "bastard feudalism" because they represented corruptions of the social order and so often led to harmful consequences.

The situation with personal fiefdoms can be very similar in business today. It is for the board of directors to exercise effective control over all areas of the organisation. Where an individual becomes too powerful in any organisation the risks increase significantly and these include fraud risks. The classic example of this is provided by the activities of Mr Leeson during his time as general manager in the small Singapore office of Barings Bank in 1992–95. He became simultaneously head trader and head of the back office settlement operations in Singapore. So, there was an absence of effective segregation of duties and because of this Mr Leeson was able to override and circumvent the bank's controls. This was compounded by the lack of robust management review and oversight of Mr Leeson's operations in Singapore by his superiors elsewhere in the Barings group. There were no doubt many reasons for this but one in particular has significance here. The profits that the Singapore operation appeared to be generating from Mr Leeson's trading activities were becoming significant to the results of the bank as a whole. Consequently, it may be thought that the directors and senior managers lacked the incentive to improve the systems to monitor his trading or to be sceptical and begin asking the probing questions that might have uncovered the fraud earlier. Mr Leeson was literally out of control and Barings Bank was soon out of business.

(b) Delegations of authority and authorisation limits

Introduction

Mechanisms to delegate authority are widely used in organisations to ensure that power is devolved from the top (the board of directors) to senior managers and other personnel responsible for the day-to-day operations. Effective delegation of authority is required to ensure streamlined and efficient operations coupled with a strong control framework and culture, which should reflect each organisation's tone from the top in terms of expectations and values. In order to be effective these mechanisms should address three requirements. They should:

- Cover the range of activities the organisation is engaged in (or is expected to engage in the future);

- Empower management to make the operational decisions expected of them; and

- State clearly the maximum authority levels for each level of the organisation's hierarchy for budgeted and unbudgeted expenditure.

An essential control

I expect to see in place clear authorisation limits setting out who within the organisation can spend what amount of money in all the businesses that I work in today. The point of real interest to me is to understand whether or not these limits are always respected by the managers and staff within the business. Sometimes, this does not happen and there is tacit (or even explicit) agreement to limits being exceeded by senior management if, by such actions, it is thought that short-term profitability will increase. Consider the example of Monsieur Kerviel's activities at the French bank, Société Générale. He was trading far beyond his authorised limits but a consistent line of his defence was always that this conduct was known about and condoned by his managers in the bank. So long as he was generating profits for the bank, of course. According to Monsieur Kerviel at his trial, he was encouraged to take risks and his unauthorised activities only became a problem for his managers when the massive trading positions that he had built up started to come under pressure. When these positions were ultimately unwound and resulted in huge losses, his actions were immediately denounced as fraudulent trading by the senior management of the bank.[4]

In my view, delegations of authority and authorisation limits on spending are an essential feature of fraud risk management. Breaches of these limits should always be treated very seriously as, in addition to the immediate area of concern, they indicate that the controls framework is fundamentally unsound.

(c) Physical and computer security over assets, records and information

Introduction

I am no expert in security matters. However, I have been fortunate enough to work with some of the leading experts in this field and I well understand its importance as a component of an anti-fraud controls framework. It is a huge subject which I cannot do justice to here, so I will confine myself to some overall best practice principles and then add to these some observations from my own experience.

For our purposes, the term security breaks down into two component parts: physical security and computer or information security.

Physical security

Physical security in its broadest sense may be defined as the protection of buildings, equipment, people, hardware and data from circumstances and events that could cause serious loss and damage to an organisation or injury to its personnel. Traditional physical security measures range from the obvious locks on doors to sophisticated buildings security systems with full integration of alarms, CCTV, access control, guarding officers and central monitoring facilities. The onset of the 21st century has brought with it new risks also. Counter-terrorist surveys are now an important element of a physical security system today as the many terrorist outrages in recent years have highlighted the increased threats in this area which must be taken seriously. Also, the huge increase in data has meant that tight security over the storage and transmission of data files is essential too. There is a related point concerning the threat of the theft of information by organised criminal gangs, whether from a company with a view to profiting from price-sensitive material or from individuals with a view to making money from identity theft. One essential control measure that all of us need to take today is to purchase a document shredder and then to make sure that we use the shredder to dispose of all old documents in a thorough manner.

Computer security

Computer security and information security are separate disciplines for professionals but there are clear linkages between the two. In fact the content of an individual computer is vulnerable to few risks unless, and until, that computer is connected to other computers on a network. Today the use of computer networks, especially the internet, is all pervasive of course. There are three broad aspects of computer security:

- Confidentiality (or privacy) which means that information should not be accessed by unauthorised parties;

- Integrity which means that information is protected against unauthorised changes – computer hacking clearly carries a risk of compromising the integrity of databases; and

- Authentication which means that the users are who they claim to be.

Information security is the process of protecting information around the above framework. This is crucial because more companies store business and personnel information on computers than ever before and much of this information is highly confidential. Effective information security systems provide a range of policies, security products, technologies and procedures. Examples are firewall information security and virus scanners, though these will not be sufficient on their own to protect all information from external, professional hackers and there is no such thing as a totally secure system. Information security systems act as a deterrent because they make it harder for hackers to gain access. Iris recognition systems are an example of modern high levels of security here.

Importance of passwords

The final point that I want to make is something that I have observed from time to time when working with clients and it concerns a failure to respect the basic control of passwords. Many organisations seem to be unaware that one of the biggest potential threats to information security is their own people, those who actually operate the computers day to day. I have worked in public sector organisations where all the workers in a department know each other's passwords and routinely log in to another computer during the day. This is justified in terms of operational efficiency. In fact, it is a significant weakness.

I have also seen passwords written on "Post-it" notes that are visible and therefore easily accessed by anyone who happens to be passing. This is simply sloppy and poor practice. In the same way that we all keep our bank cards and our PIN numbers separate, with the PIN numbers kept secret, no employee should ever keep a note of his or her password where it can be easily accessed. Secure passwords are essential and there are a number of simple steps that can be taken here. First, all computer operators, including agency workers, help-desk staff etc., should be made fully aware of the importance of security. Also, changing passwords frequently (computer experts recommend doing so at least once every three months) and using combinations of letters and numbers makes it more difficult for hackers to gain access.

So, simple but effective measures are available and, as always, raising awareness of risk is often the key to improved control. I have never witnessed the poor practices around password controls mentioned above in a financial services environment because in that industry sector there is good awareness of the risks around information security. There are also tough sanctions for any employee who does not adhere to the controls in this area.

Control inhibitors and concealment strategies

Introduction

As we have seen, the Fraud Triangle established three characteristics which are always present in occupational fraud schemes: motive, opportunity and rationalisation. The second leg of the Fraud Triangle, (opportunity) has two components parts: the fraudster needs to have both the opportunity to commit the crime and also the opportunity to conceal the crime. He or she does not want to get caught and receive a prison sentence. So, the fraudster is always looking for weaknesses to exploit in the internal control system and ways to keep the fraud secret by defeating individual controls.

Set out below are five concealment strategies frequently used by criminals (mainly directors and managers here) when committing fraud within an enterprise.

Management override of controls

The possibility that managers can override internal controls is present in every organisation. Because managers are primarily responsible for designing, implementing and monitoring the internal control system, they are likely to be well aware of the weaknesses in the system too. In addition, individual managers are perfectly capable of abusing their position to coerce or convince a subordinate to process a transaction without the normal checks being applied. The AICPA has described management override of controls as "the Achilles heel of fraud prevention",[5] especially concerning abuse of the financial reporting process. Here opportunity often combines with powerful incentives and fraudulent financial reporting may well be the result. Internal controls that otherwise operate effectively cannot be relied upon to prevent, deter or detect financial statement fraud in these circumstances. The AICPA acknowledges that management override of controls is very difficult to detect. It is looking primarily to the work of the audit committee to reduce this risk through actions such as maintaining scepticism, strengthening committee understanding of the business and cultivating a vigorous whistle-blower programme.

Collusion

Collusion may be described as a secret agreement between two or more individuals for a deceitful or fraudulent purpose. It is an important concept in the fraud context because not only is collusion difficult to detect but if it exists in an organisation it will undermine the strength of segregation of duty controls. Collusion can exist between individuals who all work for the same organisation. Alternatively a collusive scheme may involve a third party outsider – this might typically be a corruption scheme under the ACFE's fraud typology.

There is also the important variant of pseudo-collusion to be aware of. Pseudo-collusion occurs when an employee looks to take advantage of certain behaviours of work colleagues for personal benefit. For example, an employee who is aware that his or her supervisor, who authorises invoices, never checks any of the details supporting those invoices, might think that there is an opportunity for gain by presenting bogus invoices from a company which he or she controls to the supervisor for signature. In this situation the employee may very well think that there is little chance of the bogus invoice being detected because of the observed lack of diligence on the part of the supervisor. I described in the introduction to this Chapter the situation that I found many years ago at the large UK retailer involving the cheque signatory, Mr Black. There was a risk of exactly this kind of pseudo-collusion in that situation.

Both collusion and pseudo-collusion are very difficult to detect other than by a combination of controls such as awareness raising, job rotation and whistle-blower programmes. These are specific anti-fraud controls and we will look at each of them in detail later in this Chapter and the next.

Processing a transaction below the "control radar"

Most control systems will have a series of break points built into them, that is to say a series of triggers whereby transactions exceeding certain stipulated criteria require review and sign-off by a second, and usually senior, employee. Typically, these will be financial triggers, commonly known in business as authorisation levels. So, for example, imagine that an organisation works around a $20,000 break point, so that all transactions of $20,000 or more require the signature of a second manager before they are authorised and can proceed. As we have seen, internal fraudsters are often experienced members of staff and will therefore be well aware of where these break points are in the system. In our example, the fraudster will be unlikely to submit fraudulent transactions to the value of $20,000 or more because of the scrutiny of the second manager, which significantly increases the chances of detection.

It is also important to be aware that the fraudster is likely to want to receive as high a return as possible for every fraudulent transaction that he or she carries out because each one will carry an element of risk. So, there is a strong probability that the fraudster will look to initiate the fraudulent transactions at values that are just below the control radar, which in our example is set at $20,000. There is an important message here for directors and managers, as well as for fraud auditors. An effective piece of fraud-focused auditing would be to look specifically at those transactions falling just below the monetary amount of the control radar. In our example, an audit sample comprising all items in the last year processed in the range $19,500–$19,999 might produce some very interesting results! We will return to this example in the next Chapter when we look at data mining and other fraud detection techniques.

False documentation

One of the ways that a fraudster may seek to circumvent controls is by producing false documents – forgeries in other words. Many business controls are based on receiving information or documents from outside third parties to support and confirm information generated internally. Reconciliation controls are typical in this respect, as are confirmation controls. Because the information comes from an independent source (the outside third party) these types of controls are thought to be very strong and a lot of reliance will be placed on them by managers. Forgeries undermine them, of course.

Since the advent of desk-top publishing in the 1980s the risk of false documentation has increased because of the ease with which a fraudster can produce documents that at first sight look perfectly genuine but are in fact forgeries from his or her personal computer.

Both the Barings and the AIB Group frauds featured false documents. Mr Leeson's prison sentence of 6.5 years given in Singapore in December 1995, as the result of a plea bargain (and therefore shorter than it would otherwise have been no doubt), was made up of two parts: six years for misreporting details about the status of Barings' futures contracts and six months for forging documents to deceive Barings' external auditors, Coopers & Lybrand. The fraud carried out by Mr Rusnak, the currency trader working at AIB Group's US subsidiary Allfirst in Baltimore, entailed the use of false trades to cover up huge losses in his forward positions. Mr Rusnak produced forged documents for these trades and presented them as third party confirmation letters. Logos of his supposed counterparties' institutions were found by investigators in a file on his personal computer labelled "fake docs"!

Blocking the flow of information

Long delays in receiving promised information are among the most frustrating realities of the business world with which an auditor has to deal. Often there are perfectly understandable commercial reasons for these delays. Sometimes however there are more sinister reasons. The long delay might be caused by the fact that the individual who is responsible for producing the requested information does not want to release it because he or she has something to hide.

As an example, let us return to Mr Leeson's conviction in Singapore for forgery whilst attempting to deceive the auditors, Coopers & Lybrand, referred to above. This related specifically to one of the devices that Mr Leeson had used to try to cover up his trading losses. He claimed to the auditors that a £50 million balance represented an outstanding debt from a US firm of brokers called Spear, Leeds and Kellog – there was of course no debt to be collected, this balance was part of his trading losses. The auditors accepted the explanation but asked to see a letter from the firm of brokers confirming the debt. Of course, no legitimate confirmation letter could ever be provided because the debt itself was fictitious. So, Mr Leeson delayed and prevaricated over providing the letter for as long as he possibly could do so. No doubt he hoped that the auditors would either forget about it or else give up. In fact Coopers & Lybrand did neither. So Mr Leeson was forced to forge the confirmation letter. In order to make the letter look as if it had come directly from the brokers, he faxed the confirmation letter across to the auditors. But he did this late at night using his own fax machine at home. The auditors did not question the authenticity of the fax in any way and apparently simply accepted it as genuine. Incredibly, however, the document that the auditors saw clearly bore an imprint reading "From Nick and Lisa" (Mr Leeson's wife at the time was called Lisa). This meant that the document could not have come directly from the brokers.

This episode demonstrates two things. First, the extent of Mr Leeson's duplicity and his capacity to manipulate, prevaricate and do anything to block the flow of information. But it also highlights some worrying failings of the external auditors. Helga Drummond refers to this case in her book

The *Art of Decision-Making: Mirrors of Imagination, Masks of Fate,* which examines the underlying factors behind decision-making. She attempts to explain the passivity of Coopers & Lybrand here by suggesting that they might have "unconsciously screened out" the "From Nick and Lisa" reference and she goes on to say that even if they had recognised its significance they may not have acted upon it but rather might have tried to rationalise it away. One reason for this, Ms Drummond says, is that fraud on a massive scale such as this was at that time still relatively rare (Drummond, 2001, p. 33).[6] I take a different, more simplistic view, however. At the most basic auditing level it is never good practice to accept faxed copies rather than originals as audit evidence because forgeries are far more difficult to detect when looking at faxes. In addition, of course, the "From Nick and Lisa" reference was apparently clear for all to see on the document and yet no-one in the audit team seems to have thought that it was suspicious. In my view, this incident demonstrates an alarming lack of awareness, scepticism and diligence on the part of the auditors.

Specific anti-fraud prevention controls

Introduction

One of the main conclusions in the ACFE's 2008 RTTN is: "The implementation of anti-fraud controls appears to have a measurable impact on an organisation's exposure to fraud." The ACFE examined a number of specific anti-fraud controls and measured the median loss in the fraud cases reported in its survey, depending on whether organisations did or did not have a given control in place at the time of the fraud. It concluded: "In every comparison, there were significantly lower losses when the controls had been implemented."

One important observation in the ACFE's 2008 RTTN was that the two controls associated with the largest reduction in median losses were among the least well-used controls in those organisations included in the survey. The two key controls highlighted by the ACFE in this section of their report are: first, surprise audits; and secondly, job rotation and/or mandatory vacations. We cover surprise audits in Chapter 8 and look at job rotation and mandatory vacations below.

Directors and managers need to be aware of the specific anti-fraud controls that are available and also which of those are likely to prove the most effective in their own organisations, in practice. These anti-fraud controls aim specifically to minimise the opportunities both to commit fraud and to conceal it successfully. There are both preventative and detective controls to manage fraud risk. The prevention controls focus on policies, procedures, training and communication that stop fraud from occurring. The detective controls on the other hand focus on activities and programmes that highlight in a timely manner situations where fraud has occurred or is occurring. Taken together they provide a rich and varied menu of available responses to the fraud threat, from which directors and managers can select the approach that is most appropriate for their own particular organisation and circumstances.

We look at each of the anti-fraud controls that were included in the ACFE's study (together with others, such as staff vetting controls) at various stages of the book. In this Chapter we address six of the key preventative measures in detail and, using one of the characteristics of controls that was discussed in Chapter 6, we divide them between those that may be classified as "hard controls" and those that are "soft controls", as follows:

Hard Prevention Controls	Soft Prevention Controls
Staff vetting procedures	Employee support programmes
Job rotation & mandatory vacations	Fraud awareness training programmes
Anti-fraud policies	Management review of internal controls

There are a number of additional fraud prevention controls that are looked at elsewhere in the book, in particular the audit (Chapter 5) and the code of conduct (Chapter 10). The whole audit process plays an important preventative role in addition to helping with fraud detection. Elements of prevention in the audit role include: the existence of an independent audit committee; the external audit review of the financial reporting process to produce the independent audit opinion on the annual report and accounts; and an internal audit function, properly resourced and trained and prepared to carry out proactive fraud audit work. The organisation's code of conduct also plays an important part in setting the organisation's tone at the top and helping to establish its anti-fraud culture.

There are also of course a number of important deterrence strategies and detective controls that have proved to be highly effective in fighting fraud. The three key detective controls that are addressed in detail in Chapter 8 on fraud detection are:

• Surprise audits;

• Whistle-blowing hotlines; and

• Data mining exercises.

The six key fraud prevention controls

Introduction

For now let us concentrate on the six key methods available to prevent fraud, as set out in the table above. Directors and managers should be aware of them, they should consider their suitability in relation to their own organisation's risk profile and they should be prepared to invest resources where necessary to strengthen existing controls or introduce new ones in order to reduce the fraud threat to acceptable levels.

Preventing fraud, rather than detecting or investigating it, should always be the top priority for directors and managers. It is always difficult, time-consuming and stressful to be forced to react to the consequences of a fraud incident, with all the attendant damage to profits, reputation and morale that this entails. There is much truth in the old saying: "Prevention is better than cure".

Fraud prevention – the three hard controls

Let us start by looking at the three hard controls: staff vetting; job rotation and/or mandatory vacations; and an anti-fraud policy.

(a) Staff vetting
Overview
Hiring new people is a risky business. I say this with reference to the true meaning of the word risk, because new hires present both opportunities and threats to an organisation. The subject matter of this book means that we will inevitably focus on the threats here, on the downside risk, but it is important to say that working with good people is often given as the key to success by CEOs and business commentators alike, rightly in my view. All organisations want to recruit the best talent available to them as the quality of "human capital" is increasingly seen as the key differentiator from one company to another in terms of business success.

Organisations need to be realistic however. The problem for them is that threats around recruiting new people both exist and may be increasing, both from organised crime groups and from individuals who want and need a job at a time when unemployment is rising and job vacancies are falling. Background screening and recruitment checks are the first line of defence here.

Also, the risks associated with new hires may be difficult to manage in a proportionate way in current economic conditions. As more candidates chase fewer positions, already overstretched Human Resources departments have to cope with a huge number of application forms. Outsourcing and the use of recruitment agencies for part or even all of the process is common practice in many large organisations today. This will probably help in terms of efficiency. But as always, although the recruitment process can be outsourced, the overall responsibility for the outcomes of that process remains with the organisation.

In my view it is important that the contracts and service level agreements that provide the framework for these outsourced arrangements with the recruitment agencies always include a "right of audit" clause. That is to say, the organisation needs to be able to check for itself that the agreed criteria in the contract are in fact being carried out in practice by the outsourced provider (for example, by sending its own internal audit team in to go through the agency records). Of course, there is little point in having a right of audit clause in the contract unless it is acted upon. Therefore, an organisation's internal auditors should allocate time periodically for these assignments so that they gain assurance that the very important recruitment checks are in fact being carried out.

Directors and managers need to design an appropriate control system that will provide their business with reasonable assurance that criminals, associates of criminals and people who lie on their CVs and application forms will be revealed during the selection process. The best way to do this is by reference to risk.

The crucial background checks

There are a number of different aspects and considerations involved in recruiting staff and it is not appropriate here to consider the whole interview process or such component parts of it as health checks, aptitude tests and psychological assessments. We are concerned here with the background checks and pre-employment screening process that seek to verify the credentials of new employees and to check that they meet any stipulated pre-conditions of employment. These checks are carried out on information provided by the applicants both on their CVs and also when completing application forms which the company might use in order to request certain specific information. During the course of these checks it is always important to establish whether any of the applicants have concealed important information or otherwise misrepresented themselves.

The objective of the staff vetting process is to provide management with reasonable assurance that all offers of employment are subject to satisfactory pre-employment checks and that the people employed within their organisation can be trusted. The whole process needs to be both efficient and effective if it is to work to best advantage and, in order to achieve this, the checks should be designed according to risk. Everything done should always comply with the law and the whole process should be fully transparent to all the applicants.

The main purpose of pre-employment screening and background checks is to verify the identity of applicants, confirm their previous performance and employment history and ascertain their integrity by reference to their previous conduct. Set out below are the various components of the vetting process, with the key risk components highlighted.

- **Identification documents.** This should be relatively straightforward (for example, by reference to passport and driver's licence). In my experience the one area of risk that I have come across here is around the failure of so-called "right to work" checks on immigration status. Clearly, with people increasingly being willing and able to travel around the world to find work, these checks must be carried out. My own example of problems in this area comes from the airline sector.

Example: immigrants working at a UK airport. In 2005, I was working as part of a team on a value-for-money project at one of the UK's airports looking in particular at the efficiency of a number of outsourced contracts. One such contract involved the airport operating company outsourcing the staffing of a major project to an international construction and consulting company. We took advantage of the "right of audit" clause included in the contractual terms to spend some time reviewing the relevant documentation on the construction company's own premises. During the course of our work we became concerned at a number of aspects of the staffing arrangements on the project, including instances where the airport operating company had been charged for the time of several individuals who were not actually working at the airport on the days set out on the invoice according to their own timesheets. The most alarming aspect however was the lack of documentation available concerning a number of the workers used for the project. These workers were clearly temporary staff, hired for the specific purposes of working on this contract and it was clear to us that there was no evidence on file that basic identification checks on any of these workers had ever been carried out. In these circumstances there was a high risk of illegal immigrants working at the airport, something that our client quickly put in measures to address.

- **Verification of academic qualifications (usually the highest level achieved only).** Again these are fairly standard checks but sometimes they are either not done at all or else they are not followed through. This can create exposures. First of all one of the prime purposes of these background checks is to ensure that the candidate does indeed possess the minimum standards for the job and academic qualifications are clearly part of this. For example, it is a common requirement in business today for the level of minimum academic standard to be set at "educated to degree level". If no checks are made it is very easy for an applicant to claim that he or she has achieved a degree when in fact they have not done so. More importantly, from time to time a senior executive will be exposed for falsely claiming an impressive list of academic qualifications on a past CV. This can create significant problems for the organisation concerned, not least in repairing damage to its credibility and reputation. A good example of the risks here is provided by the case of Patrick Imbardelli, a senior executive with InterContinental Hotels Group.

Example: Mr Imbardelli and InterContinental Hotels Group. In 2007 Mr Imbardelli was forced to resign from his £300,000 a year job as a senior executive with the hotels group InterContinental after making false claims about his academic qualifications on his CV. At the time, his imminent appointment to the main board had been announced, but it was during the screening process for the higher-profile job that discrepancies emerged. Mr Imbardelli had falsely claimed to have three qualifications: a Bachelor of Business degree from the University of Victoria in Australia, and a BSc and a MBA both from Cornell University in the US. In fact, whilst he had attended classes at both institutions in the 1980s he had never actually graduated from either of them. A quote from a spokesperson from the hotel group to the press at the time sums up the key issue of trust in cases such as these perfectly: "We treat this as a very serious matter. The fundamental basis of trust has been undermined. He will not receive any compensation."[7] This case also highlights another issue with staff vetting. Mr Imbardelli had joined the hotels group in 2000 following an acquisition. He proved himself to be a very able and successful hotelier and was promoted to Managing Director of the Asia Pacific part of the group in 2003. However, neither in 2000 nor in 2003 did InterContinental Hotels Group ever check out Mr Imbardelli's CV. The failure to carry out such checks in circumstance of acquisition, like this one, or else in situations where long-standing employees come to be considered for promotion to senior executive positions is quite common and arises out of a misunderstanding of risk. False qualifications are a ticking time bomb which, when it goes off, will cause reputational damage both to the individual concerned and also to the organisation affected.

- **Verification of Professional Qualifications or Memberships.** The issues here are similar to those for academic qualifications although they are often much more important because in certain jobs and professions technical competence will be job-critical. Consider the positions of a medical doctor or an engineer or a lawyer for example. In many businesses, an accountancy or related qualification is often seen as an important prerequisite for success in becoming a Chief Financial Officer. Such a qualification is not always considered necessary however as the careers of Mr Fastow at Enron and Ms Callan at Lehman Brothers (discussed above) demonstrate – both may be said to have been under-qualified and over promoted. However the point is that both Enron and Lehman Brothers knew they were promoting people without certain professional qualifications. A much more serious risk comes when the qualifications are falsified because here the exposure is unknown. So, basic checks to verify professional qualifications are always recommended and they will become critical in certain industries and in certain situations.

- **Employment Reference Checks.** The objective here is to obtain verification of an applicant's employment history together with supported explanations for any gaps in that history. In addition to false qualifications, it is through exaggerated job titles, misrepresented employment dates and concealed dismissals for dishonesty that applicants most often try to mislead potential employers with the information they supply on CVs and application forms. This part of the vetting process is far from straightforward. Not only do most organisations follow up character references with only those individuals who are nominated by the candidates, but the references supplied by previous employers are often brief, basic and banal at best for fear of being sued. A confirmation that: "Ms Y worked at the company from 1 March 2010 to 30 June 2011" is not particularly helpful. Yet it is important that employment reference checks are carried out as robustly as possible, for example, by talking to the individual who supplied the reference about the candidate on his or her office telephone extension it may be possible to achieve better assurance. Certainly, the failure to carry out such checks can expose the organisation to significant risk. I remember very well the following example from the Polly Peck case.

Example: Polly Peck and a failure to take up references. As part of the initial review of Polly Peck's affairs by the administrators, I was asked to visit the premises of its Russell Hobbs subsidiary in Wolverhampton in the UK in January 1991. Russell Hobbs was (and still is) the UK's leading small electrical appliance brand, particularly famous for its kettles. As soon as I had met the Finance Director and told him that I was from the administrators of Polly Peck, he said that he could guess what I had come to talk about: "it must be to do with the recent fraud involving an employee in our credit sales team that has cost us over £100,000" he said. In fact this was the first time that I had heard of this fraud so I decided simply to say nothing and listen to the story. Apparently the fraudster had only recently joined the company. He had materially misrepresented his career history on his CV by omitting to mention on it the fact that he had spent three years in prison in the recent past following a conviction for fraud against a previous employer. I asked whether references had been supplied and followed up by the company, only to be told that the Human Resources department had been under great pressure at the time and had not in fact followed up the references given. The Finance Director did not seem as concerned by this as he might be, which surprised me a little until I learned the reason why – the company had insurance cover for this type of fraud and he was relying on recovering the losses from the insurance company. I then had to inform him that I doubted very much whether the insurers would ever pay out in this case. They would almost certainly seek to void the insurance contract on the grounds that Russell Hobbs had been contributorily negligent in the fraud by failing to follow up on the fraudster's references. This indeed was what happened and the administrators of Polly Peck never received anything by way of recoveries from this particular fraud.

- **Checking International Criminal Records.** Checking an applicant's details against criminal records databases is an important and relatively modern control and organisations should always consider carrying this out for their new hires. In particular, the check provides some assurance against penetration by criminal gangs (although criminals are increasingly looking to place those associates of theirs who have "clean" criminal records into businesses). Also, in the particular context of fraud risk management, criminal records checks provide some assurance that convicted criminals are not being employed unknowingly. This is especially relevant to financial criminals because, as we have seen in Chapter 3, these individuals tend to exhibit high recidivism rates. Directors and managers need to be aware also of the limitations of such checks, however. First, criminal record checks are primarily of benefit in relation to applicants for more specialist roles than we are considering here, in particular roles involving a high degree of contact with children or vulnerable adults. Secondly, this is not an easy task if the applicant has lived in a number of locations around the world because there are many differences between countries as to what constitutes a crime, the reliability of convictions, the quality of data etc.

- **Credit Reference Searches.** Broadly, credit reference searches involve examining the financial history of an applicant, assessing how well he or she is able to manage their personal finances and looking for evidence of financial pressure. In my view this is the most important staff vetting control that an organisation can carry out in order to minimise its fraud risk. Remember that the Fraud Triangle and other behavioural research into the motives of fraudsters suggest that financial pressure is one of the most important drivers of occupational fraud, if not the most important driver. Credit reference searches represent a smart control, therefore, one that is designed to match risk. Apart from companies in the financial services industry, however, I am not aware of many organisations making use of this control and I think this is a mistake. Just to be clear, the search should examine only the information on an applicant that is publically held and the fact that the search is a standard part of the organisation's recruitment process should be made clear to the applicant from the outset. If the applicant refuses to give permission for the credit search to take place then of course the search must not proceed. However, the organisation is entitled to draw conclusions from such a refusal. Typically a credit reference search will include: checking for evidence of financial pressure such as non-payment of debt (e.g. County Court judgements – CCJs – in the UK), bankruptcy or insolvency; cross referencing an applicant's current and previous addresses; and referencing the electoral roll information. Directors and managers need to be aware of this important control and should be prepared to use it. To take an extreme example which illustrates the importance of credit reference checks and the dangers of ignoring them, consider again the case of Barings Bank and Nick Leeson. Barings did not carry out a credit search on Mr Leeson when they first employed him in 1989 as a settlements clerk. However, the bank was put on notice by the Securities and Futures Authority in early 1992 following Mr Leeson's application to be registered as a dealer in the UK that Mr Leeson had failed to disclose on his application form a CCJ for unsatisfied civil judgement debts against him. The application was subsequently withdrawn. Despite this, Barings still allowed Mr Leeson to apply for a trading license in Singapore following his move there later in the year and subsequently to become the bank's head trader in that operation.

Key importance of staff vetting

Staff vetting is a very important anti-fraud control, something that Teresa completely agreed with during our interview. Teresa is an experienced internal auditor and was the Head of Internal Audit at a large local authority in the UK's public sector during the time period that is covered in the interview extract below. She was so concerned at the risk that applicants were taking advantage of weaknesses in the system that she initiated an enhanced vetting programme in certain parts of the local authority. As her interview shows, this was not an easy thing to do, with much resistance from senior management, but Teresa considers the process to have been very beneficial in stopping "CV liars" and therefore potential fraudsters from working for her organisation. This is what she had to say.

When you're dealing with staff you need to be able to trust them, it doesn't matter how small the discrepancy is you need to follow it through, set an example to other staff that actually we don't tolerate fraud. It's quite similar when we introduced the enhanced staff vetting programme.

That caused such uproar with some of the directors who just thought it was totally out of order and totally outside of our remit to do extra validation checks on people who were coming in because, you know, as a local authority and public sector employer we should be giving people a second chance if they did declare things to us. But actually again once we started that initiative we did, and it was interesting, we did find a lot of issues . . . we were piloting it in finance and benefits at the time but the number of appointments we did stop going ahead because there were "inaccuracies", shall we say, on CVs was significant. You know these were at very senior levels, you're talking about people who would have a huge responsibility in terms of budgeting and staff management and finance, procurement etc. and yet the negativity of a lot of the directors towards us doing this kind of work was phenomenal.

We used a different matrix system depending on the position that the candidates were applying for and therefore the impact they could have in terms of budget commitments, hiring, firing etc. We would do extra background checks on finance staff for example so we would do the CRB (Criminal Records Bureau) checks, we would check credit history, and that would be through the likes of Experian, checking for CCJs. We would also check to see if they had debts on the tax systems etc. We would do much more thorough checks on the applications than previously. We would never accept CVs at face value – we should never have simply accepted them in the first place. We would do checks on the references that had been given to make sure they were valid people, people that existed, also history checks in terms of were the applicants employed at the organisations they stated? Did they gain the qualifications they claimed?

It was generally with qualifications that we found the problems. People would say, for example, they were an accountant, but actually they had only started the Part 1 course and had given it up years ago, that kind of thing. Or they would say that they worked as a self-employed consultant for a company – they might have lasted one day as a temp, that kind of thing. It's really a much more robust and detailed review of the application than HR would probably have had the time or the inclination to do. Again, it got the word out that people were being vigilant.

There was a change of Finance Director and, interestingly, the new one that came in was from another borough which was actually where they'd started piloting the enhanced vetting, so it was great, because once he was appointed we kind of knew the process would be safe. But even so there was only one member of staff that was dedicated to doing the research and of course you always come up against issues. You know somebody's been abroad, it's much more difficult to get things checked out but we did make use of the internet and you can check qualifications fairly easily. Again there were people applying for senior positions who said they'd got degrees and MAs and doctorates, and what's the other classic one, not a management diploma but . . . yes, an MBA! And again some of them were from these places where you can apply online to get the certificate in a day so there were lots of interesting things that did come up and I see that as a real success. You've obviously got no evidence they would have done anything untoward but the fact that they kind of lied at the start . . .

One of the interesting points coming out of this extract is the extensive resistance to Teresa's enhanced vetting initiative coming from the top of her organisation. It was only with the arrival of a new Finance Director, who had sponsored this type of exercise at another London borough, that the initiative was secured. This is another example of the importance of tone at the top.

(b) Job rotation and mandatory vacations
Introduction
Internal fraud schemes often require almost continual attention and intervention on a day-to-day basis by the fraudster if they are to remain undetected. Because of this, it is not surprising that many frauds come to light during periods of sickness or other unexpected absences by the perpetrator. The twin controls of job rotation and mandatory vacations enable management to take advantage of these factors. Research by the ACFE indicates that they are amongst the least used but most effective of all anti-fraud controls. Only 12% of the organisations included in the 2008 RTTN survey implemented job rotation or mandatory vacation policies. However, the impact of these controls was seen to be highly significant. The median loss of those entities that did operate the controls was $64,000 compared to $164,000 at the organisations lacking similar procedures.

Job rotation
There are a number of risks associated with allowing employees to remain in the same job year after year: boredom and disillusionment can set in; the employee becomes demotivated and less efficient over time; and/or the employee, either working alone or in collusion with colleagues (especially when he or she is part of a small self-contained team, for example in a traditional cashiers office), is tempted to engage in fraud or some other counter productive work behaviours. Rotation of job duties and responsibilities can freshen up and combat boredom but it will also break up the opportunities for collusion and fraudulent activities. If jobs are rotated periodically, a new person coming in and examining the system's processes is more likely to notice irregularities if they have been occurring. This could be a particularly effective control in the accounts department, for example.

Managers should be aware that there are two issues with job rotation, however. First, it is difficult to implement in small organisations where staff numbers are limited. Secondly, if an employee, over time, gains knowledge of a number of different business areas and processes it may actually make it easier for that employee to commit fraud. Certainly, the investigators in the Société Générale case felt that the fact that Monsieur Kerviel had spent time in the back office functions of the bank before he became a trader facilitated his unauthorised trading because he thereby gained considerable knowledge about the bank's systems and controls and he also knew how to get round them.

Mandatory vacations
Vacations, periods of recreational time away from the pressures of work, are important to all of us. Annual leave entitlements are built into employment contracts as a matter of course. They are there for a purpose and each of us needs to make use of our full holiday quota each year in order to perform at our best when at work. Some employees choose not to do this, however. Whilst it might seem to be very loyal and laudable that these individuals are so committed to their work that they are prepared to forgo some of their vacation time, it is not good for either the business or the employees concerned in the long run and management should not allow this to happen.

From the fraud risk management perspective, mandatory vacations are a form of short-term job rotation in that the employee is away from his or her main area of work for the period of the holiday. While the employee is on vacation, it is more likely that any illegal activity, if it is taking place, will be detected. When mandatory vacations are institutionalised, it sends a powerful deterrence message throughout the organisation. In 2000, Alan Greenspan, then Chairman of the US Federal Reserve System, suggested that banks should enforce a simple internal risk control for their trading desks: The Two-Week Vacation Rule. Some firms in the financial services sector now enforce this rule for all employees across the board. Certainly, most banks will apply it in areas of high risk, in particular with the traders, compelling them to stop trading for two weeks every year. A period of two consecutive weeks away from the office provides reasonable assurance that any fraudulent activity that is being carried out by the employee concerned will be revealed. Accounting entries at banks typically clear within two weeks, which in theory should be enough time to allow any questionable or out of balance accounts to emerge.

It is not surprising that this control is used extensively in financial services, because it was the failure to enforce the Two-Week Rule that was one of the contributing factors in the famous fraud at Allfirst Financial, the US subsidiary of AIB Group based in Baltimore, involving the currency trader John Rusnak.

> **Example: Allfirst Financial's failure to enforce the Two-Week Rule.** The investigation report written in 2002 by Eugene Ludwig and submitted by Promontory Financial Group and the law firm Wachtel, Lipton, Rosen & Katz concerning the currency trading losses at Allfirst Financial highlighted the fact that Mr Rusnak was able to trade when on vacations:
>
> > It is for good reason that banks in the United States are required to have a guideline that bars traders from trading two weeks per year. Having a second employee take over for even the most trusted bank employee is a mechanism for uncovering fraud. Although Mr Rusnak did take vacations, the efficacy of the two-week rule was vitiated because Mr Rusnak was allowed to continue trading from his computer. He also traded at home and at night, but this trading was not monitored appropriately. The control weakness was the failure to verify this after hours trading. (Promontory, 2002, p. 43)[8]

(c) Anti-fraud policy statement
Introduction
Many organisations today do not have a separate, stand-alone anti-fraud policy. For example, less than 40% of the organisations providing data for the ACFE's 2010 RTTNs operated with one. Instead, in my experience, most choose to deal with fraud as one of a number of unacceptable

business practices (along with bribery and corruption, insider trading, money laundering etc.) that are typically covered together in a few paragraphs in the general staff handbook or code of conduct. From what I have observed, this approach rarely makes a lot of impact with the employees in those businesses.

I feel that this omission of a separate anti-fraud policy statement is not so much a mistake as a missed opportunity. By publishing a stand-alone fraud policy, signed off by the Chairman or the CEO, an organisation is able to set out its attitude to, and position on, fraud in a very direct and straightforward way. The policy demonstrates that fraud is taken seriously at the top and it enables an organisation to show clearly its commitment to fraud prevention, deterrence and detection.

Elements of the anti-fraud policy

There are a number of important elements to an anti-fraud policy. The policy should: define fraud; give pointers to staff in terms of what to look for; emphasise the importance of an anti-fraud culture; set out responsibilities, including the individual or department with overall responsibility for overseeing the policy; establish reporting lines; and act as a deterrent by setting out the consequences of engaging in fraud. If these elements are included, it will send out a clear message to employees and third parties alike that fraud is unacceptable and that all instances of suspected fraud will be treated seriously. The policy should be signed off by the board and it therefore becomes a part of the fraud risk governance structure, showing that a tough stance against fraud is fully supported right at the top of the organisation.

To be effective, an anti-fraud policy needs to be concise, straightforward and easily understood. It should include a very clear policy statement at the outset setting out the organisation's commitment to fighting fraud. Ideally this statement should be short and punchy, along the following lines:

> XYZ Ltd has a zero tolerance of fraud. All allegations of fraud will be thoroughly investigated and, where substantiated, will result in dismissal and/or prosecution.

The scope of the anti-fraud policy should be broad. It should cover all actual or suspected instances of fraud as defined in the policy and it will of course apply to all internal people – directors, managers and employees. It is very important that the policy is supported by those at the top of the organisation, who must be seen by everybody to comply with its provisions. Without this, it is unlikely to have traction or buy-in throughout the organisation. Equally, the policy should apply to outsiders too – to the suppliers, contractors, consultants and other third parties that have a business relationship with the organisation.

Response plan

An anti-fraud policy should also include a fraud response plan, perhaps as an appendix to the policy document itself. The fraud response plan is an outline of the process that will be followed in the event of a fraud being suspected or discovered. An important component will be to set out the fraud reporting channel, that is to say the policy should identify the individual or department where all frauds, suspected or confirmed, must be reported in to. The policy will then set out who will carry out the investigation, including a brief description of the methods to be used to secure evidence and how the investigation itself will be carried out.

Departmental heads or individual managers should be discouraged from trying to problem-solve whenever the particular problem involves suspected fraud. There are a number of reasons for this. First, business managers are rarely trained in investigation techniques and so could actually harm a future criminal case. Investigating fraud will also distract them from their core role of managing the business. Finally, there is always the temptation for a manager to think first about covering his or her personal position by making the problem go away and sweeping any issues arising under the carpet. This is unhelpful as it leads to misleading and inaccurate reporting. It also can be harmful to a subsequent professional investigation as time will be lost (it is often said that the first 48 hours are critical to a fraud investigation) and evidence may be compromised.

Before moving on to look at other prevention controls, there are two important points that I want to make in connection with the anti-fraud policy. The first is to do with communication and the second concerns the key concept of "zero tolerance".

Communicating the policy
As with any policy document it is critical that all those affected by the anti-fraud policy, all staff and relevant third parties, are aware of it and of what it says. This will not happen unless there is a commitment within the organisation to ongoing action and communication to promote the policy. Examples of this include: having a fraud awareness component in the induction process for joiners; putting the policy on the intranet, on posters displayed in common areas, on computer screen-savers etc.; facilitating ongoing awareness of the policy through periodic training sessions and management briefings; and including suitable anti-fraud paragraphs in contracts with third parties.

The importance of making the organisation's stance on fraud clear to contractual counterparties links back to something that I advocated in Chapter 5. There is advantage in organisations taking a holistic approach to financial crime, in particular so far as fraud and bribery are concerned. The Bribery Act 2010 requires UK commercial organisations (and those that carry out business in the UK) to have adequate procedures in place to manage bribery risk. Communication (including training) is stated as one of the six guiding principles to prevent bribery. Rather than look at bribery risk in isolation, in its own separate box, it is much more powerful and beneficial if an organisation combines bribery, fraud and other corrupt business practices and deals with them together. There is particular advantage when seeking to communicate a "zero tolerance" of corrupt business practices.

Zero tolerance concept
The term "zero tolerance" originated in the US where it has close associations with aspects of policing, in particular with the intention of eliminating undesirable conduct by the strict application of sanctions when a law or rule is broken. Today it is used in many contexts by politicians and executives alike when they want to appear to be tough. Famously, Romano Prodi began his term as President of the European Commission in 1999 with the slogan "zero tolerance for fraud", which looked a little hollow in 2003 when reports of the disappearance of millions of euros in slush funds and fictitious contracts started to surface in the media. The same "zero tolerance" phrase appears in many anti-fraud policy statements of businesses and public sector organisations today.

Every CEO would no doubt say that their organisation operates with zero tolerance of fraud – some may even believe it! However when I work with businesses I am often struck by how little credibility this concept holds for individuals in positions lower down the corporate hierarchy. In my experience, zero tolerance statements do not always translate into zero tolerance actions. Sometimes people are treated in different ways. As an example, I did a lot of work in the retail sector in the UK in the late 1990s. Here, it was not that unusual to see a young man or woman dismissed because the till they were operating was "short" by a small amount of money at the end of the day. However, this "tough message" was often diluted by various common practices in the sector at that time. For example, the practice of area managers being able to take their sons, daughters, nephews and nieces into a store and dress them in all the latest gear without paying anything at all. Also, I know from experience that organisations are often reluctant to bring charges against employees who have been caught committing fraud because of the time and costs associated with building a case.

So, zero tolerance is both a catchy phrase and a powerful concept. For organisations to be able to deliver it successfully though will require the commitment both to treat individuals consistently (regardless of position or status) and to prosecute all fraudsters (regardless of time and cost). To have impact throughout the organisation, a zero tolerance policy to fraud must be demonstrated through both words and actions.

Fraud prevention – the three soft controls

Let us now turn to the three soft controls listed above: employee support programmes; fraud awareness training programmes; and management review of internal controls.

(a) Employee support programmes
Introduction
It is widely held to be best practice (and increasingly common practice) for employers to develop support programmes designed to help their employees during times when individuals are experiencing problems of either a personal or a work-related nature. Often called employee assistance programmes ("EAPs"), these programmes aim to help workers by means of confidential counselling in areas such as: drug and alcohol rehabilitation, gambling addiction, abusive households, marital problems, mental health issues, financial difficulties and stress.

Such counselling can eliminate distractions that keep employees from reaching their full potential and also enable employees to keep working in the company, thereby saving the costs of re-hire etc. Also, running a good support programme demonstrates to employees that they are valued by their employers. It is this last benefit that is so important in the context of preventing fraud. The research into the motives of fraudsters that we looked at in Chapter 3 suggests very strongly that people who are disenchanted at work, who feel undervalued or that they have been treated in an unfair way, are more likely to commit fraud. Also, issues to do with addictive behaviour (drugs and gambling especially) carry particular fraud risks in view of the likely ongoing need of the employee for money in order to fuel the addiction.

Evidence from the ACFE supports the proposition that this is an important anti-fraud control. Some form of employee support programme was in place in over half of the entities included in the survey for the ACFE's 2008 RTTN (52.9%) and the impact of such a programme was significant in the reported results. The median loss at entities that had an employee support programme in place when fraud occurred was $110,000, compared to a loss of $250,000 at the organisations lacking such programmes.

Support programmes in action
I have not had much personal experience of working in situations where employee support programmes are active. I understand from discussions with associates, however, that these programmes can often be time-consuming. Ultimately, they may be frustrating and less than successful if the employee in question has a relapse.

However, they are important. Sharon was in no doubt about this during our interview for this book. Sharon is the deputy CEO of a large financial services institution in the Caribbean. This is what she had to say about employee support programmes in operation at her bank.

And the other thing we have, we have employee assistance programmes. Where if people are having financial difficulties they can go, they don't have to pay, and somebody will sit and do financial planning and so on with them. If you are a manager and you see an employee and you start understanding that your employee might be having some kind of difficulty then you send them on the programme because you don't want somebody where you know they are having financial problems at the bank! We also talk, especially to the young ones, when they come in we explain to them how easy it is to get into the trap where people start to pay you for information and why it is dangerous and those things, but you constantly have to try to be on top of the game and understand what to do, you can't just sit on it, it's constant. This is quite an investment of time and resources but it is necessary for you to protect your organisation.

Specific problem areas

I try to pick up some related issues on my training courses including, for example, the delegates' attitudes to the use of illegal drugs. Although alcohol abuse is more of a problem to business in terms of lost productivity, illegal drugs use continues to be an emotive subject and therefore attitudes towards it can be revealing of the prevalent culture in a particular organisation.

The first thing to say here is that enterprises from a number of business sectors that I have worked in (the construction and airline industries for example) have a strict zero tolerance of any use of illegal drugs and also alcohol in the workplace for very good health and safety reasons. The second thing is that I have witnessed in recent years a noticeable change in the attitude of delegates on my courses towards the use of drugs, in particular illegal substances, in the workplace. Many more people, especially in the UK, are prepared to acknowledge that addiction to illegal substances is in fact an illness and that the employee who has become addicted will require help to overcome the addiction. Ten years ago I found that this attitude was much more prevalent amongst delegates from Continental Europe than those based in the UK, where the reaction tended to vary between the extremes of indifference and a knee-jerk response of dismissal for the employee concerned.

In my experience, there is less of a call for instant dismissal in these circumstances today. Also, there is less indifference which is important, because corporate indifference to an issue like illegal drug use can bring its own problems. Consider the following example from my own experience:

Example: US investment bank. In 2005, I ran a series of workshops for a large US investment bank in New York, London and Singapore. During the course of this project I asked all the delegates in each of the locations the following question as part of a broad bi-polar exercise into aspects of the bank's culture:

You discover that your bank's star trader is addicted to cocaine – what do you do?

I asked the delegates to grade their answers numerically on a scale, 1 through to 5, with 1 being "tolerate, no need for any action" and 5 being "gross misconduct, dismissal and/or prosecution". Astonishingly, all the delegates in all three locations graded this answer exactly the same – they all scored it as 1! The nearest there came to any deviation from this was a comment from a manager in the New York office who said that he would have considered a higher grade (and therefore a more serious response) if the trader had been addicted to heroin rather than to cocaine! The investment bank no longer exists. I should say that I have used the same example with a number of other financial institutions since and have always received grades varying between 3 and 5. There now does seem to be more of a realisation that management needs to act in these situations. Providing assistance for employees to overcome their addictions is not only progressive but necessary and good business practice. The alternative is robust action leading to dismissal. Simply doing nothing and hoping that the problem goes away is what sometimes happens in practice but it is not a good option.

(b) Fraud awareness training programmes
Overview
This particular control is of course close to my own heart! It should be part of a general commitment to having a comprehensive training and development structure in place for all managers and staff, starting with induction training for new hires and continuing thereafter. This training programme should include education about fraud as a matter of course. Without such employee education, the goal that we discussed in Chapter 1 of everybody being responsible for fraud prevention and detection will simply be impossible to achieve.

In fact, an organisation's own people, the workforce, are its top fraud prevention and detection resource. Employees need to be trained in what fraud actually is, how fraud damages both the organisation and the employees and how to report any suspicious activities. All fraud awareness training programmes should send a positive message and be non-accusatory. They should emphasise throughout that illegal conduct in any form eventually costs everyone in the organisation through financial loss, low morale and adverse press comments leading to reputational damage.

Training in action – an effective control
Martin is an experienced manager working for a large retail bank in the UK. During our interview, he discussed the importance of organisations having a clear anti-fraud policy, which is then underpinned and reinforced by awareness training programmes. It is a very structured approach and one that many large organisations are adopting today. This is what Martin told me.

> One of the things for anything like fraud, and it's quite a common thing now, you have to have a strict policy, it has to be very, very visible, it has to be very, very clear, there can't be any sort of area for "well, I wasn't sure, I didn't know". So you'll find most organisations now will have a regular programme of reminders through either a training programme that you regularly do or screen shots that you regularly have to see. We have moved into certification of that so it's not just that you say you've seen it you have to go through a computer module, go through the whole module and then pass the test. That way you've got a complete audit trail, the time you took, the score you had and all that sort of thing. It is very important to have the evidence.

The ACFE in its 2008 RTTN identified fraud awareness training programmes as a key anti-fraud control in two distinct categories: fraud training for managers and executives; and fraud training for employees. Of those entities included in the survey, around 40% ran these training programmes (slightly more than 40% for managers and executives and slightly less for employees). Each produced over a 50% reduction compared with the median losses from fraud in the survey. These figures remained remarkably constant in the ACFE's 2010 RTTNs.

It is encouraging that the prevalence of fraud awareness training amongst organisations in the ACFE's survey of 2010 actually held up very well compared with the fraud training undertaken two years earlier. It is also slightly surprising. Training programmes cost money to run and expenditure budgets around the world have been impacted by the global economic downturn of 2008–09. Saving money by cutting back on training is an easy call for a Finance Director to make. Certainly my own experience and that of colleagues who also run training courses would support this proposition. There has been a marked drop in the numbers of delegates attending my public, open-enrolment training courses on fraud, especially in the UK but also in other countries too. There is one notable exception to this: in those industries and professions where there is a requirement on individuals to be able to demonstrate that they have attended a certain number of training modules each year for continuing professional development purposes ("CPD"). Consider the accountancy profession, for example. I lecture frequently for the Association of Certified Chartered Accountants ("ACCA") in the UK. As part of the CPD programme, the ACCA runs a series of structured update courses for their members held on Saturdays over the autumn period every year. I have lectured at a number of these events and they regularly attract over 100 delegates.

No compliance drivers – consequences

An important point to make here is that anti-fraud awareness training is not compulsory. It is not a legal or a regulatory requirement. This stands in contrast to the training requirements in other areas of financial crime management such as anti-money laundering and anti-bribery and corruption (following the Bribery Act 2010). Training in these areas is now required and is therefore a necessary and significant cost of compliance. To use anti-money laundering as the example, as a result of the increased rigour of legislation and regulations around the world in the wake of the 9/11 terrorist atrocities in the US (for example, the USA PATRIOT Act 2001, the Proceeds of Crime Act 2002 in the UK, and more recently the Third Money Laundering Directive 2007 in Europe) the training obligations of financial services firms and other organisations in the regulated sector for these purposes are now extensive. All employees including directors and managers must receive training on money laundering risk and on their personal and corporate responsibilities. This training is mandatory, ongoing and assessed. In other words, everyone must attend the courses (with evidence of such attendance), the training needs to happen every year (rather than being a one-off event) and the learning of the delegates should be tested with a pass required to demonstrate understanding compatible with minimum standards.

There are no similar compliance drivers in place yet for fraud training programmes. Consequently, training in fraud is likely to be patchy in practice – only 40% of the companies in the ACFE surveys carry out these programmes and, as mentioned above, I have seen at first hand that the numbers attending my public enrolment courses have declined in recent years. It would be disappointing if the combination of continuing pressures on costs and an absence of regulatory or legal compulsion serve to reduce anti-fraud training in future. Employee education is the foundation of preventing and detecting internal fraud. If the training is properly designed, costs do not need to be prohibitive. Set out below are some recommendations for fraud awareness training:

- Always include an element of fraud awareness in the induction process for new staff;

- Utilise the internal auditors as consultants to deliver cost-effective in-house training;

- Make use of fraud quizzes and practical examples (events that have happened within the organisation if appropriate) to make the training as interesting and relevant as possible;

- Where there is a requirement to train staff for compliance purposes (for example, in anti-money laundering or the Bribery Act 2010), broaden the scope of the subject matter to include fraud risk also; and

- Consider using alternative and/or complementary techniques to raise awareness of fraud: computer-based training ("CBT") packages, where the material is delivered directly to an individual's workstation or smartphone so that employees are trained in the most time-efficient way; or webinars, where employees sign into a short (say one-hour timespan) lecture and feedback session put on remotely by a training provider.

Practical training for small businesses

Finally, the most effective awareness raising is often carried out day to day by diligent and effective managers. This applies in particular to small and medium-sized organisations, where formal training courses are often considered to be prohibitively expensive.

Consider Bernard's response when I asked him how he went about the task of making everyone who works in his business aware of their individual responsibility to prevent and detect fraud. Bernard is the owner and Managing Director of a medium-sized manufacturing business based in London. His approach is completely different to that taken by Martin's company (see above) but I think you will agree that it is a very practical and cost-effective method – any manager can do the same if they have the will and the dedication. It is very appropriate for smaller organisations. This is what Bernard told me:

> I think you make people aware by talking to them, I don't know really if you want to call it training, by explaining to them what their responsibilities are, what their duty is and also pointing out to them the sort of things that can and do go on. I think this is what you must get over, you don't want them to think they are snooping or telling tales and I think this is one of the big concerns, you know "I don't want to shop somebody". It's these sorts of expressions that are common to all sorts of businesses. But the point is to get over the sense of responsibility and the sense of duty that people have to their employer and explaining to them the sort of things that can go on and having good staff, being selective, being careful who you pick to put into those sorts of positions, like your book-keeper for example. This person is going to be very, very important to you because he or she is the one who is going to tell you more about what's going on than you will ever see yourself so that's where I would say an effort should be made. It's about getting the background of the person right and supporting them in any suspicions that they might have and not to push it under the carpet. If they're worried about something you listen to their worries and you start probing, you never know where it's going to lead.

(c) Management review of internal controls

Overview

Some form of structured management review of internal controls is a central part of the modern governance, risk management and controls agenda as we have already seen in Chapters 4, 5 and 6. In particular, it is a key governance requirement both in the UK Corporate Governance Code and in the SOX 2002 in the US in terms of a management review of the controls in place over the financial reporting process.

There are two additional points to make about management review at this stage.

Devolved review

First, the review of internal controls should extend down to line manager and team leader level. For example, it is critical that those individuals in charge of the departments that represent high fraud risk (for example, accounts, treasury, purchasing and procurement, sales and customer service) understand that it is their responsibility to review the operation of the internal controls in these areas. They should be tasked formally with doing so as part of setting their objectives for the year, so that it becomes part of their appraisal process too.

Importance in small businesses

Secondly, management needs to be especially proactive in its review and oversight of the operations in smaller businesses. The ACFE's 2010 RTTNs concluded that small organisations are disproportionately at risk from asset misappropriation frauds (for example, cheque tampering, skimming, expense reimbursement and payroll irregularities) because they lack the anti-fraud controls and segregation of duties that are present in larger entities. So, management needs to be vigilant throughout the business: from an overall understanding of the accounts, through the business processes to the detailed transactions such as a regular scrutiny and sign-off of expense claims, if fraud risk in the small business environment is to be minimised. Unfortunately, this does not always happen. Without visible and proactive monitoring by managers, small organisations will remain at risk of suffering asset misappropriation fraud.

One of the interesting insights coming out of the ACFE's 2010 RTTNs is the way that those organisations that have been the victim of fraud have reacted to it. Over 80% of the organisations represented in the survey did take steps to modify their controls as a result of suffering a fraud event (though of course the flipside is that a significant minority, 20%, chose to do nothing!). There were found to be two aspects of control in particular that were strengthened by way of a response: increased segregation of duties and formal review of internal controls by management. A review of controls by management does not cost much money to implement – in my view it is an absolutely integral part of the job of being a manager in the first place. I also believe it to be absolutely essential to reduce fraud risk in small businesses.

Management review is not fraud-specific of course. It should be part of good governance in all organisations. In situations where this review is ineffective in practice, then that organisation concerned is likely to be exposed to a wider set of threats than simply fraud, because there will no doubt be fundamental problems with operational efficiency and with the management of business risk generally.

5-Point fraud prevention plan

Controls and procedures cost time and money to design and to implement. I understand that it may not be possible to implement all of the measures that I have set out here as being important in terms of preventing fraud from occurring in an organisation, or even most of them. Accordingly, I like to recommend to my delegates a basic, but sound, fraud prevention plan that they might choose to implement in their own businesses. The measures are not cost free (for example the awareness training programme will require a financial commitment) but I believe that, taken together, they provide a cost-effective and proportionate approach and represent a cogent strategy for most business organisations.

My fraud prevention plan has five components, as follows:

- An assessment of fraud risk throughout the organisation;

- An anti-fraud policy statement, to include a fraud response plan;

- A fraud awareness training programme that underpins the policy statement;

- Robust staff vetting procedures that are applied consistently to new hires; and

- A whistle-blowing hotline.

Summary – Five Key Learning Points for Directors and Managers

In this Chapter we have examined the internal controls that are most effective in preventing fraud from occurring in organisations. There is in fact an extensive menu of controls available to be used by directors and managers, both generic and fraud-specific. It is for senior management to decide which combination of these will be most effective for their particular organisation. However, it is important always to realise that no system can be guaranteed to be fraud-proof so we need to look at how to detect fraud also, which is the subject of the next Chapter.

Before we look at fraud detection, there are some key lessons for directors and managers coming out of this Chapter.

√ Be aware of the importance of the six key fraud prevention controls: staff vetting; employee support programmes; job rotation and mandatory vacations; fraud awareness training; an anti-fraud policy statement; and management review of internal controls.

√ Understand the importance of the three key generic controls that provide the foundation for the anti-fraud framework. These are: segregation of duties; delegation of authority levels and authorisation limits; and physical and computer security over assets, records and information.

√ Always carry out a cost/benefit analysis – some controls are more appropriate in certain organisations that in others. For example, segregation of duties is a vital part of the controls framework of larger organisations but may well be impractical in many small or medium-sized companies. For smaller organisations, a visible and proactive review by management of the business in general, and the operation of anti-fraud controls in particular, will be essential to provide assurance.

√ Consider adopting the 5-Point Fraud Prevention Plan as a proportionate and cost-effective way of increasing assurance in your business.

√ Remember that there is no such thing as a system of controls that is guaranteed to be fraud-proof. Because of this, there is always a need to combine preventative controls with detective controls for an optimal anti-fraud framework.

8 Detection

Fraud Awareness Quiz – Question 8

Fraud occurs in all business sectors and is detected through a variety of means. What do you think is the most common way that fraud is discovered?

"But he seemed like such a nice guy, he still lives with his mother"

I am sitting in the office of the Finance Director of a medium-sized retailer in south London. It is February 1997. I am taking the Finance Director through the results of my review of the circumstances surrounding a fraud that had been carried out by a long-standing and trusted member of his staff. The review has a particular focus on the control weaknesses that had enabled the individual not only to carry out the fraud but also to remain undetected for over three years.

The individual concerned, a man in his forties, had eventually been found out when he became ill and another member of staff had taken over his duties, which included the handling of all the accounting and all the cash arising from a sales unit established on the ground floor in the head office building. Many of the sales were made on a cash basis. Essentially the fraudster had been skimming some of the cash off the sales before any figures were recorded in the books. When the Finance Director had confronted him with the evidence of fraud he had confessed readily enough but otherwise he said very little and gave no indication as to his motive. Subsequently, he was dismissed from his employment with the company and, following the police being informed he had been arrested and charged with fraud. It was estimated that he had stolen over £150,000 from the company in the three years that the fraud scheme had been running.

I am talking to the Finance Director now about the most sensitive aspect of the fraud review from his point of view, namely the fact that the fraudster had not been the subject of even routine checks when at work. He had his own office, had complete autonomy in the running of the sales unit and was not subject to any meaningful management review that I can see at all. The Finance Director attempts to justify this by saying that the individual had worked at the company for years, he was well liked by everyone and seemed totally harmless – no one could possibly have suspected him of being a fraudster.

I tell the Finance Director that I have some good news for him but also some bad news. The good news is that I have found out the motive for the fraud. The bad news is that this motive is something that he and the other senior managers in the company could have, and should have, discovered for themselves a long time ago. The evidence was there all along, the problem was that nobody was looking. I start to explain. As part of my requests for information at the outset of the review, I had asked whether the company had a telephone call-log – that is to say, a record of all the calls made from each office extension on the company's network. I had been pleased, if a little surprised, when told that the company did indeed have this information and I was shown a series of large computer print-outs that comprised the call-log. Two things became clear very quickly. First, the inches of dust covering the print-outs indicated that they had never even been looked at by anyone previously, let alone systematically reviewed. Secondly, as soon as I located the office extension of the fraudster on the print-outs, I could see straight away that there was a big problem concerning this man's calls. The call-log for his office extension was littered with "0898" numbers – premium-rate telephone lines that at that time I knew were used to access two types of services only. They were either sex lines or they were gambling lines. I simply dialled two of these numbers and I knew immediately the motive for the fraud – our man was a gambling addict. He was making calls to the bookmakers as many as 10 times a day, sometimes more, placing bets. He obviously had an urgent need for cash to fund his addiction and this financial pressure provides a classic motive for the fraud.

I look at the Finance Director who has started to shake his head slowly from side to side. He is clearly shocked at this news. After a while he replies: "I can hardly believe it, a gambling addict! But he seemed like such a nice guy, everybody liked him. He still lives with his mother for God's sake!"

Introduction

Fraud is hidden. It is often carried out by individuals who have worked in their organisation for a long time and have good knowledge of its systems and procedures, as happened in the case I describe above. It is therefore difficult to detect fraud. This Chapter looks at the key detective measures, those controls and techniques that have proved to be most successful at uncovering fraud schemes in practice.

We begin this Chapter, however, with a review of the most under-used component of the Fraud Risk Management Framework, that of deterrence. Deterrence means the modification of behaviour by the threat of sanctions. A key concept of fraud deterrence is "the perception of detection". According to this concept, an individual who is considering committing fraud will be unlikely to proceed to the act if he or she believes that the consequences will be that they are caught, prosecuted and jailed. We discuss a number of deterrence measures that are available to all organisations but which are not often adopted in practice. Partly this is down to ignorance. But it is also the result of a failure of senior management to tackle resistance to change. For example, surprise or spot audits have been shown to have a big impact, but they are not popular with operational managers. Discussing fraud risk as part of routine audit or management reviews is also an effective way of demonstrating that fraud is taken seriously within the organisation. The problem here is that fraud is thought to be a sensitive subject, one that might offend people if it is raised. Consequently, the subject is often not raised at all, either by internal audit or by managers.

We then move onto look at fraud detection. Here, a number of the generic and preventative controls that we discussed in Chapters 6 and 7 can be specifically tailored to help to detect fraudulent activity. These include: reconciliations, independent reviews, physical inspections and stock counts, variance analyses and audit. In addition, there are three very important detective controls that are essential if management is to have any confidence that fraud in their organisation is going to be uncovered quickly. Each of these controls is reviewed in detail in this Chapter: surprise audits; whistle-blowing hotlines and the use of data mining software. These controls are by no means a panacea and fraud will remain difficult to detect even when all three are used within an organisation. When combined with the deterrence measures referred to above, however, they will provide directors and managers with reasonable assurance that if fraud is happening in their organisation it will be discovered as quickly as possible.

Before we look at fraud deterrence and detection techniques, we need to return to the Quiz and the answers to Question 8.

Answers to the Quiz

Fraud Awareness Quiz – Question 8

Fraud occurs in all business sectors and is detected through a variety of means. What do you think is the most common way that fraud is discovered?

This question asks delegates for their own perception of how fraud is detected. Over the years I have found that the general awareness in the area is good, with the majority of delegates on my courses correctly identifying in their answers the single most important method of detection. According to the research, by far the most important way that fraud is uncovered is by way of a tip-off, typically from staff, but also from non-company sources such as clients, customers and suppliers. The ACFE's 2010 RTTNs states that: "three times as many frauds in our study were uncovered by a tip as by any other method".

There are a number of important observations to make from the discussions with delegates around this question. The first is the continuing emphasis placed by delegates on the importance of pure chance or accident in detecting fraud, as opposed to the operation of a specific control or as a result of concerns raised by audit work or management review. I understand this and have a lot of sympathy with it. Chance has often played a very important part in whether and when fraud schemes are discovered, especially for high value frauds involving directors and/or owners. The same is true for fraud in smaller organisations where there are often fewer formal controls. The importance of chance might be declining, however. The analysis carried out by the ACFE for its 2010 RTTNs shows for the first time that, for the cases included in the survey, management review and internal audit work were the initial methods used to detect more frauds than those uncovered by accident.

My second observation is that there is always a healthy scepticism shown by delegates towards the effectiveness of the external audit process in detecting fraud. In fact, I cannot recall a single delegate who has given "external audit" as their answer to this question! They are right to be sceptical. According to the ACFE survey results, only around 5% of the frauds featured were detected by external audit. The external audit of financial statements is perhaps the most commonly used anti-fraud control of all in both the public and the private sectors but its effectiveness is poor and organisations are well advised not to place too much reliance on it to detect fraud.

There is one more important observation to make concerning delegates' comments in answer to this Quiz question. This point is actually the inverse of the one made above where we saw that external audits represent, in fraud terms, a frequently used but ineffective control. From discussions with many delegates over the years it seems that few of their organisations make use of the most effective anti-fraud control, the whistle-blowing hotline. Most frauds are uncovered through some form of tip-off. The delegates on my courses are well aware of this and yet, when asked, it is generally only those from financial institutions or from very large publicly listed companies who have experience of a whistle-blower programme operating in practice. Those from smaller organisations or other business sectors tend not to make use of this control at all. Also, whenever I raise the idea of maximising the effectiveness of the control by giving rewards to whistle-blowers, thereby giving them an incentive to come forward with their concerns, I am met with some amusement and often with outright hostility. This is clearly a controversial area. We will look at the whole debate around whistle-blowing hotlines in detail later in this Chapter but I will say here that I think it is ironic that the single most effective anti-fraud detective control (a whistle-blower programme) is viewed with such scepticism. Certainly the control of a whistle-blower programme is rarely used in practice and, even when it is in operation, it is often poorly designed and inefficient as a result.

The deterrence factor

Overview – what is meant by deterrence

Deterrence measures provide some of the most powerful yet least well used techniques for managing fraud risk. Set out below are a number of key ideas, putting the framework for deterrence in its proper context, before we look at the various options available to directors and managers in this area. These should be very attractive options because they are generally low cost actions that can deliver impressive results by reducing the fraud threats significantly.

According to the Oxford English Dictionary, the verb "deter" means to "discourage or prevent (a person) through fear or dislike of the consequences". Each of us will be aware of deterrence mechanisms in our everyday lives, often to do with aspects of policing and law enforcement. For example, anyone who drives a car is likely to be familiar with the device known as the speed enforcement camera ("speed camera") which is used to monitor compliance with speed limits. In the UK, where I do most of my own driving, this has had a noticeable effect. The first such systems were introduced in the 1960s but, certainly from the late 1990s onwards, with the introduction of digital cameras, speed cameras have been a significant and controversial feature of the road network in the UK. Rather than getting involved in the controversy, consider a very simple example of the impact of speed cameras on driving patterns on motorways in the UK. Here the speed limit is 70 miles per hour. Most people will exceed this speed limit when driving on the motorway as a matter of routine, apart from the 200 yards either side of a speed camera, when they will miraculously slow down to 69 miles an hour whilst moving past the camera, only to speed up again once they are out of camera range. The reason for this driving pattern is simple. In the UK if a driver is convicted of a motoring offence the courts can impose a fine and also endorse the individual's driving licence with penalty points. A speeding offence such as this is likely to incur three penalty points. If a driver builds up 12 or more penalty points within a period of three years he or she is liable to be disqualified from driving under the "totting up" system. So, this is a classic application of the deterrence factor – most drivers in the UK do not want to pay the fine or, especially, incur the penalty points and so are prepared to slow their speed down for the period of the application of the control.

When applied to financial crime theory, deterrence is based on the concept that, if the consequences of committing a crime are thought to outweigh the benefit of the crime itself, then the individual concerned will be deterred from going ahead and actually committing the crime. This is very much aligned to Dr Cressey's research and to the thinking behind the Fraud Triangle model that we saw in Chapter 3. In this context, deterrence may be thought of as the modification of behaviour through the threat of sanctions. Or to put this more in the terms of criminal psychology: an individual's willingness to commit fraud is inversely proportional to the perceived risk of being caught.

The perception of detection

This leads in turn to the key concept, highlighted by the ACFE and others, of the perception of detection. Put simply, those who think that they will be caught if they commit fraud are less likely to go ahead and commit the crime.

Fraud is by its very nature an activity that is carried out in secret and by stealth. It is a hidden, deceptive scheme and it is therefore almost always difficult to detect. Directors and managers need not despair however because fraud risk can be significantly reduced by increasing the perception of detection amongst everybody working in their organisation. Perception can be just as powerful as reality. Consider the following hypothetical example of how the perception of detection can influence behaviour.

An individual is under financial pressure and is considering committing fraud to provide the money to settle his debts. He starts to think about the opportunities but then remembers the internal audit visit last month and all the questions they were asking about fraud. The more our would-be fraudster thinks about this, the more he starts to believe that any criminal acts he commits might be detected, and as a result he becomes more hesitant about carrying out the crime in the first place. At the very least, he is likely to pause and think about the consequences. This hesitation will only increase if he is also convinced that dismissal and prosecution will inevitably follow the discovery of the fraud, so that the end result of actually going ahead and committing the fraud could well be a prison sentence. As we have seen, the research suggests that our would-be fraudster is likely to be a first-time offender, in which case his fear of serving time in jail is likely to be very high. Will he actually commit the crime? It is impossible to say for sure of course but the key point is that where the perception of detection is high, as in this example, individuals are less likely to proceed with the fraudulent act.

One issue that organisations need to address is whether or not they are going to inform the authorities about an internal fraud. Often there is reluctance to do this because of fears about damage to the business's reputation should information about the fraud become public knowledge through coverage in the media for example. This can be a difficult decision for directors and managers to take. If the employees know that the police will be contacted in the event of any fraud, however, then there are real benefits to the organisation in terms of increased fraud deterrence. Also, in practice, fears of reputational damage are often unfounded. In fact the situation can often be turned to the organisation's advantage in terms of taking a robust approach that protects shareholders' and stakeholders' interests alike.

As an example of this, consider what Sharon, the deputy CEO of a large bank in the Caribbean, had to say when I asked her about her company's approach to the whole area of fraud investigations, involving the authorities and possible reputational damage. Sharon's comments clearly show the benefits of taking a tough approach in this difficult area.

In the early days, we were kind of reluctant to involve the fraud squad and the police when we had a fraud because people would think this institution has these things . . . "your financial institution has people stealing" and so on. But then we started realising that what was happening was that the incidents of fraud were increasing especially in the retail bank – the amounts might not be huge but they had the potential to be huge. It was not like in the treasury or international trade where they hit a button and they can wipe you out of millions of dollars but still it could become endemic in your culture. We took a decision, we discussed it and after a while we said this thing is getting ridiculous we need to do something about it. We had all these tellers coming in and they would steal $5,000 and we said: "You know what, it has to stop." So we took a decision and it wasn't taken easily, I mean it was tough . . . we felt we simply had to call the police. So, eventually we decided – the fraud squad has to be called in once there is a fraud, end of story. Once audit looks at it and determines that it is fraudulent, the fraud squad has to be called in and really we don't care who it is, we don't care if the person is 21 years old or the person is 50 years old, even if it's a young person and you are affecting their lives. We also decided that if the police wanted to walk into our banking hall and take out somebody they must do it.

But I want to tell you that once we decided that, then the number of people on the front line stealing money just started dropping. I'm sorry to say this about human beings, human beings have to have sanction or reward so whether the sanction or reward is rooted in their religion or is rooted in the policies of the organisation that is what it is. I can tell you that up to this day we have senior managers who feel it is wrong to call the fraud squad. But as managers you really should try and reduce the fraud. What we also succeeded in doing was we created a public image so that when a newspaper calls and says this has happened we say yes because our organisation will not tolerate this, our customers are too important to us, our customers' money must always be safe and we will not stand for this. And we started to become known for protecting our customers' interests rather than "oh you have fraud in your bank" so it worked out well.

Ways to increase the deterrence factor

An organisation's principal mechanism for deterring fraud is to have a strong system of internal controls in place. However, directors and managers should be aware that it is possible to increase the deterrence factor within their organisation significantly by introducing any combination of the five measures (or any one of them individually) set out below:

(a) Surprise audits

The ACFE's research consistently ranks this as one of the most effective anti-fraud controls. It can be used both to deter and to detect fraud schemes. The key aspects of surprise audits, together with interview extracts showing how they have been used to good effect in practice, are considered in detail later in this Chapter under the "fraud detection" heading.

(b) Asking about fraud as part of routine audit enquiries

When I work with delegates on courses and we discuss the ways of increasing anti-fraud deterrence factors within organisations, I am very keen to stress the importance of management making all of their employees aware that fighting fraud is taken very seriously. To do so, the subject of fraud must be addressed, talked about and made visible. This can be done in a number of ways, but having the internal auditors make fraud-related enquiries during the course of their work is a central part.

Fraud and the "f-word conundrum"

This does not always happen in practice, however, far from it. In my experience, fraud is very often like the "invisible threat" in business today because nobody talks about it. To illustrate what I mean by this I like to take my delegates through what I call the "f-word conundrum". It goes something like this.

Fraud is a word that begins with the letter f, obviously. It's a standard word, used regularly enough in society. There is another word in the English language which also begins with the letter f, but this word is very different, it is a taboo word and it is definitely not to be used in polite society. You all know what the taboo f-word is and I have no intentions of saying it out aloud now. But I will say that in a business context something strange happens with these two words. In my experience, I hear the taboo f-word all the time in business – I hear it on the building site, I hear it on the shop-floor, I hear it in the accounts department and I hear it around the boardroom table. The word I never hear in a business context, or hardly ever hear, is the other f-word – fraud. Business people – managers, team leaders, auditors even – seem to be most reluctant to use this word, afraid even. Perhaps they think that by using it they may cause offence or that the other party to the conversation may somehow feel that they are being accused of actually committing fraud, rather than being asked about a significant business risk. All of this is profoundly unhelpful when it comes to reducing fraud risk. There is an old saying: "fraud is like mushrooms, it grows in the dark". If no-one discusses fraud, if even the auditors never raise the subject, how is a potential fraudster likely to react? Will he or she feel any perception of detection? Absolutely not, there will be no effective deterrence factor here at all. Don't let fraud become the taboo f-word in your organisation.

This failure to discuss fraud risk is all the more disappointing when it occurs in an audit context. The perspective is different, depending on whether it is an external or an internal audit, but it is important that the threats are discussed fully with management in both cases if the deterrence factor is to work properly in the organisation. Let us look at each in turn:

- **Internal audit perspective.** I appreciate that there are difficulties for internal auditors in addressing the subject of fraud openly during their assignments: they are working in the business every day and want to foster relationships on a professional but amicable basis. Discussions around fraud might not be thought to be conducive to this. If an internal audit is being carried out in an area of obvious fraud risk, however, (such as in the buying department or in treasury) and the subject of fraud is never raised, then I would consider this to be unprofessional, negligent even, as to me this represents a failure of the auditors to do their job properly. After all, who should know about the fraud threats in the buying department if not the head of that department? So, it is entirely appropriate, in my view, to talk to that person about fraud. However, I would caution against internal auditors starting to discuss fraud on an ad hoc basis. The approach needs to be properly thought through, with the approval of the Head of Internal Audit and the backing of the audit committee and of the board. One mechanism for doing this would be to include a specific question (or series of questions) on fraud in any risk and controls questionnaires that are issued as part of the internal audit process. Consistency has many benefits, not least here the fact that if a standard approach is adopted throughout the organisation, which includes questions on fraud, then all employees will clearly understand that fraud is on the internal auditors' "radar" and that they are actively considering the threats. This will send out a powerful message and is likely to increase the deterrence factor significantly.

- **External audit perspective.** Here the position has changed since the start of the century, in particular in response to investor concerns and perceived failings of the external auditors in the high profile corporate collapses at Enron, WorldCom and other US companies at that time. The SOX has made it compulsory for audit firms to include the possibility of fraud in their audit plans for companies listed on the US exchanges. Further, the new auditing standards SAS 99 and ISA 240 now require auditors to discuss fraud risk with management as part of the audit work. So, in theory, the external auditors should be focusing on fraud and addressing it directly with management. The audit committee needs to ensure that this happens in practice too.

Fraud questioning in action

The fundamental principle of taking a risk-based approach to fraud is to target controls at the areas of highest risk. As we have seen, for most organisations, the greatest fraud risk lies at the top with the directors and senior managers. In order to have the most effective deterrent measures in place, therefore, it is important that the fraud issue is raised with the two "riskiest" people in this context in the organisation – the Chief Executive Officer and the Chief Financial Officer. Consider the following set of questions, designed to be asked by an internal auditor of the CEO of a subsidiary company within the group that is undergoing an internal audit.

FRAUD QUESTIONS TO THE CHIEF EXECUTIVE OFFICER (ASSUME OF A SUBSIDIARY)

Q1 Internal auditors need to assess the risks of material fraud in every company in the Group, not only yours. So we need to ask you and other employees some very specific questions about fraud. Do you understand?

Q2 Do you believe fraud is a problem for business in general?

Q3 How do you think your company compares to others in terms of its vulnerability to fraud?

Q4 In the past, what kinds of fraud have been committed against your company?

Q5 What areas are currently vulnerable to fraud by employees or management?

Q6 Sometimes top executives commit fraud because of their personal financial difficulties. Are you currently in good shape financially?

Q7 Would you allow us to examine your personal financial statements?

Q8 Sometimes Chief Financial Officers commit fraud without the knowledge of the CEO. Do you have any reason to suspect that your CFO has committed fraud against the company?

Q9 Finally, I have to ask you one further question and it should be obvious why. Have you ever committed fraud against the company?

When I work through these questions with delegates, including internal auditors, on courses, they are generally receptive to this approach and are comfortable with the prospect of including all of the questions as part of their discussions with management up to, and including, Q5. Delegates react to the remaining four questions differently, however. These are very direct questions and all the delegates that I have worked with on this exercise consider them to be inappropriate, even delegates from the US where this type of aggressive questioning is advocated by the AICPA and other organisations looking to crack down strongly on financial crime. The last question sometimes attracts amusement, ridicule even along the lines of: "What is the point? No CEO is going to admit anything even if they had defrauded the company in the past." This is entirely to miss the point of the question. The primary purpose of Q9 is deterrence – the CEO will be left in no doubt that he or she is firmly on the internal auditors' radar screen in terms of fraud risk. There is a secondary purpose also, which is most relevant if the auditor has received fraud investigation training in the past. The auditor should be looking for the reaction of the CEO to this question, to see how he or she copes with pressure and then should be seeking at a later stage to calibrate that response with how the CEO reacts when he or she is not under pressure. This idea of calibration is the overarching principle behind the use of lie detectors. Of course, it is a difficult skill for a human and the auditor will need not only training but also considerable experience of fraud investigation work to bring this off successfully. We will return to this subject when we look at interviewing in a fraud context in Chapter 9. For now it is sufficient to point out that, whilst it is always possible, if unlikely, that the CEO will reveal something, without asking the question in the first place there is simply no chance of this.

Before moving on, there is one more important point to make about using the auditors to raise the profile of fraud throughout the organisation. In my view, specific questions about fraud should be directed primarily to senior management and departmental heads. The auditors will speak to many more junior members of staff during the course of their work, however. I think that there is one important question that needs to be asked of junior members of staff, especially in organisations that do not operate a whistle-blower programme. The question is as follows:

Have you ever been asked to do something that you thought was unethical or even illegal by one of your managers or your team leader?

This question sends out the important message that internal audit is concerned about these matters. It also provides an opportunity for the employee to raise concerns that, in the absence of a whistle-blower programme, might be very difficult to do otherwise.

(c) Surveillance and monitoring
Overview
I am no expert in the world of surveillance, counter-surveillance and security, although I have spent a lot of time working with people who are. I had my first dealings with security specialists when working on the Polly Peck case and I have made use of their expertise from time to time on fraud assignments ever since. I have used them in particular to assist in compiling the evidence needed to bring fraud investigations to a successful conclusion, as will be seen in the detailed case

study in Chapter 9. Whenever I have used these specialists I have always been very careful to make sure that they work within the law and have always obtained clearance from lawyers in this regard. I think that this is good advice for directors, managers, internal auditors or whoever is embarking on surveillance activities.

In this section we are looking specifically at organisations making use of certain surveillance techniques to protect themselves against the threats of theft and fraud through increasing the deterrence factor. Before we look at specific examples, some brief background information is appropriate here because the issue of surveillance is sometimes controversial.

The word surveillance is in fact the French word for "watching over". It sometimes carries sinister overtones today. Surveillance has come to be associated particularly with the close observation and monitoring of the behaviour and activities of a suspected person (or group of people), mainly by government agencies in the interests of national security. It is often carried out in a covert or surreptitious way.

Development of surveillance
The development of technology since the 1980s has seen a rapid advance in the sophistication and spread of surveillance: CCTV cameras, the interception of telephone calls, computer surveillance and biometric software have now largely, though not completely, replaced old-fashioned techniques such as assigning a couple of detectives to follow a suspect all day and note down his or her activities. The UK is now one of the most "watched" nations in the world, with CCTV cameras on every high street, or so it seems. The BBC reported in 2006 that there were over 4 million CCTV cameras in the country, about one for every 14 people! With the spread of these methods has come increasing concern about human and civil rights, especially the need to protect an individual's right to privacy. Consequently, legislation has developed to establish ground rules and minimum standards. This, in turn, has sometimes proved to be controversial. For example, the USA PATRIOT Act, passed in 2001 in the aftermath of the 9/11 atrocities is widely thought to be a tough piece of legislation aimed at deterring and punishing terrorist acts in the US and around the world and making the funding of terrorism more difficult by clamping down on money laundering. This is all true but the Act has also proved to be highly controversial with civil liberty groups. "USA PATRIOT" is in fact a 10-letter acronym that stands for: Uniting (and) Strengthening America (by) Providing Appropriate Tools Required (to) Intercept (and) Obstruct Terrorism. The Act dramatically reduces the restrictions on the ability of law enforcement agencies in the US to search the telephone, email communications, medical, financial and other records of anyone that the authorities suspect of being a terrorist. Despite the clear intention to increase national security in the US, this piece of legislation is often referred to as a "snooper's charter" by champions of civil liberty and is widely distrusted by them as a result.

Of course, surveillance is not confined to the actions of governments. Companies and other business entities today make much use of surveillance methods and in a much broader context than investigations, for example to ensure the efficiency of productivity and performance of their employees and to protect company interests. In terms of the latter, there are a number of monitoring and surveillance techniques that can be used to mitigate the risk of theft and fraud in the workplace (for example, we discussed briefly in Chapter 7 the information security measures that are available to guard against external threats from hackers and the like). All measures should be introduced transparently and must of course comply with the relevant data protection legislation. If done in the right way they can increase the deterrent factor significantly. These measures include the following:

- **Thorough, visible and vigilant management.** Not all surveillance techniques are new and technology driven! The age-old emphasis on proper supervision and monitoring of performance in the workplace is as important to deterring fraud as it is to good business practices generally. Managers are paid to manage and part of this should include a review of timesheets, checks on invoices and expense claims, regular "walking" of the department and the setting of fair and risk-informed targets and remuneration packages for managers and staff.

- **CCTV cameras.** A correctly specified and installed CCTV system, working 24 hours a day and located in the appropriate parts of the organisation's premises, can have a major influence on the behaviour of employees and the attitude of criminal gangs alike. It will act as a deterrent to theft and fraud both by outsiders and by employees. Key departments and areas would be cash handling areas (such as the banking hall or the cashiers department in a traditional banking environment), warehouses and storerooms, stockrooms and remote areas of the operation. The cameras need to be clearly visible to have the desired deterrent effect of course and there must always be proper legal safeguards in place. There are two key benefits of CCTV cameras for staff. First, they help to make everyone feel safer at work. Secondly they provide assurance to all honest employees that if (say) cash were to go missing from the safe, they are less likely to be implicated or tainted with suspicion about the theft because there is a monitoring system in place showing all money placed in the safe and removed from it.

- **Monitoring electronic communications.** Employers have the right to monitor the activities of employees in many situations at work. In addition to recording on CCTV cameras, monitoring includes: opening mail or email; the use of automated software to check email; checking phone logs; and checking logs of those websites visited. These activities will generally be perfectly legal providing the monitoring relates to the business, the equipment being monitored is provided partly or wholly for work purposes and the employer has made all reasonable efforts to inform the employee that his or her communications will be monitored (for example, in the contract of employment, code of conduct, specific company policies etc.). Secret monitoring is only allowed in certain specified circumstance so that it will very rarely be legal. One of these circumstances is to prevent or detect crime where the company is allowed to protect itself. So, if there are good reasons to suspect that an identified individual is committing fraud or other criminal acts that are harming the company, covert scrutiny of that individual's electronic communications is likely to be legal. Untargeted covert exercises where the emails etc. of a number of employees are looked at in the hope of finding something incriminating are sometimes termed "fishing expeditions" and will almost certainly be illegal. Of course, for these measures to work as deterrents, employees do need to be aware that the company can and very likely will be carrying them out from time to time.

(d) Enforcement of policies
Overview

The board sets the values, the objectives and the policies of an organisation, a process that is sometimes overlooked but in my view it is in reality the engine-room of the entire business. It is then the job of management to ensure that these policies are actually carried out in practice. It is absolutely vital in terms of the establishment of a controls culture throughout the organisation that this is what actually happens day to day and that managers are prepared to enforce compliance with the policies if need be. There is really nothing further to add here to the earlier comments in Chapter 6 on systems of control. It should be clear that if fraud deterrence is to be enhanced through respect for strong internal controls then the organisation's policies themselves have to be enforced.

Practical example

In order to assess the extent to which this enforcement of policies happens in the organisations represented by the delegates on my courses, I like to ask them a straightforward question as follows:

Do you have a clear-desk policy in your organisation?

Actually, the clear-desk policy itself is not really what I am interested in here. I am looking for a particular kind of answer – the delegate who answers in the affirmative to the question but does so with a big smile on his or her face. I almost always receive at least one such response from any group of delegates. This is very helpful because I know absolutely what the combination of a nodding head with a knowing smile means in this context – it means that the organisation concerned does indeed have a clear-desk policy but it also has the hypothetical "old Harry" as an employee. Old Harry has been employed by the organisation for the last 20 years, his office is on the second floor and his desk resembles a swamp! I say this to the delegates in a light-hearted way but there is a serious purpose to it. The management in such an organisation is clearly not doing its job because it is not prepared to enforce the policy of the board, in this case on the need for a clear desk. The result is likely to be harmful to the organisation in many ways, not least that deterrence of fraud is likely to be very low. For the avoidance of doubt, there are a lot of "old Harrys" out there in business even today!

(e) Prosecute fraudsters and publicise successful convictions
Overview
In order to manage fraud threats successfully, directors and managers must be aware of risk and respond to it in an appropriate and proportionate way. As we have seen, the research strongly indicates that the great majority of fraudsters are first-time offenders. In other words, they have never served a prison sentence in jail before. It is the prospect of going to jail that is likely to be the biggest worry, the sharpest fear for any individual who is contemplating committing fraud. So, if directors and managers really do want to have effective fraud deterrence throughout their organisation, they must not only have strong controls in place but they must also be prepared to contact the authorities after a fraud event and prosecute the identified suspects involved through the criminal courts. Dismissing a fraudster for gross misconduct is of course a necessary part of the process. But the threat of dismissal will not, by itself, be sufficient to maximise the deterrent effect. In order to achieve effective deterrence, the threat of dismissal needs to be combined with the prospect of prosecution because it is the thought of going to prison that really scares the fraudster.

Length of prison sentences
It should be said in passing that the length of prison sentences given to convicted fraudsters does not itself add much to the deterrence factor. In his paper: "Sentencing Frauds: A Review" published in 2006 as part of the UK government's Fraud Review, Dr Michael Levi looked at cases investigated by the Serious Fraud Office in the period 2000–05 and noted the following factual information:

The 109 persons convicted in Serious Fraud Office cases 2000–2005 received an average of 31.7 months' imprisonment; half of them got 3 years or less. The average sentence imposed on the most severely sentenced person per case was 37.7 months' imprisonment. Eight persons received sentences longer than five years; 19 people received 4–5 year sentences; and 22 people (mostly co-defendants in cases where others were imprisoned) received non-custodial sentences. (Levi, 2006, p. 3)[1]

These prison sentences cannot be considered to be "long", especially as we are concerned here with cases of serious fraud. Dr Levi goes on to say that prison sentences might not be the answer to rising crime levels:

A rise in sentencing levels might cause more fear among potential offenders, especially if they are not confident that they will escape conviction; but tougher sentencing is not a simple substitute for greater certainty of detection, prohibition of future misconduct and/or conviction. We have little evidence about fraud offenders' beliefs or knowledge of such consequences at the time when they contemplated their offences. (Levi, 2006, p. 3)[2]

The position in Continental Europe is, if anything, even more lenient. For example, Dr Levi notes that in the first trial of suspects in the Parmalat scandal (the Italian dairy group riddled with multi-billion dollar fraud), held in Milan, the longest sentence was given to the former Chief Financial Officer, Fausto Tonna and it amounted to two years and six months.

A notable exception to lenient sentencing for financial crime is in the US where a key part of the SOX is to increase prison sentences for senior executives convicted of committing fraud. As examples: Mr Ebbers, the ex-CEO of WorldCom who was convicted of masterminding an $11 billion accounting fraud, was sentenced to 25 years in jail; and Mr Skilling, the ex-CEO at Enron, was sentenced to 24 years in jail for manipulating Enron's reported earnings and concealing losses from the investing public. These are huge sentences. It was hoped by some that these harsher penalties would act as a deterrent and help to prevent fraud. In fact, there is little evidence of this happening. For example, in 2008 Phillip Bennett, the former CEO of Refco Inc. (once one of the world's largest commodities brokerages) was sentenced to 16 years in jail for conspiracy to commit securities fraud leading to losses of $1.5 billion. When passing sentence, the judge in the case described Mr Bennett as "staggeringly arrogant". This is a key point I think whenever discussing the behaviour of senior executives. Sometimes their motives are fuelled by arrogance and entitlement – the length of sentences will have little deterrent effect on them because they simply do not believe they will be caught in the first place!

However, it remains true that the threat of prison in general will deter some would-be fraudsters and this is the key point here, rather than the absolute length of prison sentences.

Importance of publicity
The final point to make before looking at fraud detection is that organisations should be sure to publicise internally the results of successful investigations if they want to maximise the deterrent effect. This applies most obviously to situations that have resulted in the successful prosecution of the fraudster but publicity of dismissals can also send out a powerful message. Consider the following example, from my own experience.

Example: BAA and the T5 project. During the period 2004–06 I acted as consultant at various times to British Airports Authority ("BAA") on its mammoth construction project for the development of a new Terminal 5 building at Heathrow airport ("T5"). At the time this was the largest construction project in Europe with a total spend of some £4.3 billion. The outcome was very successful, with the new terminal being delivered on time and in line with budget costs too. Over 60,000 people worked on the project, which took over five years to complete from its start in 2002. As with all major projects, fraud and theft were significant risks and BAA adopted a full fraud risk management programme to mitigate them. A key part of the strategy was raising awareness of BAA's zero tolerance approach to criminality, especially via its in-house, dedicated newsletter. Included in every issue of the newsletter was a section on security which detailed all cases of employees and contractors who had been dismissed from the site for theft, abuse of drugs and alcohol, bogus expense claims etc. Publicity played a very important part in minimising fraud risk on the project.

Fraud detection

Introduction

The primary purpose of detective controls in any area of business is to reduce the exposure gap – the length of time from when things first go wrong and the organisation starts to have a problem to when it finds out about the problem. The same is true of fraud. Unfortunately, the evidence suggests that the fraud exposure gap can be a worryingly long period of time. Occupational fraud schemes typically last for years before they are discovered, which suggests that the main anti-fraud detective controls are either not as prevalent, or not as effective, as directors and managers might like to see. John Rusnak was able to defraud AIB for five years before being detected, whilst Bernie Madoff's Ponzi scheme was running for well over a decade before it collapsed at the end of 2008. The ACFE reported in the 2008 RTTN that the typical fraud in its study of US businesses lasted two years from the time it began to the time it was caught by the victim organisation. This was reduced to 18 months in its 2010 RTTNs, although here the ACFE was looking at occupational fraud around the world, not only in the US.

Fraud detection is the identification of actual or potential fraud within an organisation. It is a crucial part of an organisation's anti-fraud strategy. It relies upon the implementation of appropriate systems and procedures to detect the early warning signs of fraud. Effective fraud detection will not only reduce the exposure gap, it will also add to the deterrence factor as both new frauds and historical frauds are discovered. Obviously this will save money and it serves to protect organisations and their employees, customers and owners.

Effective fraud detection involves a combination of techniques: both proactive and reactive measures, and manual and automated controls. We look at three of the most important detective measures in detail below: surprise audits, fraud reporting mechanisms (whistle-blower programmes) and data mining and analysis work. However, it is important to note that many of the measures that have been discussed elsewhere in the book are also part of a robust detection strategy. Ongoing fraud risk assessments are a vital (and often under-used) proactive fraud detection measure. Staff training and awareness programmes are important here too. We have looked at them in this book primarily from the viewpoint of preventative controls but clearly they should involve the education of both management and staff about how to identify the warning signs of common frauds and also the procedures to follow should they find or suspect fraud. Also, the review of systems, processes and controls by management and internal audit will add to the fraud detection framework.

The three key fraud detective measures

Let us now look in detail at each of the three measures that have been shown to be the most effective in terms of fraud detection: surprise audits; whistle-blowing hotlines; and data mining.

(a) Surprise audits
Background
Most audits, whether they are traditional external or internal audits as discussed earlier in this book, or they are quality control or regulatory compliance audits, are planned and scheduled well in advance. This enables both the auditor and the management of the auditee entity or department concerned to plan properly for the visit, to make sure that all the necessary documentation is ready and that any individuals that are likely to be required to answer the auditor's questions will be available on site to do so. Advance scheduling provides assurance, therefore, that the audit will be completed in the most efficient manner.

A surprise (or spot) audit is a completely different prospect. The whole point here is that the audit team's arrival will be unannounced, so that in this situation the auditee entity or department has no time to prepare in advance of the visit at all. Surprise audits are generally very unpopular indeed!

First, consider the position of the auditee. All entities are rightly concerned to promote operational efficiency. Managers will want to know the timing of audit visits in advance so that they can organise and prepare all the necessary documentation and paperwork. Also this will enable them to plan their calendars, so that they are confident that the right people will be available to assist and deal with audit issues as and when they arise. This is particularly important in smaller organisations.

Next, consider the position of the auditors. They always need to work in a cost-effective way and to do so it is generally necessary to contact the departments that they will want to speak to in advance of the audit. Of course, the auditee will not be given the detailed steps of the audit programme in advance or be told which specific transactions will be selected for the audit tests but they do need to know for efficiency purposes what processes will be audited. Again it is important that key staff members are available for questions and are not on vacation or have little time because it is a particularly busy work period. In addition, there is another aspect to surprise audits that internal auditors in particular do not like. They are associated with inspection regimes. Modern internal auditing has at its heart the provision of essential services to management. There are genuine concerns that surprise audits can lead to poor working relationships.

Small number of surprise audits in practice
It is accepted in the business world that an element of surprise is required for audit effectiveness in a small set of cases only. Cash is the prime area for this, whether it is a spot check on the petty cash or a full cash count of the monies held in the safe or, for example with casinos, the cash around the business at a particular point in time. Stock and inventory levels provide another area where surprise counts are recognised as being necessary from time to time.

However, set against this unpopularity is the simple fact that surprise audits are a time-honoured technique for deterring and detecting fraud. The ACFE research confirms this, consistently finding them to be amongst the most effective, if under-used, of all anti-fraud controls. As an example, consider two hypothetical scenarios involving Mr Smith, a manager in the procurement department of a large manufacturing company. Mr Smith has a motive for committing fraud. His department is subject to audit visits each year from both the external auditors and the in-house audit team. In the first scenario, Mr Smith is presented with the very typical situation whereby both the internal and the external audits are planned over six months in advance. To what extent might he be deterred from going ahead with his planned fraud because of these audits? It is likely that they will not concern him in the least. He will be very confident that he can "manage" the situation and control what the audit team sees and what it does not see. So Mr Smith's perception of detection here will be low. Contrast this with the second scenario which is that, although the timing of the external audit is planned in advance, Mr Smith knows that the internal audit department has the ability to carry out spot audits, arranged with 24 hours' notice only. He also knows that the internal auditors carried out a number of these spot audits in various departments throughout the company last year and have done so twice already this year. Does this situation concern him? Almost certainly it does. Should his department be selected for a surprise audit, which is likely to be the case at some time in the future, then he will have virtually no control over the process and anything untoward that he is perpetrating may well be detected. The position is totally different here because Mr Smith's perception of detection is in this case likely to be high. This may make all the difference, so that in the second scenario Mr Smith may well decide not to go ahead with his planned fraud, whereas in the first scenario it is very likely that he will do so as there is nothing to stop him, or even to make him pause in his decision-making process.

Issues

Before looking at surprise audits in the context of the business environment, a brief review of the issues surrounding auditing generally in the context of quality assurance is instructive. Surprise audits have an important part to play in inspection regimes looking at the standards of organisations that the public relies on (such as hospitals and schools) and here they are carried out from a regulatory compliance point of view. Sometimes, however, the rigour of this might be diluted by making the process of signing up for such unannounced visits voluntary rather than compulsory. This happens for food manufacturers in the UK's retail sector, where the aim is to make sure that food production facilities comply with global standards for food safety. The purpose of surprise audits in a compliance context is to ensure that the auditor sees the records and performance of the entity "live" so to speak, or as they would be under normal operating conditions, and not as they appear to be following an intensive clean-up campaign in the days immediately before the visit to make sure that everything looks good during the inspection.

Surprise audits might appear to be desirable in the regulatory context but again they are generally not popular with auditee organisations. There is the obvious concern that they will score less well on documentary evidence of compliance with standards and regulations if they have no opportunity of carrying out an internal review before the visit.

From time to time, however, the media will highlight examples of alarmingly bad practices and poor standards by organisations that have previously been awarded consistently high scores from inspection regimes that rely exclusively on pre-announced inspection visits. The central problem of pre-arranged inspections is that they lack rigour and there have been many examples of scandals in the UK in recent years to support this argument, in particular in the health and social care sectors. It is interesting to note that, in response to recent concerns raised, Ofsted, the UK's regulator of standards in education, children's services and skills, is to make major changes to its inspection regime. In July 2011 it announced plans to inspect children's social care services without notice in future. Local authority children's social care services are to be subject to two-week, on-site, no notice inspections, which stands in marked contrast to the existing process, under which the councils are given two weeks' notice of inspection visits. This new inspection framework is due to come into force from May 2012.

Benefits of surprise audits and examples

To repeat, the ACFE's research indicates that surprise audits are one of the most effective yet under-used of all anti-fraud controls. So, although they are not popular, all directors and managers who are looking to improve their own fraud deterrence and detection mechanisms should consider changing their audit framework to include at least the possibility of surprise audits.

Indeed, many organisations are starting to adopt this approach. Two of my interviewees, Sharon and Jerry, provide good practical insights into both the difficulties and the benefits of using surprise audits in the extracts below. They both work in the financial services industry, although their organisations are very different.

Let us look first at what Sharon had to say when I asked her what methods her bank used to manage the difficulties that intense pressure on her people to hit their targets might cause. Sharon is the deputy CEO of a large bank in the Caribbean.

So one of the things we do for example in the retail bank . . . we have loan campaigns in the first quarter of the year which is the Christmas quarter, that is when the retail bank makes most of its money. So we run loan campaigns at that time and all these incentives for our people are tied into the campaigns but our people also know that during that period we run spot audits all the time because that is a huge area of risk. Because actually again we learnt by trial and error. In the early days of the institution we operated with big incentives and there was one particular branch that was just doing so well all the time with this and that and the other. The only problem was that by the time a year had passed all the loans started going south. The audit investigation started – seven people were fired and we ended up with a parking lot of 100 cars!

So now we don't stop, we still run the loan campaigns and we do the incentives but now everyone knows that the auditors can come in at any time – people don't know when they are coming in, they just come in and they take a sample of loans from anybody and so on. And that has cut down tremendously on this kind of fraud. At first it starts off almost like a non-adherence, a credit guidelines type of thing and then it becomes . . . you are pushing, pushing more and more and it becomes clear that we are looking at a fraud situation. So we do spot audits.

And in terms of individual managers at senior levels having to meet their targets and so on it is exactly the same thing. If your results are out of line – because every month, each senior manager has to report to the whole senior management team on their perform-ance – and if your performance starts to look "too good" then there is going to be an audit. It might just be a spot audit or whatever, it might not be a full audit, it might be an auditor who just turns up to go through a sample of your loans and so on but it is going to be done. So people start to understand this.

I have to be careful how I run my business. I'm not saying fraud is not going to happen here but you have to really want to do it in this organisation because the checks are in place, and the minute you are caught you go home. I mean it's not like somebody breezes in and says "Ok it's a little thing, we can forget it". No, no, no you'll go home and it doesn't matter how small the fraud is. We do these spot audit campaigns every year now.

Sharon's bank is demonstrating excellent deterrence and detective mechanisms there. All employ-ees know that if they are going to try anything on it is a big risk to them because they are likely to get caught. And if they are caught they "go home" – the local expression for being fired. So, everyone in Sharon's bank knows that the consequences of committing fraud are serious.

Next, let us look at what Jerry has to say on the subject of surprise audits. Jerry is a senior manager in a large UK bank. This was his reply when I asked him about the importance of internal audits and whether they were essential to make sure that compliance requirements were actually carried out in practice, rather than the whole thing becoming simply a box-ticking exercise.

Yes that's right. They'll come in and they will check everything and anything from the obvious, like the cash manager, making sure that the tills are being balanced correctly and there's nothing going on there, even to areas like the way we store our papers, to make sure we have got the right papers in the right places, and that they are properly looked after in terms of the Data Protection Act.

Every area has their own rigour manager, rigour teams who come in unannounced to branches, they do spot visits and that's a real strict thing. Surprise audits are not seen as too intrusive, the bank uses them all the time. In fact it's a real big yardstick. In terms of the rigour visits you need to get a high score . . . I forgot what it is exactly that the branch needs to get, but certainly it is way over 85% pass on a compliance visit to make sure that there is no come-back. Otherwise heads will roll big time, heads will roll! The results of a rigour visit affect the whole branch's incentive payments, if they fail a rigour visit then no-one gets paid on incentives – it's a real big issue.

These rigour visits are a huge deal. You always know when the auditors are in your area. They will visit a branch in your area, sometimes they will then visit another branch in the same area so everyone is then put on "red alert" in case they come to your branch. But of course the point is that the first branch the auditors visit no-one knows and then you don't know where they will go after that. So that's the actual visits but then everything we do is then checked as well. You know they will check, sample check, spot check accounts opening, all our lending is spot checked to make sure we are complying with conditions of sanction when we are lending, again they will check and make sure that we've gone through the right models to make sure that the customers aren't disadvantaged or we haven't been making things up so that the lending can go through. So yes everything, a lot of checking goes on, rigour is a huge area and we have a rigour scorecard which must have over 20 areas a month that you have to watch. I think you've got 24 points overall and if you get less than 18, no, less than 20 points in a month again you fall out of the incentive and you have to go on an improvement plan. Yes, so rigour is a big thing.

But it's counter-acted because all everyone wants to talk about is sales, sales, sales. You simply have to make your sales, you have to hit this massive target, rather than someone saying: "Oh by the way you've got this huge rigour target, you're taking shortcuts here" which might mean that you fall down on your rigour. So, some of the focus is taken off rigour, it almost becomes an afterthought although you are always aware of the rigour teams and you know that it is very serious. The bottom line is that we are led very much by sales managers. So it's a real conflict of interest and we are caught in the middle – which is where things can become difficult!

Jerry has many years' experience in retail banking and the extract above from our interview leaves me in no doubt that surprise audits have a high profile in his bank and are seen as a very important control. As a manager in the bank's retail network, Jerry is well aware of them personally and clearly the bank is using the rigour teams as a key compliance tool, investing a lot of time and money in this area. However, it is interesting that towards the end of this section of the interview Jerry talks about the overarching importance of sales targets and the tensions that exist day to day in the bank in this regard. Sales focus is a key part of the bank's culture and it is always possible that procedural short-cuts might be made in such an atmosphere simply in order to hit aggressive targets. We will come back to look at some of the tensions caused in organisations through pressure when we look at business ethics in the final Chapter of the book.

(b) Whistle-blowing hotlines
Introduction
A whistle-blower is a person who raises a concern about wrongdoing in terms of either an illegal act or a dangerous activity within an organisation that they have become aware of through their work. The concern is disclosed either internally (to those in positions of authority within the organisation) or externally to the public authorities.

Whistle-blowing hotlines have been used in government agencies in the US for decades but more recently they have been seen as an important potential tool for helping to prevent and detect corporate wrong-doing. They are now widely regarded as an important feature of governance best practice. In the US, the SOX requires audit committees to establish procedures for the confidential and/or anonymous submission by employees of concerns regarding questionable accounting or auditing practices. In the UK, the Corporate Governance Code requires audit committees to "review arrangements by which staff of the company may in confidence raise concerns about possible improprieties in matters of financial reporting or other matters", whilst "speak up" mechanisms are one of the adequate procedures referred to in the official Guidance as being available to commercial organisations as a possible defence against charges of failing to prevent bribery under the Section 7 Corporate Offence in the Bribery Act 2010.

Whistle-blowing is therefore an early warning system that can alert organisations to a wide variety of illegal, corrupt or dangerous practices that might be happening in the organisation. These practices include fraud but they can also cover such areas as health and safety, environmental damage, negligence (in a hospital or a school for example) and the mis-selling of pensions or personal loans.

Crucially, the system should allow for confidential reporting to someone who is not the employee's line manager. The theory suggests that if an organisation has a good whistle-blowing policy in place that embodies this principle, then it is likely that any concerns that an employee might have will be raised with his or her employer in the first instance, rather than going outside to the public authorities. The issue of whistle-blowing was addressed by the UK's Committee on Standards in Public Life (often referred to as the Nolan Committee) in its second report in 1996. Lord Nolan's committee recommended that employers introduce internal whistle-blowing procedures, whereby staff could raise concerns about wrongdoing at work. The committee uses the term whistle-blowing to mean the confidential raising of problems or concerns within an organisation that are associated with that organisation and not in the pejorative sense of leaking information or telling tales. It states that effective whistle-blowing systems should include:

> a clear statement that malpractice is taken seriously in the organisation and an indication of the sorts of matters regarded as malpractice; respect for the confidentiality of staff raising concerns if they wish, and the opportunity to raise concerns outside the line management structure; penalties for making false and malicious allegations; and an indication of the proper way in which concerns may be raised outside the organisation if necessary. (Nolan Committee, Second Report, 1996)[3]

Whistle-blowing is to be differentiated from a complaint or a grievance, where the employee making the report is directly and personally affected and is seeking redress or justice for himself or herself from any resulting investigation. Consequently, organisations should have a different and separate set of procedures in place to deal with allegations of bullying, sexual harassment or other examples of inappropriate workplace behaviour.

We are concerned in particular here with the use of whistle-blowing hotlines as fraud reporting mechanisms. The remainder of the section concentrates on this particular aspect of whistle-blowing.

Whistle-blowing hotlines – the key anti-fraud detective control

Tip-off is the most important way that fraud is detected. This is one of the most striking and consistent conclusions coming out of the ACFE's RTTNs since their research data was first compiled in 2002.To repeat the key finding, the ACFE notes in the 2010 RTTNs that: "three times as many frauds in our study were uncovered by a tip as by any other method".

Consequently, it follows that a fraud reporting mechanism (often called a whistle-blowing hotline), which makes it as simple and straightforward as possible for staff (and others) to pass on their concerns about suspected or actual fraud, should in theory be amongst the most effective detective controls that an organisation can deploy in the fight against fraud. The theory is proved in practice for those organisations that use the whistle-blowing control. Because these systems almost always raise the awareness of how to report misconduct, intuitively one would expect that the presence of a fraud hotline would result in more tips. This is borne out by the ACFE's research for the 2010 RTTNs, which states that: "the presence of fraud hotlines correlated with an increase in the number of cases detected by a tip". Two other key findings in the report well illustrate the benefits of whistle-blowing hotlines: first, that those organisations in the survey that had a fraud hotline suffered much smaller fraud losses than organisations without hotlines; and secondly that the exposure gap before fraud was detected was on average seven months shorter in those organisations that used hotlines than in those without them.

In practice, although there are sometimes issues with both the attitudes of people towards whistle-blowing hotlines and also the design of the control itself (we will discuss these later in this section), it is very apparent that many business people are aware of the importance of tip-offs in detecting fraud. I have seen this very clearly in the answers given by my delegates to the Quiz over the years. This awareness was also evident in the interviews and discussions I had when compiling the book.

First, when I discussed this book with Jeffrey Robinson, the financial crime expert and best-selling international author, I asked him to name the measure that, in his opinion, was the single most effective anti-fraud control. Jeffrey answered me straight away: "A whistle-blower programme that works."

Also, whistle-blowing featured strongly in a number of the interviews that I carried out for the book. Take Jerry for example. When I asked him during our interview what other controls his bank were relying on to detect fraud in addition to surprise audits, he was in no doubt – the bank's newly-enhanced whistle-blower programme. He also had some important caveats about the need for a proper investigation process to be attached if whistle-blowing is to make a difference within an organisation. This is what Jerry had to say:

> We are very big on what we call the whistle-blowing helpline – this is where staff can anonymously report on colleagues if they suspect there is something untoward going on. It is very difficult to spot some of these problems otherwise – Steve, you yourself say that it's very difficult to detect fraud. We have a lot of league tables in the bank, all of them to do with sales – not to do with putting pressure on people! So every week there are league tables published – you could be at the bottom, you could be marked "red" and

there could also be someone miles ahead at the front. You will know it's impossible to do that many deals so these people stick out like a sore thumb but they're lauded by management. We will get emails or calls from the top of the bank saying "I want to congratulate (say) Steve Giles on a fantastic sales performance. He's done this many deals this month. . . . " But everyone knows it's not real and then after a while it's found out, yes he's been cheating, he's been doing whatever to exceed his targets by cheating. And then of course you don't hear any more about that person but then things are repeated, someone else will be lauded, and they, senior management, will say again: "Well look they're doing it, in Romford they're selling all these products, why aren't you selling them?" And the answer is the same – "Well because they're cheating, you know they're cheating." So now the whistle-blowing helpline has been brought in. People who are getting hammered for not bringing in absurdly high sales figures are now saying well no that's not right – you need to investigate those people. There are now a lot of investigations that are happening and some staff members are being sacked as a result. So I think that's the biggest change, this is self-regulation but by the staff. It is in addition to the rigour teams that come in. I think senior management are beginning to realise that there is a potential problem with anyone who is way out in front in terms of their sales because, when staff now blow the whistle on these guys and they see . . . well, yes they were cheating. So now if anyone sticks out too much I would like to think they are investigated as a matter of course.

I think the whistle-blower programme is much more effective than it used to be because the calls are seen to be investigated now. We never used to have investigations. Three years ago you wouldn't know of any. If someone was sacked it would be for something really, really bad, not the result of whistle-blowing. But now people are being investigated.

Of course, this can go wrong. Let me give you an example. We have business development managers, who have networks of brokers and they are there to attract lending. One of these business development managers was investigated recently, very seriously investigated. She didn't get suspended in the end, it was all overblown and a complete misunderstanding. When business is introduced by a broker the development manager has to submit the broker to a fraud check – a piece of due diligence so that they can check out, make sure it's a bona fide broker, it's a bona fide solicitor etc. so that there is no fraud ring or cartel in play. This manager had been sending out fraud checks but spelling the name of the solicitor she was using wrongly. One letter in the name was wrong but it was wrong on every fraud check that she sent out. The fraud team didn't pick it up originally but it was eventually picked up. They were going to suspend her because they thought she'd misspelt the name on purpose to hide whatever she was up to. She was hauled in for a three-hour "interrogation" and all her broker deals were stopped. In the end this particular broker and solicitor turned out to be bona fide. They have now moved to a rival bank, where the broker is now introducing all of his business. So she's lost out massively here and so has the bank so there is a flip side to it all. It can be investigated wrongly and the people that seem to be doing the investigating can be really hard-nosed so it does need looking into. Also with the whistle-blowing helpline – the downside of it is that it can be used for vindictive purposes and there have been incidences of individuals trying to get back on someone.

Despite this I would say definitely that the bank is moving in the right direction with this.

So, Jerry appreciates the importance of the whistle-blowing mechanism in his bank as a method of detecting and deterring fraud and cheating amongst the staff. However, he also points to some of the frustrations and difficulties that can arise with the operation of the control in practice. The main issues and difficulties that organisations face when using hotlines are addressed below, together with how these can best be handled in practice.

The "outlier problem"

Before moving on, there is one point that Jerry makes here concerning those individuals who achieve apparently outstanding results. This is something that Sharon touched on also in her interview extract shown earlier in this Chapter. I call it the "outlier problem". From time to time certain individuals or organisations outperform their peers and/or their competitors by huge margins. Outlier situations should always be subject to review and monitoring because there are only two ways that wholly exceptional results can be achieved: either through outstanding performance or alternatively through fraud. The directors and managers need to take a close look at any outliers in their organisation because either there are successful practices that can be used elsewhere in the business or else there are fraudulent practices that need to be stopped. Outliers have featured in various guises in this book, Mr Leeson being the most obvious example of an individual who was regarded as a "star performer" by Barings Bank for a number of years before his fraud was uncovered.

The remainder of the section sets out the essential features of successful hotlines before we conclude by looking briefly at one of the most innovative but controversial areas surrounding this whole subject, that of providing incentives for whistle-blowers.

Scepticism and mistrust of hotlines

When I work with organisations or with delegates I continue to notice an underlying attitude of scepticism towards the idea of hotlines, despite their acknowledged effectiveness in detecting fraud. This can best be summed up by the following hypothetical story that I like to tell on training courses:

> I visit the Finance Director of an old client and he tells me that last year the organisation decided to take my advice and install a whistle-blowing hotline. The costs were not insignificant in terms of the time spent planning the initiative, writing the new policy, installing the line and making everyone aware of it. Nevertheless, the directors thought that it was a worthwhile investment because they felt that they were putting in place a really strong anti-fraud control that would bring tangible benefits to the organisation. However, the Finance Director tells me that they now feel more than a little disappointed. He says that the hotline was installed some 18 months ago and since that time the organisation has only received two calls on the line – and one of those was a wrong number!

As I mentioned, this is a hypothetical story, it has never actually happened to me. Should it ever happen in the future, I would like to think that my response would be to ask the Finance Director what he thought was really going on here – what did the low levels of reporting say to him about his own organisation? Did the fact that there were so few calls on the hotline indicate that the organisation had no problems with fraud, corruption or other criminal acts? Or was the reason for the small number of calls more to do with their employees not knowing about the hotline or (more likely still) not trusting it? These are questions that all organisations need to ask if they have a hotline in place but they receive very few calls on the number. Should the answers to them be unclear, my strong recommendation would be to commission an internal audit review into the workings of the hotline, perhaps to include a staff "awareness and attitudes" survey. Fundamentally, this is an issue about the effectiveness and efficiency of the whistle-blowing hotline as a key governance and anti-fraud control. It is entirely appropriate that internal audit should carry out work in this area and report back to the board with recommendations for improvement.

The other negative attitude that I have seen regarding hotlines is mistrust. In particular, staff are reluctant to report concerns they might have about colleagues because of a number of related factors: fear that their identity as a whistle-blower might be revealed with negative consequences for their own career or reputation; fear that they do not have sufficient evidence to "prove" fraud, so that the colleague they suspect might be unfairly treated or dismissed as a result of their disclosure; or a basic dislike of the idea of "telling tales" on colleagues which they feel will inevitably result in trouble, either for themselves or for others.

There are signs that attitudes to whistle-blowing might be changing in some countries. In the US, there was seen to be a heroic quality about those responsible for blowing the whistle on the corporate scandals at the turn of the century. "Time" magazine famously made three whistle-blowers its "persons of the year" in 2002. They were all women who took huge risks to blow the whistle on what went wrong at WorldCom (Cynthia Cooper), Enron (Sherron Watkins) and the FBI (Coleen Rowley). In the UK, a YouGov survey in 2007 found that 85% of people in work said that they would raise a whistle-blowing concern internally, a result largely replicated in an Ernst & Young[4] survey in the same year on attitudes of staff to whistle-blowing in multinational companies. However, in the same survey, Ernest & Young noted a much less positive response from employees of multinationals based in countries in Continental Europe.

This is something that I have noticed myself. In 2009 and 2010 I was part of a team running an anti-fraud and corruption training programme for executives and staff of a major financial institution based in Luxembourg.

Example: Whistle-blowing policy in action. The institution had, in 2009, issued a new, enhanced whistle-blowing policy covering the actions of its employees both internally and also in their dealings with the third party individuals and organisations that were counter-parties in its extensive lending operations. A major part of the training programme was to raise awareness of the whistle-blowing policy and how it was supposed to work in practice. The employees that we worked with were generally very positive about the programme and understood very well the need for the institution's operations to be free from any suggestion of fraud or corruption. Nevertheless, there were two issues that we came up against consistently during the training programme that suggested to us that the whistle-blowing hotline might not be as effective in practice as the senior management of the institution were hoping for. First, many employees seemed to have a problem with the idea of reporting merely suspicions – as opposed to proof – of any corrupt practices that they became aware of, as was required under the new policy. They were concerned that suspicions were some way short of proof and that people and projects could be unfairly disadvantaged as a result. Secondly, most employees gave indications during the training that they would be much more likely to report concerns about the actions of third parties than they would be to report concerns about the conduct of any of their colleagues. There was resistance to the idea that some employees might be involved in fraud and also genuine concerns that their own reputation and standing within the institution would be damaged if knowledge that they had made such a report ever became public. This was indicative of a positive culture of trust and loyalty but I had a real sense that people working for this institution are extremely uncomfortable with the idea of filing a report on a co-worker.

Reporting mechanisms and hotlines – the essential features
In my view there are a number of essential features of any whistle-blowing mechanism if it is to be an effective anti-fraud control. These are summarised below.

- **Whistle-blowing policy.** There are two key points that need to be emphasised in any whistle-blowing policy. The first is that organisations need to place whistle-blowing in its proper context as a positive measure that will assist in enabling them to conduct business honestly and with integrity at all times. Many employees will be likely to have negative feelings about both the term and the concept of reporting on others – no one likes to think of themselves as a "snitch". It is important therefore to say that the policy is a key element for safeguarding the organisation's integrity. It applies to illegal and corrupt practices and it is aimed at enhancing transparency and underpinning the organisation's system for combatting all illegal acts that might damage its activities and reputation. The second crucial point is to say very clearly that the purpose of the policy is to ensure that all workers are confident that they can raise any matters of genuine concern without fear of reprisals, in the knowledge that they will be taken seriously and the matters will be investigated appropriately.

- **Scope of the whistle-blowing policy.** The policy should of course apply to all directors, managers and employees within an organisation. Best practice suggests that the scope should be extended to include anyone performing services for or on behalf of the organisation (for example, agents, brokers consultants, contractors etc.) and also to customers and suppliers of the organisation. The work of the ACFE points clearly to the advantages of such an inclusive approach. In its 2010 RTTNs, the ACFE notes that: "customers, vendors, competitors and acquaintances (i.e. non-company sources) provided at least 34% of fraud tips, which suggests that fraud reporting policies and programmes should be publicised not only to employees but also to customers, vendors and other external stakeholders".

- **Reporting obligations.** Managers and employees will normally have a duty under the whistle-blowing policy to report incidents of illegal or corrupt behaviour as soon as possible after the incident in question in accordance with the organisation's reporting lines (see below). This includes both actual incidents and also suspicions. In my experience, the requirement to report suspicions is a concept that many people working within organisations are uncomfortable with. Most employees are actually looking for certainty before making a disclosure! In reality it is often extremely difficult to obtain proof in such areas as fraud and corruption, even for trained investigators. All organisations should make it clear that they value any concerns reported in good faith, even when the employee is uncertain. The duty of the employee is to report suspicions, which can then be properly investigated. It is also worth saying that it should always be possible to raise concerns both orally by calling a dedicated telephone number (as is implied by the term "hotline") or in writing using a web-based portal.

- **Reporting lines.** The organisation should establish a number of alternative reporting channels to facilitate disclosure. As we have seen, workers may not feel comfortable discussing concerns with their direct line managers, who might be the source of the problem. So, the reporting line should go elsewhere, to someone in the organisation who is in a senior and trusted position – for example, the Ethics Officer, or the Head of Internal Audit or the Company Secretary. As an alternative (and in extreme cases) the Chairman or the CEO could be contacted. Also, some workers may be uncomfortable with the prospect of talking to anyone internally in the first instance. So, it would be helpful to have an external point of contact also. As an example, in the UK many organisations take out support packages with Public Concern at Work,[5] the whistle-blowing charity. If their workers are unsure whether or how to raise a concern or want confidential advice they can contact Public Concern at Work either by telephone or by email.

- **Confidentiality and/or anonymity.** Whistle-blowing hotlines should aim to accommodate both confidential and anonymous reporting. There is an important difference between the two, however. A fundamental feature of successful whistle-blowing programmes is that people are confident that they can raise concerns on the understanding that these reports are confidential – in other words their identity, whilst known by the Ethics Officer and the investigators for example, will not be made public elsewhere. This is a different concept to anonymous reporting, whereby the caller simply reports a concern but withholds all details of his or her identity. It is much more difficult to follow-up and investigate anonymous tip-offs simply because there is no possibility of obtaining additional information after the initial report has been made. The whistle-blowing policy should make it clear that, whilst anonymous reporting is catered for, the organisation cannot guarantee to investigate all anonymous allegations. Proper investigation may prove impossible if the investigator cannot obtain sufficient information or ascertain whether the disclosure was made in good faith. It is always preferable for whistle-blowers to reveal their identity because then the organisation is in a position to take measures to preserve their confidentiality. Finally on this point all whistle-blowers will be expected to keep the fact that they have raised a concern, the nature of the concern and the identity of those involved confidential.

- **Protection for "good faith" whistle-blowers.** All organisations seeking to have an effective whistle-blowing mechanism in place must emphasise that anyone who reports incidents in good faith under the policy will be protected from dismissal or any form of disciplinary action, retaliation or victimisation. No manager or member of staff should be able to use their position to prevent this disclosure from happening. The phrase "good faith" in these terms should be taken to mean that the employee concerned reasonably believes the transmitted information to be true. It is to be contrasted with disclosures that are made maliciously, in bad faith or with a view to personal gain. This can sometimes happen in practice and it is important to realise that whistle-blowing is not a panacea – it is a mechanism that can be abused by "bad faith" whistle-blowers to settle personal scores or to gain an advantage. It should be emphasised that there is no protection for bad faith whistle-blowers who will be subject to disciplinary action.

- **Raising awareness.** It is an obvious thing to say but, in order to be effective people need to know that the whistle-blowing hotline exists. Sometimes organisations do very little to publicise this control and to raise awareness of it. This is a mistake that can be avoided relatively easily with a few simple processes. In addition to receiving copies of the policy, employees should learn about the hotline as part of their initial induction training programme, and thereafter there should be periodic reminders on notice boards and on screensavers etc. There should also be specific training sessions aimed at showing how the mechanics of the process work in practice and also to answer any questions or concerns that employees might have. Publicity of the hotline should be extended outside the organisation also if maximum benefit from the control is to be achieved.

- **Investigations.** It is a fundamental point that if the whistle-blowing hotline is to remain credible, all disclosures are followed up and are properly investigated. The general principles of investigations apply here – these are discussed in more detail in the next Chapter. The over-arching point is that all organisations should be committed to investigating disclosures fully, fairly, quickly and confidentially. The length, nature and scope of the investigation will depend on the subject matter of the disclosure. It may be possible to resolve the matter by an internal review. Alternatively, if the allegation is one of serious fraud, corruption or other illegality then a full investigation might be required, to be carried out by, for example, third party forensic accountants. The individual responsible for receiving whistle-blowing reports will normally make the decision and will arrange, coordinate and oversee the investigation process.

Exceptionally, there might be matters that cannot be dealt with purely internally. In these cases, external authorities will need to be notified and become involved either during or after the investigation. Finally, it is important to make clear that, in addition to making sure that the investigation procedures provided for are effective, the basic rights of any individual implicated in whistle-blowing reports will always be respected. These include the right to receive a fair hearing.

- **Reporting results.** The person nominated to oversee the whistle-blowing hotline (e.g. the Ethics Officer) is responsible for reporting on the progress of individual investigations. Normally the reports would go to the audit committee but there may be another appropriate management committee to receive them.

Rewards for whistle-blowers

One of the most controversial aspects of this whole area is the idea of rewarding whistle-blowers. Most people that I discuss this with on my courses are very uncomfortable with this idea, many say that it introduces unnecessary conflicts of interest and some even view it as unethical. Certainly, it is not common practice for private sector organisations to offer rewards to whistle-blowers. This is one area where there has been more progress in the public sector. Some innovative private sector organisations are looking to follow the example of the public sector.

The US provides the model here. The False Claims Act 1986 is an attempt to enlist the citizen to combat fraud by offering rewards. The False Claims Act entitles citizens who formally notify the authorities of a fraud on the US government to a cut of between 15% and 30% of the damages recovered from the fraudster. This aspect of the legislation applies where the whistle-blower registers a claim under the Act in the courts and this is then considered by the authorities. The reward aspect is known as "qui tam", meaning that when a citizen takes legal action on behalf of the State, the citizen does so also on behalf of himself or herself. In fact, the citizens who come forward are almost always workplace whistle-blowers. The US authorities view the False Claims Act as a great success, bringing $15 into public funds for every $1 spent. In the fiscal year 2006/07, for example, the US government recovered $2 billion under the Act, of which $177 million went to whistle-blowers.

This US policy of encouraging whistle-blowing disclosures by rewarding whistle-blowers was confirmed by the Dodd-Frank Act 2010. Included in this Act, the main purpose of which is to reform Wall Street and protect consumers from the excesses of the financial system, is a provision that creates a programme within the Securities and Exchange Commission to encourage people to report securities violations creating rewards of up to 30% of funds recovered for information provided. This part of the Act has been characterised as a "whistle-blower bounty provision".

The position in the UK is different. Here the Public Interest Disclosure Act was passed in 1998. Rather than offering whistle-blowers a monetary award, this Act operates by protecting them from reprisals by their employers, provided they are not acting in bad faith. The protection can extend to re-employment but is mostly around the provision of compensation for any losses suffered by the whistle-blower. The Act promotes and protects whistle-blowing both internally and externally, whether to the authorities or publically.

(c) Data mining and data analysis techniques

Introduction

Trying to discover fraud in a modern business can often feel very much like trying to find the proverbial needle in a haystack. In fact this is a very good analogy. The "haystack" is represented by the large data warehouse of information that the organisation will have built up over the years, whilst the "needle" is the very small number of fraudulent transactions that are buried somewhere in all the huge volume of information. Data mining provides the means by which the dedicated fraud investigator, auditor or manager might be able to find the needle.

Data mining is the process of analysing large data sets from different perspectives in order to discover new or hidden patterns and relationships and then to summarise this into useful information. It is actually one part of the much wider "knowledge discovery in databases" process that combines the collection, warehousing, extraction, analysis and reporting required for the efficient management of the vast quantities of data that are now everywhere in the modern world. Data mining is the analysis part of all this. It is the process of finding correlations or patterns among dozens of fields in large relational databases.

Data mining is a relatively new term, being introduced in the 1990s. However, the manual extraction of patterns from data has happened for centuries whilst the modern technique has been born out of developments in three related fields over many years: statistics, artificial intelligence and machine learning. Data mining techniques have been used for many years by businesses and governments around the world. Consider for example, the use by companies of powerful computers to sift through volumes of supermarket scanner data and analyse market research reports. Data mining has also been used to fight crime, for example by the insurance industry to uncover fraudulent claims by identifying cases where the same individual was involved in many different claims, either as driver, passenger or witness.

Computer-assisted audit techniques ("CAATs")
Before looking at data mining techniques specifically in relation to fraud, it is worth putting them in their proper context here. Data mining is one of a number of computer-based tools (CAATs) that are available as software capable of auditing data. The use of CAATs is essential if large, modern organisations are to be audited to a satisfactory standard and in a cost-effective way. Their function is to enable an efficiently automated audit of data to take place, thereby allowing auditors to increase their personal productivity as well as that of the audit function. CAATs include various types of software designed to assist in many different types of audits, for example: spread-sheets; statistical sampling; databases; and real-time testing programmes. One key aspect of CAATs (especially when considering an area like fraud) is their ability to audit the data and transactions, especially the integrity of the data.

The power of CAATs is that they analyse large quantities of data in a customised fashion. They enable the user to interrogate the entire number of transactions in a population under review without having to resort to looking at a random sample only of those transactions. Consider an audit of expense claims in a large company employing 10,000 people. The number of expense claims in any year could easily be in excess of 100,000 so that it would be simply impossible to audit 100% of them by means of an old-fashioned substantive review by the auditor. However, scrutiny of 100% of the transactions, according to set criteria, is possible if CAATs are used. This is extremely important when trying to uncover fraud, because it is likely that the number of fraudulent transactions, if they exist at all, will be very small and will not be picked up in an audit sample selected by traditional methods.

Data mining and fraud detection
Data mining is one of the most important proactive fraud detection procedures available to organisations. It is recommended by the ACFE, the IIA and the AICPA. The reason is simple – it is a powerful, efficient and cost-effective way to increase assurance around fraud risk and to provide directors and managers with reasonable assurance that any fraud in their organisation will be uncovered. It is important to note that data mining is not a panacea – fraud remains difficult to

detect. But data mining does increase the chances of doing so. Directors and managers should incorporate data mining into their procedures as it is a proportionate response to the threats and the technique is recognised as best practice.

Data mining uses technology to identify anomalies, trends and risk indicators within large populations of transactions. The results can be used to identify relationships among people, organisations and events. It enables a limitless number of relationships to be assessed both within large databases and by comparing large databases. Because data mining identifies and highlights anomalies in the data, it is a very useful technique for identifying both the misappropriation of assets and fraudulent financial reporting. Of course, the anomalies that are identified will almost inevitably require further investigation, this time by humans!

The different data analysis software that is available

There are a number of specialist data mining software tools available. I am familiar with two of these myself: Audit Command Language ("ACL"); and Interactive Data Extraction and Analysis ("IDEA"). These products share a number of characteristics. They are both classed as generalised audit software because they work with computer systems in general and are not proprietary to any one supplier or system. They are both flexible and have huge capacity to handle data. They are also low-cost and relatively easy to use products. In my view either ACL or IDEA would make an excellent addition to any organisation's audit toolkit, not only for anti-fraud work but also for more general audit application.

There are other types of data mining software available, for example Monarch and PanAudit Plus. It is also worth noting that Excel can now be used as a practical alternative for data mining purposes. This was not really possible in the past because there were always data capacity limitations that prevented the use of spreadsheets for effective data mining. Excel is clearly the most commonly used electronic spreadsheet programme in business today and, since it is now available with greatly increased capacity, it is possible that many organisations will be able to adapt this for data mining use relatively easily.

Proactive fraud auditing using data mining software

The key point of difference between proactive fraud auditing and traditional auditing is in sample selection. Traditional auditing will aim to select a random sample of transactions from the population under review so that each item in the population has an equal chance of being selected. This sample will then be the subject of the audit tests.

Fraud auditing is the inverse of this. The objective here will be to skew the audit sample so that it contains the most risky or suspicious transactions in the population, with the great advantage that this allows the auditor to focus his or her time and attention where it matters the most. This will be done by using the data mining software to create a "fraud filter" so that unusual items, patterns or matches are highlighted. It is important to understand that the list of items high-lighted by the data mining review will not be a list of fraudulent transactions. Rather, it will be a list of unusual or suspicious items that will then have to be scrutinised by the auditor in order to understand the facts and circumstances of each transaction on the list. There could be a business explanation for some of the items on the list, some could be the result of errors but some may well be the result of fraud.

Although data mining is normally associated with an audit or an investigation activity, it can be used (with a little training) by management at all levels to enhance their ability both to analyse data and to detect fraud. Use of data mining software will enable management to: identify hidden relationships among people, organisations and events; identify suspicious transactions; spot and correct errors; assess the effectiveness of internal controls; monitor fraud threats and vulnerabilities; and not least consider and analyse thousands or even millions of transactions.

Data mining is therefore an effective detective control. For our purposes here, directors and managers should ensure that data mining is targeted in particular towards any areas of high fraud risk in their organisations.

Risk and red flags

It is fundamental that the search criteria for a data mining exercise are compiled according to risk. This means that the auditor (or manager) must program the software to look for signs of fraud, often described as red flags. The key concept here is to identify those transactions that exhibit key characteristics (red flags) and then to drill down into the high-risk areas that are identified. These tests and procedures will then be carried out across 100% of the items in the population under review. Of course, red flags will differ according to industry sector, location and the individual circumstances of each specific organisation. However, set out below are a number of examples of what can be done with data mining software, starting with break-point clustering, which looks at one of the key risk areas for internal fraud generally and then showing those red flags that might be looked for as being indicators both of financial statement fraud and of asset misappropriation.

- **Break-point clustering.** This technique looks in particular for abuses of financial authority limits. The method involves reviewing those transactions processed just below a control radar point in the system. Examples of a control radar point are the amount at which a second authorising signature kicks in for invoices or the amount above which expense claims must be accompanied by an invoice in order to be authorised for payment. Two considerations are in play here from the fraudster's point of view: first, there is an increased risk of detection, because of the extra layer of control for any fraudulent transaction submitted above the control break-point; secondly, as every fraudulent transaction represents a risk, the fraudster is likely to try and obtain the biggest return possible for each such fraudulent transaction submitted. This means that fraud is often seen in those transactions that fall just below the control break-point. So, for example, if there was concern about fraud in the purchase ledger and the second signature control was applied for all invoices of $20,000 or above, a very appropriate test would be to programme the data mining software to flag up all those invoices paid in the last 12 months in the range $19,500 to $19,999. This list of flagged up items provides the sample that is to be audited. Clearly, not all items on the list will be fraudulent but if, for example, a significant number of these invoices are from the same supplier then the auditor will want to understand the full background to the supplier relationship and review thoroughly all of the individual transactions on the list.

- **Risk of financial statement fraud.** Data mining provides external auditors in particular with the prospect of a more sophisticated analytical review of financial data than is possible without it. The first step is to compile databases of key ratios, industry characteristics and other attributes of organisations that have been the victims of financial statement fraud in the past. Then, data mining techniques can be used to calculate coefficients of correlation between known financial statement fraud schemes and the organisation that is to be audited. This can be used to pinpoint the areas of greatest risk within the organisation.

- **Asset misappropriation fraud – payroll.** An analysis of payroll data and comparison with personnel records by data mining software programmed to highlight suspicious-looking activity can help to determine if fraud is occurring. Typical red flags here include: duplicates, that is to say payees with the same (or similar) names and/or account numbers; ghosts, that is individuals who are being paid on the payroll but are showing no time and attendance, no vacations, no expenses and scarce personnel records; leavers remaining on the payroll; and a pay date that precedes the employment date.

- **Asset misappropriation – purchasing and procurement.** This will be an area of high risk in terms of fraud threats in most organisations. Here an analysis of data, including master-files, concerning suppliers, the purchase ledger, accounts payable and personnel records by data mining software can also indicate whether any fraud is occurring. Typical red flags include: round sum payments made just below the sign-off threshold; duplicate payments (whether by amount or by invoice number and date); an employee with the same details as a supplier (name, address or telephone number); and the use of a PO Box address.

Continuous auditing and Benford's Law

Large organisations should consider using continuous auditing or transaction monitoring systems on a continuous or real-time basis using built-in flags and trigger points. This will enable management or the auditors to identify and report fraudulent activity much quicker, thereby reducing the exposure gap. It will also promote quicker investigation of higher risk transactions.

An example of this would be the use of Benford's Law[6] analysis. This is the process of comparing actual results against expected results by looking for unusual transactions that do not fit an expected pattern. Benford's Law is a digital analysis technique that can be used with large random number samples. It describes the relationship of the first digit in a series of random numbers. The leading digits do not occur randomly, for example: the number "1" will appear approximately 30% of the time as the leading digit; the number "2" appears almost 18% of the time as the leading digit; and the percentage decreases down for each successive number so that it is only 4% for the number "9". For our purposes a large random number sample could be invoice values, invoice numbers or the values on expense claims. So, Benford's Law could be used to identify anomalous transactions in one of these areas because fraud will alter the natural pattern of the digits. For example, such a test could be used to identify whether an expenses policy which stipulates that all claims of $30 or over (say) must be supported by a receipt in order to be reimbursed is subject to abuse. Abuse of expense claims would be indicated if the actual results showed a large "spike" in the number "2" appearing as first digit as this is likely to be caused by many expense claims being submitted at $29.99 or slightly less in order to avoid the need for a receipt. So, Benford's Law analysis can examine expenses, general ledger accounts and payroll accounts for unusual or unexpected transactions and amounts or patterns of activity that may require further analysis.

Summary – Five Key Learning Points for Directors and Managers

This Chapter has provided a detailed review of the most important and effective fraud deterrence and detection controls that are available to directors and managers. As with our analysis of fraud prevention controls, it is for management to select the most appropriate and proportionate of these measures that best fit the individual circumstances and requirements of the organisation.

There is one part of the Fraud Risk Management Framework remaining to be examined, that of investigations and this is addressed in the next Chapter. Before looking at how best to investigate fraud, there are a number of key learning points for directors and managers in this Chapter that are worth repeating as follows:

✓ Understand the importance of the perception of detection concept and be prepared to take tough decisions to increase it. Make sure that controls are robust and are enforced so that those who are thinking about committing fraud will be deterred from actually doing so by the prospect of being caught, being prosecuted and going to jail.

✓ A whistle-blowing hotline is a very important detective control for fraud, bribery and other corrupt business practices. Carefully assess whether it is appropriate to your organisation. If it is, ensure not only that this control is in place in your organisation but also that it is working effectively too. This will require a periodic, independent review (by internal audit or others) of the whistle-blowing process.

✓ Encourage the internal audit function to include provision for a small number of surprise audits in its audit plan each year. Support the auditors when these happen as they may well not be popular in the operational and service units affected. However, surprise audits are an effective tool in the fight against fraud. Make sure they are not overlooked in your organisation.

✓ Commit to the use of data mining software by auditors and/or management.

✓ Be aware of two practical fraud risk measures: the importance of break-point clustering as a simple but effective fraud detection technique and the need to monitor the activities of outliers. Many fraudsters attempt to abuse financial authority limits by processing transactions just below an authorisation threshold. So, whether by making use of data mining software or by manual review, ensure that regular checks in these areas are carried out. Any individual or department that produces truly exceptional results (either good or bad) should be highlighted for review by management to confirm the numbers and understand what the causes are.

9 Investigation

Fraud Awareness Quiz – Question 9
Who is responsible for investigating fraud in your organisation?

Don't crash the car

It is an early morning in November 2000 and I am driving from my home in north London up to the investigation office situated in a warehouse on the outskirts of Northampton. It is a journey of 73 miles. I know this because I have been making the same trip every day for the last three weeks. The routine is pretty much identical each day: get myself out of bed early and be on the road by 5.15 am; listen to the tapes; arrive at the warehouse; open the office by 6.30 am; and then start working through the next batch of documents before the rest of the team start arriving at 7.00 am. Today, it is pitch black outside, the weather is miserable and I know it will be bitterly cold in the office first thing.

I should say something about the tapes. They are not exactly a collection of Mozart's piano concertos or a "Top of the Pops" compilation. In fact they are tape recordings of all the telephone conversations made on Mr "X's" office extension on the previous day. These are put together for me by the team's security specialist at the end of business each day. My schedule is then to listen to as much of the tape as I can whilst driving home in the evenings and then I go through the remaining recordings on my journey back to the office on the following mornings. The only problem is that, although Mr X certainly does like to talk on the telephone (and some of the comments I have heard him make about certain directors of the company are inappropriate to say the least), he has not said anything of real interest or relevance to the investigation so far. As the days pass, I can't help wondering if this is not all a waste of time and money? Was the source of the tip-off simply ill-informed or perhaps our whistle-blower was engaged in a malicious and vindictive act, designed to cause difficulties for an ex-colleague? I know that both of these scenarios are possible.

I seem to be listening to the same content again today: Mr X shooting the breeze with his mates – sometimes colleagues who work for the company, more often outside contacts; Mr X talking to his wife; Mr X arranging his social life; Mr X negotiating with suppliers – always in general terms, he seems to save the specifics of business for his meetings. There is not even much in the way of good gossip or scuttlebutt today – it seems like it is going to be a very dull journey.

"Hello darling how are you?" Mr X is calling his wife. "I'm fine darling, how are you?" I have heard all this stuff before, I know their routine by now. "Everything's fine here. What have you got planned for lunch today?" "Oh, nothing special, maybe I'll go round to see Jean, you know". Then, I hear something truly astonishing. Mr X suddenly lowers his voice and says to his wife: "It looks like we've got that £10,000 from XYZ Ltd . . ." She in turn drops her voice and replies simply and clearly with just one word: "Fabulous." That's all there is. Without pausing, Mr X now returns his voice back to standard pitch and he and his wife go back to chatting normally as if nothing has happened.

After listening to hours of tapes, this revelation comes completely out of the blue and lasts for less than 30 seconds in total. It absolutely substantiates the allegations made against Mr X of receiving back-handers from suppliers and shows that we really do have a problem with this man and with his department. It is all that I can do to avoid crashing the car.

Introduction

This Chapter on fraud investigations is basically divided into two component parts. In the first section I set out in full a narrative of the events of the fraud investigation case, of which the story set out is a short extract. I have presented it as a case study, although a study where all the details are kept anonymous for obvious reasons. In the second part of the Chapter we then analyse the key ground rules of fraud investigations from a general and best practice perspective and look at some other real life examples from the interviews with business directors and managers that I conducted for the purposes of this book.

There are a number of points to make at the outset in order to introduce the case study. The incident described above happened to me during the course of a large fraud investigation that I was involved in at the turn of the century. I was hired by the board and senior management of a FTSE Top 100 company to manage the case on their behalf. In total, the work lasted for almost 18 months and resulted in a successful outcome as the company recovered the losses it had incurred as a result of the fraud. Looking back, it was in many ways the complete fraud investigation because it comprised all the classic elements: meticulous planning; a changing crime hypothesis; the use of specialist covert investigation techniques; document analysis; interviews conducted in pressure situations; evidence gathering, storage and use; liaison with the police; working with lawyers to prepare the case for civil litigation purposes; and detailed discussions with the company's insurers around settlement of the insurance claim. It is because of this that I have used it as a detailed case study to show the various stages of a real-life fraud investigation. I believe it gives directors and managers a good insight into how fraud investigations can be handled in practice in order to give the best chances of a successful outcome.

There is an old saying that I remember from my days in forensics: you need two key attributes to be a good fraud investigator: first, you must be lucky; and secondly you must have a good "sense of smell". Whilst there may be some truth in this, I believe that a structured, methodical, forensic approach to fraud investigations is always best. A forensic approach means carrying out work to a standard that would be expected in a court of law and there are some key guidelines and benchmarks of performance here. These are addressed in the second part of this Chapter.

Before we look at the case study we need to return to the Quiz and the answers to Question 9.

Answers to the Quiz

Fraud Awareness Quiz – Question 9
Who is responsible for investigating fraud in your organisation?

This question asks the delegates directly about the final part of the Fraud Risk Management Framework – investigation. The answers of course vary from delegate to delegate depending on the type of organisation and the responsibility structure in place, but I always look for a common theme. Typical responses are: the investigation team; security; internal auditors; forensic accountants; the police. There is nothing wrong with any of these answers of course, but I always check one thing with the delegates – do the individuals they have nominated possess the training and skills to carry out fraud investigation work proficiently? Because the "correct" answer to the question, the one that I am waiting to hear, is: "specialists" or "experts".

In fact, the answer to this question is the inverse of the response that I most often receive to the very first question in the Quiz, which asks who has responsibility for preventing and detecting fraud. As we have seen, the majority of delegates answer Question 1 with the single word: "everyone". Whilst it is always powerful to engage everyone within an organisation in preventing and detecting fraud, it would be a mistake indeed to allow everyone to take part in fraud investigations. This might seem a ridiculous proposition but I have seen it operate in practice, for example where the manager of a department that has uncovered a problem will choose to investigate it himself or herself without reporting it through the proper channels, in the hope of resolving the issue without anyone outside of the department ever being aware that there was a problem in the first place. This scenario will often turn out badly. Most managers have neither the training nor the experience to investigate fraud so that the results are almost inevitable: lost time, evidence tampered with or not secured and little chance of recoveries of the money lost.

There is one area that I like to explore further in the discussions on this question and that is where delegates have given "internal audit" as their answer. Fraud investigators need to have experience and/or training in order to bring a case to a successful conclusion. Areas such as the conduct of interviews under extreme pressure and the handling of evidence in a way that is acceptable to a court of law are critical and if mistakes are made here then all of the time and money expended on the investigation process will likely be wasted. Most internal auditors do not ordinarily possess these skills and directors and managers need to recognise this. However, this does not mean that internal auditors should never be involved in fraud investigation work – on the contrary, I think they have much value to add. It is important that directors and managers understand the requirements of investigation work. Once these are recognised, the solution is in fact quite simple – plug the skills gap! This can be done in one of two ways: either by hiring one or more outside experts to work with the internal audit team on specific investigations (for example, a forensic accountant or a security specialist); or by increasing the fraud expertise of the internal audit department through recruiting an expert or by training-up the existing staff so that one at least of their number is able to carry out investigation work proficiently.

Fraud investigation case study

Project "Fuschia" – A Case Study

The opening

1. Initial preparations

The case begins for me with a phone call. It is John, the Head of Internal Audit ("IA") at a very large FTSE 100 public limited company in the UK ("the Group") and he has both a story and a proposition for me. Do I remember Mr X? "Yes, vaguely" I reply. John then proceeds to tell me that the Group Chairman has just received an anonymous letter in which the unnamed source has made a number of serious allegations against Mr X about corruption with suppliers. The Chairman is very concerned – he wants the allegations to be thoroughly investigated.

I recognised the name as soon as I heard it and now things start to come back to me about Mr X. I seem to recall hearing similar stories about him earlier. John confirms that these allegations are along the same lines as a number of other rumours about Mr X that IA is already aware of. They all point in the same direction – basically, that Mr X has been receiving backhanders from suppliers in return for awarding those suppliers contracts and repeat work. John shares his Chairman's concerns that there could be a big problem in the business and he is determined to get to the bottom of it. He is in the process of putting together an investigation team to do just this, but he has one practical problem. He himself is due to leave the Group in the near future to take on another position elsewhere. So, he is looking for a case manager, somebody to lead the investigation after he has gone and take it all the way to trial if necessary. He and I have worked together in the past – is this something that might interest me? I don't need long to think about it: "Yes, absolutely" I reply and we arrange to meet in the Group's head offices in London on Monday morning. It is September 2000 and I have just come to the end of a long running assignment for another client. The timing of John's call is perfect for me.

I should say something about Mr X. He is a director of one of the Group's subsidiary companies and he heads up the property team based in the Midlands in offices just outside the city of Northampton. As soon as John mentioned Mr X I recognised the name. This is the same man who had been singled out to me on a previous assignment for the Group as someone who was engaged in dubious practices. I remember it clearly because of the unusual circumstances. The comments were made at the end of a disciplinary hearing by an ex-area manager who had just been sacked. The circumstances were such that, when I heard what the ex-area manager had to say and the way that he said it, I had a strong "gut feeling" that this information could be highly significant. I remember that this was not a view shared by the Director of Human Resources at the time who had told me, as soon as the disciplinary meeting had concluded and the ex-area manager had left, that he did not believe a word of it. He knew Mr X. Mr X was highly rated within the Group and had been ear-marked for promotion, perhaps even to the main board in due course. The Director of Human Resources could not believe that he would risk all this over something so stupid. I was not so sure myself. Accordingly, I had passed the information onto IA soon afterwards and had heard nothing since until now. It seems that the suspicion conveyed to me was only one of a number of allegations. Clearly, there are others who have similar concerns about Mr X's conduct.

I meet John as agreed on Monday and I am introduced to the rest of the investigation team. It is a small team, comprising five of us in total, excluding John, and the strategy is that we will use additional resources as and when required. I have worked with two of the team previously: Darren from internal audit and an investigator called Brian who the Group uses from time to time on difficult assignments. They are both very professional people and I am looking forward to working with them again. The other two are: Wayne from the Group's security department; and the external lawyer Chris, a partner from a large firm of solicitors who has worked extensively on international financial crime cases in the past and who has been engaged by John previously on a number of important and sensitive issues for the Group.

We discuss strategy and tactics. Our primary goal is to resolve the issues thrown up by the allegations of corruption made in the anonymous letter in a way that is efficient, thorough and fair to all parties – including Mr X, of course. Confidentiality in everything we do will be critical to success. John has already decided that we need to carry out a full-on covert investigation into Mr X and his activities. Reporting lines have been set up. John has the backing of the audit committee for this and he will report to the Finance Director who will take matters to the main board as and when required. However, he tells us that there is a good deal of scepticism about this operation at board level as Mr X has produced impressive results, driving costs down and always hitting his targets. A number of the directors know him personally and like him. John has decided that we will give the covert operation one month to run in full, with the option of extending this into a second month and take the opportunity then of looking at what is going on within Mr X's department, depending on results.

We brainstorm how the fraud might be working in practice. On the one hand it could be very simple according to the following hypothesis. Mr X probably uses a small number of "key suppliers" to carry out the major parts of the property programme, including the store re-design and re-development work. He asks for bribes from all or some of these suppliers in return for which he will corrupt the tender process to ensure that these suppliers win the work in the first place and retain it thereafter. I point out that there is a problem with this simple theory. Corruption schemes are fundamentally inefficient, they add extra costs into the process which then have to be paid for by the victim company. Normally this is achieved by suppliers inflating the costs of their work in order to cover the amount of the bribes. In this situation, however, everything that I am hearing points in the opposite direction – Mr X is actually reducing costs and bringing in projects below budget. This is counter-intuitive. So, whilst on the one hand things might look simple, on the other hand this might be a difficult case to crack. Or, as Chris the lawyer points out, there is a third possibility – this is all based on rumour and supposition at present, there is as yet no evidence. There might be no case at all.

We discuss mechanics and practicalities. The team will be based in a small office in one of the Group's warehouses outside Northampton. Darren, Brian and Wayne are all based in the Midlands, so this will be convenient for them. I live in north London and will drive there and back each day. Chris, the lawyer, will work from his offices in London and will be available for consultation as and when required. John says that there are lockable and fire-proof cabinets in the designated office so that there will be plenty of storage space for all the evidence that we will gather during the course of the investigation.

Finally, John tells us that he has already given the investigation its codename – project "Fuchsia".

2. The covert investigation – planning stage

We decide that there are to be three lines of inquiry for the first month of the investigation and we will retain the option of extending the time period, depending on results. They are as follows:

- First, we will set up an operation to record all conversations on Mr X's business telephone line. Chris the lawyer confirms that, in his opinion and given the facts and circumstances of the case, we are entitled to do this by the various pieces of legislation relevant at the time, including the new Regulation of Investigatory Powers Act 2000 ("RIPA"), governing surveillance and investigations (and covering the interception of communications) to obtain private information about an individual. There are a number of procedures that have to be followed in order to ensure that any evidence obtained is admissible in court further down the line. Brian, the investigator, has extensive experience of this kind of work and knows exactly what to do.

- Secondly, the team decides that it might be very useful to do a search of all the rubbish and garbage that Mr X throws out of his home each week. Brian knows people who specialise in this type of work (known as "garbology"!), he has used them on a number of investigations in the past and gives us his assurance that they always operate within the law. There are strict legal requirements here. It is of course illegal to take private property. It is also illegal to take anything that an individual has put in his or her rubbish bin whilst the bin is still on the individual's property. This would be trespassing. The only time such activity is legal therefore is when the bin has been placed outside of the individual's property prior to refuse collection by the local authority. Even then the courts will apparently throw out any evidence obtained simply by removing the contents of the bin. Rather, in order to have good prospects that such evidence to be admissible in a court of law, the contents of the bin must first be removed, taken away and photo-copied, the original contents returned to the bin and the photo-copies presented to the court! At this stage I voice an objection, saying that in my experience such exercises rarely produce anything useful and are often an expensive waste of time. I am over-ruled on this one.

- Finally, we need to review and analyse the available records and documentation. It will be relatively straightforward to access the accounts information of relevance to the case relating to Mr X's department: total spend per annum, split by supplier; the number of projects run; the policies and procedures that govern the tendering process; and a list of the main suppliers that are used. It will be more difficult to gain access to the department itself. If the investigation work on Mr X's telephone and rubbish bins does not come up with any evidence of corruption, it will be important that we see what is going on in his department at first hand. Only then will we be able to gauge the culture in that part of the business: how the staff work and interact together; whether there is any meaningful segregation of duty controls; or whether Mr X is able simply to override formal procedures and do exactly what he wants to do. All this will be important in deciding whether the anonymous tip-off has any substance to it or is simply malicious. In order to start the ball rolling for this, we decide that IA will notify Mr X that it plans to do some work in his department towards the end of October. I will be involved as an outside "value for money consultant", a role that I have played in the past and one that allows me to ask questions that are highly relevant in a fraud context. Fraud is after all the ultimate in a business failing to obtain value for money.

3. The covert investigation – operational stage

The mechanics of the investigation are now in place. The garbology team does its work on Thursday nights. Friday is the day of the week when the waste collection is carried out by Mr X's local authority, which means that he always puts his rubbish bin out ready for collection on Thursday evenings. Brian has set up the telephone wire-tap on Mr X's office extension and arranged things with Wayne, the security specialist, so that tape record-ings are made of the conversations on that line each day which are then made available for me to listen to on my daily journeys to and from the investigation office. At the same time, we have obtained background information on the activities of Mr X's department, in particular details of the main suppliers used, the spending patterns and how the tenders for new work are controlled. Darren and I go through this documentation each day in the office, starting early and working late – a typical investigation schedule. We also put the plan in place to set up a value-for-money audit that will be carried out in Mr X's department next month.

For the first two weeks nothing out of the ordinary happens at all. The first two garbology runs are made – we find nothing of interest in Mr X's rubbish. I listen to the tapes each day. The reception is good, the dialogue is very clear but again there is almost nothing of relevance to the investigation in what I am hearing. There is one amusing conversation in the middle of the second week when Mr X is talking to a supplier and is trying to set up a mutually convenient time for them to meet in December to discuss business. The supplier suggests a date only to be told by Mr X, after a pause as he consults his diary, that this date is impossible: "Sorry that day is no good for me. Looking at the diary, I already have a meeting booked with some 'tosser' of a value-for-money consultant at mid-day. How are you fixed for the next day?" The value-for-money consultant he is referring to is of course me! Also, it is clear from the documents that Darren and I are going through that, although Mr X does like to work with the same group of suppliers on many projects, the required tender documentation is in place for every major piece of work and, at least at first sight, it appears as though all of the controls over the process have been correctly followed. I can't help wondering from time to time if we are looking for something which simply isn't there.

4. The covert investigation – results

Then everything changes in Week 3. First of all, after two and a half weeks I finally hear something on the tapes that really matters, something that provides the first piece of corroboration of the allegations of corruption made against Mr X in the anonymous letter. This comes completely out of the blue during a conversation between Mr X and his wife as follows:

"Hello darling how are you?" Mr X is calling his wife. "I'm fine darling, how are you?" I have heard all this stuff before, I know their routine by now. "Everything's fine here. What have you got planned for lunch today?" "Oh, nothing special, maybe I'll go round and see Jean, you know". Then, I hear something truly astonishing. Mr X suddenly lowers his voice and says to his wife: "It looks like we've got that £10,000 from XYZ Ltd . . . " She in turn drops her voice and replies simply and clearly with one word: "Fabulous." That's all there is. Without pausing, Mr X now returns his voice back to standard pitch and he and his wife go back to chatting normally as if nothing had happened.

When I reach the office, having successfully avoided crashing the car, I immediately go to the schedule of key suppliers that Darren and I have been drawing up. Sure enough, XYZ Ltd is on the list. For me, any reservations that I might have had concerning the substance of the anonymous letter now disappear. We are looking at a clear case of corruption here: Mr X is receiving money from XYZ Ltd which company is, in turn, one of a small number of key suppliers that Mr X chooses to use on most of his projects. I don't believe in coincidences. Of course, we need more evidence, but once I inform John we are both agreed – this is serious.

We don't have long to wait for the next key piece of corroborative evidence to come out of our covert investigation. It arrives in our office on the Friday morning of Week 3. Before we see it Brian calls to alert us to what has been found: the garbology team rang him during the night with some incredible news. Apparently, included in the rubbish from Mr X's bin that they were sifting through were the originals of bank statements relating to an account in the Cayman Islands, addressed to Mr X at Mr X's address. The bank account has over £500,000 in it. Very shortly afterwards Wayne arrives with the copies of everything that was recovered from last night's work and the news is confirmed – we have copies of the bank statements in our possession. They are good copies too, no folds or fudging. This is something that a jury can readily see and understand.

So, it turns out that my doubts about the covert operation have been misplaced in this case after all. Without it, we would have taken far longer to investigate the anonymous letter, perhaps never being in a position to resolve the allegations one way or the other with any degree of certainty. But we know now. Privately, I am astonished by the fact that Mr X has not even bothered to shred the bank statements before putting them in the bin – not only that, they show no signs of being crumpled or folded up either. Mr X has become complacent – he has managed to put aside a lot of money and he obviously does not think that he is going to be caught any time soon!

5. Acting on the results

The first thing we have to do is to inform the key players of these developments.

John and I arrange to see the Finance Director on Monday morning. When we meet, he is clearly very concerned at what we have to tell him. We have no indication of the scale of the corruption so far, whether any other suppliers are involved or indeed whether any other staff members are implicated. There is a Group board meeting to be held the following week and the Finance Director says that he will use it as the opportunity to inform his fellow directors of the issue and obtain their approval for the best course of action. It is decided that we will continue with the covert operation for the next two weeks at least and that John will update and fully brief the Finance Director again before the board meeting. This is likely to be a key meeting. I contact Chris by telephone. He is impressed with the findings, particularly so with the discovery of over £500,000 in an overseas bank account as this provides a potential source of funds for the recovery of losses in any future litigation. He highlights an important practical point. He says that we must be prepared to go to Court as soon as a decision is taken to proceed against Mr X in order to be sure of securing these funds. We can do so by obtaining an injunction that will freeze the assets in the bank account pending further order or final resolution by the court. Effectively, this injunction will prevent Mr X from accessing the funds and moving them to other bank accounts of which we are unaware. Chris has wide experience of these matters and assures me that this will be possible despite the fact that the funds are held in an account in the Cayman Islands. He tells me that he will start to prepare the necessary papers for this and will wait for further instructions from us.

The final people that we consider contacting at this stage are the Group's insurers. Although John and I both agree that it is important to keep the insurers fully informed in a matter such as this (not least because the Group may well look to obtain recoveries, if only in part, from its insurance policy) we decide that it would not be appropriate to do so until the board has been informed and we know how the directors wish to proceed. A call to the insurers is on my "to do" list and will become urgent should the board decide to take action against Mr X.

John and I put together the briefing for the Finance Director and the Group board. The last week of the covert operation has produced more results, with the search of the bins producing a number of schedules with numbers and calculations on them – we have no idea what they refer to at this stage but they may prove extremely useful in the future. Also, Mr X has been very busy on the telephone, most of the discussions being of no relevance to the investigation but he has been particularly indiscreet in his comments made about a number of the Group directors. John thinks that this could be relevant and we decide that it will be useful for the directors to hear a compilation tape of the key conversations that have been recorded – a sort of "edited highlights" version, lasting no more than 10 minutes. I contact Brian and he will arrange for this to be available in time for the board meeting.

6. Decisions taken

I am in John's office in the Group's London headquarters. I am waiting for him and the Finance Director to come back from the board meeting that will decide how the investigation will proceed from now onwards. We had briefed the Finance Director prior to the board meeting. He did not need any persuading that the issues were serious and like us he felt the situation called for robust action. John had gone with him to the board meeting to add his views. There are three areas in which decisions are needed:

- First, what to do with Mr X internally. On the basis of the evidence so far, our view is that he should be suspended immediately and escorted from the premises enabling the investigation to proceed openly without him being there. Subsequent confirmation of the corruption should result in Mr X being dismissed.

- Secondly, the calculation and recovery of the losses incurred by the Group. This will entail civil litigation against Mr X and any other parties to the conspiracy. We know already that XYZ Ltd is involved and it is at least likely that some of the other companies used as key suppliers by Mr X will be involved too. A number of individuals, as yet unknown, will be part of the scheme also, no doubt.

- Thirdly, whether or not to involve the police and to bring criminal prosecutions against all those found to be involved in the corruption scheme. This is in many ways the most difficult decision for a FTSE 100 company to take because of the likelihood of the story becoming public via the press and the risk of damage to its reputation as a result.

The Finance Director and John enter the room and tell me how things have gone in the board meeting. They had outlined the case and played the highlights tape. The directors had reacted with a mixture of concern, disappointment and anger to what had been said. The decision was unanimous: Mr X is to be suspended immediately, the investigation is to continue with a view to bringing both civil and criminal actions against those involved (depending always upon the advice of the lawyers as to the likely chances of success) and the board is to be kept fully informed of progress.

John contacts Wayne in Northampton and instructs him to proceed against Mr X. This has all been prepared beforehand. Mr X will be taken by Wayne to see the Director of Human Resources (who is in the Northampton office today for these purposes) where he will be told of the allegations against him and that he is suspended from this point onwards, on full pay, pending the results of the investigation. He will be asked to attend a disciplinary meeting in due course and, in the meantime, he is not to have contact with anyone from the Group. Following this meeting, Wayne will collect Mr X's security pass and escort him from the premises.

The opening part of the investigation has been concluded. John is leaving the Group next week and it is now down to me to take the case forward to a satisfactory conclusion.

The middle game

With Mr X's suspension, the investigation moves from being a covert operation to being an open, if confidential, exercise. It lasts for six months as a concerted exercise, with a few loose ends taking longer to tie up. The case will actually take just over 18 months before it is finalised. The bulk of the work is carried out by me and Darren, the internal auditor, with Chris the lawyer also being actively engaged in providing legal advice at all the key stages of the process. Darren and I spend the majority of our time carrying out three essential activities:

- First, reviewing and analysing the available evidence. There are of course a number of sources of this, for example: the various papers and schedules that we recovered from the search of Mr X's rubbish; the accounting records, contracts, documentation and correspondence generated by, and relating to, the operations of Mr X's department; and the information contained on Mr X's computer. In relation to this last point, I should say that the first thing that we did following the suspension of Mr X was to instruct the IT manager to take possession of his computer and provide us with a copy of everything on the hard drive.

- Secondly, conducting a programme of interviews and follow-up work. These interviews are held with the key individuals connected to the case: members of Mr X's department, work colleagues from other departments, outsiders who had had dealings with Mr X but are not on our "suspect list", either as individuals or in terms of the companies they work for. These interviews are essentially information gathering exercises. We need to find out as much as we can about Mr X's operations and this needs to be done as quickly as possible. The information provided by the interviews is very helpful in getting us up to speed.

- Thirdly, carrying out background research. The document review and the interview process highlight a number of companies and individuals that could be implicated in the corruption scheme. We make much use of online searches and corporate information provided by Companies House – all publically-available data. We do not resort to attempting to obtain information by illegal methods, for example, by procuring individuals' banking records. We know that this possibility does exist (there is a basic and long-standing trade in personal information here, whereby private details such as bank statements are copied and made available by bank employees in return for a sum of money) but, aside from the obvious ethical concerns, this action would serve us no purpose. Our objective is to build a case that will stand up before a court of law and all information obtained illegally will simply be deemed inadmissible by the court. In other words, we will not be able to use it.

The work over the next six months is intensive and forensic in nature, ensuring that everything is prepared in a way that will stand up to scrutiny in the courtroom, if it comes to that. There are frequent consultations with Chris and also updates given to the Finance

Director and the main Group board. There are seemingly endless frustrations and days when nothing seems to fit together. In short, it is a typical fraud investigation.

The significant developments and major breakthroughs on the case are set out below, grouped together into their component parts.

1. Analytical review of the evidence

With Mr X suspended and out of the way, we concentrate our efforts on the activities of his property department. From looking at the analysis of money spent over the last three years, it is clear that most of the major projects to re-design or renovate or re-fit the Group's extensive network of office and retail outlets involved using the same companies. In fact, Mr X contracted the majority of the work out to four businesses. Our research on these businesses shows that two are large, international organisations (one of which is XYZ Ltd), whilst the other two are much smaller, locally based firms. This could indicate some form of a cartel arrangement, although we cannot jump to any conclusions because a proper tender process appears to be carried out on all large projects. We conduct a number of tests on the rigour of these tendering arrangements, including contacting some of the unsuccessful bidders under the pretext of a "quality evaluation exercise" – going through a questionnaire with the manager concerned to see whether, in the manager's opinion, the process was efficient, professional and fair. One of the managers that Darren contacts by telephone is very angry – no, his company has not been treated fairly! He says that the whole thing is a "stitch up" and that everyone in the business knows that Mr X always chooses the same suppliers. This will be the last time that his company pitches for any work with the Group as there is never any chance of success and it all becomes a pointless waste of time and resources. Even allowing for the natural feelings of a losing bidder, this is a forceful call and it clearly makes a big impression on Darren.

We make a key discovery when we find out that each of the two large companies operates a rebate scheme. That is to say (in this particular type of rebate scheme) an arrangement exists whereby the supplier's customers are repaid an amount of money each year, the payment representing a percentage of the total money spent by the customer with the supplier once the total spend exceeds certain agreed trigger points. Not only that, it is also very clear (from all the paperwork, the systems notes and the information provided by the employees in the department from the interviewees), that Mr X always kept the rebate scheme strictly to himself – he handled all the details. All the correspondence, any queries that came up and finally the cheques received from the suppliers themselves all went through Mr X in the first instance. It is no surprise that I am unable to reconcile the amounts that ought to be received by the Group in respect of these rebates, according to the correspondence and documentation, with the actual amounts received and booked as income in the Group's own management accounts. The Group should be receiving a lot more of these rebates. In fact, according to my calculations, there is a shortfall of over £2 million spread over the three-year period of the review.

Our review also shows that the two smaller firms used frequently never had to submit themselves to a formal tender process for any of the work that was allocated to them on the various projects. Instead, Mr X would use them all the time for certain types of supplies. He never chose to obtain alternative quotations for these supplies, even though from time to time on projects the money spent on these items would exceed the purchasing guidelines, thereby triggering the "three written quotes" control that was part of the system. Mr X simply overrode this control. We are told that these businesses were all treated by Mr X as "preferred suppliers" – apparently, he always said that they were outstanding in their respective fields and that they consistently produced excellent work. When we probe further it is clear that none of the property team was prepared to challenge Mr X on this. Also, it was pointed out by a number of the managers that the suppliers always came in below budget, so what was the point of querying the way that they had been appointed?

The budgeting aspect still bothers me. If kickbacks are being paid and rebates are being diverted, how can the department consistently come in below budget? I have an idea that the budgeting process itself has been manipulated somehow by Mr X. I have no means of checking this myself so I contact an industry expert in this area – he is busy in the short term but he will be available to help us in the near future.

2. "Eureka moment"

In addition to the budget conundrum mentioned above, the other part of the case that I am determined to get to the bottom of concerns the papers that we have obtained as a result of the garbology work on Mr X's rubbish. Included in these papers are copies of a number of schedules showing columns of figures and various annotations all in Mr X's handwriting, but I do not understand at all what their significance is. It is clear to me that they are important though because I have checked the numbers appearing in one of the columns on the schedules against the value of the invoices raised by each of the suppliers for work done on the projects and duly paid by the Group – they are an exact match. The other columns are at this stage meaningless. I decide to take the schedules home one weekend to work on them. I spend time studying them, looking for patterns. It seems to me that an amount is being sliced off the top of each figure corresponding to the invoice value and this amount is then divided up. But the numbers do not make any sense: the amount of the top slice varies and the division does not correspond to a two-way split, which is my working hypothesis.

It is getting late in the day, I am drinking a glass of gin and tonic when I notice something. A pair of initials (GG) has been handwritten by Mr X in various parts of the schedules. I had initially assumed that these were isolated items. It now occurs to me that the photocopy might have obscured a number of connecting brackets – GG (whoever he or she is) might be getting a slice of the action! I work through some numbers again, re-perform the calculations and suddenly it all fits. There is a three-way split of the excess, rather than the two-way split that I had originally assumed. The numbers work perfectly. What I am in fact looking at is clear evidence of corruption. There is an overcharge to the Group on invoices raised for work and materials by the two small contracting firms and this overcharge is being divided up equally between Mr X, whichever contracting firm was responsible for raising the particular invoice and the mysterious GG.

All in all, it has been a very good weekend's work.

Actually, the identity of GG does not remain a mystery for long. I am sure I have seen this pair of initials somewhere before. As soon as I arrive in the office on the following Monday morning I go through our research files, looking in particular at the various accounts, correspondence and other documentation that we have collected on the two large international companies that we have under review. Sure enough, I find that one of these companies (XYZ Ltd) has listed down, as the sales director of one of its divisions, a gentleman with the initials GG!

3. Results from the interviews

Darren and I run the interview programme in parallel with the ongoing review of the documents. We are aiming to speak to anyone and everyone who we think might be able to provide information that will help us with the case. Of course we cannot speak to the one person who we would most like to talk to about all this – Mr X himself. The other frustration and indeed practical difficulty for me is that, because the Group has chosen to say nothing about the reasons why Mr X has been suspended, the "rumour mill" in his department is running wild. People don't know me and simply assume that I am from the police and am conducting a criminal investigation! So, I make sure that I start every interview by carefully explaining that I am a consultant helping the Group to understand what has been happening in Mr X's department in the light of a number of allegations made against Mr X – I am not a policeman and the sole purpose of the interview is to gather relevant information. The fact that Darren and I carry out all the interviews together helps to calm the situation as he is from IA and is known to many of the interviewees from the Group.

We learn a lot about Mr X during the course of the interviews and from our research. He is 40 years old, has worked for the Group for over five years and comes from a background in retail. He is a hard-working manager, an expert in his field and is highly articulate – he is clearly held in high regard and is seen as something of an inspirational figure by a number of the younger employees in his department. He delivers impressive results and the profile of the property department has risen around the Group generally since his arrival, benefiting everybody who works there. He is not a great socialiser, rarely staying late at office functions or parties, and does not appear to have an excessive lifestyle. In fact he comes across in everything that we hear about him during the interviews as a decent family man – not as a stereo-typical fraudster at all.

We learn some interesting details, circumstantial evidence but important to the case nonetheless. Mr X and GG have known each other for years, they go "way back" to Mr X's time in retail. Not only that, we are told that GG is very close to the Managing Director of one of the smaller firms that we are looking at – the two of them live in the same village and even went to the same school!

The interviews uncover another aspect of the case. It is a director of one of the Group's suppliers who first puts us onto this during the course of our interview with him. He is in the middle of telling us how much he has enjoyed working with Mr X, of Mr X's personal drive and commitment and that he simply cannot believe the allegations. He then says something that really does surprise us: "Of course, all this business has ended our joint project, killed it stone dead." When I ask what joint project he is referring to he says that Mr X and some of his team have set up their own business and are working out their notice period with the Group. He was happy to work with this new business on a large property design project rather than putting this work with the Group because the rates offered by Mr X are better. The fact that Mr X would himself be involved provided him with assurance on the quality of the work.

The idea that Mr X was working out his notice period is news to us, nobody has mentioned this before. When we make enquiries on returning to the office we discover that there is a very good reason why nobody has mentioned it to us before – it has not happened! Neither Mr X nor anyone in his team has ever given notice of an intention to leave the Group. It appears that there is more than a suggestion of moonlighting going on here – of Mr X and some of his managers developing new business opportunities, to the detriment of the Group, whilst still being paid by the Group.

In order to check this, Darren and I do some analysis work on the diaries kept by Mr X and his managers to record the dates of meetings, assignments etc. Sure enough, the diary entries for Mr X and three of his managers show a marked degree of congruence, especially during the last six months or so. We have already spoken to the three managers concerned but there is no doubt that we need to see them again now.

This time the interviews are different. We explain carefully to each of the three managers what the purpose of this second interview is, namely to go through with them certain new allegations against Mr X that might concern their own conduct. However, the main Group board has already decided that these employees will not be prosecuted either through the civil or the criminal courts if they assist with the investigation. Mr X remains the focus of their fire and testimony from these managers is likely to provide persuasive evidence in the case against him. Accordingly there is no need for us to give the cautions at the start of these interviews which would otherwise be required under the UK's Police and Criminal Evidence Act 1984.

The three managers all broadly accept that they have been engaged in developing a new business venture whilst still employed by the Group. They are therefore in breach of their terms and conditions of employment. It is clear that all three did so because they were excited at the prospects of the new business venture, but also out of loyalty and attachment to Mr X. It is evident that their feelings towards Mr X changed somewhat during the course of the interviews. Two examples of this are instructive.

During the first interview with the only female manager in Mr X's team, she tells us that she felt a particular empathy with Mr X because, like her, he had a degree in history from university – none of the other managers in the department had even been to university, let alone read for an arts degree. I tell her that I am very surprised to hear this. I say that I have been through Mr X's personnel file, I have seen his academic record and I can tell her categorically that, although he achieved an "A level" qualification in history, he never went to university. The look of surprise and disillusionment on her face on hearing this news is obvious – Mr X is clearly a very plausible liar.

During the last of this series of second interviews, the third manager is telling us all about the great sense of togetherness that existed amongst the four of them, they got on so well together and the camaraderie between them was "brilliant". He said that a lot of this was to do with the fact that, although Mr X was the leader of the group, they were all committed to the new business venture, they were all in it together and they were all taking the same risks. When I tell him that I am surprised at this, that I do not see an equal sharing of risks at all, it is his turn to ask me what I mean by that. I reply by saying that the fact that Mr X has over £500,000 salted away in an off-shore bank account might mean that in fact they have not all been operating on a level playing field risk-wise at all. I ask him if he knew anything about this. By the look of shock on his face I can clearly see that this is the first time he has heard of Mr X's off-shore bank account. He becomes angry too.

4. Litigation commences

Things are happening quickly now. First, Mr X has been summoned back to the office for a disciplinary hearing at which he is given the opportunity to say something in response to the allegations of corruption against him. He chose to remain silent. At the end of the meeting he is dismissed from the Group's employment.

Secondly, working with Chris our lawyer we have developed our statement of claim, the first stage in the civil litigation process. This sets out our estimate of the losses that the Group has incurred as a result of the corrupt acts of the various parties against it, together with an outline of our case and reference to the evidence that has been obtained to support the case. The statement of claim is delivered to each of the defendants: Mr X, each of the four business entities that we are investigating and GG on an individual basis. We are claiming back from each defendant the amount that we believe that defendant has defrauded the Group out of. We believe that each defendant has the resources to settle their component part of the claim. The accounts of each of the businesses are healthy and show substantial net assets. Our researches indicate that the two individuals, Mr X and GG, are wealthy. For example, Mr X has over £500,000 in a Cayman bank account. Also, each individual lives in a substantial property. It is true that each property has a mortgage attached to it (meaning that the mortgage lender has a first charge over the property that would have legal precedence over our claim in court) which will limit any recoveries from this source. However, we have protected the Group's interests as best we can by notifying the UK's Land Registry of our legal claim, thus preventing either Mr X or GG from raising a second mortgage against the excess equity (the value of the house over and above the value of the mortgage) in their respective properties.

The second area of litigation is the criminal process. Working on instructions from the main Group board, we inform the police authorities of the actions of Mr X and the others in the corruption scheme. Darren and I have a series of meetings with the local Detective Sergeant who will be handling the case and provide him with files of documents put together during the investigation, together with copies of the tape recordings made. Chris has told us that the criminal process must take precedence over our civil action in terms of timing, so that the civil case will not proceed to court until the criminal case has been decided one way or the other. I know from experience that the police investigation may take a long time to reach a conclusion so there are likely to be some frustrating times ahead. Nevertheless, if the criminal court does find Mr X guilty then the corruption case will almost certainly succeed in the civil court where the burden of proof on the prosecution is considerably lower.

We learn that Mr X is subsequently arrested and released on police bail.

5. Quantum of loss statement

As part of the case, I put together the quantum of loss statement to support the statement of claim in the civil action. As its name implies, this is a formal statement of the losses incurred by the Group as a result of the fraud and this is the basis of the Group's claim for recovery of those losses.

In addition to the elements of corruption noted above, we include in the part of the claim relating to Mr X a calculation of the estimated losses suffered as a result of the moon-lighting activities by Mr X and the three managers – a quantification of the time spent on work that was not wholly undertaken for the benefit of the Group, plus the opportunity cost of lost business. There are two further elements included in calculating the quantum of losses incurred. First, the best estimate possible of the costs of the investigation. Of course, no money would have been spent on this had there been no fraud in the first place. Secondly, a calculation of the extra bank interest paid by the Group as a result of the fraud. The losses incurred as a result of the corruption scheme will have negatively impacted the Group's bank balance throughout the period of the fraud, causing more interest to be charged by the bank as a result. The Group is entitled to recovery of these extra interest charges.

The total quantum of loss from our calculation is slightly in excess of £4.8 million.

This is the amount that we are trying to recover for the Group from the various defendants, with the individual claims from each defendant being set out in detail in the statement of claim. Of course, the Group will not be able to recover through civil litigation more than it has lost – hopefully the case is sufficiently strong to convince the court! Darren and I believe that we have put together a very strong case. Chris and the barristers that the Group has retained to take us through the litigation process confirm this, telling us repeatedly that we have a "strong arguable case" but almost every lawyer will say that to his or her client. There is of course a more objective judge of the strength of the case – the Group's insurers.

6. Keeping the insurers informed

I take the time to contact the insurers as soon as the main Group board takes the decision to proceed against Mr X. The Group has in place fidelity insurance cover. As a result it is indemnified against employees who dishonestly commit fraud for personal benefit or cause the insured to sustain a loss. I am informing the insurers that the Group may well have a future claim on its fidelity insurance policy. Of course, the burden of proof will be on us to convince the insurers that the losses are real, that they are the result of the actions of Mr X and that the Group is doing everything in its power to recover the losses before having recourse to the insurance cover.

Darren and I hold a series of meetings with the insurers, carefully taking them through all of the various elements of the claim. They are convinced that we have a strong case and take a lot of confidence from the fact that we succeeded in freezing Mr X's bank account in the Cayman Islands - the amount of £500,000 represents over 10% of the claim and is very likely to be recovered. In particular, they approve of our strategy in terms of the litigation process, including the decisions both to proceed against Mr X and also not to proceed against the three employees involved with him in the moonlighting part of the claim. We had decided that these individuals, having few valuable assets that we could seize as part of the legal process, will be more helpful to us as witnesses in the case against Mr X (who does of course have substantial assets).

It is crucial that we take the insurers with us in terms of the litigation strategy. The Group's fraud insurance carries subrogation provisions, which provide that if the insurance company pays out on a claim it will acquire the rights of the insured to sue the wrongdoer. In other words, the insurance company can itself take over the civil action and thereby seek to recover the losses that it has paid out under its policy. This has implications for the Group and for the conduct of the investigation. We cannot interfere with the subrogation provisions in any way (for example, by entering into settlement agreements with any of the defendants without the express consent of the insurance company) if we wish to retain the insurance cover.

Darren and I spend a considerable amount of time with the insurers and the Finance Director also meets them on occasion. It is time well spent – the insurers are fully on board.

The end game

There is a flurry of activity as soon as we issue the statement of claim to the defendants. We receive short initial responses from their respective lawyers all denying the allegations. We then receive more detailed replies, each seeking to rebut that part of the claim relating to their respective clients. All the lawyers protest strongly against our use of the evidence relating to the recording of telephone conversations on Mr X's business extension and to the papers recovered from his rubbish bin. They say that they will apply to have this evidence declared inadmissible in court. Chris assures us that this is standard procedure. His view is that this evidence, which is a very important part of the case, was obtained legally, it is highly relevant to the case and so the court will allow it to stand as evidence in any trial.

Once the initial legal dust settles, the correspondence becomes more measured. We enter the part of the legal process known as "Discovery" during which each side puts together the various pieces of evidence on which it proposes to rely in court. Chris is hugely busy now, collecting together all relevant documents, ordering and indexing them in files so that they can be easily located before being sent to each of the defendant's solicitors.

Settlement discussions begin, exploratory and tentative at first then gaining pace and substance. We feel that the two large companies might well be very keen to settle the claim in order to limit reputational damage likely to accompany any press coverage of a corruption case. The Finance Director is very helpful here, talking directly to his counterparts on the main boards of the defendant companies.

This type of approach is particularly effective with the company XYZ Ltd, which has clearly been carrying out its own internal investigations into the matter. All the indications are that this process has found evidence of wrongdoing by GG within XYZ Ltd too – although not dismissed, GG has been moved internally within the company and no longer has any responsibility for sales. When speaking to the directors of XYZ Ltd, the Finance Director takes the line that each of the two companies, XYZ Ltd and the Group, has suffered as the result of having a rogue employee at a senior level within their organisation. Mr X and GG have clearly entered into secret arrangements that have benefited themselves. Neither he nor anyone at the Group was aware of what Mr X had been doing and he is sure that the same thing applies at XYZ Ltd. It is in each company's interest to settle the litigation before it gets to court. This argument gains traction and so the lawyers get involved and settlement discussions start in earnest. Of course, we have to make concessions. Equally, XYZ Ltd is obliged to make an opening offer and then to revise that offer. Our claim against XYZ Ltd is for slightly less than £1.5 million plus investigation costs and interest. We are prepared to waive the costs of the investigation and the interest element also. We are even prepared to go further if need be. There is a feeling that we can reach agreement at around half of the claim figure. In all the circumstances, Chris recommends such a settlement and the insurers are prepared to accept it.

However, before the deal can be concluded we learn that XYZ Ltd has experienced a fire that has destroyed one of its warehouses. It is a serious situation and the directors' attention is properly focused back on the business operations. So, progress on the settlement deal comes to a shuddering halt.

Progress on the criminal case appears to have stalled also. Although the Detective Sergeant remains friendly, he has clearly got other cases that are higher up on the police force's agenda than a complicated corporate fraud and corruption case. These kinds of cases not only tie up a lot of police investigation time but they also represent an area of crime that is notoriously difficult to prosecute successfully through the criminal courts.

It is now over a year into the case. Darren and I have nothing tangible to show for all the time, effort and resources that have gone into the investigation, certainly not in terms of actual monies recovered for the Group. We have various pieces of civil litigation out-standing together with a number of ongoing settlement negotiations but no successful outcomes so far. There has been limited progress at best by the police on the criminal case against Mr X.

Neither I nor Darren is working on the case full time now: Darren has resumed his internal audit work in IA and I have other projects that take me away from the Group for most of my time. The case is "ticking over" only, we seem to have reached stalemate and it is all very frustrating. There has been one development that helped me to fill in the missing piece of the fraud hypothesis, namely if Mr X is engaged in a corruption scheme how is he able to produce results that come in consistently below budget? I had met with the industry expert and the answer is in fact very straightforward – Mr X rigged the budgets! He consistently overpriced the costs of the work to be done by around 20% in terms of the schedules he put forward as the project costs, leaving him and his co-conspirators plenty of scope to defraud the company and still come in below budget. It seems that nobody was prepared to challenge or question Mr X's budgets.

Then, one morning, I receive a call from the Finance Director and quite unexpectedly this gloomy viewpoint all changes. The Finance Director asks me if I can attend a meeting in the Group's London headquarters in two days' time. It is important and I am pleased to say that I can make myself available. The meeting is being set up at the request of the Group's insurance company and the Finance Director suspects, from everything that he has heard, that the insurers want to discuss the possibility of them taking over the running of the litigation themselves. If true, this would be a game-changing moment because it would also mean that the insurers are prepared to pay out on the policy.

I arrive at the meeting to join Darren and Chris alongside the Finance Director. I try not to get carried away at the prospect of a settlement – we have been at this stage before on the investigation, only to be frustrated by last-minute difficulties. In the event, I need not have worried this time. The representatives from the insurers arrive, we know them well by now and the meeting is very business-like. Incredibly, after only 30 minutes' discussion the deal is done. The insurers will settle the claim at just over £4 million and in return will be given the right to pursue the civil litigation themselves. This is a very satisfactory result for the Group and it vindicates all the hard work and effort that had gone into the investigation.

It is now 5.30pm that same evening. I am standing in a wine bar in the City of London and with me are Darren and Chris. Chris invited us all out to celebrate the success, but unfortunately the Finance Director could not make it. Chris goes to the bar to order some drinks. Darren makes a comment to me that Chris will come back with half a bottle of champagne by way of celebration. I am sceptical. He is a partner in one of the largest firms of solicitors in the country – I imagine he can afford to buy a whole bottle. Five minutes later we have our answer – Chris returns with three glasses and half a bottle of champagne! Who knows, I joke with Darren, maybe he will make a good investigator one day after all!

That is the end of the case so far as I am concerned. Although I learn later that the police decided to drop the criminal charges against Mr X, the investigation has been a success, with substantial recoveries for the Group and minimal reputational damage.

Fraud investigation – best practices

Introduction

This section looks at the framework of investigations and establishes the essential ground rules for success. The circumstances of each individual fraud case will be different so that the investigatory tactics that are likely to produce the best results will vary from case to case. However, there are a number of key components that are likely to feature in most investigation situations: handling the initial allegations; setting the overall objectives; personnel and reporting lines; using covert techniques; evidence handling; rules for interviewing under conditions of stress; dealing with the police and the litigation process; quantifying the claim and keeping the insurers informed; and communication issues, both internal and external. These areas are not mutually exclusive and there will be many cross-over points in practice, as the case study above clearly demonstrates. For the purposes of clarity and efficiency, however, each one is addressed in turn below.

Before we look at the detail, it is worth re-stating the two overarching principles behind fraud investigations: firstly, they should be carried out by experts in this field; and secondly they require that a forensic approach is taken from the outset in order to provide the best chances of success. Directors and managers should not themselves become involved in the detail of fraud investigations. Senior managers do have an important role to play, however. They should understand the process and should retain control of it, both in terms of setting strategy and of controlling costs. Without this, fraud investigations are unlikely to have successful outcomes.

When commencing an investigation it is always prudent to assume that the case will end up before a court of law. This will mean that a forensic approach is appropriate. Webster's Dictionary defines the word forensic as: "belonging to, used in or suitable to courts of judicature or to public discussion and debate". A forensic approach is one that is appropriate and acceptable to a court of law: objective, thorough and detailed, well documented and with proper respect for the rules of evidence and court procedure.

All fraud investigation work needs to be forensic in nature, therefore.

Handling the initial allegations

Objectives

The first objective of any investigation should always be to resolve the underlying allegations efficiently, thoroughly and fairly. This is vital, not least the third element in this, that of fairness, especially towards those individuals who are implicated, as their reputations and career prospects are at stake. There is a well-known saying that is highly relevant here, which is: "there is no smoke without fire". Fraud investigations start with allegations against one or more individuals, often coming from an anonymous source. Sometimes the allegations turn out to be groundless. So they need to be tested against the available evidence and there are two imperatives for this: speed and confidentiality.

Confidentiality

To take the second imperative first, maintaining confidentiality at all stages of a fraud investigation is clearly important, but it is particularly so in the initial stages. Where a whistle-blowing hotline is in place, allegations of fraud will generally be made in accordance with the policy so that a nominated officer (such as the Ethics Officer or the Head of Internal Audit) will receive notification directly. Where no formal hotline exists, it is important that a mechanism exists so that all allegations of fraud are directed to an appropriate focal point in the organisation (for example, the Head of Internal Audit or, in smaller companies, the Finance Director). There are a number of practical steps that can be taken to promote confidentiality:

- Allocate the initial work to a very small team, perhaps only one individual;

- Carry out the initial checks on a covert basis, either by desk-top review (for example of personnel files or expense claims), or by setting up a pretext for working with, or having discussions with, the subject of the allegations. I have used the pretext of conducting a value-for-money exercise myself on a number of occasions: value-for-money reviews are unlikely to be challenged (especially in times of difficult economic conditions) and they enable me to ask pertinent questions around selection of suppliers, tendering processes and approval of invoices that are often highly relevant in a fraud context;

- Involve others on a strictly "need to know" basis. Often it is necessary to brief certain individuals within the organisation in order to gain access to information (for example the Head of IT or the Director of Human Resources); and

- Consider allocating a codename to the project. Codenames should be chosen that are neutral, unconnected with the subject of the investigation and unlikely to attract attention. In the case study, the codename was "Project Fuchsia" which did the job for us on that occasion.

Speed

Dealing next with the equally important factor of the speed of the process, the crucial point at the outset is the need for some part at least of the allegation to be verified by available evidence. There is no requirement for every allegation made to be looked at in detail but it is important that there is some credibility established before the individual implicated is confronted and a full-blown investigation commences.

If there are a number of allegations made, always look at the most simple and straightforward one first. If the available evidence suggests that there is substance to the allegation then this might be the trigger for a more formal process to begin. If there is no evidence to substantiate this particular allegation, move on to the next one. As a safety net, always allocate a time-frame for review. For example, if no evidence is found after, say, two weeks or one month, then a line should be drawn under the covert work and nothing progressed, thereby preserving the confidentiality of the suspect's identity.

Initial suspicions confirmed

If any or all of the underlying allegations are confirmed by the initial covert review then there is a well-established procedure that I recommend should be adopted by all organisations. The individual who is the subject of the allegations should be suspended immediately (on full pay), asked to hand over security passes etc. and escorted from the premises. He or she should be told not to have any contact with the organisation or its employees for an agreed period of time (for example, one month) after which they will be required to attend an interview.

This may seem to be an extreme reaction but it is essential if the subsequent full investigation is to be able to proceed as efficiently and effectively as possible. The suspect needs to be removed from the organisation so that he or she cannot interfere with the investigation process by seeking to influence interviewees or to tamper with documentation. It is the approach we used with Mr X in the case study to good effect and I recommend this approach to all directors and managers who are in this situation.

Setting the overall objectives

Strategy versus tactics

When I was a boy at school I became interested in chess. I played the game a lot and became quite proficient, reaching men's county standard by the time I was 16 years old. Then I realised that I would never be as good as Bobby Fischer, other interests kicked in and that was the end of my chess career! The reason that I mention this here is that one of the attractions to me of chess (and perhaps why I was reasonably good at it) was that I could always see that everything in the game, every single move, was important and contributed towards the final result (win, lose or draw). This might seem obvious, but often my opponents seemed to approach the game in a more disconnected way, with an opening system selected at random, some risky tactics in the middle which led to an end game that was totally unpredictable. I used to enjoy playing this type of opponent as I found that I usually won!

I have always approached fraud investigations in the same way as I used to approach a game of chess. The case study above is presented in the classic three-stage process of a chess game: the opening, the middle game and the end game. This is how I think of it. The individual components of the investigation (for example, the choice of personnel, techniques and timing) can have important short-term consequences for the progress of an investigation. But these are primarily tactical considerations. It is the long-term, strategic view of the case that is always fundamental to its success or failure.

The importance of the end game

Directors and managers need to think long and hard before they embark on a full-scale fraud investigation, which is likely to be both costly and risky. The risk comes from the uncertainty of what the investigation will reveal – it is impossible to predict what forensic analysis might uncover during the course of the work. So it is very important to focus on the endgame.

I encourage my clients always to think hard at the outset about how they want the investigation to turn out, about what precisely are their long-term objectives. My advice to the delegates on my courses is the same. There are a number of choices for directors and managers at the start of the investigation process and it is important that they understand the implications of each, make an informed decision and commit to an investigation strategy from the outset. This strategy of course should be based purely on considerations of what is in the best interests of their organisation.

The various objectives of a fraud investigation (which are not mutually exclusive) are to enable the organisation to achieve one or more of the following:

- Identify and dismiss the culprit, together with any collaborators whether inside or outside of the organisation;

- Prosecute the culprit(s) through the criminal courts;

- Recover all the losses incurred by the organisation as a result of the fraud through a combination of civil litigation and insurance claims;

- Learn lessons from the circumstances of the fraud and re-design the anti-fraud controls in the organisation to provide better assurance that fraud will not recur in the future; and

- Make the problem "go away", in terms of removing the suspect from the organisation quickly and by agreement, thereby negating any need for an investigation. This will also remove the threat of the employee subsequently claiming damages in an employee tribunal. Agreement in these circumstances is normally secured by way of a payment and the promise of a reference from the organisation in return for the signing of a confidentiality agreement by the individual. These are known as "compromise agreements". This limited objective is not something that I would recommend to a client in a fraud situation but sometimes it represents the most cost-effective option and is therefore an attractive solution. I have been hired several times in the past to carry out reviews of specified individuals in an organisation, normally middle or senior managers, aspects of whose behaviour has been questionable. My recommendation in this type of case would be to start by reviewing the individual's personnel file, looking to verify qualifications and references, and his or her expense claims. Discrepancies in either of these two areas will provide reasons for dismissal without compensation if the company so chooses, so they tend to lead to a swift settlement in my experience.

Consequences of making wrong decisions at the outset

The implications of dismissing a fraudster and of commencing civil and criminal proceedings as a result are discussed in detail later in this section, together with the issues surrounding the civil litigation process. Before we look at these, there are a number of important consequences of taking the wrong decisions at the outset of a fraud investigation that directors and managers need to be aware of.

One immediate area of difficulty is where the individual is suspended, but the subsequent investigation fails to find sufficient evidence to justify court action. What happens then? It is critical that the Human Resources department is fully involved in all decisions to discipline, dismiss or prosecute employees if the risks of expensive and time-consuming tribunals are to be minimised.

Set out below are two brief examples from my own experience of the consequences of making wrong decisions at the outset of an investigation.

Example: Managing Director not prepared to testify. The first concerns a fraud in a large private company that involved bogus invoices submitted and authorised by the Finance Director. The case was straightforward and the MD, who knew the fraudster well, was outraged at the deception, which he took extremely personally, and instructed myself and the lawyers to prepare a civil action to recover the money and also to inform the police, so that the FD would face criminal prosecution also. Much time was spent helping the police and preparing for the criminal action when suddenly and completely unexpectedly the MD announced that he was not prepared to testify in court under any circumstances. This completely unbalanced the criminal case to the extent that it did not proceed and wasted a lot of company time and money. If the MD had made this clear at the start of the process much of this could have been avoided.

Example: An unexpected twist. The second example illustrates how sometimes the investigation process can take unexpected twists. Whilst at Deloitte and Touche I was asked to investigate a purchase ledger fraud carried out in a university. The university's Finance Director was my point of contact, it was he who initiated the investigation and I must say that right from the start I found him to be a very difficult individual to deal with. He made it clear that he knew "everything about fraud investigations", he was dismissive of our approach and generally he conducted himself in an arrogant way. During one of our first meetings I asked him for some information about one of the university's bank accounts, which he duly supplied and I said that I would be following this up with the bank manager. As it happened, the bank manager was on holiday at the time, so I was unable to speak to him for a couple of weeks. When I finally made contact with him, something very surprising came out of the discussion – the Finance Director had provided me with incorrect information! At first, I simply assumed that this was the result of an error, so I arranged a meeting with the Finance Director to go through this again. This meeting was wholly unsatisfactory and I became concerned that I was being misled. However, nothing prepared me for what happened when I got back to my office later that day. There were a number of messages for me to call the University Vice-Chancellor urgently (this was of course in the days before the widespread use of mobile phones!). When I did so the Vice-Chancellor demanded to know what I had said to his Finance Director because, immediately after my meeting with him that morning, he had resigned and left the building! As things subsequently transpired, we found that the Finance Director had himself been authorising payments to his girlfriend, whom he had introduced to the university, for non-existent consultancy services paid out of the bank accounts that I had been enquiring about.

Reporting lines and the investigation team

Governance structure

There should be clear reporting lines in place to deal with fraud events. A member of the board should take responsibility for financial crime risk management. He or she should retain overall control of fraud investigations that are either large and/or particularly sensitive where, for example, a director or senior manager is implicated.

As mentioned above, directors and managers should not themselves become involved in the detail of fraud investigations. This extends in particular to "hands on" managers holding positions as departmental heads, line managers or team leaders. In my experience people holding these positions tend to be committed individuals who are used to being in charge and to supervising their teams closely – should there be a problem in their unit, for example, of whatever nature, they will want to deal with it themselves. In practice this means that team leaders or line managers will want either to fix the problem or to bury it – they do not have the skills to achieve the former, whilst the latter is undesirable and contrary to concepts like zero tolerance. They are often too close to the people and the problems to view the circumstances of the case objectively and dispassionately. They are simply the wrong people to handle allegations of fraud and corruption.

Investigations should be led day-to-day by experienced managers from non-operational departments, such as internal audit, compliance, ethics or security. There should be reporting lines in place, via the audit committee to the board, for large investigations or those where a director or senior manager is implicated. An important point relates to the reporting method chosen to keep key individuals informed of progress of the work, whether these are directors, other members of the investigation team or the insurers. I have a strong personal preference for oral briefings rather than written progress reports. Written reports take up valuable time, they may quickly become out of date as the investigation develops and, unless always addressed to the lawyers, they might have to be disclosed to the defence during the legal proceedings. Of course, a full written report will be required at the conclusion of the investigation, but until then regular oral briefings given to the interested parties are, in my view, sufficient.

Composition of the investigation team

The size of the team that conducts the day-to-day investigation work will vary according to the scale, nature and complexity of the underlying fraud. In my experience, when investigating large frauds a team with a good skills mix, comprising individuals from both within and outside of the company, works very well. There is normally a relatively small "core team" supplemented when required by individuals from within the organisation with relevant skills such as in Human Resources or IT. This provides the necessary balance which is important for success in large cases.

Smaller investigations will be run with fewer people of course. Often there is only one investigator working the case day-to-day which inevitably creates difficulties. It is really important for quality assurance purposes, however, that even the smallest of investigations is supervised.

Internal members of the fraud investigation team will usually come from either the compliance, security or the internal audit departments. As mentioned earlier, many large organisations in the US and now some in the UK too are looking to beef up their own internal fraud expertise by hiring people with specific investigation experience or with a relevant qualification, such as the accredited Certified Fraud Examiner from the ACFE. This makes a lot of sense at a time when fraud risks are increasing in response to challenging global economic conditions.

For those companies without internal expertise, it is possible to strengthen the investigation team from an anti-fraud perspective by hiring in specialist skills from outside of the organisation for the duration of the case. There are three areas in particular where directors and managers often call in such specialist assistance:

- Forensic accountants (see below);

- Lawyers, experienced in the key areas of financial crime litigation and asset recovery – very often, these will need to be appointed from an outside firm because the in-house lawyers will lack this specialist expertise; and

- Investigators. The specialist investigators that I have worked with in the past have come from one of two backgrounds: either the police or the revenue services. Those that I have worked with have been resourceful and committed individuals, with a healthy dose of scepticism around the explanations they are given and very focused on securing convictions. I have only one caveat to make – investigators need controlling. Left to their own devices, they will happily run up bills of tens of thousands of dollars to investigate a fraud of one thousand dollars only. Because of their backgrounds this is perhaps inevitable but it is something that directors and managers need to be aware of.

Forensic accountants

Many organisations will look to their auditors first as a source of assistance if they encounter a fraud, especially if it is large. Certainly, every major accounting practice and professional services firm today has a specialist forensic accounting division, not only the "Big Four". However, there is one important caveat around conflicts of interest here that directors and senior management should always consider. If the fraud is large, the question arises as to whether or not the auditors should have discovered it during their work. Should the audit work be deemed to be negligent, then the audit firm will be a potential source of recoveries, specifically from its professional indemnity insurance cover. Even if legal action against the auditors is unlikely, my advice to clients is always to commission an investigation in these circumstances that is truly independent, which means appointing a firm other than the auditors to carry it out.

Organisations today have plenty of choice when it comes to selecting a forensic accountant. It is not only accounting practices that offer forensic accounting services. Specialist investigation companies have developed much broader expertise than the simple personal investigations firms, almost private detective agencies of 30 years ago. Examples of these are Kroll, which describes itself as the world's leading risk consultancy, and Control Risks, which again styles itself as a risk consultancy specialising in the management of "political, integrity and security" risks around the world. Each offers forensic services as part of an overall risk consultancy product. Considerations of cost will be important here of course, but also expertise and, as the requirements of each individual assignment will vary, so it is important to consider the options.

Forensic accountants, whether from an accounting or an investigation firm are ideally suited to assist in fraud investigations because they bring accounting techniques and concepts to situations that have legal consequences. There is no established "job description", however. I remember reading once that a good forensic accountant needs to be part cop, part accountant, part lawyer and part psychologist!

Certainly, to be good at investigating fraud, forensic accountants will need a broad mix of skills: solid technical accounting abilities; meticulous preparation and analysis, with good attention to detail; high motivation levels; an investigative mentality (that is to say, a thorough, questioning and sceptical approach); a resilient and resourceful temperament; the ability to deal effectively with people at all levels and good communication skills generally. As in so many other areas of business today, it is the underpinning personal qualities of integrity, reliability and competence that give a forensic accountant his or her personal credibility.

The use of covert techniques

Law enforcement

Clandestine or covert techniques are used extensively by law enforcement agencies today. They may be defined as those methods used to gather information about a person's movements, communications or other activities in such a way that the person concerned is unaware that such an attempt may be taking place. They are particularly useful in combatting sophisticated crimes such as fraud, where it has become increasingly necessary for investigators to gather a body of compelling evidence of a suspect's involvement in a crime prior to confronting or arresting the suspect.

Covert techniques are not confined to use only by specialist counter-terrorism officers or units investigating serious and organised crime. They are used much more widely to respond to all levels of criminality and all types of crime as a result of the development of intelligence-led and proactive policing. Covert methods are particularly effective in "live" investigations where the criminal conduct is still taking place and they can produce compelling evidence for the court, for example the covertly recorded conversations of co-conspirators. Their deployment should always be proportionate. Also, and most importantly, it must always be within the law. Each jurisdiction will have its own legislation to regulate the use of covert investigation techniques by law enforcement agencies (e.g. the USA PATRIOT Act and the Regulation of Investigatory Powers Act 2000 in the UK). Also, the authorities must always be mindful of developing human rights legislation and convention around the world.

Types of covert techniques
Covert techniques are also available for use by organisations in the public and the private sectors. As with the law enforcement agencies, it is fundamental for directors and managers to ensure that the law is always followed. Specialists should be used for covert work and they will need to be controlled. So the legal position should always be checked out before the coverts are deployed. Only by doing so can directors and managers ensure that the evidence obtained will be admissible in court and also that they avoid the reputational damage of commissioning illegal activities.

There are two main reasons why covert techniques are used in internal fraud cases. The first is that they can provide confirmation of allegations made against a suspect. This was particularly helpful in the case involving Mr X described above as without the evidence that the coverts uncovered it is probable that the corruption scheme, or at least the extent of the scheme, would have remained hidden. The other reason is to assist in obtaining successful prosecutions in court. Evidence such as the bank statement we uncovered showing £500,000 in Mr X's account in the Cayman Islands is likely to have a big impact, in particular on jury members.

There are three key types of covert techniques that might be useful to organisations when trying to uncover fraud, depending always upon the circumstances of the case, as follows:

- **Desk-top research.** This is an important, if rather mundane, part of the process. It falls into two component parts: research of external sources and internal review. With widespread access to the internet, the external review is a much quicker, cheaper and more thorough process than in the past. Today it is possible to learn a lot about suspects, whether individuals or corporates, very quickly – everything from press reports to Facebook entries could be relevant here. Internal review involves accessing information about a suspect without him or her being aware that this is happening. Key areas for review would be the suspect's personnel file and expense claims. In my experience, the majority of individuals who are committing fraud and abuse on a large scale within organisations are also committing it on a small scale. The abuse of travel and subsistence claims is often part of a more general pattern of criminality.

- **Analysis of communications.** Fraudsters are likely to make use of mobile and fixed-line telephones, email and the internet to further their criminal schemes. Organisations in both the public and the private sectors are entitled to monitor such communications, to the extent that they are carried out by the suspect using the organisation's property. So, a review of the suspect's email traffic will play an important part in most covert investigations. The case study above demonstrated the use of listening in to telephone conversations made using company equipment. All of this must be done in accordance with the law and employees must be aware that the organisation has the right under the law to monitor their office communications in certain circumstances. We have seen in earlier Chapters that this right should be set out in the contract of employment and underpinned by specific policies. A typical policy here might be termed an Acceptable Use Policy, governing the use of the organisation's information and communications equipment and systems. This policy should clearly state that communications equipment is provided exclusively for the conduct of the organisation's business and should not be misused.

- **Garbology.** As was seen in the case study, the review of the contents of a suspect's rubbish bin can provide valuable evidence for an investigation. Garbology (sometimes referred to as "dumpster diving") can produce impressive results. Care is required, however. These operations are costly, they need to be scrupulously carried out in order to comply with the law and they may well fail to uncover anything of value to the investigation. This last point is increasingly relevant as there is greater awareness of personal security today than in the past. Most of us today are aware of the need to protect our own sensitive information – identity, bank account details, passwords etc. It is always wise to shred documents before putting them in the rubbish. So, we should all acquire a shredder and use it – good advice for all of us, including the fraudster!

Evidence

Definitions and basic principles

Evidence may be defined as the means employed for the purpose of proving an unknown or disputed fact. In the case of fraud investigations, the strength of the evidence obtained will be fundamental in assessing whether the underlying allegations against an individual are credible and, ultimately, in deciding whether the case succeeds or not before a court of law.

The first thing to consider is the criteria for admissibility of evidence. In order for evidence to be admitted by the court, the correct rules and procedures must be followed. Lawyers for the defence will always look for ways to strike-out evidence put forward by the prosecution, so it is important always to consider carefully the legal requirements. Generally, the standards are more exacting in the criminal courts than in the civil courts, for the reasons set out below. However, there are three broad tests for a piece of evidence before it is accepted by the court and can be considered as part of the case. First, it must be relevant, that is to say it must assist the court in determining whether some fact at issue is more or less likely. Secondly, it must be material to the case, which means that it is relevant to, and supports, an assertion made during the course of the trial. Finally, as we have seen, the piece of evidence must be obtained fairly. Anything obtained illegally or improperly will be excluded. Evidence that is found to be irrelevant, unreliable or prejudicial is also likely to be excluded.

There are two types of evidence in court cases: testimony and exhibits. Perhaps the most traditional form of evidence given before a court is that of oral testimony by a witness who is present in the courtroom on the day. This remains a key component of criminal trials. In civil cases, oral witness testimony is largely replaced by written statements. The statement must be signed by the witness and contain a statement to the effect that the witness believes everything in it to be true. So, one of the procedures required during the investigation is to convert those interviews that are most useful to the case into witness statements that are then considered by the court. Apart from testimony, all other documentary or real evidence (that is to say, material objects such as photographs) should be exhibited to the court in a statement. This means that each document should be formally produced into evidence by a witness. Each exhibit should be identified, using the initials of the person making the statement, and there should be consecutive numbering within the statement. The quality of this evidence and the rigour of the cross-referencing within it, play an important part in the overall credibility of the case.

Burden of proof

Most western countries operate around the fundamental legal principle of the presumption of innocence. This is most readily understood by the phrase "innocent until proven guilty". The onus is on the prosecution therefore to prove its case to the standards set by the court. The term for this is the burden of proof.

The standards set by courts for that must be met by the prosecution in order to discharge this burden of proof successfully vary according to the jurisdiction. However, the highest standards will be applied in criminal cases. In the UK and the US the burden of proof in criminal cases is "beyond reasonable doubt". Guidance given by judges to juries in the UK is that, in order to convict the accused, they must be persuaded "so that you are sure".

The standards for burden of proof for civil litigation will be set lower than for criminal cases. For example, the civil standard in the UK is "the balance of probabilities". This is often referred to as being "more sure than not" that the accused is guilty of the offence.

Evidence handling

The great majority of the documentary evidence that is gathered, read, analysed and included in the court papers during the course of a fraud investigation is likely to have come from the organisation itself. It can of course comprise a wide variety of documents including: accounting schedules and spreadsheets, invoices, minutes of meetings, cost estimates, correspondence with suppliers, diary sheets etc. There will be two presumptions around the submission of business records as evidence for court: first that they have been prepared as a normal part of doing business; and secondly that they were prepared reasonably near the events at issue. Normally, the courts will accept photocopies as evidence rather than insisting on seeing the originals. However, the defence has the right at any time to challenge the reliability of the evidence submitted, so that the originals might have to be produced in exceptional circumstances. All computer-generated schedules are classed as secondary evidence but are legally valid. Particular care needs to be taken over evidence obtained from the suspect's computer. It is always prudent to commission a computer expert to provide a written verification statement to confirm to the court that neither the computer, nor the evidence obtained from it, have been tampered with in any way subsequent to the suspect being escorted from the premises.

The prosecution will need to provide a full record and audit trail of how a piece of evidence was obtained, together with full documentation to support every transfer or movement of the evidence thereafter. During the course of the investigation, the various pieces of evidence obtained should be logged, and then stored in lockable and fire-proof cabinets prior to copying by the lawyers for litigation purposes.

Circumstantial evidence

Often fraud investigators fall back on circumstantial evidence to prove some or all of their case. Without going into the detailed legal definitions, circumstantial evidence may be seen as indirect evidence which can be used to draw inferences about a series of events in a case. It is not as strong as direct evidence. For example, in the recent insider dealing case involving the Galleon hedge fund, it was the wire-tap evidence against Mr Rajaratnam that had the most powerful impact on the jury, as it included his own words in conversations with his associates who leaked the information. But circumstantial evidence is generally admissible in court and many convictions have rested largely on it.

It is rare to get a complete set of documentation that proves the guilt of the suspect in a fraud case. As a result the investigators will seek to draw inferences from the available circumstantial evidence that builds up into a compelling case against the suspect. For example, the combination of statements from cooperative witnesses together with what documentation is available might be sufficient to prove undue influence, especially if there is an indication of unexplained wealth acquired by the suspect. It might then be possible to use circumstantial evidence to identify and turn an inside witness in a cartel situation (perhaps a middleman or a bribe-payer) against the suspect. This inside witness will no doubt be able to provide direct evidence of the payment of bribes.

Guidelines for interviews

Overview
Interviews form a key component of most fraud investigations. As with everything else here they must be carried out in accordance with all relevant legislation. The rules regarding the conduct of interviews are generally contained within broader pieces of legislation that attempt to strike a fair balance between the powers that the police require to carry out their jobs effectively and the rights of members of the public. Examples are the so-called "Miranda Rights" statements in the US, following the Supreme Court decision in the case *Miranda v Arizona* (1966)[1] and the Police and Criminal Evidence Act (PACE)[2] in the UK, passed by Parliament in 1984 and amended in 2005.

For investigators of occupational fraud cases, there are really only three reasons for carrying out interviews. The first reason is to gain information about the circumstances of the case and about the suspects. The great majority of fraud interviews are actually information-gathering exercises. As such, they do not require fraud experts to carry them out, although there are a number of important steps to take to promote the chances of a successful interview as set out below. The second reason is to provide witness statements for court purposes. As discussed above, witness statements are a key part of the evidence of most prosecution cases in a fraud trial. The final reason for carrying out a fraud interview is to extract a confession from the suspect and any co-conspirators. Success here may well save much time, effort and uncertainty in the court process later on. This type of interview should be carried out by experts and is discussed in more detail below.

The information-gathering interview – best practices
Most people who have worked in the public sector or in private sector organisations will have conducted interviews and will be familiar with most, though perhaps not all, of the procedures and techniques set out below. However, the most important, overarching requirement is that these interviews are carried out professionally – they might well turn out to be critical in building the case.

Best practices for information-gathering interviews in a fraud context include those listed below.

- **Being prepared.** This is a vital prerequisite for a successful fraud interview, as it is for any other interview situation. Have an interview brief prepared ahead of time, rehearse the questions beforehand and make sure that any documents that are likely to be required are sourced and available. Proper preparation is the passport to efficient and productive interviews.

- **Location and timing.** The interviewer should always retain control of the process. Part of this will be to make sure that the interviews take place at locations and at times that are generally suitable to the interviewer. Always make sure the formalities are noted down properly: the name of the interviewee, together with the date, time and place of the interview.

- **Gaining cooperation.** Employees have a duty to cooperate in an internal investigation provided what is being asked of them is reasonable. So, at the outset the interviewer should take the time to ask the interviewee for their assistance and be careful not to restrict his or her ability to end the interview or leave the room at any time. Try to establish rapport and put the interviewee at ease. Explain the purpose of the interview.

- **Number of interviewers.** I always prefer to have two people conducting fraud-related interviews wherever possible. One should take the lead and ask most of the questions, with the other listening and clarifying any points of difficulty or ambiguity that might arise. An individual interviewer may not be able to react quickly enough to unexpected developments, especially if he or she has to take detailed notes as well as ask the questions. On the other hand, three people being present might be seen to be oppressive towards the interviewee. So far as the number of interviewers in a fraud case is concerned therefore, two is the perfect number.

- **Recording of interviews.** My preference is to record all interviews carried out in a fraud context, rather than relying on traditional hand-written notes. Recording is actually a quicker and more efficient method, it enables the interviewers to concentrate on the questions and the subsequent answers and it results in a more accurate transcript of the interview. It is important to ask the permission of the interviewee before doing this – no secretly taped interview will be admissible as evidence in court. The recording should be typed up as soon as possible after the interview and the interviewee should be asked to sign it to indicate that it is a true and accurate record. If permission to record the interview is not given, then hand-written notes should be made during the interview. In these situations, I like to ask the interviewee to read the notes at the conclusion of the interview and initial them. This is particularly important if something unexpected or controversial is said during the course of the interview which might be an important factor in the case. The point must not be open to challenge later on. Hand-written notes should be typed up as soon as possible after the interview.

- **Interview protocol.** There are three broad types of questions that an interviewer can choose to ask when carrying out an interview: open questions, closed questions and leading questions. As the purpose of this type of interview is to gain information, open questions are best as they encourage the interviewee to do most of the talking. Examples of open questions are: "Tell me what is your procedure for authorising purchase ledger invoices?" or "You work in HR, could you take me through the checks that are carried out on new employees please?" Open questions like these encourage the interviewee to speak about the subject and the interviewer should allow him or her plenty of time to do so without interrupting. The interviewer should try always to clarify any ambiguities in the answers. When all the questions have been asked, the interview should be concluded in a professional manner. Here closed questions should be used to re-confirm the facts. An example might be: "Thank you for your time today, I really appreciate it. Can you just confirm that it is Mr Smith and not Ms Jones who authorises the purchase ledger invoices?" Also, the interviewee should always be asked whether he or she has anything more to add or whether there are any other areas that should be discussed. Leading questions, where the expected is suggested in the question, are not effective in fraud interviews: they provide little new information and they are likely to be challenged in court as an attempt to lead the witness.

Interviewing the suspect

Interviewing the prime suspect is a very different prospect to all the other interviews carried out in a fraud investigation. Here the objective is not focused around the need to gather information at all. In fact, this interview should not take place until all relevant material, documents and insights into the case have been obtained. Consequently, it is important to note in terms of the chronology and the timing of the interview process that the main subject in the case should be the last person to be spoken to, the final interview.

The main reason for interviewing the suspect is to try to secure his or her confession to the fraud. In most cases this will be a difficult task, but it is by no means impossible if it is approached in a professional manner. It is important that this interview, more than any other, is carried out by an experienced investigator who is trained in the art of conducting interviews under conditions of stress. In my experience, it is best if the second interviewer is someone who has not been part of the core investigation team in order to add some objectivity to the process. The Director of Human Resources is often an ideal person for this role.

The suspect is likely to have been suspended for between one and three months prior to the interview, during which time the investigators will have gathered together the available evidence to make their case. The interview itself must be conducted fairly. After the usual preliminaries, the interview will consist largely of the investigators putting each piece of this evidence in front of the suspect in a logical sequence, one piece after another, and asking for explanations of what has been happening. By means of this thorough, methodical approach the investigators are able to build up psychological pressure on the suspect – he or she will be able to see that there is a strong case against them and denials might well seem increasingly desperate. Rather than saying bluntly: "We know you committed the fraud, it is obvious!" it is more effective in my experience merely to hint at this by saying something like: "I hear what you are saying, but all the evidence is pointing in another direction – how do you explain it all?"

There is one useful tactic that I have used a number of times towards the end of the interview to try to elicit a confession and that is to display some sympathy towards the subject. Without ever offering any deal, it is possible to alter the suspect's mood by making statements like: "It seems pretty clear to me from all that I have heard that you intended to pay the money back at the earliest opportunity" or "Speaking personally now, it seems to me that none of this would ever have happened if the company had only treated you right in the first place." The object of these kinds of remarks is to give the suspect every opportunity to confess, to make it as easy as possible for him or her to do so.

Another important aspect to consider here is the issue of lying. At some stage the suspect is likely to start telling lies in an attempt to provide false explanations, cover his or her tracks and/or deflect blame. How easy is it to spot a lie in these situations? Actually, it is very difficult to detect when a person is telling a lie in practice. It is precisely because of this that polygraph testing (commonly known as lie detector tests) has been used extensively in the US and elsewhere around the world in the areas of counter-terrorism, counter-intelligence and criminal investigations.

Use of the polygraph is not confined to the authorities, however, and individuals, courts and businesses all make use of it from time to time. It works around the principle of calibration. The basis of the polygraph is that, by attaching a series of monitors to the subject's body, it detects changes in body functions that are not easily controlled by the conscious mind, such as breathing rate, perspiration, blood pressure and pulse. The idea is to ask the subject a series of questions, starting with simple ones where there is no pressure, then moving onto the core questions which are difficult and subject to pressure. The test monitors the vital signs throughout so that significant changes on any of the questions can be identified. In general, a significant change (such as a faster heart rate, higher blood pressure or increased perspiration) indicates that the person is lying. When a well-trained examiner uses a polygraph he or she can detect lying with a high degree of accuracy. Because the examiner's interpretation is subjective, however, and because different people tend to react differently when they are lying, a polygraph test is not perfect and can be fooled. I remember reading somewhere that two ways that a person can fool a polygraph are for him or her either to grind their teeth together or to scrunch up their toes!

I have never used a polygraph myself. However, when I have interviewed the main suspect in a case I do try to apply the same basic principle of calibration used in the polygraph tests. I will start the interview by putting a number of simple questions to the suspect for example name, job title and number of years worked at the organisation. I will then look closely at the suspect's body position, tone of voice, facial expression etc. as he or she answers these easy questions. I then ask a very different type of question: "All the evidence that I have found points to you being the culprit here – tell me, why did you steal £500,000 from your company?" I will now look for signs of an unconscious reaction by the suspect in terms of sweating, blinking, change in tone of voice etc. which may confirm to me that he or she is lying.

Interviewing the main suspect in a fraud investigation is a very difficult assignment. Nevertheless, the view of the ACFE is that, if carried out in a thorough, professional manner, the interview can bring about the confession of the suspect. The success rate is reckoned to be around one in three cases.

The litigation process and involving the police

Overview

There are two distinct types of legal action that can be brought as a result of the fraud investigation: criminal litigation and civil litigation. Each is entered into for a different purpose. An organisation will initiate civil litigation primarily to recover the losses it has incurred as a result of the fraud. The aim of criminal proceedings is very different however. Normally an organisation will only inform the police of the fraud if it intends to start a criminal process which could result ultimately in the individuals who committed the fraud being sent to jail. The two types of action are not mutually exclusive. Typically, civil litigation will result naturally from the investigation process, providing of course that there is sufficient evidence to provide a reasonable prospect of success in court for the victim organisation. The decision then to involve the police is sometimes more difficult, however, involving considerations of the higher standard of proof required and the possibility of the story being reported in the media with consequent issues around the organisation's reputation.

We will look at the key points for directors and managers in each of these two types of legal action in turn, beginning with the civil litigation process.

Civil litigation

The main purpose of taking action through the civil courts in a fraud case is to recover losses. This natural desire for recoveries, combined with the lower burden of proof on the prosecution here than that which exists in the criminal process, makes civil litigation a frequent recourse of organisations that have been the victims of fraud. The basis of the civil action will be a formal statement of claim to the court setting out the extent of the losses suffered by the organisation and seeking restitution from the various parties involved. The evidence to support the claim will be bundled together by the lawyers and exchanged with the equivalent bundle of evidence supplied by the defendants' lawyers well in advance of the trial date.

In my view there are three really important considerations for directors and managers to make when contemplating civil litigation:

- **Settlement negotiations.** All litigation is contingent and expensive. No matter how strong a case might appear to be and how bullish the opinion of the lawyers, the case might still be lost at trial. I have a vivid personal memory that illustrates this very well. I was sitting in the Court of Appeal in the UK (the second highest court in the land) listening to the appeal proceedings of one of the civil actions that Touche Ross had taken out on behalf of the creditors against a bank in the Polly Peck case. We had won at first hearing. The courtroom itself was an intimidating place, with dark panelling around the benches. I remember looking at the panel immediately in front of me and noticing that someone had scratched into the panel a single word – "Anarchy". Hugely ironic given the location I thought. However, I soon found myself sympathising completely with the feelings behind this particular piece of graffiti because, despite our earlier success and without any warning from our lawyers, we ended up by losing this particular appeal hearing! So, it is well worth the victim organisation exploring settlement negotiations with the other parties before the case is heard in court. My advice here is quite simple: be fully prepared to go to court but negotiate hard for a settlement, so that the case is only heard in court if absolutely necessary.

- **The statement of claim.** As a matter of tactics, I have always advised my clients to be as aggressive as possible in the amount of losses that are included in the statement of claim in civil litigation. Of course, it is essential that the losses can be substantiated and that the claim is not seen by the judge as being frivolous. However, individual components of the claim can be dropped as the case progresses if it is clear that they cannot be substantiated. The costs of the investigation and lost bank interest as a result of the losses should always be included. The real benefit of submitting an aggressive claim for recovery of losses of course will be seen in the settlement negotiations. For these to succeed some form of compromise between the parties will be necessary and this will involve elements of the claim being reduced. An aggressive claim from the outset makes the settlement negotiations more palatable and provides the flexibility for success.

- **Obtaining recoveries.** A fundamental requirement of success in civil litigation is that the defendants must have sufficient resources to pay for the recoveries that the court might award. These resources might come in various forms: money in bank accounts, both onshore and offshore; property assets; investments; shareholders' funds (in the case of a company). The defendants will not always be totally helpful and open in their disclosures of their assets. Consequently, one of the criteria for selecting lawyers and/or investigators to work on the case should be their experience and track record in successfully tracing assets. As a matter of precedence, the court is always likely to be very reluctant to award the family home of one of the defendants as part of the recoveries – judges do not normally consider it proportionate to make a family homeless in order to compensate a business for financial loss. Finally, it is always worth considering the position of the auditors in a corporate fraud case. They will certainly have the ability to pay should the court find them liable because all audit firms carry professional indemnity insurance cover. However, it is often difficult to succeed in a negligence claim against the auditors around failure to detect fraud, because their duties are owed to the shareholders (rather than to the company) and they have no specific duty to detect fraud. Having said all that, one of the largest recoveries made by Touche Ross for the creditors of Polly Peck was the result of settlement negotiations with the company's auditors in respect of a claim for damages for negligence and/or breach of contract relating to the audits for the two years ending December 31 1988 and 1989.

The police and criminal proceedings

As we have seen earlier in the book, there are significant advantages if an organisation is prepared to embark on criminal proceedings in terms of the prevention and deterrence of fraud. It is the prospect not only of being caught but also in particular the probability of this resulting in a prison sentence, that is likely to deter a would-be fraudster from actually committing the crime. Certainly, the concept of taking a zero tolerance approach to fraud has built within it the assumption that the police will be called in following the discovery of a fraud event. So why is it that in practice many organisations choose not to involve the authorities at all?

There are a number of practical difficulties associated with prosecuting fraud in the criminal courts. First, the burden of proof is "beyond reasonable doubt", a high standard that may not in fact be possible to achieve given the available evidence. As a result, the authorities may decide not to take the case to trial or, if they do, the defendant may be found not guilty. Secondly, the criminal process will always take precedence over any civil action, which will become stalled if the police are unable to progress the criminal case quickly. One way of addressing this potential issue is to ensure that the internal fraud investigation is finalised before the police are informed, so that a complete evidence file is handed over to the officers to whom the case is allocated. The police themselves are sometimes seen as an issue. Many police officers lack the training and skills to investigate fraud effectively. They also lack the time. Police forces have performance targets to meet, which are geared towards solving the most serious crimes (murder, rape etc.) and to completing cases quickly. A complicated commercial fraud case which could well take years to resolve with only moderate prospects of success at court is not likely to be high on the list of police priorities. The final issue is often around concerns for the organisation's reputation. If the authorities are called in and the case does proceed to trial, then it may well receive coverage in the media. Because corporate fraud and corruption cases always seem to attract negative headlines and comment, directors and managers will be concerned at the reputational damage that this may well cause their organisation. We address some of these communication issues below.

Insurance – the quantum of loss statement and making claims

Not all fraud events will result in an insurance claim of course. The terms of the policy, any excess contained within it, will mean that it will make no sense commercially for an organisation to attempt to recover losses from the small, low level frauds that will inevitably occur from time to time. For a large fraud, however, the situation will be very different.

The importance of insurance to a private sector organisation fighting fraud has been stressed throughout the book. First, adequate insurance cover for internal fraud, especially fraud carried out by senior management, should exist. This is part of good governance and risk management. Secondly, the organisation must keep its insurers fully informed whenever a fraud event which might be the subject of a claim occurs. This includes the litigation strategy and potential settlement discussions with any of the accused parties. Spending time with the insurers, briefing them on the progress of the investigation and on developments in any legal actions that are taking place is the best way to ensure that, if the losses from the fraud are not capable of being recovered in full elsewhere, the insurance company will pay out on the claim and not seek to dispute it. As was seen in the case of Mr X, insurance cover is often the key to a successful outcome for the investigation.

The basis of any settlement with the insurers will be a formal claim based on the amount of money that the organisation has lost as a result of the fraud. This will have to be substantiated of course and one way of doing this is to have an independent forensic accountant certify the amount of the claim in a formal quantum of loss statement. Such a statement can be very helpful because not only does it provide comfort to the insurers, it also subjects the claim to the type of scrutiny that it is likely to face during the litigation process itself.

Communication issues

Introduction

We saw earlier in this Chapter that fraud investigations should be kept confidential, especially in their early stages. However, it is impossible in practice to maintain the pretence of "business as usual" internally once the suspect and any co-conspirators have been suspended from work and frog-marched off the premises. Questions will be asked, as a matter of course. Equally, the organisation will have no control over the publicity that any legal actions resulting from the investigation attract in either the local or the national press or any other media.

These are difficult areas for directors and managers. In practice it is often easier to handle the external communications than it is to deal with what is happening within the organisation in terms of rumours and gossip. Each case is different of course, but set out below are a number of essential pointers to be aware of if the communication issues are to be dealt with effectively.

Media contingency planning

Fraud is sexy. It has always attracted a lot of media attention and no doubt it always will. Directors and managers should recognise this and ensure that there is a media contingency plan in place in their organisation as soon as any large-scale fraud investigation is started. Large businesses will have their own public relations experts and press officers. The appropriate individuals need to be drafted in to help with this aspect of the investigation. For smaller organisations, the senior management will need to decide which person will handle any enquiries from the media. Lawyers should be consulted about precisely what can and what cannot be said publically about the case.

The golden rule here is that there should be only one point of contact internally with the media – it might be at director level, or it could be the Head of Internal Audit. However, it is very important that the press, for example, are not able to quote from two different sources (for example, both the Chairman and the CEO) as this might produce different, even contradictory, messages.

The other point for directors and managers to be aware of when dealing with the media in the middle of a fraud case is that there is often very little that they can safely say especially if the case is proceeding to trial and the whole matter has become "sub judice". It is always helpful in these circumstances to have a short outline statement prepared in advance that seeks to present the organisation in a positive manner. An example of this would be the following: "PQR Ltd. has a zero tolerance of fraud and corruption and takes all allegations of fraud extremely seriously. We are currently helping the police with their enquiries into this matter and cannot say anything more at this time."

Managing internal communications

Reactions internally to a fraud investigation can vary enormously. Directors and managers need to be aware of the key issues here. The first is what to do when the investigation process first becomes public knowledge within the organisation. This is likely to happen as soon as the suspect is suspended, escorted from the premises and told not to return or have any contact with the organisation for a period of time. Given that the suspect is likely to be a senior individual within the organisation, this action is going to arouse a mixture of curiosity, concern and fear amongst co-workers. In my experience, the lawyers are likely to advise against the organisation putting out any written statement explaining the circumstances of the suspension. This will be because of fears of being sued subsequently by the suspect. However, simply to say nothing will be to leave things purely to the internal rumour-mill which, inevitably, will quickly be operating at full capacity. If possible, a short oral briefing by senior management saying simply that the organisation is following up a number of allegations made against the suspect, who has been asked to stay away for the duration of the investigation, can be helpful. Some reassurance towards those employees who work closely with the suspended suspect is also important, as they will be concerned about their own positions and reputations. Providing always, of course, that there is no likelihood that these employees were colluding with the suspect – without absolute confidence of this, no such reassurance can be given.

In my experience, there are always a number of positive outcomes for the business grappling with the realities of a fraud investigation. The first is that the level of awareness of fraud risk is likely to increase significantly throughout the organisation. Deterrence factors too will be enhanced because there is now evidence of senior management action against fraud. Finally, all fraud events should result in a review of internal controls, with changes being made so that it is less likely that the organisation will be a victim in the future.

Summary

This section has provided a wide-ranging review of the most important areas of a fraud investigation, from tactics and techniques through to commencing litigation and achieving recoveries of the losses incurred. By way of a summary, set out below is a seven-stage investigation process that I recommend all organisations to follow in these situations. It provides a practical methodology for directors and managers, starting with the first suspicions and running through to the key decision around whether or not to commence litigation.

- **Step 1.** Assess the credibility of the underlying allegations quickly and confidentially.

- **Step 2.** If the initial suspicion is confirmed, suspend the suspect and escort him or her from the premises.

- **Step 3.** Set the objectives of the investigation – in particular, what is the desired end-game?

- **Step 4.** Obtain expert legal advice.

- **Step 5.** Pull together all the available evidence through an analysis of documentation, a review of external sources and a programme of interviews.

- **Step 6.** Interview the suspect at the end of the evidence-gathering process; and

- **Step 7.** If no confession is obtained from the suspect during this last interview, assess with lawyers and insurers whether the evidence obtained is sufficient for civil and/or criminal litigation purposes.

Fraud investigations – practical examples

The people who I have interviewed for this book are business men and women, they are not fraud experts. However, they have all encountered fraud within their organisations at some point in their careers and have had to deal with it. Set out below are extracts from three of the interviews. In the first, Frazer talks about how his organisation handles the investigation process itself and then Bernard and Charles provide overviews of some of the fraud cases that they have encountered.

Frazer is a senior manager in one of the UK's public sector departments. During our interview the discussion moved on to how his department dealt with fraud cases and I asked him whether the investigations were always carried out by internal staff. This is his reply:

Yes, and this is interesting. Fraud investigations here always have been carried out by internal people. In some respects they might have been carried out by the wrong internal people and I think possibly the choice of investigator has been more around "who is available?" than who was necessarily the appropriate person. So what we are doing, and again this is in progress, we are developing a pool of investigators based on people we know who have carried out investigations in the past, who did it well. We're making sure that they are appropriately briefed and trained but without sending them all on long training courses, we need to get some proportionality here.

But what we are setting up is . . . I guess you would call it a steering group, compliance group, an "expert group", "central excellence", whatever it is, made up of a number of people whose roles predominantly look at this sort of thing. So we might have the head of security, we might have the head of internal audit, we might have me and what we would be looking to do is to have some refresher training or some training in terms of best practice for the sorts of investigations we have so that we can properly support the investigators in carrying out the one or two cases that they might work on in a year. So we would increase our experience and use that experience to support that investigator. Also the central group would then be a focus for discussion about increasing or decreasing risk and that would form the basis of our regular reporting back to our directors, chief executive and audit risk committee.

So we're not there yet and I think one of the criticisms has been that we have been slightly sporadic and inconsistent on how we have carried out investigations, whether we've learnt lessons from these, whether we have had punitive action, how we've stored evidence, that sort of thing. Some of our people have previously been forensic accountants, some are PACE-trained because they are ex-policemen now working in our organisation, also we have some who are experts on procurement. So we tend to pick a specialist with an aptitude as opposed to an investigator who uses a specialist.

It is possible that we could involve the police. Having discovered that the information is reliable, we would then go down that criminal investigation route. If at any point we discover criminal activity we then have to make a decision about whether or not to inform the police, at which point it will be handed over to the police as a criminal investigation. However, most of ours are probably civil and I think, I'm just trying to think of a criminal case, we do investigate some things but I haven't come across one that has been dealt with as a criminal case. We do have third party fraudulent use of our e-cards and all of those are reported to the police but we're indemnified by the providers – they carry out their own investigations which we are not privy to.

Bernard is a very experienced businessman, who has worked in a variety of roles in a number of different manufacturing businesses before launching a management buy-out for a company that he still owns and runs today. He has had direct experience of investigating and dealing with a number of fraud cases during his career. Bernard told me about two of them during our interview:

The first was quite interesting and was where the managing director of the company was actually selling off the assets of the company as his own. He had owned the company once upon a time. His company was then acquired by a large group and some years, two, three, four years later, this managing director who people knew owned the company effectively (although of course he didn't own it, he'd sold it), he actually started selling off some of the assets of the company and putting the money into his own pocket. This was difficult to prove but we did prove it. A certain amount of luck comes into it, an enquiring mind, being vigilant, putting something together which is what happened and the managing director was confronted and he was dismissed. But that was a very difficult situation, where people thought he still owned the business but he actually didn't, it didn't belong to him anymore.

But the other thing I want to mention is with any sort of investigation to do with fraud, the biggest problem is to keep it confidential. The fewer people that know about it the better and if it could be almost kept to two or less, which isn't always easy, it's best of all. You really need to keep it well under wraps and not do anything overtly suspicious that would forewarn the suspect. But people do silly things. The managing director was actually investigated over concerns that he was fiddling his mileage claims. Again, that was down to vigilance on behalf of the staff. That was a book-keeper who had picked up something, didn't like it, thought it was odd, dates didn't quite tie up and that's another thing, just thinking about dates which is good for fraud, claiming expenses which has happened again in two or three different places. If somebody is travelling between companies, they've claimed the same expenses which could run into many thousands of pounds from different areas and people do it even though they are earning vast salaries, as was the case with this guy.

And the second fraud was one that was very distressing, where we had the police involved. It was a more recent case where a very long-serving, trusted member of the company was running a business on the side. This individual had been an employee for 22 years or more and he was actually running a business on the side! Again that was quietly investigated, it took some months, many months really, to put it together, six or seven months to really put the case together. And then he was challenged and, of course, everything came out.

The police were involved, he was taken to court. Unfortunately he didn't go to prison but he had a suspended sentence and all the money was repaid, other monies were repaid, he had to re-mortgage his house and whatever and so he did and everybody else knew in the village where he lived. So that was, again, that was someone who was trusted but being thorough in your investigation, being right in the investigation of any fraud is the most important thing. It doesn't matter where it is or how big it is, it doesn't matter whether you are talking about millions of pounds or £10 here and there, it's to be thorough and to be right. It's all too easy to have hunches and I can remember many, many years ago when I was in transport, that a lot of thefts were going on from the transport company, they did a lot of deliveries into the West End of London and the directors had a gut feeling as to who was behind it all. It was nothing more than that, just a gut feeling. So at 3.30 in the morning the police raided this guy's house and he was there with his wife and small child. They found absolutely nothing, they were totally wrong and it caused major upset and I always remember that. In any fraud investigation case you must be thorough and get your facts absolutely right before you get the police involved.

Charles now works as a business strategy consultant but he has a wide experience of corporate life in a variety of different locations too. I asked him during our interview whether he had ever come across any fraud issues during the time earlier in his career when he was working in the United States. This is what he told me:

Yes, I did actually. We had to fire one quite senior manager for falsifying documents. This was at a factory site. He was a senior guy, quite a good guy. Everybody liked him and we all felt he would make it to the very top management team. One of the things that was critically important for us in the business at that point in time was rapid turnaround of orders, getting rid of the backlog so it was all about customer responsiveness and we found that he had been altering the dates on orders to make his performance look better. When it was brought to my attention as Finance Director I found that it had apparently happened before and he had been given a private warning. But this was now the second time that it had happened and we decided we were going to let him go, as simple as that. It wasn't really part of the financial team's responsibility to do this, it was very much a supply side thing but I was in on the decision about what was going to happen. Very reluctantly we decided . . . well this is falsifying company records, he has done this deliberately, he knew it was wrong, he had been warned, he had to go.

His motivation was to improve the perception of his own performance. There wasn't a direct and immediate financial gain for him but nonetheless the net effect of what he was doing was to improve his own standing and at the expense of the business too. He just wasn't solving the real business problem that we had at the time.

He left the business completely quietly, there was no problem or fuss. With the first warning, whilst it was private, it was all documented, I checked with the HR people who said: "no it's very straightforward", which it was. And he didn't dispute it.

Summary – Five Key Learning Points for Directors and Managers

This Chapter has addressed the very important area of fraud investigations from both a theoretical and a practical perspective. Investigations should be carried out by experts but it is very important that there are reporting lines to senior management who decide strategy and have oversight of the process.

We look at business ethics in the next Chapter and this provides the appropriate context in which to place all the issues that we have addressed in terms of fraud and financial crime throughout this book. Before doing so, there are a number of important messages for directors and managers if they are to give themselves and their organisations the best chance of obtaining successful conclusions to fraud investigations, as follows:

✓ Assume always that a fraud investigation will end up in court. Be prepared for this and adopt a forensic approach to the investigation throughout.

✓ Ensure that your organisation has access to fraud investigation expertise either internally (through the appropriate training of existing staff or by recruiting an anti-fraud specialist) or externally (by using forensic accountants and/or specialist investigators).

✓ Always use specialists when conducting covert investigations. Make sure that their activities are closely supervised, both from the cost point of view and also to ensure that they comply with the law. Evidence obtained illegally will not be allowed to be used in court and the organisation might incur reputational damage if it is seen to have engaged in illegal activities.

✓ Focus on the end-game. Set clear objectives for the investigation which should always be directed towards the best interests of the organisation. Understand the differences between civil and criminal litigation and do not allow personal emotions to interfere with a professional and objective assessment of the merits of the case.

✓ Be clear on where the recovery of losses will come from. This is normally from one or more of: the defendants, the auditors or the insurers. Be realistic about the extent of the recoverable assets of the defendants and the chances of a successful action against the auditors. Make sure the insurers are kept fully informed throughout the investigation process as they often hold the key to recoveries.

10 Ethics

Fraud Awareness Quiz – Question 10

Imagine that you are the Head of Internal Audit and are faced with the following situation: by chance you learn that one of your sales executives provided false and inflated academic qualifications on his CV and application form when he applied to join the company two years ago. Since he joined he has made an excellent impression and last year he hit all his bonus targets making him one of the company's most highly rated managers. What do you do?

The RICE model

It is May 2006. I am standing in front of a flipchart in a room in the training centre of one of the fastest growing banks in the Caribbean region. The training centre is located in the town of Chaguanas in central Trinidad and Tobago, about 15 miles in-land from the island's capital, Port of Spain, a short distance in miles although the journey has taken me almost an hour to complete from the hotel this morning. This is the first of a series of talks and training sessions that I am due to give to the executives and managers of the bank over the course of the next two weeks. There are 20 managers in the room for this session. By way of introduction, I say how delighted I am to be back again in beautiful Trinidad and Tobago and I thank everyone at the bank for making me feel so at home. I refer in passing to the weather (it happens to be raining!) and to the heavy traffic (coming from London, I know all about traffic problems too!), people laugh and this helps to break the ice. I then come to the subject matter of the course – "Business Ethics".

I am aware that the delegates might be sceptical about the value of this training. Before leaving the UK, I had mentioned this project to a number of my business colleagues and associates. It had certainly attracted a lot of interest. Of course, the location of the training gave rise to a good deal of comment and many rather envious contrasts were made between the beautiful Caribbean islands and the dull and wet United Kingdom. But it was the content of the course that had given rise to most discussion. My colleagues thought that the idea of talking about business ethics for two weeks was unusual, some of them thought the idea was highly amusing, one big joke even. They advised me to pack my swimming trunks and suntan lotion. They said that clearly I would be spending most of my time lying on the beach or sitting around the swimming pool drinking highballs rather than teaching because these would be amongst the shortest lectures in history! What they were all trying to say was that, in their view, there are no ethics in business. And there are no ethics in banking especially! In reply, I joked with them all that I was very disappointed to hear these out–of–date and rather cynical comments, yet in reality I understood exactly why they were thinking in this way. This cynicism was the direct result of the continuing headlines and corporate scandals involving a combination of greed, criminality and incompetence in the business world generally and in the financial services industry in particular. I remember wondering at the time whether these attitudes might not be shared by the people I would be working with in Trinidad and Tobago and thinking that if they were then I might be in for a difficult two weeks indeed.

The audience is very quiet as I begin the presentation. I am hoping that they will react positively to the overall message of the programme – that good business ethics is central to sustainable success for every organisation. But I am not entirely convinced that they will. So I start with one of those "stranger than fiction" true stories that I hope will demonstrate straight away the importance of the subject and the message.

I tell them about the growth in interest in the idea of having codes of ethics for commercial organisations during the 1980s and about the development of value statements in the 1990s. Value statements are brief commentaries encapsulating the core values and beliefs of a business and are signed off by the Chairman or the CEO on behalf of the board of directors. I use the example of the RICE model to illustrate this. "RICE" is an acronym and each letter represents a very powerful word in business ethics. I write the initials on the flipchart and ask the delegates to tell me what words they think each letter might represent. A manager shouts out "responsibility" as his idea of what the word representing the letter R might be. It is a good answer but in fact R stands for "respect" in this particular value model. Then we move on to the letter I and this attracts a number of responses from the floor, interestingly they all come up with the same word – "integrity". This is a word that appears in the values and ethical codes of almost every company that makes the commitment of time and energy to produce these things. To complete the acronym, I tell the delegates that the letter C stands for "communication", whilst the final letter E is for "excellence". So, this is the RICE model – Respect, Integrity, Communication and Excellence. I ask the delegates what they think about it, how would they feel if they worked for an organisation that had this model as its core vision and values? I remind them also that this model was considered to be very innovative back in the 1990s. Although there is some scepticism, the comments coming back are generally positive.

Now I am moving on to the real point of the example. I ask them to tell me the name of the company that first developed the RICE model and used it as its own value statement. What do they think? There is a lot of discussion in the room now and various company names are shouted out, generally examples of successful businesses: General Electric Company, Wal-Mart, Ford and others. Then someone comes up with an altogether different suggestion. It is in fact an outrageous answer. It is the name of a company now universally reviled and thought to be so far removed from all notions of best practices in terms of business ethics that this has to be a joke answer, surely. The answer shouted out is Enron. There is much laughter in the room now but I do not join in. I simply nod my head slowly and people begin to realise that this is in fact the correct answer! I say to the delegates that, although it seems hugely ironic now, the RICE model was an important part of Enron's Code of Ethics and Vision and Values platform during the 1990s and it attracted a lot of favourable comments. These values were summarised and included in Enron's Annual Report in 1999.[1] As a result, Enron was often held up to be an example of best practices in managing business ethics at that time.And I am delighted to see that the delegates in the room get the point, they understand the irony, absolutely! There is immediately much more energy in the room and everyone seems to be totally engaged with the course now. Secretly, I breathe a sigh of relief – business ethics might be a difficult sell in the UK but its importance is clearly well understood here in this bank in Trinidad and Tobago. I know now that I am going to enjoy my time here during the next two weeks very much.

Introduction

I have now run many more business ethics courses since that first one in Trinidad and Tobago, described above. But I always start each course in the same way, with the example of Enron and the RICE model. I feel that this story shows more powerfully than any other example that I can think of, what can happen when the most fundamental principle of business ethics, the need to match the stated values of an organisation with the actual behaviour of the people working in it, especially those at the top, does not work. Values without action are meaningless. It is so easy for any organisation to "talk the talk" in terms of business ethics by using words like integrity, trust and respect. It is so much more difficult in practice sometimes to "walk the walk", especially under commercial pressure to hit short-term targets. Yet the failure to match corporate values with employee behaviour creates cynicism amongst employees within an organisation and mistrust amongst stakeholders outside of it. Enron provides a clear and strong example of this.

This Chapter looks at the fundamental principles of business ethics, at the concepts of integrity and trust and at the Golden Rule. It places these principles firmly in the modern business context by looking at the key area of pressure, in particular the extreme pressure that organisations sometimes put on their people to encourage them to hit performance targets. This can impact negatively upon workplace behaviour. The modern business ethics toolkit is examined and the main tools reviewed: value statements; codes of ethics and conduct; reporting lines; and ethical training and development programmes. Finally, we look at a number of practical aspects of business ethics through a sample of interview extracts to provide a flavour of what the phrase actually means in practice to experienced directors and managers.

Ultimately, business ethics is the result of the combination of the culture of the organisation and the behaviour of its people. As we have seen throughout the book, problems with either corporate culture or deviant behaviour increase fraud risk. In my experience one of the most important ways of promoting good business ethics is by thorough case-based ethical training. This entails looking at scenarios involving ethical dilemmas, those "grey areas" of business life where values might be in conflict, and using your organisation's business values to find the optimal solution to them.

Question 10 of the Quiz asks delegates to solve one such ethical dilemma that happens from time to time in real life. Let us see what answers the delegates on my courses have come up with over the years by way of a solution to this dilemma.

Answers to the Quiz

Fraud Awareness Quiz – Question 10

Imagine that you are the Head of Internal Audit and are faced with the following situation: by chance you learn that one of your sales executives provided false and inflated academic qualifications on his CV and application form when he applied to join the company two years ago. Since he joined he has made an excellent impression and last year he hit all his bonus targets making him one of the company's most highly rated managers. What do you do?

I like to ask delegates on my courses this question because it goes straight to the heart of one of the tensions in business that can interfere from time to time with good governance and good ethics – that is the difficulty of reconciling short-term and long-term objectives by organisations under the day-to-day pressures of business life. It also picks up, almost as a by-product, the concept of zero tolerance that many companies will say is their policy when dealing with such issues as fraud, deception and inappropriate business practices in the workplace.

There are no right and wrong answers when looking at a question like this. Every organisation will need to look to its own codes and value statements to find the reference point that will provide it with the approach that is best suited to its own individual circumstances. Nevertheless, there are certain answers that are more powerful than others when looking at the question from a counter-fraud perspective.

There are two broad and distinct types of responses that I have come across over the years: the first is quick and straightforward, the second is long, drawn-out and agonised. In my experience, I rarely encounter the two attitudes on the same course or workshop as generally it is the course location, rather than the industry sector, that will determine which way the overwhelming majority of the delegates on a given day will be likely to react to this question. So, there might be some national characteristics at play here.

I have seen the first type of response – the quick and straightforward reaction – most obviously demonstrated by people attending my courses in Continental Europe (Switzerland and Luxembourg in particular), in Singapore and in the Caribbean. Here the great majority of delegates will read the question, they will take somewhere between 15 seconds and 45 seconds to process the information and then they will all come to the same conclusion: if the facts are proven, then the sales executive should be dismissed. The executive has lied, it will therefore be impossible to place trust in him in the future and the consequence is that he must "go home" (to use the Trinidadian expression for firing someone). There might be one or two dissenters from this view on courses in these parts of the world but generally agreement is reached very quickly on this question and we can then move on.

Elsewhere in the world, I have seen very different viewpoints, most noticeably from people attending courses from the UK. Most UK delegates tend to answer in any way that serves the same overall purpose – the retention of the sales executive's services by the company. I have heard many different arguments deployed to say why the sales executive should be retained, including, for example, the following: the executive can clearly do the job so there is no problem; the executive needs to be spoken to but so long as he is supervised closely going forward there is no problem; the HR department should have checked the references thoroughly, that's where the problem lies; and if Lord Sugar is prepared to accept individuals who have fudged their CVs and application forms, why should this be a problem for us?

To explain this last point, it refers to the UK version of the popular television series "The Apprentice" first shown in the US where Donald Trump is the star of the show. In the UK version, it is Lord Sugar, the pugnacious and successful British entrepreneur, who runs the show. In one of the programmes in the UK series, a contestant was found to have misstated the length of time he had spent at college studying a particular course on the CV that he submitted as part of the selection process for the show. It was clear, even on TV, that the man knew that he had been caught out lying and that he expected to be fired. This firing process is one of the hooks of the show. At the end of every episode Lord Sugar will point to one of the candidates and declare "You're fired!" (except when it happens to be the final episode of every series, when he declares "You're hired!" to the winner instead). In this particular episode, rather than fire the individual who had lied, Lord Sugar decided to keep him and in fact he ended up hiring the man at the end of the series! To be fair, Lord Sugar has made it clear in his autobiography[2] that throughout his business career, which has often been controversial, he has always believed in fair and straightforward business dealings. As he says in his book: "It's what you do in practice that gains you business credibility, not hype or empty promises." Perhaps this example from "The Apprentice" demonstrates that there are sometimes no right or wrong decisions when it comes to business ethics. In my view, however, Lord Sugar has set an unfortunate example here.

Although I understand all of the arguments set out above from my UK delegates and the commercial reasons for them, I have to say that they are fundamentally flawed from the ethical viewpoint.

So, when I work with groups that are minded to hang on to the sales executive in this question, I try to influence the discussion by pointing out the deliberate "ethical red herring" that I have included, namely that the executive in question is one of the company's most highly-rated managers and hits his bonus targets. From all the answers that I have heard from delegates it seems that many business people, especially in the UK, fall for this red herring hook, line and sinker! The reason why the delegates want to retain the sales executive is quite simple – they read in the question that he is a successful guy! This is the practical, commercial point of view, and business is all about delivering results after all, is it not? However, the problem with this line of thinking is that it focuses on the short term and ignores the impact that such a decision is likely to have throughout the business. One of the fundamental principles of business ethics is that everyone in the organisation should be treated equally. If codes of conduct, ethical charters and statements of core values are to gain the respect of all employees and so have real traction within an organisation, then they must apply to everyone in that organisation regardless of position, status or the results that have been achieved. The success or otherwise of the individual concerned must not be the driver of the decision-making process in these types of situation. Instead, the focus should be on the merits of the case. When the issue is to do with behaviour in the workplace, it should not matter whether the conduct in question is carried out by a successful sales executive (as here, apparently), or by the Chairman of the organisation, or by an average performer in the accounts department or by the receptionist – scrutiny should always focus on the conduct and not on the position held by the individual concerned.

There is an old saying attributed to Charles de Gaulle, the French general and President, that I think is very relevant in this context and that I always try to pass on to the delegates: "The cemetery is full of irreplaceable men." The point is very simple – no-one is irreplaceable. People respond to challenges and new "star performers" will emerge if given the opportunity.

I then like to ask the delegates what we know for certain about the sales executive on the basis of the information provided in the question. They can all see that the one thing that we do know about him for sure is that he is a liar. And actually a lot flows from this. If he is capable of lying to get a job, how reliable are the results that he has generated in order to hit his bonus targets? After all, the most successful salesman at Barings Bank in 1993 and 1994 was a certain Nick Leeson. So, it would certainly be sensible to check these results. Will you ever be able to trust this salesman, especially when times are tough and his own performance comes under scrutiny? Some delegates think that it will be possible to manage the executive closely in the future, to be more hands-on with him, thereby reducing this risk. However, I say to them that in my experience successful salesmen rarely respond well to being closely managed – they tend to need a degree of autonomy in order to be fully motivated. Finally, I ask the delegates what would happen to the idea of zero tolerance in this hypothetical organisation if the sales executive is allowed to remain in his job. Clearly, the credibility of this approach to criminal and unethical behaviour would be lost.

So, although there are no right or wrong answers to this particular question, I definitely encourage the delegates to take a robust approach. In my opinion, the sales executive should indeed "go home".

The business ethics framework

Introduction

The word ethics is derived from the Greek and it means character or manners. Ethical theory has its origins in the work of the ancient Greek philosophers such as Socrates and Aristotle and addresses issues concerning morality – questions about right and wrong, good and evil, justice and crime. Ethics or moral philosophy has developed out of these theories into a set of principles of right conduct, a theory or a system of moral values. The *Encyclopaedia Britannica* defines ethics as: "the branch of philosophy concerned with the nature of ultimate value and the standards by which human actions can be judged right or wrong".

From a practical point of view it is helpful to understand that business ethics is the study of business situations, activities and decisions where issues of right and wrong are addressed, with a view to helping us to make better decisions at work. Ethical business behaviour in the workplace is actually determined by the interaction of many things: the law; government regulations; industry practices; professional standards; cultural and social mores; corporate culture; and one's own internal moral code.

Although all of these factors interrelate, in practice one of them is often more important than all the others. When I ask delegates to consider which one is the most important driver of behaviour in business, they almost always give me the same answer, which is "one's own internal moral code". Actually, although no doubt we all would like to believe that our own moral compass will always guide us in terms of how we will react to different situations in the workplace, the evidence suggests that corporate culture has the most important influence on how people in business conduct themselves in practice. We will look at the importance of corporate culture, especially in pressure situations, later in this Chapter.

The golden rule of reciprocity

The ethical theories of the ancient Greeks have been taken up and adapted by the world's great religions. However, I always try to steer well clear of entering into any debates with delegates on the merits of the various religious beliefs that might be represented around the training room on any given day. Instead, I emphasise the one common thread that connects business ethics with the work of the ancient Greek philosophers and with the religions of the world, one idea that is fundamental to all three. That is the Golden Rule of Reciprocity. Put simply, the Golden Rule states that:

We should treat others in exactly the same way that we want others to treat us.

Sometimes delegates question this, saying that they are unsure whether the Golden Rule has any place in the commercial world. When I am asked this, I reply that, although the Golden Rule might look like a religious statement it is in fact a universal statement about culture and relationships which are central to sustainable business success. If in the real world of commercial cut and thrust organisations try to win business by lying, bribing, cheating or deceiving their customers (rather than by relying on open and straightforward business competition, by having an excellent value proposition and a competitive pricing structure) they may achieve short-term success but it will be unlikely to last. All of the examples that I have used throughout the book point to this conclusion. The Golden Rule is central to sustainable success for any organisation.

I set out below another example from my personal experience that shows very well the consequences of a failure to treat customers honestly and with respect. The example demonstrates the ultimate risk that cheats and liars face in the business worlds: in the end, when their customers find out about these methods, they simply take their business elsewhere.

Example: supply chain problems. A number of years ago I was commissioned by a client to look into the efficiency of their procurement and supply chain operations. They had a number of issues in this area, as most organisations do, but I discovered a very big problem with one of their long-standing suppliers, who I happened to include in my sample for review. Whilst going through this supplier's invoices, I noticed that the design of the supporting schedules which listed out in detail all of the items that had been sold to my client (by type, quantity, price etc.) had changed at the start of the year under review. I noticed something else also – the prices shown on these new supporting schedules were all wrong. They were all overstated and by odd amounts. There was clearly some glitch in the computer programme, somehow introduced when the schedule design was changed no doubt. My client had not noticed it and as a result had paid more for the goods than they should have done. This was a big account, so the numbers were likely to be significant. As I continued the analysis, I found out something else that was surprising too. After seven months of errors, the prices on the supporting schedules suddenly corrected themselves! All the invoices were correctly priced thereafter. I discussed these findings with senior managers at my client and they were both surprised and very concerned. This was all news to them. There had been no official price changes during the year and no communication from the supplier concerning what might or might not have been happening with the invoices and supporting schedules. I calculated that my client had over-paid by slightly in excess of £100,000. So, what to do? This could have been a deliberate act on the part of the supplier, in which case it was fraud. However, the fact that the pricing was now correct led me to believe that error, rather than fraud, was the more likely cause. My concern was around the following hypothesis: the supplier's managers had indeed discovered the problem, had adjusted the computer programme so that the pricing was now accurate but had chosen not to say anything about it to my client, hoping that my client would never find out about it, in which case they would simply pocket the extra £100,000 in profit to which they were not entitled. The Finance Director and I met with the supplier's senior sales people and, during the course of a really difficult meeting, my suspicion was confirmed. When I presented the evidence, the supplier replied to the effect that it was all a mistake and that it was no fault of theirs that my client had not found out about it earlier. Clearly, they had no intention of informing my client otherwise. There were two outcomes from this meeting. First of all, it was agreed that my client would receive a credit note from the supplier for the £100,000 overpayment. Secondly, once the credit note had been received, my client never bought anything from that supplier ever again.

So, in my view it is clear that the Golden Rule is as important in business deals as it is in our personal lives. A sustainable business is an ethical business. This is one rule that really should not be broken if an organisation is looking to achieve success over the long term.

The key concepts of integrity and trust

Almost all organisations and businesses today will choose to include the words integrity and trust in any statements they make about ethics or values in official communications. The following is a typical corporate statement:

> Integrity is the cornerstone of our business. We conduct our affairs in a manner consistent with the highest ethical standards.

Organisations might think that statements like this are well crafted, but they give the appearance of being banal and meaningless unless they are backed up in practice by the actions of all employees. The first stage of this is awareness raising – it is essential that everyone who works in the organisation understands what its values are and also their importance. When I worked with the Caribbean bank on the project as described at the start of this Chapter, I included the statement above in my slide presentation. I did not introduce this particular slide in any way when it was shown and found that, out of over 300 managers and staff that I worked with during the two weeks of the assignment, no more than half a dozen of them recognised it as coming from their bank's own mission statement, and one of those was the person who had drafted it! There is an important lesson for all directors and managers in this. It is essential always to make sure that the organisation's values and standards are properly understood throughout the business.

What does the word integrity actually mean? According to the Oxford English Dictionary it means "moral uprightness and honesty". I always think of it in terms of doing things right, first time, every time and operating within the law at all times. Consistency of performance in these areas leads to an organisation being trusted, both by its staff and also by third parties including customers, suppliers and the public.

Trust is another vital component of reputation. Being able to generate feelings of trust is critical if an organisation is to achieve long-term success. I once heard someone define the word trust as "the residue of promises fulfilled" and I think this is a powerful definition. It suggests why most politicians struggle to generate trust – they make promises in order to get elected which they often struggle to deliver subsequently when they face the practical realities of being in office.

Business ethics and the law

Each of us, individually, is responsible for our own actions, for acting ethically. Indeed, most of us like to believe that we are law-abiding citizens, although the reality is sometimes very different. In fact, most of us break the law on a reasonably regular basis. I have already used the example of the lack of respect for the law shown by drivers of motor cars in the UK in terms of failing to drive within designated speed limits, despite the fact that the speed limits exist for very good health and safety reasons. The same is true with the use of hand-held mobile phones whilst driving. This is illegal in the UK, again for obvious safety reasons and yet people continue to drive at the same time as conducting a conversation with a mobile phone in their hand (even worse, some people drive whilst texting!).

The same issues arise in business organisations. Most organisations would say that they have zero tolerance of violations in three areas of their business in particular: laws and regulations; public and employee safety; and the truthfulness of records and statements. Yet as we have seen in the many examples throughout the book, this is very often not the case in practice. Pressure to perform and to hit short-term targets is often the cause of these violations.

When I work with organisations on ethical training and development programmes, I like to test people's attitudes to good ethics and honesty both in the workplace and in their private lives by means of a series of questions. Most managers and employees are prepared to admit that they have used office pens and stationery for private purposes. Some will go further and acknowledge that from time to time they may have used unlicensed software or illegally copied music. Very few people who I have worked with, however, will admit to submitting false expense claims or to lying on an insurance claim in order to gain a financial advantage.

So, what is going on here? Well, it is clear that most people bend the rules in some shape or form both in their private lives and also when at work. In most cases, there are limits to this of course, depending upon each individual's attitude and circumstances: their perception first of what he or she considers to be "wrong" and secondly when he or she considers that the risks become too great. Greater consistency is needed in the workplace. All organisations need to set out their own rules about their expectations of business behaviour and communicate these to their employees. These rules need to be robust enough to withstand the pressures of work. Such rules appear in various forms within organisations: ethics charters, value statements, codes of conduct, policies and procedures. We will look at these in detail later in the Chapter.

The law defines minimum acceptable standards of behaviour. It is essential that an organisation operates within the law and abides by all relevant regulations. This is absolutely necessary in order to build trust and to retain reputation. So, there should be a compliance programme in place to provide reasonable assurance of this, exactly as set out in the COSO Framework. However, simply adhering to the letter of the law and relevant regulations will never be sufficient to build trust or to demonstrate integrity because this is what all organisations should be doing as a matter of course. More is needed. Organisations need to keep to both the letter and the spirit (or intent) of the law. I saw a good example of this whilst working on a project for the Gambling Commission[3] in the UK in 2007.

> **Example: Gambling Commission reforms.** The project required me to look at all aspects of compliance and enforcement of the law and regulations of the gaming industry in response to the changes introduced by the UK's Gambling Act 2005. One of the Gambling Commission's three licensing objectives is to protect children and other vulnerable persons from being harmed or exploited by gambling. The legal gambling age in the UK is 18 years of age. However, right from the outset the Gambling Commission encouraged all operators in the industry to "think 21". That is to say, all staff working in the industry were asked to check the IDs of anyone entering their premises that appeared to be under the age of 21, rather than concentrating on people who looked to be younger than the legal minimum age of 18. It was felt that this would make it far more difficult for a 16 or 17-year-old youth to be able to gamble. Although controversial within the industry, this move was designed to assure the public that casinos and betting shops were prepared to act responsibly by looking at the intention and spirit of the law in terms of protecting young people, rather than simply adhering to the strict letter of the law.

In my view, business ethics actually begins where the law ends. It is about the "grey areas" of business where values can often be in conflict, in particular where short-term commercial drivers – the need to hit monthly or quarterly targets, either as an individual or as an organisation – produce intense pressure to achieve results at all costs. Many of the questions posed are difficult or controversial. Studying and paying attention to business ethics will help an organisation to make better decisions, not unequivocally right decisions.

The "3Rs" ethical roadmap

Whenever individuals or organisations are concerned about their actions, the "3Rs" ethical roadmap can provide helpful reference points. The behaviours that this roadmap sets out should be straightforward and routine but sometimes commercial realities, pressure or complacency interfere with how the business decision-making process works in reality. The "3Rs" are set out in turn below.

- **Respect.** This means treating everyone with dignity and courtesy. Respect includes using company supplies, equipment, time and money appropriately, efficiently and for business purposes only. It means protecting and improving the workplace environment and abiding by all laws and relevant regulations.

- **Responsibility.** Each of us has a responsibility when at work to our customers, co-workers, employers and of course to ourselves. Behaviours here include: providing timely, high-quality goods and services; working collaboratively and carrying your share of the load; and meeting all reasonable performance expectations.

- **Results.** In my view, results must be obtained both legally and ethically if sustainable growth is to be achieved. This is sometimes in practice the hardest "R" to match up to and we have seen many examples in this book of organisations and individuals that have tried to hit targets or relieve pressure by manipulating results.

Individual responsibility

There is a well-established ethical toolkit (charters, codes, training etc.) by which organisations gain assurance on business ethics today and we will look at this later on in the Chapter. Employees will be expected to comply with these procedures of course but the reality is that each of us is very capable of rationalising away our unethical behaviour. The following statements may well be familiar: "everyone else does it so that makes it OK"; "I am going to pay it back next month"; "the boss does it so why shouldn't I"; "I simply don't have the time to carry out all of these checks"; "it's not my job to do that"; and "they will never spot it so don't worry about it."

There is organisational responsibility in the workplace but also individual responsibility. Each of us has a personal responsibility to do the best that we can to behave ethically in business. We are all human, of course, which means that none of us is perfect. We all need to work at this. I try to address this issue directly when I work with clients by focusing on the key areas in the workplace environment where, under pressure, we may all fall into bad habits. I do this through the medium of the following simple self-assessment questionnaire. There are 10 questions as follows:

ETHICAL SELF-ASSESSMENT QUESTIONNAIRE:

In the previous three months have I . . .

- Submitted bogus or inflated expense claims?

- Used or taken company resources for personal purposes or conducted personal business on company time?

- "Thrown a sickie" when I really wasn't ill?

- Engaged in negative gossip or spread rumours about someone?

- "Bad-mouthed" the company or management to colleagues or third parties?

- Knowingly ignored or violated a company code, policy or procedure?

- Manipulated figures on a timesheet, budget or report?

- Been less than honest (lied or grossly distorted the truth) to clinch a deal or hit a target?

- Accepted an inappropriate gift or excessive corporate hospitality?

- Tried to hide, failed to admit to or correct a mistake I made?

In my experience, these are the key areas of concern for all of us in terms of our conduct. Some of the questions relate directly to certain aspects of fraud that have been discussed earlier in the book. What all of the questions do, however, is to address those particular sub-optimal behaviours that are the most frequent and corrosive of business ethics in terms of our individual responsibilities.

Corporate culture

Each individual is different and each person has their own standards, moral codes and cognitive drivers of behaviour. As we saw earlier, however, it is not so much individual characteristics that are the most important influencers of behaviour in the workplace but rather corporate culture. One of the most important pieces of research in this context was carried out by the American social psychologist Stanley Milgram at Yale University in 1961–62. This involved conducting a series of experiments on obedience to authority. He found that 65% of his subjects, ordinary residents of New Haven, were willing to give apparently harmful electric shocks of up to 450 volts (a potentially lethal dose) to a victim for no other reason than because a scientific authority commanded them to do so. In fact, the victim was an actor, who did not actually receive any electric shocks – something that was only revealed to the subjects at the end of the experiment. Milgram himself drew a chilling conclusion from this research and it is something that everyone in the business world should be aware of: "A substantial proportion of people do what they are told to do, irrespective of the content of the act and without limitations of conscience, so long as they perceive that the command comes from a legitimate authority".[4]

Culture in this context may be said to be the combined set of individual and corporate values, attitudes, competencies and behaviours that determine a company's commitment and style. A healthy corporate culture will exist where the atmosphere is positive and where behaviour is openly assessed, challenged, developed and rewarded. This is the inverse of a blame culture and we have already seen the negative consequences to organisations that operate with a blame culture.

The tone of the entire organisation will be set at the top, so what the directors and senior managers actually do, how they conduct themselves day-to-day, the values they choose to promote and reward, will all be critically important to how everyone else in the organisation acts. Much has been written about the importance of tone at the top and many, but not all, of the examples of corporate fraud that we have looked at in this book were caused directly by the criminal, bullying and intimidatory actions of those running the victim organisation. In my view there are four components of corporate culture that are crucial if strong business ethics are to be promoted, as follows:

- Directors and senior managers need to set a proper example, always promoting the values of their organisation as this is the best way to reinforce honesty and ethics.

- Treat everyone equally. This is fundamental – favouritism, tolerating different treatment for senior and/or "successful" people produces cynicism and indifference throughout the organisation to its stated values.

- Do not set unachievable targets. So-called stretch targets that challenge individuals and business units to improve performance are respectable tools of management. Targets that are impossible to meet are entirely different however. Setting impossible targets can only result in one of two outcomes, neither of which is desirable: either the employees will fail or they will cheat.

- Communicate a zero tolerance of unethical behaviour throughout the organisation.

Pressure, incentives and short-term targets

Pressure is a major influence on behaviour. We saw in Chapter 3 that the most important reason for fraudulent behaviour in the workplace is some form of financial pressure. In a more general sense, one of the most important causes of poor ethical decision-making within organisations is the pressure that senior management and their workforce are under to hit short-term performance targets. Quarterly reporting is ubiquitous now and it has a lot to answer for!

Directors and senior managers are constantly looking to grow their corporations and to maximise shareholder returns, not so much in the long term, as this has little meaning for individuals, but in the short term. Jeff Skilling at Enron provides a good example of this. He was so focused on short-term profit maximisation that he made it a condition of his joining Enron in 1991 that Andersen, the auditors, agreed to sign off on the mark-to-market accounting policy (as opposed to traditional historical cost accounting) that he wanted to use there. According to Mclean and Elkind, this was a "lay-my-body-across-the-tracks issue" for Mr Skilling (Mclean and Elkind, 2003, p. 39).[5] His reasoning was simple. The effect of mark-to-market accounting would, generally, be to accelerate the profits taken on long-term projects – rather than spread them out evenly over the length of the project, which might be 20 years or longer, they could be brought forward into earlier years provided the value of the project had increased. Now this was virtually guaranteed at Enron because it was the Enron managers themselves who would determine the project values! Mr Skilling saw himself as a smart man who had brilliant ideas and he wanted to enjoy the benefits of those brilliant ideas himself. Sustainability was not a big driver for him – after all, he was not going to be around at Enron in 20 years' time! Although no doubt more modest, all employees will have their own targets to meet and, if they are ambitious, they will be desperate to hit them either in order to earn bonuses or, in difficult economic conditions, to better safeguard their jobs.

Lord Browne, the ex-CEO of BP plc points clearly to the tensions between short-term and long-term business targets in his autobiography *Beyond Business*.[6] He describes in the book that when he first heard that he was going to be promoted to the role of Chief Executive at BP he thought in terms of a 10-year plan and what he could achieve for the company during that time. As soon as he started working in the job as CEO, however, he says that his attention become absolutely focused on hitting the next quarter's numbers in order to satisfy the expectations of the market. Rather than a 10-year plan, Lord Browne's vision was quickly changed to 40 quarterly targets.

Incentives can have a huge influence on behaviour, depending on their value to the individuals who stand to gain from them. We saw earlier in the book that they are thought to have encouraged high risk-taking by traders in financial institutions. Some of the key reforms in the aftermath of the financial crisis have been designed to change this by: reducing the percentage of the bonus that could be taken by bankers in cash; spreading the time-period of the bonus out in terms of when it became due; and introducing clawback provisions in the event that the bonus was linked to fraud or mis-information.

Much of the poor current reputation of the financial services industry has to do with behaviour that is widely seen as being unethical and much of this unethical behaviour has been driven by incentives. In the US one of the key drivers of the sub-prime lending crisis was the lucrative incentive schemes available to mortgage originators such as Countrywide Financial and their salesmen in the form of commissions and fees made on completion of the loan deals. The payment of these incentives was not contingent upon the borrowers, mainly poor families, being able to repay the loans in the future. The result was a widespread failure to apply traditional underwriting standards and prudent lending criteria.

In the UK, there has been a public outcry against the widespread practice in recent years of the banks selling expensive Payment Protection Insurance ("PPI") schemes as part of the deal when consumers take out a loan, mortgage or credit card even when this was not in the customers' best interests. The bankers were driven to do this by the incentives that they could earn. Considerations of business ethics did not apply, apparently.

This was a point that I put to Jerry during our interview for this book. Jerry is a very experienced retail banker in the UK. He has worked through the "PPI era" and, despite coming under pressure to do so, he told me that he did not sell the product himself because he did not agree with it. I suggested to him that, whilst banks like to portray themselves as being customer-focused, in reality they are all incentive-driven businesses. This is Jerry's candid reply.

I definitely agree with that. Our motto at the moment is that we put the customer at the heart of everything we do, which is absolute rubbish. The customer is the last person we think about. We are going through a huge lending push at the moment, because of the famous "Project Merlin" where all the banks have promised the government that they will lend amounts of money to businesses to try to stimulate the economy. We are being told by the bank that we have to phone customers up, we have to be seen to be pro-active, so phone customers up just so that we can go to the government and say: "Look how many pro-active calls we've made, look how many pro-active appointments we've booked". Despite this, all our interest rates went up again two weeks ago. You know if you want to borrow over £25,000 the basic rate is 20% on an unsecured business loan.

> There is a sliding scale, true but for an average client on an average grade it is still 19.5%. So you know, we are going to the government saying look at all the calls we've made, we are really being proactive. But we are not really "helping", we are not helping the customers with interest rates and things like that.

Jerry went on to talk about another form of pressure that exists in his bank, the pressure to hit performance targets. Here the incentive for doing so is not so much to gain extra remuneration in the form of commissions or bonuses. It is much more basic – it is all about employees trying to keep their jobs. If they do not meet their targets the bank will put them on Personal Improvement Plans ("PIPs"). This is what Jerry had to say about PIPs:

> It all depends on the manager. Some managers like to use PIPs a lot – I mean, they are described as an aid. During the year almost everyone would be on a PIP from one area or another. It could be sales, but sales within different areas so it could be your selling of our packaged products, it could be your selling of account opening, it could be lending where you are not hitting the target or it could be customer service that you are put on it for. When you go onto a PIP you have a certain amount of time, I think it is four weeks, to show an improvement in your performance. It's a two way thing, so you have to say what you want from the manager and he or she will help you. But if you don't hit the target at the end of the four weeks then it's extended. If then after that you don't hit it you will receive a written warning. Finally you will get managed out of the business or you will get managed out of your role. You will be displaced because you can't perform, you can't hit your targets and that happens a lot. So if you're managed out where do you go from there? You are going to go out but you're not going to get a good reference if you then leave the bank because you couldn't do your job. So that's the kind of pressure that is applied.
>
> That means that you're only as good as . . . Well, I was going to say only as good as your last year but we are now on quarterly targets. So now you are only as good as your last quarter and in theory you are only as good as your last week! We have now a five week rolling programme so actually you are only as good as your last five weeks. It simply doesn't matter what you have done before. If in this five week period you haven't hit your target it's like: "Well why not?" Then we have daily conference calls to ask: what have you been doing? These calls are in the morning. Then at the end of the day you will get another call: what have you done, why are you not doing this, why haven't you done that? It's daily. It really ramps up the pressure.

This is extreme pressure and it is not difficult to see that, faced with the prospect of being put on a "PIP" as a consequence of failure, bank employees might be prepared to fudge figures, keep errors hidden or indeed ultimately engage in some form of fraud.

The business ethics toolbox

Introduction

All organisations need to be able to deal with pressure situations and commercial realities. Developments in business ethics over the last 50 years or so have provided organisations with a number of tools that are available for use by directors and managers in order to provide them with assurance on behaviour and standards of conduct by everyone in the workplace. There are four main tools in the box: value statements; codes of conduct and ethics; confidential reporting lines; and ethical training and development programmes. We look at each in turn below.

Value statements

Put simply, value statements are expressions of an organisation's core beliefs. Organisations spend time and effort writing them in order to identify and connect with their stakeholders both internally (mainly with employees) and externally (mainly with customers). They should be seen as guiding principles, positive statements summarising the core mission and aspirations of the entity. An organisation's corporate values should be expressed and reflected in the way that the people working in the organisation act day-to-day.

By recounting my use of Enron's RICE model in the story at the beginning of this Chapter, I may have placed value statements in a mostly negative context. I will try and balance this shortly by turning to a more uplifting example, that of Johnson & Johnson. It remains important, however, that directors and managers are aware of the dangers involved in making claims about the way the organisation acts and treats its stakeholders that are simply not borne out by the reality. Clearly, in the Enron example, the values of respect, integrity, communication and excellence set out in the model seem to have little connection with the arrogance, deceit and greed that have come to characterise behaviours at that particular corporation. There are other examples too where the actions of people, sometimes senior managers, appear to be a long way removed from the principles and values put forward by the organisations they work for. The risk to the organisation here is both external (of reputational damage) and internal (of cynicism).

Consider the situation of McKinsey & Co., the global management consultancy firm. The firm has been implicated in the Galleon insider dealing scandal (discussed in Chapter 5) through the actions of two of its ex-senior executives, Anil Kumar and Rajat Gupta, who have both become embroiled in the case. The behaviour of these two gentlemen that is alleged by the authorities is far removed from the McKinsey core values, especially the value of client confidentiality, which goes to the heart of McKinsey's business. The firm claims to be "the trusted adviser to the world's leading businesses, governments and institutions." Yet, this is hardly consistent with insider dealing – the use of confidential client information for private gain. McKinsey states on its website: "We are a values-driven organisation. For us this means to always . . . " There are then set out on the website the organisation's five core values in a series of short, pithy and no doubt powerful sentences. The third of these values addresses confidentiality and is expressed as follows:

> **Keep our client information confidential.** We don't reveal sensitive information. We don't promote our own good work. We focus on making our clients successful.[7]

How does this value of strict client confidentiality match up to the reality of the actions at McKinsey's, in particular the actions of the people at the top of the organisation? Well, in 2010 Anil Kumar, a former leading partner and director of McKinsey pleaded guilty in court to one count of securities fraud and one count of conspiracy to commit securities fraud in connection with the Galleon case. He admitted to providing Mr Rajaratnam with confidential inside information about the clients he was working on whilst at McKinsey's over a five-year period from 2004–2009 in return for $1.75 million. He subsequently testified for the authorities against Mr Rajaratnam in return for the expectation of a more lenient sentence.

Matters could get worse for McKinsey because Rajat Gupta, the prominent Indian business leader, has also been arrested in connection with insider trading in the Galleon case. Mr Gupta has had a high profile career; for example, he is a former director of Goldman Sachs and Procter & Gamble. However, for our purposes it is important to understand that he was Managing Director of McKinsey & Co. from 1994 to 2003. Mr Gupta has pleaded not guilty to the charges.

Dominic Barton, the current global Managing Director of McKinsey, has candidly described the case as "incredibly distressing and embarrassing" in an interview with the Financial Times newspaper in July 2011. In the interview he says that he believes that the firm will not know for many years to come the possible damage done to its brand as a result. However, he pledged to make the organisation stronger and said that McKinsey had already instituted a rigorous review of its values and practices that had prompted changes to policies, compliance and training.

However, it would be wrong to be too cynical about value statements and their impact on organisations and stakeholders. These statements can be very powerful and influential if they are adopted and used by the people to guide their conduct, especially those at the top. One of the most famous of all value statements is that used by Johnson & Johnson, the US multinational pharmaceuticals, medical devices and consumer health group.

The values that guide Johnson & Johnson's decision-making are spelled out in a very simple one-page document called "Our Credo". This was drawn up in 1943 by a member of the company's founding family. As the company website states:

> Our Credo is more than just a moral compass. We believe it's a recipe for business success. The fact that Johnson & Johnson is one of only a handful of companies that have flourished through more than a century of change is proof of that.[8]

And success has not always come easily for the company, especially during the crisis concerning the Tylenol poisoning scare of 1982. Tylenol at the time was Johnson & Johnson's most profitable medication. However, someone started tampering with the capsules, putting cyanide poison in them. Seven people died as a result and widespread panic followed. The company's market value fell by $1 billion as a result. However, its directors and managers demonstrated excellent crisis management at this time. They acted quickly, with complete openness about what had happened. They immediately withdrew the product from sale completely, across the whole country, thereby showing themselves to be prepared to bear the short-term cost in the name of consumer safety. This established a basis for trust with their customers and their results recovered quickly. The Credo was used widely within the company as a reference point during the crisis. The Chairman at the time, James Blake, was quoted as saying: "After the crisis was over we realised that no meeting had been called to make the first critical decision. Every one of us knew what we had to do. We had the Credo to guide us."

The Johnson & Johnson Credo has undergone some changes since the 1980s. However, it retains its credibility within the business and its core values continue to have widespread respect. The Credo is set out in full below.

Our Credo

We believe our first responsibility is to the doctors, nurses and patients, to mothers and fathers and all others who use our products and services. In meeting their needs everything we do must be of high quality. We must continually strive to reduce our costs in order to maintain reasonable prices. Customers' orders must be served promptly and accurately. Our suppliers and distributors must have an opportunity to make a fair profit.

We are responsible to our employees, the men and women who work with us throughout the world. Everyone must be considered as an individual. We must respect their dignity and recognise their merit. They must have a sense of security in their jobs. Compensation must be fair and adequate and working conditions clean, orderly and safe. We must be mindful of ways to help our employees fulfil their family responsibilities. Employees must feel free to make suggestions and complaints. There must be equal opportunity for employment, development and advancement for those qualified. We must provide competent management and their actions must be just and ethical.

We are responsible to the communities in which we live and work and to the world community as well. We must be good citizens – support good works and charities and bear our fair share of taxes. We must encourage civic improvements and better health and education. We must maintain in good order the property we are privileged to use, protecting the environment and natural resources.

Our final responsibility is to our stock holders. Business must make a sound profit. We must experiment with new ideas. Research must be carried on, innovative programs developed and mistakes paid for. New equipment must be purchased, new facilities provided and new products launched. Reserves must be created to provide for adverse times. When we operate according to these principles, the stockholders should realise a fair return.[9]

Codes of ethics and conduct

A code of ethics and/or conduct is an important management tool because it establishes the organisation's expectation of its people in terms of business ethics. It should apply to everyone in the organisation, including directors and senior managers. It should establish simple and fundamental principles of action that all employees can use as reference points if they ever should get into areas of difficulty or doubt around their own actions. These principles will be required to be followed by both the organisation itself and by the employees (and increasingly by service providers also) in all their actions day to day. As part of this, all those to whom the code applies will be expected to avoid engaging in any conduct or activity that may raise questions about the organisation's honesty, impartiality or reputation or may otherwise cause it embarrassment. Management must be prepared to enforce the standards in the code no matter who violates them.

The code is an important document that should be signed off by the board. Many codes start with a personal statement by the Chairman or the CEO, emphasising his or her personal commitment to the principles and values contained therein. It is important that board commitment is underpinned by a clear management structure that facilitates the effective operation of the code. For example, in a development being led in the US an increasing number of large organisations are choosing to appoint an individual with the specific title of Ethics Officer in either a full-time or a part-time role. One of the responsibilities of the Ethics Officer is normally to ensure that the code is effectively implemented, which will necessitate clear reporting mechanisms (to the audit committee and/or the board), together with monitoring and auditing processes to provide the prospect of continuous improvement going forward.

As we have seen, the effective management of business ethics is addressed in the SOX. Here, s. 406 requires companies that are listed in the US to disclose whether they have codes of ethics and also to disclose any waivers of those codes for any members of senior management. The code of ethics applies in particular to the CFO and the company's other senior financial officers.

An organisation's ethical standards should be reflected in the fundamental principles that guide its practices. Typically, these fundamental principles will include the following: acting in accordance with all laws and relevant regulations; conducting the organisation's business with integrity; behaving fairly and honestly at all times; and respecting others.

So, one fundamental aspect of the code is to re-affirm core values and principles. Another is to address working relationships. The code will usually state the organisation's commitment to promoting working relations that are based on integrity, loyalty and mutual trust. Aspects of behaviour should normally be addressed in the code together with "difficult areas" where the code will provide employees with signposts showing how such situations should be handled in practice. Examples of what might be covered in this part of the code are as follows:

• The organisation's attitude to alcohol, drugs and substance abuse, gambling in the workplace and sexual relationships at work;

• The very important area of the need to avoid conflicts of interest situations, which is often addressed by carefully explaining what external interests might cause difficulties and by referring to the organisation's gifts and entertainment policy;

• The need for confidentiality around information and data handling;

• The need to protect the organisation's assets, both tangible (such as what is and what is not acceptable use of the entity's information and communications equipment and systems) and intangible (such as reputation); and

• The organisation's policies towards the environment and health and safety issues.

The consequences of failing to comply with the code in any of these areas will normally be dealt with on a case by case basis. But there should be a clear statement that any breaches of the code will be treated as a disciplinary offence and may result in dismissal and/or prosecution if serious.

In addition, of course, the code should include reference to corrupt business practices: fraud; bribery and corruption; insider dealing; collusion; coercion; money laundering and terrorist financing. This is where the organisation's zero tolerance of all corrupt business practices should be clearly stated along with a description of the consequences of such action – investigation followed by disciplinary action that might lead to dismissal and, in the case of criminality, to prosecution. Unless stated elsewhere, for example in a separate anti-fraud policy, the organisation should set out clearly what it considers to be fraud. So, for example, it will need to address in particular the key "grey areas" around falsification of sickness, qualifications and references, expense claims and signatures on documents.

The code is designed, therefore, to assist employees in situations where the "right" answer may be unclear and so may dissuade good people from making wrong choices in moments of weakness or crisis. However, it can only do so if everyone reads it and understands it. This is often an area of concern because in my experience many organisations will address the code formally with each of their employees on one occasion and on one occasion only during their entire working career with the entity. That is normally done at the least appropriate time – the day on which the employee joins the organisation. When this happens, the directors and managers of the organisation concerned will have no assurance that their employees understand what is expected of them. This can cause practical difficulties for the organisation in a disciplinary process and is likely to attract criticism from any tribunal convened in an unfair dismissal case. But more importantly it means that the power of the organisation's message in terms of its principles and values is simply dissipated and will have little or no influence with the employees.

This practical problem is being addressed in many organisations today through an "affirmation requirement". This means that each year all employees are required to sign a declaration confirming both that they have read the code and that they have understood it. A number of my clients and some delegates on my courses remain resistant to this idea. From discussion, it seems likely that the main reason for this resistance is that the concept of annual sign-offs is not established as part of the corporate culture, so that people will seek to resist change by claiming that this annual sign-off is merely a routine exercise devoid of any meaning. Therefore, the argument goes, what is the point? I always advise against taking this attitude for two reasons. First, there are clear practical benefits of annual sign-offs for any entity that is embroiled in a disciplinary situation because the employee will have more difficulty in arguing that he or she was unaware that what they were doing was wrong. Secondly, and more importantly, the annual sign-off does provide a mechanism to give senior management assurance that their people do indeed know what the organisation stands for and understand its principles, values and ethical framework. When added to other measures such as an ethical training programme discussed below, it becomes part of a structured business ethics improvement plan. In my view the affirmation requirement is an essential control here.

Confidential reporting lines

Some form of confidential reporting mechanism is an essential part of a business ethics pro-gramme. We discussed one of these mechanisms, whistle-blowing hotlines, in some detail in Chapter 8. We did so because tip-offs and disclosure are the most effective way that fraud and corruption schemes are uncovered in practice. It is important of course that the code of conduct and ethics refers to the organisation's whistle-blowing policy if it has one. There may well be other reporting lines, for example around grievances and inappropriate workplace behaviour, which will typically be handled by the Human Resources function.

There is not much to add here to the detailed discussion in Chapter 8. However, it is worth re-emphasising the key point about whistle-blowing hotlines because it is one that applies to all of these reporting mechanisms. That is the crucial aspect of confidentiality. If these reporting lines are to be effective controls over the organisation's ethical framework they must be respected and trusted by everyone. The building blocks of this trust are clear: a commitment from the board to protect anyone who makes a disclosure in good faith; reporting to a respected individual who is not the line manager; absolute guarantees on confidentiality and protection against retaliation; fair and professional disciplinary and investigation processes; and a proper feedback loop.

Ethical training and development programmes

I have conducted many ethics briefings and training sessions over recent years. Most of these have been done on an in-house basis rather than as public courses. That is to say, I have been com-missioned by an individual organisation to help them to roll out a dedicated programme for their people, as happened in the case of the business ethics training course in Trinidad and Tobago that I describe at the start of this Chapter.

I think it is fair to say that almost all the delegates who have attended these courses have done so, at least at the outset, with a heavy heart, with the feeling that this will be a dull day full of meaningless platitudes. I know from experience that many arrive with the attitude that they have much better things to do with their time and that the whole exercise is pointless in any event because "you can't teach ethics". Actually, in my view this is all entirely misconceived: business ethics is all about human behaviour so that it is intrinsically interesting; the training should be firmly focused on the organisation itself, its policies and what happens there, so that it is practical and not theoretical; and competence in ethics is an acquired reasoning skill that can be taught. In practice, I know that this training works. Delegates do learn a lot about the organisation, about things that can go wrong and (perhaps) about themselves. The majority of delegates actually end up enjoying the experience too. How do I know this? Well from discussions with delegates during the day, gauging the engagement levels in the room and from reviewing the course feedback scores, which are an ever-present feature of modern training programmes.

Each ethical training and development programme that I have run in-house is of course different because it will be tailored to meet the specific requirements of the client. However, they are all conducted on a traditional face-to-face basis. Over the last few years, I have been involved in delivering training by other methods also.

There are a number of alternatives to face-to-face training that are available today, different ways for organisations to raise awareness of business ethics and deliver an appropriate training and development programme without relying on traditional training delivery. Computer-based training ("CBT"), with individual modules delivered to an employee's workstation is increasingly seen as a cost-effective and efficient means of imparting knowledge. The employee can then work through the training module whenever it is most convenient to him or her, thereby minimising disruption to their work. There is no travelling involved either, so time and money are saved. Most of these CBT training modules are accompanied by an assessment mechanism usually in the form of a multiple choice test, where a minimum score must be achieved before the training module is completed.

An often-mentioned danger with CBT is that the programmes can be tedious so that the retention rate for employees is low. In order to counter this, I am working with colleagues to design training modules that are short "skill burst" sessions with video dramas or interview-type ("talking heads") content included. These packages can be delivered straight to the employee's smartphone – the ultimate in training efficiency!

Despite the differences, there are a number of important features that should be common to all ethical training and development programmes, as follows:

• The organisation's commitment and approach to business ethics should be an important component of induction training for all new hires in the organisation.

• The training should be continuous. That is to say, it should be ongoing and not a one-off event. So, there should be different pieces of training each year for every employee.

• Training in ethics should be mandatory and not optional.

• Records should be maintained of the ethics training that is carried out. For traditional face-to-face delivery this will mean keeping an attendance register. For CBT, there must be some form of audit trail built into the programme so that the organisation is able to keep track of those employees who have carried out the training satisfactorily (in other words those who have worked through the material and passed the accompanying tests) and those who have not.

• The training must be supported by the board and senior managers. There are various ways of demonstrating this support. At its most obvious, directors and senior managers should put themselves through the training programme, attending courses and completing the CBT modules also. Where CBT is used, a short video clip of the Chairman or CEO at the outset of the training module, emphasising the importance of the training, his or her personal commitment to it and the beneficial outcomes for the organisation can be very important.

- The training should always include a case-based component. That is to say some examples of situations that contain an ethical dilemma of the type seen in Question 10 of the Quiz. These cases should reflect issues that are relevant to the organisation, perhaps incorporating recent situations that have been dealt with or areas of policy that either have changed or are thought to cause confusion and uncertainty in the workplace.

In my experience, a blended and varied approach to training always works best. So, a mix of face-to-face sessions and CBT spread over a number of years might well provide the optimal training solution here.

Business ethics in action

The importance of business ethics and corporate culture came up at various times during the interviews that I carried out for this book. There were some very interesting observations made by the interviewees, a selection of which is set out below.

First, consider Charles' response to one of the questions that I asked him. Charles has wide-ranging business experience, working in the UK, the US and also in Continental Europe at various stages of his career. He spent many years working for a large, privately owned US business and I asked him specifically whether there was an ethics programme in place in that organisation when he was part of the senior management team there. This is what he had to say:

> Not a programme as such, no. But there was a two-page statement on ethics and what was expected from managers within the business and I think it was good sense, it was well written. In addition to that, our business had, like so many companies do, a list of values that we called principles but they included principles on how we should deal with one another. Unlike most businesses I think that ours really genuinely lived those principles. So there were those in place. Anything more than this I think would have been a little bit contrary to the spirit of the business at the time.
>
> The people in our business used these principles day-to-day. Often I now go into businesses and there are statements of values which are fairly irrelevant and the actual behaviour on a day-to-day basis is quite different from those but no, in our business there was a pretty good alignment of those and there were lots of anecdotes and stories, you know, passed around the business which supported those things.
>
> We had programmes for all employees in our business. Sometimes these were dismissively referred to as "sheep-dip" programmes but they were actually pretty good. But the focus of those was really how to manage well or how to lead well and the ethical side of things was almost taken for granted, a sort of culture of high expectations if you like and so certainly there weren't any finger wagging programmes about . . . you know this is good and this is bad and you ought to know the difference by now.

Next, consider Martin's comments. Martin has had a long and successful career with a large retail bank in the UK and he has seen many changes during his time there. He is well aware of the importance of culture and ethics, both corporate and individual when assessing fraud risk. His comments below highlight the importance of changing culture and values in his organisation and the consequent rise in risk of fraud that this brings.

Now we come to the organisational culture and how does that reflect in the type of person employed. Now, just thinking back to when I joined the bank . . . at that time they didn't seem to recruit people, whether consciously or unconsciously, that, I don't know, that stood out dramatically. Instead they picked people who seemed "steady" if you know what I mean. Everybody that worked in my area all through those early years, they were all steady people that joined from school and had worked their way progressively through the grades and patiently through the grades. They weren't people who were in a hurry because people in a hurry take short cuts so they were people who steadily built a career with an endgame that said: "when I get to a certain age I will have a fully-paid pension, have a comfortable retirement, and in the meantime I've got job security". It attracted a certain sort of person.

The interesting thing is whether culturally that has changed in that the mix is very different today. You can equate it almost to 1950s Britain compared with the current 21st century London. The mix today is very exotic and I don't mean that in a racial sense. I mean it's an international one with those people from different cultures and backgrounds and with different values. There is much, much more portability today, people move around incredibly quickly. People come in from somewhere abroad, they might be here for a year, they go to America, they come in from Australia, they do six months and then they decide this isn't for them and they go somewhere else. So they haven't come through the ranks in the organisation, they've not taken in any values from us as a result. That's not to say that these people are going to run away with money but it does provide the organisation with a different challenge. Whereas here, in this particular branch, we've still got people who started a long, long time ago, worked their way through, it's almost like you'd trust them with your life really because they are just those sort of people, they have been around and they still want to be around.

In an international bank, the movement of people is far more drastic. And the contract between the workforce and the bank has also been damaged. This is the other side of the coin. That portability is only really a reflection of the bank's ambition which has led to growth and then retrenchment and then redundancy and therefore the contract with the staff, to a certain extent, is broken. So people look at things in a completely different way.

I think historically the bank would have looked for, very early on, and would have taken a close interest in what you did outside the bank, what sort of person you were. There was a sort of consciousness that it wasn't the place to go out and get roaring drunk. For example, you couldn't be seen in a betting shop. Anything that looked like risk was not encouraged and would have meant that people's careers would have been stymied quite early on. There was also the checks and balances that were a bit subtle behind the scenes and with modern life these have gone. I'm not trying to say that was any better, it's just that it gives you some different dynamics.

Lifestyle pointers are always something too. We are taught to keep a close eye on clients in terms of the people they employ. The classic being the financial controller who turns up in a very, very nice car and when the chat gets going he always seems to be on nice foreign holidays. You try and work out what he should be on salary-wise. He seems to be living a lifestyle that's far in excess of that. Steve, this is stuff that you would have done with your forensic work years ago. It does come up. So, similarly you need to be aware of any member of staff that looks as if they are living high on the hog. Of course, you can't write it down and it's a difficult thing. It's breeding managers who will stop and think: "that doesn't seem right".

Years ago the bank used to fairly closely control the finances of its staff but obviously that has changed dramatically now. Even if you end up banking personally with the bank there are no obvious managerial people above you looking down on what you are doing. Whereas years ago you had to get your manager to sign anything that you wanted to do financially, if you wanted a mortgage he had to agree it, a personal loan had to be signed off by him and then signed off by a credit officer as well and you had to demonstrate financial probity and all that sort of thing, produce an income and expenditure statement etc. etc. In fact you had to do all the things that customers have to do but even with a bit more rigour. That's all gone now.

Finally, consider what Adrian told me. Adrian used to be the Compliance Officer in a large international financial institution. During our interview, I asked him where he positioned compliance in an organisation and what the key drivers of its success were. He gave me a powerful answer, not to do with policies and procedures but centred on corporate culture and business ethics. This is what Adrian said.

It's all very good talking about job descriptions but I really, really think, looking at fraud in particular, in the context of the compliance function it really is a special kind of person to be able to manage it because there are so many things, so many skills that you have got to have – personal, detective, trusting, committed, aloof to a certain extent, completely devoid in terms of emotion but looking at things in an analytical way. If you don't have that combination of skills then you are never going to find the right person, regardless of job descriptions. Why, if you don't have the right person then you can't get the right buy-in and if you can't get the right buy-in you can't put in the right controls. You cannot create the right culture. It comes down to culture. The culture, you have got to influence it, you have got to set it and you cannot simply manage it. Culture, the tone is set at the top and if you cannot influence your immediate peers in order to get the culture that you want, you run the risk that something might go wrong somewhere.

Compliance is critical because it sits at the positive centre of everything. That's where you look at compliance. It has to be at the centre of the organisation and it has to be a feeder, a communicator, a facilitator between areas and departments. It makes sure that people are adhering to and following procedures and it acts as a constant reminder, reminding management when things are lax. You manage with tough empathy. This means always being honest, not being false in any way so you shock, you use the truth to make sure that you get the message across, you motivate or you change behaviour. You manage with tough empathy.

But integrity is everything. If there's no integrity, well that's the cornerstone of a relationship gone right there. With integrity anybody can make mistakes and you should always give people a second chance. How do I measure a second chance? Once I was in a situation where I was informed that one of the bank's messengers was involved in smuggling tobacco. So, I knew the guy, I knew him quite well, I thought he was a nice guy, I understand why he was into tobacco crime, he doesn't earn enough money, I know, fine. But it puts the bank in a difficult situation. So, I bring him in and I say, look I heard that you were involved in this, he said "no". So I gave him another opportunity – I heard that you had been stopped by the police – "no it wasn't me". I tried again – my sources have told me. "No, no, no". OK I gave him three chances to own up so I now had to say: "Look unfortunately I don't believe you, now you must go and tell the manager that you are leaving or I will tell him what's really happened". The guy still sees me down the street, he says "hello". I gave him three opportunities to redeem or reveal himself. I would have helped him out, no question, but he shut me out so I had no other option. I wasn't prepared to run the risk of bringing the bank's reputation down, tarnishing the bank's reputation. I gave him three chances – no, no, no each time. So I say that I give you one more chance to tell the boss yourself, I won't get involved just say you are leaving and leave it at that. And he did that. But he still says "hello" when I see him in the street, even now. That means tough empathy, that's what tough empathy is.

Integrated approach

Adrian's comments about the need to manage with "tough empathy" are very perceptive I think. In fact the phrase sums up very neatly the approach to business ethics that I recommend to both my clients and my delegates alike. This is the integrated approach, one that combines tough compliance measures with the promotion of the organisation's positive values. The following areas help to illustrate this integrated approach:

- A purely compliance approach within organisations will place the emphasis on absolute adherence to the law, regulations and procedures, whereas an organisation that promotes employee engagement and positive behaviour will always emphasise the importance of being true to the organisation's stated values. The integrated approach balances values and rules.

- A compliance approach will always seek to prevent unethical conduct, whilst a values approach turns this thinking on its head by promoting ethical conduct. The integrated approach does both. It promotes ethical conduct but has a zero tolerance of all unethical conduct.

- A compliance approach will promote formal accountability mechanisms (staff appraisals, disciplinary procedures etc.) underpinned by external enforcement when needed (such as by auditors, lawyers, or the police). A values approach will encourage people to take personal responsibility based on internal commitment to the organisation. The integrated approach will certainly stress the importance of internal commitment but will have external enforcement structures in place also.

The integrated approach is a balanced approach and one that I admire and support very much. Without a grounding in values, compliant conduct is undirected and without a clear goal. It may be described as blind. On the other hand, without respect for compliant conduct verbal and internal commitments to values are hollow and have no meaning. They may be described as empty. The challenge for directors and managers is to root compliance, all the policies, controls and procedures that we have discussed throughout the book, thoroughly in the overall context of the organisation's values and fundamental principles.

When I work with delegates I sometimes use sporting analogies to illustrate the point make. An example is set out below and I have used this often when addressing issues co business ethics.

Business ethics – golf or football? The integrated approach is absolutely the approach that has been adopted with so much success over the last 100 years in the sport of golf. Golfers, whether they are amateur or professional, have huge respect for golf's values – etiquette, courtesy towards one's opponents, fairness and accepting the part played by chance (known as the "rub of the green"). However, this is underpinned by an equally strong insistence on playing always by the Rules of Golf and a zero tolerance of any violations. Golfers will very likely be disqualified from competitions if they make a mistake in following the rules. If cheating is involved, however, the sanctions are severe. An amateur golfer caught cheating (a difficult thing to prove and the subject of a number of court cases over the years) will in all probability be thrown out of his or her golf club. If a professional golfer is found to be cheating then he or she is very likely to be suspended from playing professionally anywhere in the world for a period of time and ultimately could be banned for life. This is the integrated approach as set out above seen in action on the golf course. Because of this we can all have confidence that if Tiger Woods, Rory McIlroy, Suzann Pettersen or any golfer wins a tournament they have done so fairly and because they happened to play the best golf of any of the competitors taking part. In contrast, consider another sport, that of association football. Here, there seems to be little respect for the rules of the game and cheating on the pitch is a matter of routine. At the same time, there is little respect shown either to the officials (referees and linesmen) or to the opponents and these individuals are regularly subjected to intimidation and provocation on the pitch respectively. The compliance mechanisms and disciplinary procedures in football are weak and inconsistent. The sport's governing body, FIFA, is itself periodically beset by allegations of corruption. Winning and the short-term success that it brings is all that matters in football. The players themselves face few meaningful sanctions whatever their behaviour and sometimes they appear to be all-powerful, precisely because it is they who win football matches.

Association football is a more popular sport around the world than is golf by a wide margin today. It has tradition and dynamism and the media to thank for that. However, which has the more sustainable business model? This is a much more arguable proposition. Directors and managers would do well to ask themselves whether they want to run their organisations along the golf model or the football model.

Summary – Five Key Learning Points for Directors and Managers

We have ended the book by looking at business ethics. Equally, we could have started it here because ethics provides the entire context in which the fight against fraud is located. If business ethics are not well established within an organisation, then fraudulent behaviour will become more likely. In the same way, if values are promoted but the policies and procedures of the organisation are not respected then opportunities for fraud will present themselves. Actually, there is a simple enough business maxim at work here: a well-run business is an ethical business.

As with every area that we have looked at in the book, we conclude the Chapter with a summary of the important messages for directors and managers, as follows.

✓ Make a commitment to consistency in how you treat all stakeholders, especially your employees. Everyone in the organisation, regardless of position or success, should be treated equally in terms of violations of standards of business ethics, even if this means taking tough decisions that might be thought to harm the business in the short term. Only by making this commitment and having the determination to carry it out will respect for ethical codes and concepts of zero tolerance be earned.

✓ Include an affirmation requirement for the code of conduct and ethics. All employees should be required to sign a declaration each year confirming both that they have read the code and that they understand it.

✓ Be prepared to take the lead on business ethics. Commit to the golden rule of reciprocity. Understand the importance of the actions that you take at the top of the organisation day-to-day and also the need to be highly visible and supportive of ethical training and development programmes. Be aware of the modern business ethics toolkit and make use of it.

✓ Understand the importance of pressure in the workplace, in particular the tendency of extreme performance targets and incentive schemes to force people to focus absolutely on short-term results. Business ethics, in these situations, loses relevance.

✓ Manage with tough empathy. This means rooting compliance drivers (the policies, controls and procedures that we have discussed throughout the book) firmly in the values of the organisation.

Epilogue

Distinguished merit

I am standing in the small and beautiful Trafalgar Cemetery just outside the old city walls. It is May 2011. This is one of my favourite places in the British overseas territory of Gibraltar, which is the peninsula at the extreme southern end of Spain at the entrance of the Mediterranean Sea, and I always try to spend some time here whenever I am lucky enough to be working in Gibraltar. It is a gorgeous evening, very quiet and peaceful in the cemetery now that all the tourists have finished doing their shopping in Main Street and returned to their cruise ship. I walk over to stand in front of one of the two gravestones in the cemetery that are marked out by small bouquets of poppies to commemorate the fact that here are buried two casualties of the Battle of Trafalgar, Admiral Nelson's famous naval victory over the combined French and Spanish fleets in October 1805. The inscription on this tombstone reads as follows:

> To the memory of Captain Thomas Norman of the Royal Marine Corps and late of His Majesty's ship Mars, who died in the naval hospital of this place on the 6th day of December 1805, in the 36th year of his age and having suffered several weeks with incredible patience and fortitude under the effects of a severe wound received in the great and memorable sea fight off Trafalgar. His brother officers on the station have consecrated this humble but sincere testimony of their sense of his distinguished merit and of their regret for his premature fate.

I have never heard of Captain Thomas Norman before, he is not famous like Nelson. The phrase "their sense of his distinguished merit" is striking, however, it makes an impression on me. Captain Norman was an ordinary sailor not a hero and, as a naval officer, his rank indicates that he would have achieved no more than moderate success. Clearly, however, his actions as a man earned him the respect and admiration of his fellow officers. I see very clearly the irony of this situation, the contrast between the qualities of this ordinary man that I am reading about here on the tombstone and the characteristics of the people who I am in the process of writing my book about – a book about fraud and the fraudsters who commit it! This makes me think, first, about my time here in Gibraltar and then about the book that I am writing.

The purpose of my visit to Gibraltar is twofold. I am to give a lecture tomorrow on the UK's new Bribery Act 2010 and its practical implications for businesses and individuals in Gibraltar on behalf of the GACO. Then in the evening I am due to attend as a guest the first running of a new foundation course, to be delivered by local teachers, providing school leavers with an introduction to the financial services industry. Financial services are a central part of the local economy and provide much employment in Gibraltar, but young people here often have little idea about banking or insurance and the job opportunities that these business sectors provide. The course is designed to address this gap and I am really looking forward to seeing how the first classroom session works out in practice. I have a particular interest in it because I and a friend based in Gibraltar were jointly responsible for writing it and pulling together the course materials. But this project has been the long-term aspiration of members of the GACO committee (Ivan, Doreen, Ben and others). It has been driven forward entirely by them and by the local teachers. Each of these people has given much time and energy to it, outside of their work hours and for no monetary reward, in order to help the young people in their community. This is a highly innovative venture, it deserves to succeed and in my view it displays more than a little of the same characteristics that no doubt comprised the "distinguished merit" so admired in Captain Norman by his fellow officers.

I have brought my laptop with me on the trip, of course, both in order to show the slides for the lecture and also so that I can continue to write my book on fraud whilst in Gibraltar. The book is in its early writing stages but already I know what the most frequently used word in it is going to be – "fraudster", someone who commits fraud. I have deliberately chosen to use this word exclusively in all of my examples and descriptions because "fraudster" is a suitably neutral and professional term – this is going to be a business book after all and not a moral treatise. I took this decision because I felt that the use of the word "fraudster" throughout the book will help to ensure consistency of treatment of the various named cases and individuals.

Now standing in the Trafalgar Cemetery I am suddenly not so sure. There are many other words that I could use to describe these individuals in the book, some of them much more loaded with meaning and judgement than "fraudster". Slowly I think through a list of these, a collection of juicy nouns and adjectives and phrases and I smile to myself. It would be very satisfying to use some or all of these words at various points in the book but I know that by doing so I would make my publisher nervous.

So instead I make a commitment to myself. I will not change the basic plan but I will make sure that somewhere in the book I say something very straightforward about the consequences of all this. There is nothing admirable about committing fraud no matter how "clever" the fraudsters think they are being or how much they try to persuade themselves that their actions are justified in some way or other. Fraud brings misery and loss to all those who are affected by it. When committed against companies and businesses it can bring severe financial damage to investors and creditors of course. But very often the people who are most affected are the ordinary men and women who are the employees of an organisation blighted by fraud and who are threatened by the loss of their jobs and, sometimes, their life savings as a result.

I have a clear idea already in my mind about the various examples of fraud that I will use throughout the book. Some are from my own experiences and others are from headline cases. I think about some of the individuals that I know I will be writing about, names that have become synonymous with some of the biggest fraud scandals of recent times: Leeson at Barings Bank; Lay, Skilling and Fastow at Enron; Ebbers and Sullivan at WorldCom; Rusnak at Allied Irish Banks; and finally Bernie Madoff, the gigantic swindler of modern times. When they are listed together like this they make a somewhat motley crew. All have become infamous because of their involvement in corporate fraud. What else do they have in common? Well, most obviously they are all men. Arrogance seems to be a clear second group characteristic, greed may well be a third. However, there is another common thread, not so frequently commented on but every bit as important as the others in my view. This is a group that is entirely lacking in any sense of "distinguished merit".

References

Introduction

1. The circumstances surrounding the collapse of Polly Peck and the High Court decision to accede to the directors' application to place the company in administration was widely reported in the UK press at the time. See Financial Times, 26 October 1990 for a good example of the coverage.
2. The trial of Mr Nadir in 2012 has attracted widespread media attention. See www.bbc.co.uk/BBC Home/BBC News/UK for a good summary.
3. Trollope, A., *The Way We Live Now* (London: Chapman and Hall, 1875).
4. See the *Telegraph* article "Banker Christian Littlewood gets longest jail sentence for millions in insider trades" (2 February 2011) for a good summary of the case.

Chapter 1

1. The Institute of Internal Auditors; The American Institute of Certified Public Accountants; Association of Certified Fraud Examiners: "Managing the Business Risk of Fraud: A Practical Guide" (2008).

Chapter 2

1. Association of Certified Fraud Examiners (www.acfe.com). The ACFE describes itself as the world's leading anti-fraud organisation and premier provider of anti-fraud training and education. Its website is a source of much authoritative insight and research into occupational fraud. In particular, the semi-annual reports titled Report to the Nation on Occupational Fraud and Abuse ("RTTN") are a particularly valuable source of information as they contain detailed analysis of thousands of fraud cases reported by their members. The first report was produced in 1996 and then a second in 2002, since when they have been updated every two years. The latest report came out in 2010 when, for the first time, it is presented as a global study of fraud trends because it includes cases from around the world in its analysis, rather than only cases originating in the US. As a result, this report is titled Report to the Nations on Occupational Fraud and Abuse ("RTTNs").
2. International Auditing and Assurance Standards Board of the International Federation of Accountants: "International Standards on Auditing No. 240: The Auditor's Responsibility to Consider Fraud in an Audit of Financial Statements" (2003).
3. Auditing Standards Board of the American Institute of Certified Public Accountants: "Statement on Auditing Standards No.99: Consideration of Fraud in a Financial Statement Audit" (2002).
4. Wachtell, Lipton, Rosen and Katz, Promontory Financial Group: "Report to the Boards of Directors of Allied Irish Banks plc, Allfirst Financial Inc. and Allfirst Bank Concerning Currency Trading Losses" (2002).
5. Leeson, N., *Rogue Trader*. (Great Britain: Little, Brown and Company 1996).
6. The British Airways case was widely reported in the UK media at the time – see the Telegraph article "Sickness is a pain in the neck for BA" (29 January 2004) as an example.
7. *Le Monde* (January 28, 2008).
8. See the CBC news website for a good summary and timeline of the WorldCom case: www.cbc.ca/news/background/worldcom
9. Cooper, C., *Extraordinary Circumstances: The Journey of a Corporate Whistleblower* (New Jersey: John Wiley & Sons Inc., 2008).
10. National Fraud Authority: "Annual Fraud Indicator" (January 2010).

11. Gee, J., Button, M. and Brooks, G., *The Financial Cost of Fraud* (London: MacIntyre Hudson/CCFS, 2009).
12. See the CNN website for a good summary of the Andersen trial: money.cnn.com/2002/06/13/news/Andersen_verdict.
13. KPMG's "Fraud Barometer" (30 January 2012).
14. This comment of the priest attracted much interest in the UK press – see the *Telegraph* article "Priest advises congregation to shoplift rather than turn to mugging or prostitution" (21 December 2009) as an example.

Chapter 3

1. Chartered Institute of Personnel and Development: "Recruitment and Retention Survey" 2008.
2. Hollinger, R. and Clark, J., *Theft by Employees* (Lexington: Lexington Books, 1983).
3. Cressey, Dr D., *Other People's Money: A Study in the Social Psychology of Embezzlement* (1953).
4. Leeson, N., *Rogue Trader* (Great Britain: Little, Brown and Company, 1996).
5. Albrecht, S., Howe, K. and Romney, M., *Deterring Fraud: The Internal Auditor's Perspective* (Alamonte Springs, FL, Institute of Internal Auditors Research Foundation, 1984).
6. Ditton, J., "Perks, pilferage and the "fiddle": the historical structure of invisible wages" *Theory and Society* IV (I): 1977.
7. Kerouac, J., *On The Road* (Viking Press, 1957).
8. Wolfe, D., and Hermanson, D., "The fraud diamond: considering the four elements of fraud" *The CPA Journal*, December 2004.
9. PricewaterhouseCoopers, "Global economic crime survey 2011" (www.pwc.com).
10. Trollope, A., *The Way We Live Now* (London: Chapman and Hall, 1875).

Chapter 4

1. Bank for International Settlements, "Basel II: International Convergence of Capital Measurement and Capital Standards: a Revised Framework" (www.bis.org 2004).
2. Bernstein, P., *Against the Gods: The Remarkable Story of Risk* (John Wiley & Sons, 1998).
3. The Joyti De-Laurey trial attracted much media attention in the UK at the time – see the *Telegraph* article "City secretary guilty of £4.5m fraud" (20 April 2004) as an example.
4. Inter Organization Network 2011 Status Report: "Gender Imbalance in the Boardroom: Opportunities to Change Course" (www.ionwomen.org).
5. Joint Australia/New Zealand Standards Board, "Risk Management Standard" (1995).
6. There are many books about Admiral Nelson and the Battle of Trafalgar. One of the most comprehensive and fluent accounts of the Trafalgar campaign is provided by Clayton, T. and Craig, P., *Trafalgar: The men, the battle, the storm* (Great Britain: Hodder and Stoughton, 2004).
7. Basel Committee on Banking Supervision: "Sound Practices for the Management and Supervision of Operational Risk" (www.bis.org/publ/bcbs195.htm, June 2011).
8. See BBC News Europe (8 September 2011) for a good summary of the Galliano case.
9. There has been extensive media coverage of the BP oil spill arising from the Macondo well blow-out in the Gulf of Mexico, as well as a report from the US National Commission investigating the tragedy. See the in-depth archive at the *Financial Times* for a good summary (www.ft.com/indepth/bp-oil-spill).
10. See Smith, C. and Quirk, M., "From Grace to Disgrace: the Rise and Fall of Arthur Andersen" *Journal of Business Ethics Education* 1(1): 2004, 91–130) for a comprehensive summary of the Enron/Andersen case.
11. McLean, B. and Elkind, P., *The Smartest Guys in the Room: the Amazing Rise and Scandalous Fall of Enron* (United States of America: Portfolio, 2003).
12. Ministry of Justice, "Bribery Act 2010: Guidance about procedures which relevant commercial organisations can put in place to prevent persons associated with them from bribing" (2011).
13. The European Parliament, "Directive 2005/60/EC on the prevention of the use of the financial system for the purpose of money laundering and terrorist financing" (2005).
14. Joint Money Laundering Steering Group, "Guidance for the UK Financial Sector on prevention of money laundering/combatting terrorist financing" (2009).

Chapter 5

1. Financial Reporting Council, "The UK Corporate Governance Code" (June 2010).
2. Garrett, B., *The Fish Rots from the Head: The crisis in our boardrooms, developing the crucial skills of the competent director* (Great Britain: HarperCollinsBusiness, 1996).
3. Garrett, B., *Thin on Top: Why corporate governance matters and how to measure and improve board performance* (Great Britain: Nicholas Brealey Publishing, 2003).
4. There have been many books and articles written about the Enron scandal. In my view, the most comprehensive and authoritative account is provided by: McLean, B. and Elkind, P., *The Smartest Guys in the Room: the Amazing Rise and Scandalous Fall of Enron* (United States of America: Portfolio, 2003). There is also a documentary film based on this book: "Enron: The Smartest Guys in the Room" (2005) directed by Alex Gibney.
5. McKinsey & Company, "Global Investor Opinion Survey" (2002).
6. Permanent Subcommittee on Investigations of the Committee on Governmental Affairs, United States Senate, "The Role of the Board of Directors in Enron's Collapse" (8 July 2002).
7. The Cadbury Committee, "Report of the Committee on the Financial Aspects of Corporate Governance" (Great Britain: Gee, 1992).
8. Ibid.
9. National Commission on the Causes of the Financial and Economic Crisis in the United States: "The Financial Crisis Inquiry Report" (US Government Edition, January 2011).
10. Financial Reporting Council, "The UK Corporate Governance Code" (June 2010).
11. Financial Reporting Council, "The UK Approach to Corporate Governance" (October 2010).
12. The appointment of Sir Stuart Rose to Executive Chairman at Marks & Spencer plc promoted much discussion and debate in the UK media at the time. See *Director Magazine:* "Split Role for Rose Threatens Combined Code" by Tom Nash (May 2008) for a good summary of the issues.
13. *The Guardian*, "Tony Hayward on BP oil crisis: I'd have done better with an acting degree" (9 November 2010).
14. Financial Reporting Council, "2009 Review of the Combined Code: Final Report" (December 2009).
15. *Financial Times*, "Citigroup chief stays bullish on buy-outs" (9 July 2007).
16. The Powers Committee, "Report of Investigation by the Special Investigative Committee of the Board of Directors of Enron Corp." (1 February 2002).
17. The Galleon case attracted widespread media interest, especially in the US. See the *New York Times* commentary and archival information at topics.nytimes.com/top/reference/raj_rajaratnam for a good summary of the case.
18. Transparency International (www.transparency.org).
19. The World Bank, "The Costs of Corruption" (8 April 2004).
20. Ministry of Justice, "Bribery Act 2010: Guidance about procedures which relevant commercial organisations can put in place to prevent persons associated with them from bribing" (2011).
21. For a full text of Mr Raju's resignation letter see *Indian Express*, "Full text of Raju's letter to board" (www.indianexpress.com, 7 January 2009).

Chapter 6

1. Committee of Sponsoring Organisations of the Treadway Commission, "Internal Control – Integrated Framework" (1992).
2. Chartered Accountants of Canada, Criteria of Control Board, "Guidance on Control" (1995).
3. Financial Reporting Council, "Guidance for Directors on the Combined Code" (1999, revised 2005).
4. Committee of Sponsoring Organisations of the Treadway Commission, "Enterprise Risk Management – Integrated Framework" (2004).
5. Auditing Practices Board, "Scope of an Audit of Financial Statements of Private Sector Entities" (2010).
6. *Re Kingston Cotton Mill Co (No 2)* [1896] 2 Ch 279, CA.
7. Institute of Internal Auditors (www.theiia.org).
8. Auditing Standards Board of the American Institute of Certified Public Accountants, "Statement on Auditing Standards No. 99: Consideration of Fraud in a Financial Statement Audit" (2002).

9. International Auditing and Assurance Standards Board of the International Federation of Accountants, "International Standards on Auditing No. 240: The Auditor's Responsibility to Consider Fraud in an Audit of Financial Statements" (2003).
10. Special Committee of the Board of Directors of Hollinger International Inc., "Report of Investigation" (August 30, 2004).
11. Permanent Subcommittee on Investigations of the Committee on Governmental Affairs, United States Senate, "The Role of the Board of Directors in Enron's Collapse" (8 July 2002).
12. See www.findlaw.com/hdocs/docs/enron/empltr2lay82001.pdf for a copy of the letter written by Ms Watkins to Mr Lay in August 2001.

Chapter 7

1. Association of Certified Fraud Examiners, "Report to the Nation on Occupational Fraud and Abuse" (2008).
2. Association of Certified Fraud Examiners, "Report to the Nations on Occupational Fraud and Abuse": 2010 Global Fraud Study (2010).
3. McFarlane, K.B., *The Nobility of Later Medieval England* (Oxford: Clarendon Press, 1973).
4. See www.bbc.co.uk/news/10259720 for a good summary of Monsieur Kerviel's defence position at his trial.
5. American Institute of Certified Public Accountants, "Management Override of Internal Controls: the Achilles' Heel of Fraud Prevention" (2005).
5. Drummond, H., *The Art of Decision Making: Mirrors of Imagination, Masks of Fate* (Chichester: John Wiley & Sons, 2001).
7. See sgforums.com/forums/1744/topics/261415 for a good summary of the story of InterContinental Hotels and Mr Imbardelli.
8. Wachtell, Lipton, Rosen & Katz, Promontory Financial Group, "Report to the Boards of Directors of Allied Irish Banks plc, Allfirst Financial Inc. and Allfirst Bank Concerning Currency Trading Losses" (2002).

Chapter 8

1. Levi, Dr M., "Sentencing Frauds: A Review" (2006).
2. Ibid.
3. Committee on Standards in Public Life: "Second Report – Local Public Spending Bodies" (Cm 3270-1, May 1996).
4. Ernst & Young FIDS Surveys, "Blowing the whistle on fraud, bribery and corruption" (2007).
5. Public Concern at Work (www.pcaw.org.uk).
6. For the application of Benford's Law to the fraud problem see in particular: Durtschi, C., Hillison, W. and Pacini, C.,"The Effective Use of Benford's Law to Assist in Detecting Fraud in Accounting Data" (Journal of Forensic Accounting, 1524–5586, V: 2004, 17–34).

Chapter 9

1. United States Supreme Court: *Miranda v Arizona*, 384 US, 436 (1966).
2. UK Parliament: The Police and Criminal Evidence Act 1984 (amended 2005).

Chapter 10

1. Enron: "Annual Report 1999: Our Values" (2000).
2. Sugar, A., *What You See Is What You Get: My Autobiography* (Pan Macmillan, 2010).
3. The Gambling Commission (www.gamblingcommission.gov.uk).
4. For a good summary of the work of Stanley Milgram and the "Milgram Experiment" see www.stanleymilgram.com a website compiled by Dr Thomas Blass.

5. McLean, B. and Elkind, P., *The Smartest Guys in the Room: the Amazing Rise and Scandalous Fall of Enron* (United States of America: Portfolio, 2003).

6. Browne, J., *Beyond Business* (Great Britain: Weidenfeld & Nicolson, 2010).

7. McKinsey & Company: "Our Values" (www.mckinsey.com).

8. Johnson and Johnson: "Our Credo Values" (www.jnj.com).

9. Ibid.

Index